D0876154

The Paradise Myth in
Eighteenth-Century Russia

Studies of the Harriman Institute,
Columbia University

The Paradise Myth in Eighteenth-Century Russia

Utopian Patterns in Early Secular Russian Literature and Culture

STEPHEN LESSING BAEHR

Stanford University Press, Stanford, California

Stanford University Press
Stanford, California
© 1991 by the
Board of Trustees of the
Leland Stanford
Junior University
Printed in the
United States of America
CIP data appear at the
end of the book

Published with
the assistance of
Virginia Polytechnic Institute
and State University

Title-page illustration:
An eighteenth-century reproduction of
an Old Russian print entitled "Paradise"
(from Dmitrij Tschiżewskij,
Paradies und Hölle:
Russische buchmalerei.
Recklinghausen: Verlag Aurel
Bongers, 1957).

To Irina

Contents

Preface

Many years ago, while working on utopianism and anti-utopianism in Dostoevsky (especially the golden age myth and its destruction in *The Possessed*, *The Adolescent*, and "The Dream of a Ridiculous Man"), I started to wonder where visions of an ideal world had begun in Russian literature and what role they had played. In tracing the roots of such visions, I found myself moving further and further into the past. By the time I reached the Primary Chronicle, I had come to conclude that since that famous day in 987 when the emissaries of Kievan Prince Vladimir reportedly experienced "heaven on earth" at an Orthodox cathedral in Constantinople, the quest for an earthly paradise has been one of the central focal points of Russian literature and culture; only later did I understand that paradise has also provided one of the prime means of propagandizing the Russian status quo.

The present book is the first of a projected series on the use and abuse of paradise and utopia throughout Russian literature and culture. It focuses on the crucial period from approximately 1682 (the accession of Peter the Great) to 1796 (the death of Catherine the Great), when Russian culture was being transformed from sacred to secular. During this period, visions of an earthly paradise recurred in panegyric and pastoral poetry, portrait painting, the utopian novel, allegorical fireworks and masquerades, Masonic ritual and literature, and even the winter garden. As has often happened in Russian culture from Muscovite times through the Soviet period, "paradise" frequently became synonymous with "Russia," which was depicted as the locus of perfection not only by nationalists (whose patriotism brought paradise to their lyres) or by those who wanted to earn the favor and rewards of the tsar but occasionally by those who wanted to "educate" the tsar, the tsar's courtiers, and the literate populace by stressing the means of making Russia an ideal land.[1]

Two main factors help explain the importance of the paradise myth in eighteenth-century Russia: the optimism generated by two of the most successful rulers in Russian history (Peter the Great and Catherine the Great), who moved Russia from backwardness toward equality with the West and won important military victories that aroused great patriotic emotions among the populace; and the persistence in much of this period of a Byzantine- and Muscovite-influenced "culture of consent,"[2] which demanded affirmation that "whatever *is* is right" (i.e., is perfect, like paradise) and encouraged even major writers like Lomonosov to sign their odes to the reigning monarch with the word "slave."[3]

This book reflects the ways that eighteenth-century Russia adopted and adapted the topoi of the European paradise myth to create a distinctly Russian potpourri.[4] Although these Russian conventions at points recall the allegorical statues of Egyptian pharaohs whose nameplates changed with a change of leadership, they nevertheless canonized sincere hope for a nation that had not long before undergone major national traumas during the Time of Troubles and the Schism of the Orthodox Church; while the conventions often functioned mechanically in individual works, they reveal a great deal about the literature, culture, and social concerns of the eighteenth century when examined macrocosmically. Today, these topoi provide an important perspective, as well, for understanding the roots of such nineteenth-century conservative ideologies as "Official Nationality" and Slavophilism[5] and to some extent even twentieth-century socialist realism.

Like socialist realism, Russian literature in the first two-thirds of the eighteenth century was by and large a "state literature," supporting the powers-that-be with propaganda.[6] Conventions like the paradise myth became a frequent propagandistic tool and helped to make Russian literature of the first two-thirds of the century overwhelmingly "monologic" (depicting a static, ordered world where truth is knowable and embodied in the state and its divinely appointed tsar).[7] Unlike most contemporary Western writers, who (under the influence of the scientific and critical worldview of the Enlightenment) used the conventions of the paradise myth to idealize faraway lands and hence criticize existing reality, most Russian writers of the eighteenth century used these conventions to idealize, mythologize, and "utopianize" the Russian status quo and the Slavic past. Much of the literature using the paradise myth in eighteenth-century Russia was thus closer to the literature of European Renaissance courts than to that of the contemporary Enlightenment, reflecting a "culture gap" between Russia and the West that is significantly larger than is generally acknowledged.[8] Only in the last third of the eighteenth century and the first third of the nineteenth did Enlightenment influences start to shape a "new" Russian literature based on individuality and freedom, which frequently attacked or parodied the premises and conventions of the myth; without understanding these conventions, one cannot fully comprehend the "golden age" of Russian literature.

The book begins with a lexicon, grammar, and rhetoric of paradisal places and then examines ways these "utopian patterns" helped to shape eighteenth-century Russian literature and to provide a bridge between sacred and secular cultures in Russia. Chapter 1 presents a typology of paradise, discussing Western conventions that were to become omnipresent in eighteenth-century Russia; this discussion purposefully excludes Russian examples in order to illustrate the kinds of foreign influences that predominated during this period. Chapter 2 focuses on the role of these patterns in the creation of a "political theology," which attempted to sacralize the secular state. Chapters 3 and 4 are organized around two images central to the paradise myth: the rebirth or renaissance of Russia, often linked with the earlier myth of Russia as "Third Rome" (Chapter 3); and Russia as an Edenic garden bearing paradisal "fruits" ranging from ideal monarchs to useful sciences (Chapter 4). Chapter 5 discusses the myth in the allegorical rituals and literature of Freemasonry, and Chapter 6 studies the Russian utopia and "eutopia" (a hybrid of the panegyric ode and the utopia that is virtually unique to Russia). Finally, Chapter 7 deals with the reactions against the paradise myth during the late eighteenth and early nineteenth centuries and its replacement by the myth of an iron age, as major Russian writers from Radishchev to Pushkin began to revolt (in true Enlightenment style) against the "official" literature on which they had been raised, while others (including Gogol) parodied paradisal conventions in a still unrecognized way.

Much of the research for this book was done during the course of two IREX grants in the Soviet Union. I am grateful to the staffs of the rare book divisions at the Library of the Academy of Sciences in Leningrad and the Lenin Library in Moscow and those of the archival divisions of the Lenin Library and the Saltykov-Shchedrin Public Library in Leningrad, who overwhelmed me with materials. Thanks to their help, I have been able to draw on a broad spectrum of sources, including major and minor literary and artistic works, full runs of journals, bound collections of short eighteenth-century texts, program books for courtly festivities, and Masonic manuscripts. From a plethora of possibilities, I have chosen illustrations and examples for their typicality, interest, and illumination of more general patterns in eighteenth-century Russian literature and culture.

Parts of individual chapters of this book appeared elsewhere in earlier (and often significantly different) versions. Small parts of Chapters 2 and 7 appeared as "Regaining Paradise: The 'Political Icon' in Seventeenth- and Eighteenth-Century Russia," in *Russian History* 11 (Summer-Fall 1984):148–67, which was reprinted with some modifications in *Russian Literature Triquarterly* 21 (1988):61–80. Three parts of Chapter 3 led previous lives under the following titles: "From History to National Myth: *Translatio imperii* in Eighteenth-Century Russia," in *Russian Review* 37 (January 1978):1–13; "In the Re-Beginning: Rebirth, Renewal, and *Renovatio* in Eighteenth-Century Russia," in A. G. Cross, ed., *Russia and the West in the Eighteenth Century: Proceedings of an International Conference* (Newtonville, Mass.: Oriental Research Partners, 1983), pp. 152–66; and "*Fortuna Redux*: The Courtly Spectacle in Eighteenth-Century Russia" in A. G. Cross, ed., *Great Britain and Russia in the Eighteenth Century: Contacts and Comparisons* (Newtonville, Mass.: Oriental Research Partners, 1979), pp. 109–22. A relatively small part of Chapter 5 appeared in "The Masonic Component in Eighteenth-Century Russian Literature," in A. G. Cross, ed., *Russian Literature in the Age of Catherine the Great* (Oxford: Meeuws, 1976), pp. 121–39. And Appendix C appeared as "Pavel L'vov's *The Russian Pamela*: A Utopian Excerpt," in *Russian Literature Triquarterly* 20 (1987):107–10. I am grateful to the editors of these journals and volumes for permission to use this material.

In the all-too-many-yeared process of writing this book, I have received a great deal of intellectual, personal, and financial support, which it is my pleasure to acknowledge. My greatest debt is to my wife, Irina Mess-Baehr, whose tough-minded advice has helped me to remove many errors of literature, logic, and language. The reader for Stanford University Press, Professor Mark Al'tshuller, and the anonymous reader for the Harriman Institute of Columbia University provided constructive and valuable criticism that has greatly reduced the girth of the book and I hope has made it more readable for others. Professor I. Z. Serman read the penultimate draft and provided useful suggestions.

For suggestions on previous drafts of individual chapters in various forms, I am grateful to Professors Robert Belknap, Istvan Csicsery-Ronay, Milton Ehre, Robert Entzminger, Richard Gustafson, Robert Maguire, Marc Raeff, Karen Rosenberg, Harold Segel, Savely Senderovich, William Mills Todd III, and John Yiannias. Helen Tartar, Peter Kahn, Nancy Lerer, and John Feneron of Stanford University Press have given excellent editorial advice. For financial support, I am grateful to the International Research and Exchanges Board for their two fellowships in the U.S.S.R.; the Andrew W. Mellon Foundation for a very pleasant and productive year as a Mellon Faculty Fellow in the Departments of Slavic Languages and Literatures and Comparative Literature at Harvard University; the National Endowment for the Humanities for a one-year research fellowship that allowed me to complete a draft of the book and to begin its sequel; the University of Virginia for two summer faculty fellowships that began the book; and Virginia Polytechnic Institute and State University for two similar fellowships at the intermediate stages of writing and two quarters of sabbatical leave at the end. Together, these individuals and institutions have allowed me to finally reach the point that Horace mentions in his *Epistle* I, 20 ("To His Book, About to Make Its Own Way in the World"): "For mart and street you seem to pine / With restless glances, book of mine! / . . . / Still, if you must be published, go; / But mind, you can't come back, you know!"

The modified Library of Congress system of transliteration is used throughout the book with the exception of well-known names, where the standard English version (e.g., Dostoevsky, Tolstoy, Gogol) is used, except in bibliographical citations of Russian sources; in quotations, archaic endings have been modernized to eliminate inconsistencies between eighteenth-century and modern editions. Names of tsars are anglicized (e.g., Catherine instead of Ekaterina). Unless noted, all translations are mine; all italicized quotations represent my emphasis as well unless otherwise stated.

The Paradise Myth in
Eighteenth-Century Russia

CHAPTER ONE

The "Language" of Paradise: A Typological Introduction

When Peter the Great repeatedly referred to his newly founded Petersburg as "paradise,"[1] he was integrating some traditions from old Russian culture with a commonplace Western image that would become omnipresent in Russia through the end of the eighteenth century. Using the Western word *paradiz* instead of the Russian word *rai*, Peter stressed the new orientation he hoped to give his country and its capital.[2] But, knowingly or not, he was also preserving a precedent from Kievan times when some rulers called their homes or towns *Rai*.[3] Before examining the Orthodox, Byzantine, and old Russian cultural traditions that helped to shape the eighteenth-century Russian paradise myth (Chapter 2), we shall study in this chapter some of the Western conventions borrowed by eighteenth-century Russians to describe paradise. In subsequent chapters, these conventions will provide a heuristic device for reexamining the literature and culture of eighteenth-century Russia, where the paradise myth became central under the influence of Peter's westernizing reforms.

Paradise Defined

The eighteenth-century Russian paradise myth was the product of a gradual merger in Western literature of various classical, biblical, and patristic traditions of perfect times and places into a single "megamyth"—a compendium of the historical myths depicting the good life. Although this amalgamation had begun as early as classical and biblical times,[4] it culminated only during the European Renaissance, when the similarities between classical

and biblical myths were often stressed more than their differences.[5] As Arthur Golding's 1567 English translation of Ovid's
Metamorphoses explicitly asked:

> Moreover by the *golden* [*age*] what other thing is ment,
> Than *Adams tyme in Paradyse*, who beeing innocent
> Did lead a blist and happy lyfe untill that thurrough sin
> He fell from God? From which tyme foorth all sorrow did begin.[6]

By the time they reached eighteenth-century Russia, most
classical and biblical myths of the good life had become virtually interchangeable;[7] whether labeled "paradise," "golden
age," "Elysium," "Fortunate Islands," "promised land," "Eden,"
"heaven on earth," "Arcadia," "peaceable kingdom," or even
"Hesperides,"[8] the ideal place or time was often defined or described through identical details, drawn from a single reservoir of
paradisal motifs.[9] Many of the most productive details came from
Ovid's description of the golden age in *Metamorphoses*, which
became a primer in mythology known to virtually every schoolchild; through it, such motifs as eternal spring, communal property, and, especially, the presence on earth of Astraea (the virgin
goddess of justice who left the earth when mankind became corrupt and whose return would signal a new golden age) became
hallmarks of the paradise myth. Among details from other works
that were sufficiently marked to define paradise when used alone
were: rivers of milk and honey, swords beaten into plowshares,
the wolf lying with the lamb, and abundant food without work.
(For a more complete list, see Appendix A.) Paradise was also
frequently defined through the rhetorical topos of *locus amoenus*
(the "pleasant place"), depicting gardens, flowers, birds, warm
breezes, and springs (see Chapter 4).[10] These definitional details
often combined with several recurrent lexical and syntactic patterns to create an international and intertemporal "language" for
defining and describing ideal worlds.

The paradise myth contained a number of mechanisms for ex-
tending its definitional vocabulary. The myth thrived on detail,
mirroring on the lexical level the essence of paradisal content—
abundance.[11] Many works using the myth generated new details
through a process of *synonymization*, through which definitional
details assimilated contiguous, nondefinitional words or phrases

and made them function as synonyms of the words "ideal" or "perfect" for the duration of a text or section and thus lose their normal denotations.[12] Often this occurred when nondefinitional words were included in a list with definitional ones, which came to function as dominants, creating a single semantic field that deemphasized lexical distinctions.[13] The myth thus created "gilt by association," allowing every text to produce its own context of perfection. (For an extended example of this process, see the reading of Robert Herrick's "The bad season makes the Poet sad" at the end of this chapter.)

One of the most important lexical patterns of the paradise myth was the *negative formula*, which defined ideal places and times not through the presence of positive qualities but through the absence of negative ones.[14] For example, Ovid in *Metamorphoses* defined the golden age as having no war, work, poverty, laws, judges, or foreign travel.[15] So important was this negative formula to the paradise myth that the repetition of the adjective "no" at the beginning of several consecutive phrases of a literary text often signaled a description of paradise (or its opposite if all the terms negated were good). The negative formula provided a particularly good vehicle for social criticism, picturing paradise as excluding undesirable qualities present in the society of the author (which was often implicitly compared to hell);[16] in the literary utopia, for example, the negative formula often portrayed the elimination of social problems and was marked by such details as "no slavery" (in a slaveholding society), "no bribery" (in a bribe-taking society), and so on. Through the negative formula and synonymization, all ages, authors, and cultures have been able to translate the ideals of the definitional vocabulary into their own idiom, emphasizing qualities that they believe to be desirable and excluding qualities they believe detrimental to perfection.[17]

The Grammar of the Good Life

Just as the paradise myth limited the denotations of words, so did it frequently restrict the underlying grammatical patterns of a text or section, reflecting the fact that literary themes (here: the description of the perfect place) have often determined both

lexis (the choice of vocabulary) and syntax (the method of combining subject-verb-object). Like the lexical patterns in a text
using the paradise myth, the syntactic patterns usually repeated
themselves once established. Many texts using the myth tended
toward parataxis, adding one paradisal detail to another with no
logical or inevitable order and no necessary point of conclusion.[18]
Word economy was inimical to the myth, which often generated
new details in the manner of a repeating decimal; abundance
and redundance were closely linked.[19]

The vocabulary of the paradise myth was often concentrated in
the predicate of individual sentences, which were attached to a
subject through a number of specific subject-verb structures. The
most elementary sentences were simply metaphors that linked
the paradisal lexicon to a subject through a copulative verb, producing the structure:

"A is B"

where A was a subject (often one to be praised) and B a defining detail of the paradise myth. Thomas Campion's 1605 lyric
"Cherry Ripe" exemplifies this *metaphorical pattern* in its praise
of the persona's beloved: "There is a garden in her face / Where
roses and white lillies grow; / A *heavenly paradise* is that place /
Wherein *all pleasant fruits* do flow." Here the beloved's face (metonymic of the beloved herself) is praised by metaphorical association with a paradisal garden of fruits and flowers (especially
the lilies and roses linked with perfection in the Bible).[20] In Campion's poem the description of the "heavenly paradise" uses the
same details and syntax as that of its earthly counterpart, reflecting the fact that at least since Revelation (which describes the
heavenly Jerusalem using some details from the Eden story in
Genesis) heavenly and earthly paradises were merging semanti-
cally as well as physically.

Utopias, pastoral poems, panegyric works, and works describing an ideal past often used the *descriptive pattern*:

"There they have . . ." / "Then they had . . ."

with a predicate of definitional and assimilated vocabulary. If the
ideal place or time was described by a first-person narrator, the
structure became:

> "There [Then] I saw . . ."

The narrative of the returned traveler Raphael Hythloday in book 2 of More's *Utopia* presents a particularly good example of this structure. When the paradise myth was used for praising one's own country, this pattern became:

> "Here [Now] we have . . ."

Like many of the patterns of the paradise myth, this descriptive pattern was often used in propagandistic texts, including the panegyric odes of Renaissance Europe and eighteenth-century Russia.[21]

In panegyric literature, the heroic and messianic patterns also appeared quite often. The basic subject-verb structure in the *heroic pattern* was:

> "He/she established . . ."

or

> "He/she has brought . . ."

When combined with the "negative formula," this structure became:

> "He/she eliminated . . ."

where the predicate consisted of words excluded from the paradise myth. The heroic pattern frequently celebrated the accomplishments of a monarch or other leader, as in the first of Sir John Davies's 26 "Hymns of Astraea," written for England's Elizabeth I:

> *The Maid* which thence descended:
> *Hath brought again the golden days,*
> And all the world amended.
> Rudeness itself she doth refine,
> Even like an Alchemist divine,
> Gross times of iron turning
> Into the purest form of gold.[22]

Here, as in many panegyric lyrics of the time, Elizabeth ("the Maid") is identified with Astraea, whose return to earth would bring a new golden age, and with an alchemist who has transformed the age of iron to that of gold.

Instead of the normal third-person subject, literature praising a hero or monarch sometimes used a second-person subject,
resulting in the pattern:

"You have brought . . ."

Davies uses this underlying pattern in Hymn II:

Blessed Astraea, I in part
Enjoy the *blessings you impart,*
The *peace,* the *milk and honey,*
Humanity and civil art,
A richer dower than money.[23]

Projected into the future, the heroic pattern (which used a
past- or present-tense verb) became the *messianic pattern,* which
was frequently used for prophetic statements:

"He/she will bring . . ." (+ positive vocabulary)

or

"He/she will eliminate . . ." (+ negative vocabulary)

Like the heroic pattern, the messianic pattern often praised a
reigning monarch, as in the *Aeneid* when the shade of Anchises
says to Aeneas: "This, this is he . . . , *Augustus Caesar,* son of a
god, who *shall* again *set up the golden age* amid the fields where
Saturn once reigned."[24] Many of the most famous examples of
this messianic pattern were biblical, such as the following messianic prophecy from Isaiah:

And there shall come forth a rod out of the stem of Jesse, and a branch
shall grow out of his roots. And the Spirit of the Lord shall rest upon
him, the spirit of wisdom and understanding. . . . [W]ith righteousness
shall he judge the poor. . . . *The wolf* also *shall dwell with the lamb, and the
leopard shall lie down with the kid . . . ; and a little child shall lead them. . . .
[A]sps and cockatrices shall not hurt nor destroy* in all my holy mountain.
[Isa. 11:1–9, King James version]

The underlying structure of this passage is "he [messiah] will
come and bring" and "he will eliminate." For example, the last
sentence in effect states that the savior will eliminate dangerous
serpents (and hence, symbolically, the enmity between man and
nature) in creating a millennial paradise.

This messianic pattern was also used with second-person subjects, assuming the form:

"You will come and establish . . ."

or

"You will eliminate . . ."

Probably the most influential work to use this version of the paradise myth was Virgil's Fourth Eclogue, which prophesied that a child would restore the golden age during the consulship of Pollio:

Only do thou, pure Lucina, smile on the birth of the *child, under whom the iron brood shall first cease, and a golden race spring up* throughout the world! . . . For thee, child, the earth shall untilled pour forth. . . . Uncalled, the goats shall bring home their udders swollen with milk, and the herds shall fear not huge lions; unasked thy cradle shall pour forth flowers for thy delight. The serpent, too, shall perish. . . . Assyrian spice shall spring up on every soil. [Virgil 1:29–33]

Although the second part of this quotation appears to be in the third person, the underlying structure has the form:

"You [child] will bring . . ."

Messianic narratives sometimes used a first-person variant of the descriptive pattern to create a *prophetic pattern*, describing a future paradise:

"I saw . . ."

Probably the most famous example of this appears in Revelation:[25]

And *I saw a new heaven and a new earth*: for the first heaven and the first earth were passed away. . . . And *I John saw* the holy City, *new Jerusalem*, coming down from God out of heaven, prepared as a bride adorned for her husband. . . . And I heard a great voice out of heaven saying . . . God himself shall be with them . . . ; and there shall be no more death, neither sorrow nor crying, neither shall there be any more pain: for the former things are passed away. [Rev. 21:1–4]

Through the combination of its definitional and assimilated vocabulary with its subject-verb structures, the paradise myth has provided a rhetorical structuring principle for many literary and nonliterary texts. Knowing these patterns, the attentive reader can often recognize the applicability of the paradise myth to the interpretation of a work from its very first line. For example, if we were to see a poem beginning "A place there is diffusing rivers four" (the actual beginning of a poem by the fifth-century writer Dracontius), we would be keyed to the probable relevance of the paradise myth by the combination of the descriptive syntactic pattern with the detail of four diffusing rivers from the Eden legend. Our suspicion would be confirmed by the paradisal details of the following lines:

> With flowers ambrosial decked; where jewelled turf,
> Where fragrant herbs abound that never fade.
> The fairest garden in the world of God.
> There fruit knows naught of season, but the year,
> There ever blossoms earth's eternal spring.[26]

As in this poem, works using the paradise myth have often been marked by anaphoric words like "here," "there," "where," "then," or "when" repeated at the beginning of two or more successive lines or phrases; indeed, repeated contrasts in a work of literature between the spatial adverbs "here" and "there" or the chronological adverbs "now" and "then" have often been sufficient to mark an opposition between paradise and hell.[27]

Occasionally, first-person syntactic structures in the paradise myth have been tools of irony—especially the first-person messianic pattern ("I will bring") and descriptive pattern ("There I saw"). Since in literature a person claiming to be a messiah is often a madman or a fool (with such obvious exceptions as the Bible), the first-person messianic pattern frequently provided a means of mocking a self-proclaimed savior. Some excellent examples are contained in Gonzalo's famous speech in act 2 of Shakespeare's *Tempest* ("Had I plantation of this isle, my lord") and Jack Cade's vision of the Cockaigne that his revolution would bring in *Henry VI*. Both characters display high ideals despite low capabilities.[28] Although Gonzalo does repeat some well-honored ideals of the paradise myth in his speech (largely "borrowed" from Montaigne's "On Cannibals"), the context establishes him as one of Shakespeare's "wise fools." Credibility in such works, as in any first-person narration, depends on the reader's assessment of the narrator. Thus, the description of what looks like a paradisal Land of the Houyhnhnms in book 4 of *Gulliver's Travels* loses its credibility when the reader realizes that Gulliver has

become an unreliable narrator, a madman whose praise of a society of superhorses (narrated through the "There I saw" pattern)
cannot be trusted.

Purposeful contradictions between paradisal form and infernal content have also created irony in literary works. For example, paratactic strings of paradisal conventions were sometimes linked not with an ideal place but with hell, frustrating
the reader's expectation (created by title or context), as in the
following example from Voltaire's *Candide*: "Nothing could be so
beautiful, so smart, so brilliant . . . as the two armies. Trumpets,
fifes, oboes, drums, cannons formed a harmony such as was
never heard even in hell" (p. 20). Voltaire's use of the word "hell"
where the reader has been lured to expect "paradise" (from the
context of beauty, brilliance, and especially harmony) typifies
such irony. Similarly, many anti-utopias have created irony by
having a narrator recite surface panegyrics to a "paradisal" state
that context subsequently shows to be a totalitarian hell.

Coordinated Themes and Images

The lexical and syntactic patterns of the paradise myth were
often strengthened by association with a number of ancillary
themes, motifs, and images. The myth frequently depicted the
creation of an ideal community where nature (including human
nature) is benevolent, emphasizing such themes as the renewed
friendship between man and beast (as in Virgil's Fourth Eclogue
or the Book of Isaiah); the return of a lost prelapsarian language
allowing complete communication between man and nature; the
existence of an *axis mundi* in the form of a tree, mountain, or
cosmic pillar connecting, and hence unifying, heaven and earth
(such as that appearing in Bacon's *New Atlantis*, which draws the
narrator's attention to the Book of Solomon); the return of an-
drogynous beings (unifying both sexes in themselves as Adam
supposedly had before the creation of Eve); and the use of al-
chemy to restore base metals to gold (through a process called
coniunctio or the unification of male and female opposites).

In works using the paradise myth, groups were often given
precedence over individuals, the social over the personal, the
communal over the private. The words "mine" and "yours" were

frequently associated with the undesirable and the word "ours"
with the good, just as "we" usually predominated over "I"; the
individual was marked as "good" only to the extent that he or
she fulfilled the norms and needs of the community.[29]

In depicting the total victory of good over evil, the myth often
portrayed a symbolic re-creation of the world in the place enjoying the good life—a restoration of the paradisal conditions of
the first age of man.[30] Since the cosmogonic transformation from
chaos to cosmos traditionally has been associated with the transition from darkness to light, images of brightness and sun often
have been associated with the ideal place and images of darkness
with its opposite;[31] the East (direction of the rising sun) was often
the location of paradise (as in Eden itself, which was said to be
"in the East").[32] Repetition of the cosmogony was often accompanied by other themes and imagery of ideal beginnings, including
virginity (the untouched or beginning sexual state), childhood
(the time before corruption), and primitivism (the preservation
of the beginning state of mankind by simple people like shepherds or noble savages).[33] Frequently, womb symbols and other
symbols of birth, rebirth, or re-beginning were used.[34] After depicting this return to beginnings, many works portrayed (either
implicitly or explicitly) a complete absence of time, for without
time chaos and evil (i.e., change for the worse) could not be re-
introduced, and paradisal good could survive in timeless perpetuity. Since plot depends on change and disequilibrium, works
occurring in a paradisal place frequently were plotless.[35]

Many works using the paradise myth have depicted a "sacred
space"—a place separated from the rest of the universe by some
physical or symbolic boundary that provides an ethical demarcation between "good" and "evil" or between the "sacred" and the
"profane."[36] Thus literary utopias were frequently set on inaccessible islands or on the moon, and paradisal lands in faraway
places like the land of the Hyperboreans (etymologically "beyond the North"); similarly, the golden age was defined as a
time when men had no communication or commerce with other
civilizations. Imagery of barriers, such as walls (e.g., post-Fall
Eden), high mountains[37] (e.g., those surrounding El Dorado in
Voltaire's *Candide*), or water (e.g., the island utopia), often emphasized this opposition between the sacred and the profane.

Paradise as Propaganda

The patterns discussed in this chapter have frequently been used for panegyric and propagandistic purposes, praising some person, place, period, product, or concept through a "spatial correlative"—a paradisal place corresponding to the goodness of the subject praised.[38] Many texts have praised a subject by making its name synonymous with perfection, assimilating it into the paradise myth for the duration of a text or section by including it in a syntagmatic chain of the ideal, as, for example, in Homer's *Odyssey* when the disguised Odysseus says to his wife Penelope (who does not recognize him):

Your fame has reached heaven itself, like that of some perfect king, ruling a populous and mighty state with the fear of God in his heart, and upholding the right, so that the dark soil yields its wheat and barley, the trees are laden with ripe fruit, the sheep never fail to bring forth their lambs, nor the sea to provide its fish—all that as a result of his good government—and his people prosper under him. [*Odyssey*, Book XIX, p. 291]

Odysseus lauds his wife here by associating her with a "perfect king" whose just rule brings paradisal plenty to his kingdom. However, like many discourses using the paradise myth, his rhetoric does not stop with the description of the ideal kingdom but uses this description to put his wife into the right frame of mind to grant a request: "Yet just because you are so good . . . do not insist on finding my lineage and my country." As in this example, the paradise myth frequently functioned as a rhetorical technique of persuasion, and its lexical and syntactic patterns were often used for political propaganda.[39]

To illustrate the relationship between paradise and propaganda and the functioning of the paradise myth in a literary text of a period that strongly influenced eighteenth-century Russia, let us examine Robert Herrick's 1648 sonnet "The bad season makes the Poet sad":

Dull to my selfe, and almost dead to these
My many fresh and fragrant Mistresses:
Lost to all Musick now; since every thing
Puts on the semblance here of sorrowing.

5   Sick is the Land to'th'heart; and doth endure
    More dangerous faintings by her desp'rate cure.
    But if that golden Age wo'd come again,
    And Charles here Rule, as he before did Raign;
    If smooth and unperplext the Seasons were,
10 As when the Sweet Maria lived here:
    I sho'd delight to have my Curles halfe drown'd
    In Tyrian Dewes, and Head with Roses crown'd.
    And once more yet (ere I am laid out dead)
    Knock at a Starre with my exalted Head. [Herrick, p. 114]

Herrick's sonnet mourning the overthrow of Charles I by Cromwell is divided into two opposing parts with a clear dividing
point in line 7 ("But if"). The first six lines of the poem describe
an "infernal" space—the England of Cromwell, a "sick" land that
has displaced the paradise of Charles I and created a "bad season" for the poets; lines 7–14 describe the paradise that would
reappear if the reign of Charles could be restored.[40] This division mirrors a general opposition in the two halves of the poem
between death and life, sickness and energy, dullness and creativity (especially poetic creativity),[41] and, implicitly, the iron age
and the golden age—all of which reflect the opposition between
Cromwell and Charles.

These oppositions create two syntagmatic chains that function
like dominoes: the chain of lines 1–6 assimilates all its motifs
into the infernal myth and makes them functional synonyms of
the word "bad"; the chain of lines 7–14 assimilates its motifs
into the paradise myth and makes them synonyms of the word
"good." By the end of the first chain, Cromwell is associated with
hell; by the end of the second, Charles has become linked with
paradise.[42] This link with paradise is emphasized by the use of
the messianic syntactical pattern ("He will eliminate"/"He will
bring") to structure the entire second part. The lists below sum-
marize the complete process of assimilation into the paradise
and infernal myths.

Infernal = Cromwell	Paradisal = Charles
dull	Mistresses (Muses)
dead	Musick (Poetry)
lost	golden Age

sorrowing	Charles's Rule
sick	smooth and unperplext
faintings	Seasons (Eternal Spring)
desp'rate cure	Sweet Maria (Henrietta
	Maria, Charles's wife)
	Curles . . . in Tyrian Dewes
	Head with Roses crown'd
	Knocking at a Starre

Significantly, all of the nouns assimilated into the paradise myth begin with capital letters—the only words receiving such emphasis with the exception of "Land" (Eng-land), which is the focus of the poem and would also become synonymous with the good and be assimilated into the paradise myth "if that golden age" of Charles's reign would "come again."

As in Herrick's work, the paradise myth provided a potent means of propagandizing *any* place or time (and the person or concept associated with it) as perfect.[43] The messianic and descriptive patterns of the myth were used particularly often in propagandistic praise of the powers-that-be and in voicing nationalistic feelings, linking one's country and its leaders with paradise by including them in a "syntagm of perfection."[44] In several periods and places, including the courts of Renaissance France and England, the paradise myth provided an important organizing principle for literary and propagandistic works. As I shall demonstrate in the remainder of this book, the Russian eighteenth century was one such period. To understand the role of the paradise myth in this century of transition from sacred to secular and from traditional backwardness to modern Western culture, I shall examine briefly in Chapter 2 the historical background of the paradise myth in Russia and then proceed to a detailed study of the integration of Russian and Western ideals of paradise in many diverse areas of the eighteenth century.

CHAPTER TWO

Sacred into Secular

The Russian paradise myth was strongly shaped by the Orthodox Church and the Byzantine heritage that the church brought with it to Russia. Even after the secularizing reforms at the end of the seventeenth century and the beginning of the eighteenth, the influence of Orthodoxy remained enormous not only in literature and the arts but also in ideology, where a Muscovite tendency toward "political theology" (the expression of political ideas through a "general framework of liturgical language and theological thought")[1] was intensified as part of a general transfer from church to state of concepts, themes, imagery, stylistic techniques, and terminology. This chapter examines several Orthodox, Byzantine, and Muscovite ideologies that helped to shape the eighteenth-century paradise myth and studies the role of the myth in the attempt to create a "religion of state" during this period of secularization in Russia.

Heaven on Earth

Within the Eastern church, the ability to return to a paradisal state was emphasized far more than in the Western church.[2] Several key aspects of the paradise myth in eighteenth-century Russia stem either directly or indirectly from the idea of spiritual reform in the Eastern church, which Gerhart Ladner has defined as "the return to Paradise, the recovery of man's lost image-likeness to God, and the representation on earth of the heavenly *Basileia*" (the Kingdom of God).[3]

Imagery of heaven on earth and the earthly paradise was cen-

tral to the theology of the Eastern church, frequently symbolizing the church itself or linked with its rituals. As St. Irenaeus
wrote, "The church is planted as a paradise in this world."[4] From
Origen's third-century equation of baptism with the entry into
paradise to Eusebius's fourth-century *Ecclesiastical History* (where
the church is referred to as the earthly likeness of heaven), to St.
Ephraem's fourth-century *Hymns on Paradise* (where the church
is said to be "similar to paradise"),[5] and to St. Germanus's eighth-
century writings (where the church is called "the heavens on
earth, where God, who is higher than the heavens, lives"),[6] the
idea is repeated that the church is a terrestrial paradise—an
earthly image of the Kingdom of God in heaven.[7]

The Eastern church, from the teachings of its Fathers to its
prayers, stressed the ability to experience through Orthodoxy a
foretaste of the joys that await the true believer in heaven; the
church was even called a "spiritual paradise" at several places
in its liturgy.[8] As an eighth-century hymn still used today in the
Orthodox Christmas vespers states: "The Cherubim have moved
away from the tree of life, and *I partake of the delight of paradise*
from which I had been ejected because of disobedience. . . .
Today the age-old bond of Adam's condemnation has been un-
tied. *Paradise has been opened to us, the serpent has been crushed.*"[9]
This Orthodox emphasis on the ability to experience paradise
on earth through the church[10] was transferred to Russia after
its conversion; under the influence of Orthodoxy, the search for
heaven on earth became a central theme in Russian culture.

Literary reflections of this theme appeared in Russia as early
as the Primary Chronicle, where under the heading for 6495
(A.D. 987) the emissaries of Prince Vladimir reported to their
prince about their experience in a Greek Orthodox church: "We
did not know whether we were in heaven or on earth because
there is no such sight and no such beauty on earth and we do not
know how to tell about it. We only know that God dwells there
with men."[11] I would argue that these famous lines (written at
least 125 years after the Christianization of Russia) use both the
Eastern patristic symbolism of the church as an earthly paradise
or heaven on earth[12] and the general Christian conception of the
church as a "provisional paradise" that anticipates the ultimate
uniting of heaven and earth at the end of time (Rev. 21:3).[13] In-

deed, the symbolism of heaven on earth in the Chronicle reflects
the same theology that underlies the architecture of the Orthodox dome church (including that of Hagia Sophia, presumably
visited by Vladimir's emissaries), symbolizing through its cupola
the descent of heaven to earth and the biblical conception of
heaven and earth as a single world.[14]

Depictions of the church as heaven on earth reflected a characteristic of Byzantine theological thought that John Meyendorff has called "realized eschatology"—the assumption that the
transfiguration and deification of man are accessible *now*, not just
in the future.[15] Much Byzantine political thought was premised
on equivalent theocratic assumptions and strongly influenced
the development of Muscovite political ideas[16] and, in turn, of
many works of Russian literature and culture through the end
of the eighteenth century. As we shall see later in this chapter, the Orthodox idea of the church as heaven on earth was to
help shape the paradise myth in secularized eighteenth-century
Russia, when the *state* came to usurp this "function."

The Political Icon

In both theology and politics, the Byzantines assumed that any
earthly ideal imitates some heavenly model—an idea reflecting
the very essence of the Orthodox icon. As part of its political
heritage from Byzantium, Russia received the doctrine that the
ideal state is a theocracy—an empire guided by God. Sir Steven
Runciman has written:

Just as man was made in God's image, so [in Byzantine political theory]
man's kingdom on earth was made in the image of the Kingdom of
Heaven. Just as God ruled in Heaven, so an Emperor, made in His
image, should rule on earth and carry out His commandments. . . . [If]
the copy . . . could be achieved, with the Emperor and his ministers and
counsellors imitating God with His archangels and angels and saints,
then life on earth could become a proper preparation for the truer reality
of life in Heaven.[17]

The perfect state, in other words, was conceived as being in the
image and likeness of heaven just as the Garden of Eden had
once been. George Fedotov has argued that this "social extension

of icon veneration" underlies all Eastern Orthodox theocracy: "The tsar is, as it were, the living icon of God just as the whole empire is the icon of the heavenly world."[18]

Under the influence of this Byzantine concept of the ideal state and the theology of the icon that it reflected, the biblical idea that God made man in His own image and likeness (Gen. 1:26–27) became an important marker of political and personal perfection in Russian culture, frequently using the words *obraz* ("image") and *podobie* ("likeness"). Such "imagery" reflected the inherent presence in the icon of a vision of paradise regainable to the true believer—a view of a transformed and transfigured world where man could regain his likeness to God lost in the Fall. Under the influence of this Byzantine theological principle, the moral-religious opposition between *obraz* (which sometimes came to connote not only "image" or "icon" but "the form and embodiment of beauty," "the visible symbol of the beauty of God") and *bezobrazie* (that which is "without image, shapeless, disfigured, ugly," "monstrous," or "deformed") became central to Russian literature and culture.[19]

As a result of a renewed Byzantinization of Russian culture under Tsar Alexis (reigned 1645–76), Byzantine political theory continued to play an important role in Russia through at least the late eighteenth century and helped contribute to the sacralization of the tsar that often accompanied the paradise myth in this period.[20] As Eusebius had stated in his "Oration in Praise of the Emperor Constantine" (A.D. 335), the Christian state is mimetic of the Kingdom of God in heaven, and God is the archetype of the Christian king.[21] Under the influence of such Byzantine ideas many Russian works depicted the perfect state as obtainable only through a perfect ruler, who was in the "image and likeness" of God, chosen by Him to remake the earth in the "image" of heaven and thus reestablish paradise on earth.

This idea of the good monarch as the image and likeness of God and his land as the earthly image of heaven was both strengthened and tempered in Russia under the influence of Agapetus's "Hortatory Chapters" (a "mirror of princes" written for Emperor Justinian that circulated in many manuscripts and had three different printed translations in eighteenth-century Russia).[22] Agapetus stressed that if a king remakes himself in the

image and likeness of God, then his subjects will be re-formed
in the image of their king. Implicit in these chapters was the assumption that if a monarch correctly uses his "kingly dignity"
and scepter, which are given him by God "in the likeness of
the heavenly kingdom" (*po podobiiu nebesnogo tsarstviia* in Stepan
Pisarev's 1771 Russian translation), he will create the just society
on earth.[23] By assuming that kings are placed on the throne by
God, Agapetus contributed to the theory of divine right that frequently accompanied the paradise myth in eighteenth-century
Russia. But by stating that with this God-given power comes
the responsibility for the monarch to follow all laws himself,
Agapetus's work also gave support to those wishing to restrain
the power of the tsar.[24] Agapetus intended his praise of the emperor to apply *only* when the incumbent carried out his duties of
humanity, justice, and humility. But as we shall see, this didacti-
cism was often lost in the eighteenth century, when the paradise
myth frequently became part of the propagandistic arsenal of
Russian panegyric poets, reflecting the influence of Muscovite
ideology with its frequent conception of Russia as "sacred and
perfect, needing no change or improvement."[25]

The Third Rome and Sacred Imperialism

Byzantine political theology contributed to the secular paradise
myth in eighteenth-century Russia not only directly but also
through the intermediary of what Richard Pipes has called the
Muscovite "ideology of royal absolutism," consisting of four
basic elements: the idea of Moscow (Muscovite Russia) as the
Third Rome; "the imperial idea," connecting the rulers of Moscow to the imperial line of the Roman Emperor Augustus; the
depiction of Russian monarchs as universal Christian sovereigns;
and the ideology that the Muscovite sovereigns received their
authority from God.[26] These Byzantine-influenced ideas became
particularly strong in Muscovite Russia as a result of a number of factors: the immigration to Russia in the late fourteenth
and the fifteenth centuries of many prominent Bulgarian and
Serbian intellectuals, who produced new Russian translations of
Byzantine political tracts that helped bolster Muscovite sacred
imperialism (including Agapetus's "Hortatory Chapters");[27] the

fall of Byzantium (the "Second Rome") to the Turks in 1453; the marriage of Ivan III to the niece of the last Byzantine emperor in 1472, leading to claims that Moscow was the successor of the Byzantine empire;[28] and the final Russian rejection of the domination of the Mongol Horde in 1480. Together, these factors helped infect Muscovy with messianism. From this time forward, the tendency of Russia to depict itself as a "perfected theocracy" and to idealize its present situation—two mainstays of the paradise myth in eighteenth-century Russia—became particularly well developed.[29]

The ideology of Moscow as the Third Rome embodied the theory of *translatio imperii* ("translation of empire")—the idea that in any period a single nation would be the dominant cultural and political force in world civilization and that this force would move from one state to another with the passage of time.[30] Drawing its authority from biblical passages, this theory gained importance in Western Europe during the Middle Ages, when it presented theological justification for the replacement of one universal monarchy by another[31] and became a rhetorical vehicle for propagandizing the mission of one's country as both sacred and universal—a resurrection of the old Roman combination of *sacerdotium* and *imperium*.

With the fall of Byzantium and the consequent application of the theory of *translatio imperii* to Moscow, the paradise myth began to appear explicitly in Russian secular literature. One of the earliest comparisons of Russia to the earthly paradise occurs in the "Discourse Against the Latins" (c. 1461), which condemns the 1439 Council of Florence that had attempted to unite Eastern Orthodoxy with Roman Catholicism ("the Latins"):[32] *"Like the God-planted paradise of the spiritual East [myslennogo vstoka] or like the garden made by God with flowers and shining with piety in the universe* [i.e., Eden], *the God-enlightened Russian land is rejoicing, the land of the pious Prince Basil, tsar of all Russia."*[33] This passage describes the Russian state through two images that had previously been used for the church: a "spiritual paradise" and a God-planted Eden. Similarly, the "Tale of the Princes of Vladimir" (late fifteenth or early sixteenth century) depicts the tsars of "holy Russia"—"those God-appointed holders of the scepter"—as being "like the trees of paradise planted by God."[34]

Even after the secularization of the seventeenth and early eighteenth centuries, this idea of Russia as a paradisal country led by a God-appointed tsar remained an essential assumption of much secular Russian literature.

The assumption that Russia had become like paradise also underlay the most famous Russian application of the *translatio* theory: the monk Filofei's early-sixteenth-century epistle to Grand Prince Vasilii III, which continued to circulate through the eighteenth century in Russia:[35]

Old Rome fell because of its church's lack of faith, the Apollinarian heresy; and in the Second Rome, the city of Constantine, the pagans broke down the doors of the churches with their axes. . . . And now there is the Holy synodal Apostolic church of the reigning third Rome of your tsardom, which shines like the sun in its Orthodox Christian faith throughout the whole universe. And that is your realm, pious tsar, as *all the empires of the Orthodox Christian faith have gathered into your single empire . . . you are the only tsar for Christians in the whole world. . . .*

Listen and attend, pious tsar, that all Christian empires are gathered in our single one, that *two Romes have fallen, and the third one stands, and a fourth one there shall not be; your empire will not fall to others,* according to the great Evangelist.[36]

One of the "fruits" of the Third Rome theory was the addition of the imperial orb or "apple" (*iabloko* or, later, *derzhava*) to the regalia of the Muscovite ruler. This orb, which took the form of a golden apple (hence the name "*iabloko*"), symbolized the rebirth of the Roman empire under a Christian *kosmokrator* ("ruler of the world")—the Muscovite tsar—who, like Christ, was to reverse the consequences of the apple-caused Fall of man and restore the world to the Edenic state of its beginnings.[37]

This connection between Russia, the Third Rome, and paradise was seen occasionally in the visual arts as well. For example, one icon entitled *The Church Militant*, painted to mark the victory of Ivan IV at Kazan in 1552, shows three rows of soldiers on foot and on horseback led by the Archangel Michael toward a garden on a hill, representing paradise, where the Mother of God sits on a throne with Christ in her hands.[38] On one level, this icon represents the victory of Christianity over Islam, leading mankind into the "spiritual paradise" (the Christian Church) and away from "Sodom" (Islam). But on another level, as John

Stuart has noted, this paradisal garden may also be interpreted as Moscow—the Third Rome—and Sodom as Kazan.[39]

Until the second half of the seventeenth century, the myth of the Third Rome and other versions of the paradise myth were used largely by ecclesiastical propagandists of the state rather than by poets or by the state apparatus itself.[40] But in part as a result of a power dispute between Patriarch Nikon and Tsar Alexis, the paradise myth became part of official state propaganda. In deposing Nikon (and thus proclaiming the superiority of the state over the church), Alexis began the process of secularization that was to be frequently supported by the paradise myth until the last part of the eighteenth century.[41]

Reacting against Nikon's depiction of the church as a "second state" and its patriarch as a "second tsar,"[42] Alexis's son Peter I stated in his 1721 Ecclesiastical Regulation, substituting a state-controlled synod for the Patriarchate: "[T]he common people, not knowing the difference between the spiritual and the autocratic power, and being impressed by the greatness and fame of the supreme pastor [patriarch], think him a second sovereign, equal or even superior in power to the autocrat, and believe the church to be another and higher state."[43] The paradise myth, which frequently served to idealize, propagandize, and mythologize autocracy, often tried to reverse this perception by portraying the state as another and higher *church*.[44] As Pierre Pascal has written: "[A]fter Nikon, Russia no longer had a church: It had a religion of state. From there to state religion it required but one step."[45] In the rest of this chapter, we shall examine the ways the paradise myth helped to develop this "state religion." By portraying the Russian state, instead of the church, as heaven on earth, the tsar as an "earthly god" or the "icon of God," and his Russia (the "new Zion") as transfigured through his efforts, the myth strongly contributed to what Joseph II, the Holy Roman emperor, called the "one religion—that of directing all citizens equally toward the good of the state."[46]

The Spiritual Paradise

At least fifty years before Peter's Ecclesiastical Regulation, there began a widespread appropriation of church concepts, vocabulary, and symbols for redefining the new secular state and its tsar.

In this general transfer of images from church to state (which resulted in part from the absence of any conception of a secular state in previous Russian history),[47] the images of a spiritual paradise and of heaven on earth were gradually converted from sacred to secular use.

The secular use of paradisal imagery probably resulted in part from the revival in the second half of the seventeenth century of the Byzantine and Kievan metaphors of the church as heaven on earth in connection with the battle between Patriarch Nikon and Tsar Alexis. Simeon Polotskii reflected this revival in the prose preface to his encyclopedic collection of verses called *The Garden of Many Flowers* (1677–80): "I have tried to add this many-flowered garden of mine to the house of God, *the holy Eastern church, [which is] like a spiritual Eden [edemu myslennomu], a spiritual paradise [raiu dukhovnomu], a heavenly garden,* for the glory of the creator of all things and for the spiritual use of all who are trying to live devoutly."[48] Supporters of both patriarch and tsar used similar imagery to propagandize their claims. Proponents of Patriarch Nikon published a book of verses entitled *The Spiritual Paradise (Rai myslennyi,* 1659), claiming the ultimate power in the church for the patriarch, who is compared with Christ, "the great pastor of all."[49] In contrast, Simeon Polotskii's "Greeting 10" to Tsar Alexis (1678) used paradisal imagery to argue that the church is subservient to the tsar:

God ordered the cherub to guard the earthly paradise so that no one would dare to enter it and entrusted a sword to him, this servant of his. The sword was fiery and turned very fast so that the Garden of Eden would remain intact, and the tree of life was entrusted to him so that it would remain untouched. *You, o tsar,* the true servant of God, *are like the cherub,* although you are made of flesh; *to you from the living God is entrusted our spiritual paradise—the holy church.* In it there flowers the tree of life, which gives life to the souls of the faithful who together comprise the body of Christ. . . . *You* [tsar] *are the chosen cherub of this paradise,* and because of this a sword has been given to you by the Lord so that *you will be its keeper and protector.*[50]

These lines, written after the victory of the secular "sword" over the sacred, stress the idea of the tsar as guardian of the church and reflect the movement toward a secular state that Alexis's victory represented.[51]

Occasionally, the image of a spiritual paradise was transformed to refer to the Mother of God as a "spiritual garden"
(*myslennyi sad*),[52] using the frequent Christian allegorical interpretation of the Virgin Mary/Mother of God as the "enclosed
garden" (*hortus conclusus*) of the Song of Songs. This allegory
was quite popular in both the verbal and the visual arts in
seventeenth-century Russia, producing such titles as Antonii
Radivilovskii's 1676 collection of poems called "The Garden of
Mary" (*Ogorodok Marii*) and Nikita Pavlovets's icon *The Mother
of God as an Enclosed Garden*.[53] The link between the Mother of
God and paradise may help explain a rather curious image in
eighteenth-century Russian panegyric poetry in which female
tsars were compared to a "paradise of the spirits" (*rai myslei*).

The most famous usage of this image occurs in M. V. Lomonosov's 1759 Name Day Ode to Tsar Elizabeth:

O source of bounty, Angel of peace, O goddess of glad hearts, on Whom
the purple mantel is like the dawn and the crown of peaceful days is
like the sun. O *beautiful paradise of our spirits, O clear image* [*obraz iasnyi*]
of the cloudless heavens where we see the gentle spring in your face, in
your lips, in your eyes, and your morals. Is it possible in your kingdom
to see the horrible war in Europe? [Lomonosov, 1950, 8:648]

Here the words *rai* (paradise) and *mysli* (spirits, thoughts) combine to form the phrase "the beautiful paradise of our spirits"
(*myslei nashikh rai prekrasnyi*);[54] however, the "spiritual paradise"
implied by the combination of these two words is no longer the
church or the Mother of God but Tsar Elizabeth, who is seen as
an "icon" or "image" of "the cloudless heavens," as the church
itself had earlier been portrayed. This image of Elizabeth as the
"spiritual paradise" reflects the broader eighteenth-century tendency to transform vocabulary dealing with the Mother of God
to praise female tsars.

Under the influence of Lomonosov's 1759 Name Day Ode,
lesser poets also used the component images of the "spiritual
paradise" to praise the reigning tsar. For example, Ermil Kostrov's 1780 Accession Day Ode to Catherine II begins:

Why are the loud sounds of new applause ascending rapidly to the
clouds? And why are the hands of zealous Russians stretched out to the
bright heavens? Who is being blessed by these happy lips? To whom

are they weaving [*pletut*] just praises? *Catherine, [you are] the paradise of our spirits [Ekaterina myslei rai].* Our hearts are striving towards you.[55]

Here the poet (who poses as the chronicler of Catherine's applauding subjects) equates the tsar with the spiritual paradise as part of his process of "praise weaving," imitating the old Russian style of "word weaving" (*pletenie sloves*)—a paratactic style, based on the accumulation of many synonyms, that was used particularly frequently in the lives of saints.[56]

In consonance with the general movement of images from church to state and court, the image of heaven on earth was itself secularized during the late seventeenth century. Simeon Polotskii (one of the most important sources for the secular paradise myth of the eighteenth century) wrote, "I dare to call Russia heaven."[57] Later this theme echoed in the works of Lomonosov, who in his 1761 Accession Day Ode to Elizabeth wrote:

The creator leads, and Peter the Great follows. He raised us. Hurry, O Russians, tap the Urals for the statue [*na obraz*] as a sign of his victories: so that his immortal face may shine in all corners of the earth, as bright and great as the sun, and so that it may be seen from unknown places, and so that *Russia, the equal of heaven,* may show the world as many great deeds as there are stars.[58]

In his December 1761 Accession Ode to Peter III, Lomonosov was even more explicit when he wrote regarding Russia's flourishing state: "I see heaven on earth."[59] In the process of secularization, the Russian state had thus "usurped" the role of the church as heaven on earth, just as it was to borrow other Orthodox and biblical rhetoric, concepts, and imagery to depict itself as the new locus of paradise.[60]

The Transplanted "Image"

In the transfer of symbols from sacred to secular, the Byzantine practice of using the concept and vocabulary of the icon for political propaganda was resurrected in Russia, creating a paradisal vision of the return of man to the image and likeness of God under the influence of the new secular state and its tsar. One early visual example appears in Simon Ushakov's 1668 painting *The Planting of the Tree of the Russian State* (Illustration 1). Called

Illustration 1. Simon Ushakov, *The Planting of the Tree of the Russian State* (from John Stuart, "The Flowering of Moscow," in *Art Treasures in Russia*, ed. Bernard Myers and Trewin Copplestone. New York: McGraw-Hill, 1970).

an icon (*obraz*) by Ushakov himself, this painting depicts Ivan I (the first of the "gatherers of the Russian lands" into the Muscovite state) and Metropolitan Peter (whose shrine made Moscow the spiritual center of Russia) planting in the Moscow Kremlin a tree whose branches are covered with medallion portraits of Russian tsars and church officials.[61] In the center of this "cosmic tree" connecting Russia to heaven is a reproduction of the Vladimir Mother of God icon (whose transfer from Vladimir to Moscow had symbolized the rise of Muscovite political power) and above the tree, in heaven, is Christ.[62] The tree grows through the center of the Kremlin's Cathedral of the Assumption (the coronation cathedral of the Russian tsars).

The focus of this painting on "planting" is significant, reflecting an important theological image often applied to the church. Just as God "planted a garden eastward in Eden" (Gen. 2:8), so the Church Fathers often used planting in their writings to represent the founding of the church, the earthly image of the heavenly paradise. Indeed, Ushakov places Christ and the Mother of God in approximately the same positions in his "tree of state" that they would occupy in the typical Orthodox dome church: Christ at the top center looks down as He usually does from the central cupola; the Mother of God is in the middle of the painting, symbolic of her role as intercessor between heaven and earth (as her midway position between ground and cupola symbolizes in church frescoes). The symbolism of the dome church (portraying heaven as descending to earth) is thus transferred, in effect, to the new secular *state*, which, like the church, becomes "a paradise in this world"—an "icon" or "image" of heaven on earth.

On the tree of state are pictured roses and grapes. The roses, which have no thorns, had in patristic symbolism often represented paradise—the place where the rose without thorns grew (hence, symbolically, the church); the grapes had also represented the church, which made Christians the "branches" of the "True Vine" (Christ).[63] Such patristic symbolism was well known in seventeenth- and eighteenth-century Russia. Indeed, in one catechism of the Slavonic-Greek-Latin Academy students were asked whether the rose without thorns grew in paradise. They were given the response that Saints Basil the Great, Ambrose, and John of Damascus had answered in the affirmative since God created the thorn only after the Fall.[64] As Ushakov's painting reflects, by the last third of the seventeenth century such patristic symbolism was being applied not only to the church but also to the state.

This transplantation of symbols from sacred to secular also extended to the tsar, who was pictured as the icon or "image" of God on earth, just as his state was viewed as an earthly image of the heavenly kingdom.[65] For example, Simeon Polotskii proclaimed to Tsar Alexis, "You are the *image* [*icon*] of God" ("*Bozhii ty obraz, tsariu Aleksie*").[66] From the late seventeenth through the early nineteenth century, this symbolism resounded throughout Russian panegyric and patriotic literature.[67]

A paradigm for this pattern appears in Lomonosov's "Ode on the Arrival in St. Petersburg from Moscow of Empress Elizabeth in the Year 1742 After Her Coronation."[68] Using a typical convention of the time, Lomonosov has God appear as a character (referred to as the "Ancient of Days" from Dan. 7:9) and proclaim that Elizabeth is His image/icon through whom He rules: "May you [Elizabeth] be eternally blessed . . . and with you all of your people, whom I have entrusted to your authority. . . . *Nations now honor my image* [*obraz*] *and my spirit infused in you.* . . . Through you I will punish evil, through you I will reward good deeds. Rule with my sanction; I will always be with you" (lines 51–80). Lomonosov's God makes it clear that He is on the side of Russia, offering a blessing to nations friendly to His new chosen land and a curse to its enemies.[69] As He states, the latter have "raised their swords against me, . . . for I myself am defending Russia" (lines 93, 100). In short, God's own words in this poem point vividly to the political theology of the mid-eighteenth century, which posited an iconic relationship between Russia and heaven and between God and tsar. Despite a 1680 ukase that forbade Russian citizens' comparing the tsar to God, this practice continued—and was encouraged—throughout the eighteenth century.[70]

By depicting the monarch as the icon or image of God, eighteenth-century Russian literature often implicitly compared (or even equated) the monarch with God's perfect Image, Christ the King, who would overcome the Fall and lead His subjects back to paradise.[71] This comparison reflected not only the fre-

quent Byzantine equation of the ruler with Christ but also the
Russian idea that power is a burden to be avoided, except by the
one whom God has chosen to suffer.[72] In the writings of Feofan Prokopovich and his contemporary Feofilakt Lopatinskii—
some of which were edited by Peter the Great himself—tsars are
explicitly called "gods" and "christs."[73] In other literature and
official ceremonies of the late seventeenth and the eighteenth
centuries, the name of the tsar was often blatantly substituted
for the name of Christ, for example when Peter was welcomed
to Moscow in 1709 after the victory at Poltava with words addressed to Christ on His entrance into Jerusalem: "Blessed is he
that cometh in the name of the Lord. Hosannah in the highest,
Lord God appear to us."[74] Gavriil Buzhinskii in a sermon on the
first anniversary of Peter's death called him "the resurrection
and the life."[75] And Catherine the Great was called "the beginning and end of all things."[76] Indeed, one of Peter the Great's
associates, Ivan Kirillov, even kept a portrait of Peter in his icon
corner, bowed to it, and lit candles in front of it—actions fitting
the tsar's status as the "image" of God.[77]

Even in works that avoided the direct equation of monarch and
Christ, there often appeared epithets for the tsar like "earthly
god," "the Russian God," and "Godlike" (*Bogopodobnyi*: "in the
likeness of God").[78] As Lomonosov wrote in his 1755 "Speech
in Memory of Peter the Great": "If one must find a man who is
similar to God in our comprehension, then I cannot find any possibility other than Peter the Great."[79] And just as the name God
was usually printed in capital letters in the eighteenth century,
so was the name of the monarch, implying an obvious analogy.
Finally, syntactic parallelism sometimes reinforced the idea of
the monarch as the icon of God on earth, as in one anonymous
poem published in 1783: "Great is GOD in his deeds, great is
Russia's MOTHER [Catherine II]."[80] The tutor of Peter the Great's
son may thus have been quoted accurately when he said of Peter:
"He is so pleased when they equate him with God."[81]

Through such analogies and equations, the ruler cult from
which the icon had in part originated and the medieval idea of
divine kingship were, at least rhetorically, restored in Russia.[82]
On one level, this transformation of earlier traditions provided
the ideological underpinnings for the emergence of modern

absolutism in Russia.[83] On another level, these iconic descriptions of the monarch set the stage for a conception of Russia as a messianic land—a country led by an "anointed one" (Greek: *khristos*; Hebrew: *mashiah*) that was or would become the promised land for the people of the world. Just as man lost Eden and his original likeness to God, so by imitating the monarch's divine nature could subjects now reform themselves and make their land into a new Eden.

This "mimetic ethic" provided the foundation for a vision of Russia as heaven on earth that was to play a central role in Russian courtly culture of the eighteenth century. The basic principle is prefigured in Simeon Polotskii's poem "The Example" ("Obraz," c. 1678): "All people conduct themselves according to the example [literally, "image"] of the tsar and imitate his life with their own. . . . Through the sanctity of the tsar, the people are also sanctified."[84] A similar mimetic ethic runs throughout much of the literature of eighteenth-century Russia: a good tsar will create a paradisal kingdom, a bad tsar an earthly hell.[85] Conversely, as Pavel L'vov wrote in his novel *The Temple of Truth* (1790), the monarch who creates the good life for his subjects is "the image of God on earth."[86]

By the early eighteenth century many works depicting the monarch as the image and likeness of God also portrayed a paradisal or Edenic Russia. Thus the connection we observed in Ushakov's icon between the Russian state and the earthly paradise foreshadowed a broad cultural pattern of the eighteenth century. This pattern is reflected in Lomonosov's 1742 Arrival Ode, discussed above, where after God's announcement that Elizabeth is in His image, Russia is described as a country where "swords will be beaten into ploughshares and spears into pruning hooks" (one of the descriptions of the millennial kingdom in Isa. 2:4) and where "in winter there is golden spring" (one of the descriptions of the golden age in classical writers like Hesiod and Ovid).[87] This new Russian world of order, peace, and perfection was filled with divine grace and celebrated the sanctification of God's image on earth.

The Transfigured Tsar

The world depicted in the icon is not the everyday, post-Fall world but a world transfigured—changed by the light of Christ to resemble its pre-Fall state. This paradisal world of the icon reflects the Orthodox belief (celebrated in the holiday of the Transfiguration) that matter can be restored to its original Edenic harmony and beauty.[88] This belief was reflected in secular literature of the seventeenth and eighteenth centuries, which occasionally portrayed a transfigured tsar creating a paradisal world. As Leonid Ouspensky has observed, "A man's transfiguration communicates itself to all the surroundings, for an attribute of holiness is the sanctification of all the surrounding world."[89] The external manifestation of this harmony was often shining light, reflecting the divine light present in transfigured creation.[90]

By the reign of Tsar Alexis, the image of the tsar as "the light of all Russia" had become fairly common in Russian literature. As Simeon Polotskii wrote in some early verses to Alexis, "Rejoice, bright Tsar from the East, shining upon Russia with light from the eye of God."[91] Through at least the early nineteenth century, the tsar was described as a secular version of the transfigured Christ; there were references to his "bright face," his "shining," and the "light" and "rays" that he emitted. He was often called a "luminary" (*svetilo*) and described or addressed with the epithet *svetleishii* ("the very bright"—the equivalent of "His Highness"); and his Russia was sometimes called a "radiant place" (*svetloe mesto*) where people "rejoice radiantly"—in other words a paradise.[92] Sometimes it was said that a "heavenly light" shone in his eyes, and that in his presence "nights are bright as days." And several times his throne was explicitly compared with Mount Tabor, where Christ was transfigured.[93]

In accordance with this pattern, when Vasilii Petrov in his poem "On the Conclusion of Peace with the Ottoman Porte" calls Catherine II "the beginning and end of all things" and "the image of the all-powerful Deity," and then asks her to "pour [her] light from [her] lofty throne" (*s gornego prestola*), it is clear that he is equating her with the transfigured Christ.[94] This image of light shining from Catherine provides a leitmotiv to the poem, which goes on to depict her giving the ignorant the key to paradise.

Similarly, Ivan Golenevskii's untitled ode to Catherine II depicts her as a "beautiful angel *shin*[*ing*] *in the likeness of God*" and goes on to credit her with the re-creation of a golden age in Russia.[95]

More conventional solar imagery was also used in the eighteenth-century Russian paradise myth to express the connection of a monarch with God, the gods, and the Good.[96] For example, Aleksandr Sumarokov's "Ode to Empress Catherine II on the First Day of 1763" begins with a depiction of Catherine as the light driving out all darkness (the party of Peter III) from Russia, resulting in the appearance of a "golden-dawned day" in her land; typical of many poems of the time, this work associates Peter (who had himself been "shining" when on the throne) with falsehood and hell, and Catherine with truth and paradise.[97] Although such solar imagery reflected centuries of literary convention and the absolutist equation of the king with the sun (most recently under the influence of France's Sun King and Versailles), the importance of transfiguration to Orthodoxy often presented overtones that were unique to Russia, emphasizing the restoration of a lost paradise to an earth brightened because of Russia's tsar.[98]

God's Chosen Country

The imagery examined thus far often combined to represent Russia as God's chosen country.[99] Within this variant of the paradise myth, the Russians, as a result of their "true belief" (the etymology of "Orthodoxy"), were often portrayed as having obtained the Promised Land awaited by the Jews in the Old Testament, and the Russian land was depicted as the new Israel or new Zion. Thus Peter the Great's associate Aleksandr Menshikov called Petersburg "the holy land,"[100] and Vasilii Trediakovskii (in his 1728 "Verses in Praise of Russia") depicted Russia as "a creation of God"—a land divinely granted "riches, plenty, and a treasury of goodness" because "all of [its] people are Orthodox."[101] This idea of Russia succeeding Israel as God's chosen country reflected the heritage not only of the Bible and of the theory of "translation of empire" but also the more recent images of Moscow as the "New Israel" and Kiev as the "second Jerusalem."[102]

The equation of Russia with Israel occurred particularly frequently in war poems, where Russia's enemies often were identified with Egypt, the biblical enemy of God's chosen people.
For example, Lomonosov's 1759 Name Day Ode to Elizabeth
compares Russia to Israel and Prussia (its opponent in the Seven
Years' War) to Egypt. God appears as a character and, para-
phrasing Exodus, says to "Moses" (Elizabeth): "I in my fury will
harden the conceited heart of Egypt. . . . I will arm Israel invinci-
bly with most holy strength."[103] Just before this speech, Lomonosov contrasts Russia and Prussia through a series of oppositions
between "here" (*zdes'* = Russia = paradise) and "there" (*tam* =
Prussia = hell)—a device typical of the paradise myth.

God's love for His new chosen people was occasionally portrayed as providing messianic hope for other countries as well,
as in Lomonosov's 1748 Accession Day Ode to Elizabeth: "And
your sword, entwined with laurels, stopped the war [in Europe]
while still unsheathed."[104] Similarly, Aleksandr Karin's 1760 ode
to Elizabeth proclaims that "Europe, drowning in battle, has
raised its woeful voice, placing hope in you that your great
spirit will save everyone."[105] The belief of many Russians in the
messianic mission of their country was thus being expressed
in terms that anticipated Slavophile conventions of the mid-
nineteenth century, stressing Russia's role as a peacemaker to
a war-ravaged Europe. Such messianism sometimes combined
with a "paradisal populism," as in Lomonosov's 1762 Accession
Ode to Catherine, where the poet enumerates the virtues resulting from God's love of the Russians, "Count the heroes which
we have, from the farmer to the monarch, in the courts, in regiments, on the sea and in the villages, in our territory and on
foreign soil, and at the holy altar." This great potential of the
Russian people will allow Catherine, "a goddess" whom "the
Almighty with His strong hand" has placed on the throne, to
establish "a beautiful paradise" in Russia.[106]

In consonance with these Old Testament patterns Russia was
even called the "promised land" (*obetovannaia zemlia*). For example, Kheraskov's June 28, 1764, Accession Day Ode to Catherine II states that "those empires are happy which are blessed
by God" and speaks of the "Promised Land" to which God
had summoned those people who obeyed his commandments.[107]

The poem continues this metaphor, describing Catherine as a new Moses leading her people to a promised land of milk and honey.[108] Similarly, as Ermil Kostrov wrote in his ode to Catherine of October 5, 1782, depicting the joys at Catherine's statute for the Administration of the Provinces [*Gubernii*]: "In this way once, the chosen tribe, a people loved by the Creator, . . . had taken the law on Mount Sinai; in this way once, the face of their leader had shone . . . ; Israel is now trembling in horror, while Russia is clapping its hands with joy." [109] Russia is thus seen as replacing a jealous Israel as God's new promised land.[110]

The related image of a Russian Zion—a holy land reserved for God's chosen people—also appeared in Russian poetry of the eighteenth century, as in Lomonosov's 1761 "Ode on the Accession of Peter III," which pictures "the joyful Russian Zion." [111] Similarly, Sumarokov began a poem with the line "The Muscovite Zion has been illuminated," using the image of the Lord as an "everlasting light" to Zion (Isa. 60:20) in referring to the illuminations and fireworks celebrating the marriage of the future Paul I to Maria Fedorovna; the implication of the return of "Mary" (Maria) to save Russia was probably quite purposeful in this poem. Through such associations of sacred culture with the secular state and the resulting depiction of a new earthly paradise in Russia, the state was able to use and abuse religious patterns for propagandizing its leaders and their goals. Although the audience for this propaganda was often ill defined (and frequently turned out to be the monarch and his or her court), such paradisal imagery became a mainstay of much eighteenth-century Russian culture and often became a sine qua non of panegyric literature.[112]

Christian into Classical

Secularization and westernization were often accompanied in Russia by "classicalization"—the allegorical or metaphorical use of classical myth. As a result, the new paradise being created in eighteenth-century Russia was often described through mythological imagery, which continued to sacralize the secular state.[113] Two institutions strongly stimulated the rise of a mythologically oriented culture in Russia during the second half of the seventeenth and most of the eighteenth centuries: the church-supported, university-level academies like the Kievan Academy and Moscow's Slavonic-Greek-Latin Academy; and the Academy of Sciences in St. Petersburg.

With the westernization of Russia came a westernization of education, and it has been fairly stated that "the Petr of Kiev [Peter Mohyla—the founder of the Kievan Academy] prefigured the Petr of Moscow and, especially of *Sankt-Peterburg* [Peter the Great]";[114] Mohyla's adoption of Jesuit educational practice had great influence on Muscovy as a result of its 1667 "conquest" of Kiev.[115] Among the elements of the Jesuit educational system borrowed by Mohyla was an emphasis on allegorized classical myth in rhetoric and poetics courses.[116] This mythological emphasis in Russian schools was reinforced after the founding of the Academy of Sciences, which, in addition to its functions connected with the natural sciences, was charged with composing panegyric odes, public speeches, and allegorical courtly festivals; Jakob von Staehlin, the Professor of Rhetoric and Poetry, did so much to bring the allegorical court culture of Western Europe to Russia that Princess Dashkova later called him "the professor of allegory."[117] Indeed, many of the phenomena discussed in this book under the general rubric of the "paradise myth" would not have been possible were it not for these institutions, which helped translate Russian concerns into the language, rhetoric, and mythology of Western literature.

Although references to classical Greek and Roman mythology had been considered "pagan" by the Orthodox Church, they began to appear in school poetry written at the Kievan Academy as early as the 1630's. To make these mythological references more compatible with Christian culture, attempts were sometimes made to assimilate them to Christianity, as in a 1632 reference to "the queen of the sciences—the *Orthodox-Catholic Minerva*."[118] Such hybrid titles were to continue in Russia through the early eighteenth century, when Peter the Great was referred to as "the Orthodox Mars."[119]

Mythological references were particularly frequent in *school drama*—a genre introduced into the curriculum of Russian schools by the late seventeenth century under the influence of Jesuit educational practice; this genre was to have major impact

on panegyric literature in Russia through the end of the eighteenth century.[120] Written by teachers and students of poetics
and rhetoric and performed by students, these school dramas
combined classical mythology, medieval allegory, and contemporary politics.[121] As the prefect of Moscow's Slavonic-Greek-Latin
Academy, Iosif Turoboiskii, stated, these dramas provided "not
only spiritual but also political training."[122] These dramas paved
the way for the use of mythology (including the paradise myth)
as a weapon of ideology in eighteenth-century Russian literature
as a whole. Under their influence, eighteenth-century Russian
allegory frequently opposed Absolute Good (usually representing Russia) to Absolute Evil (often its enemies) and the Sacred to
the Profane in genres ranging from allegorical fireworks to masquerades, the panegyric ode, the Masonic novel, and the literary
utopia.[123] As the representative of the Good or the Sacred, Russia
was frequently depicted in these genres as the "good place"—
the *eu-topos* of Thomas More's pun (see Chapter 6 below).

The myth of the golden age first appeared in Russia in the late
seventeenth or early eighteenth century and became a component (and sometimes even an allegorical character)[124] of school
dramas and other works of school rhetoric by the early 1700's, as
in Turoboiskii's "The Most Glorious Triumph of the Conqueror
of Livonia" (1704), written in honor of the victories of Peter the
Great over the Swedes during the early part of the Great Northern War. In praising the acquisition by Russia of territory on the
Gulf of Finland (including the newly founded St. Petersburg),
Turoboiskii compares Peter's "liberation" of the area to Perseus's
freeing Andromeda and taking her as his wife. This "marriage"
of Petersburg and its surrounding areas to Russia is then equated
with Christ's marriage to the church, which is itself identified
with the tsar's marriage to his country.[125] The work depicts a
"golden age" for this marriage and praises "[Peter's] Orthodox
army," which is giving his country "a golden age, an age of secu-
rity, an age of happiness."[126]

The Golden Age appears as an allegorical character in Dmitrii
Rostovskii's 1704 *Nativity Play*, where Christ's birth is shown to
reflect God's intention of restoring paradise to mankind. In the
Antiprologue, Human Nature declares that she "was made in the
image of God,"[127] and Hope reassures her that the Golden Age,

Peace, Love, Meekness, Happiness, and Eternal Joy will help her to regain paradise. But Reason enters and presents Hope as a deceiver, bringing the Iron Age (which threatens the Golden Age), War, Hatred, Fury, Malice, and Tears. A battle occurs between the retinues of Hope and Reason, but Hope is the ultimate victor as a result of the birth of Christ. Despite the appearance of the classical Golden Age (rather than the biblical Eden) as a character, Rostovskii's drama clearly relates the *Christian* ideology of paradise: the assumption that, despite the attempts of Reason and Envy, Christ will restore paradise to mankind and unite heaven and earth. As Heaven says to Earth, "I will be called earth and you heaven, just as God will be called man and mortal man called immortal God" (p. 227).

As the eighteenth century progressed, classical and biblical myths of similar content began to be used interchangeably in most literary genres, creating a single reservoir of mythological imagery (as had occurred much earlier in Western Europe).[128] This general equivalency of classical and biblical myths was reflected, for example, in the appendix to N. G. Kurganov's popular *Russian Universal Grammar* (1st ed., 1769), which stated that classical myths are simply "symbolic figures"—a system of secular imagery that often has biblical equivalents (p. 234). Like the Renaissance translator of Ovid, Arthur Golding, Kurganov wrote, for example, that "the *golden age means the viceless life of Adam and Eve in the earthly paradise*, where they had everything that they needed without having to work." Kurganov also identified Ovid's bronze age with the biblical Flood and Pandora's box with the tree of knowledge of good and evil from which Adam and Eve ate the fatal fruit.

As the equation between Christian and classical began to develop in Russia, the monarch was portrayed not only as the image of God but also as the image of classical deities.[129] For example, Simeon Polotskii implicitly depicted the monarch as the image and likeness of *Apollo* in his 1668 poem "Phaeton and Echo":

I am the image of God's glory [*Obraz bozhiia slavy*], Phoebus, born of light. And who among creatures is similar [*podobny*] in his brightness? Who has seen or heard of such? I pray you to tell me. "There is." Where?

"Here." What is his name? Who is he? "Aleksei." Of what rank is the person who has such a gift? "He is tsar."[130]

Through his identification with Apollo, Aleksei here becomes a secular figure of Christ—the *"image* of God" who is "born of light" (John 1:7–10, Heb. 1:3, etc.).

Such equations of monarchs and gods rhetorically revived the classical idea of "apotheosis," defined by one source translated into Russian in the eighteenth century as "an old pagan ritual used for including one's male and female rulers, benefactors, etc., among the ranks of the gods."[131] In Lomonosov's 1743 Name Day Ode to Grand Prince Peter, for example, Mars says about Peter the Great: "He was a God, he was your God, Russia."[132] The poem goes on to depict Peter taking on human character- istics (specifically "flesh") and descending to Russia from "on high" (*s gor'nikh mest*).

The rhetoric of apotheosis became part of a virtual "religion of state" in late-seventeenth- and eighteenth-century Russian literature, which depicted the state and its ruler as objects of reli- gious veneration, reviving a custom of Hellenistic Greece and im- perial Rome.[133] By mid-century, divine epithets for the monarch and for Russia had become so conventional that they became a virtual sine qua non of panegyric literature. Such rhetoric re- curred even at private banquets attended by the monarch and his or her court, as in the following 1776 speech recited in French to Catherine II ("Minerva") and other members of the royal family by the young daughter of Prince Aleksandr Viazemskii:

It seems to me that this palace has been transformed into a *temple* con- secrated to your august names. Dear objects of our desires, *you are our divinities*. Yes, I see Minerva, the goddess of wisdom, sciences and arts; Phoebus Apollo, the god of light; and Hebe, the ornament of empire. You have left Olympus to embellish these places. You have inspired in us that divine ecstasy and that celestial joy that only the gods have the power to produce.[134]

Such apotheoses of monarch and court were frequently accom- panied by the paradise myth, implying that the presence of a deity would help make Russia heaven on earth.[135]

The Virgin Goddesses of Paradise

By the second half of the eighteenth century, two goddesses were often identified with the reigning monarch (who was female for most of the period): Minerva and Astraea.[136] Both represented qualities of the paradise that the monarch was supposedly creating: Minerva, the goddess of reason and war, embodied qualities by which Russia could catch up with and surpass Western Europe—qualities of reason, "science" (in the broadest sense of "learning"), and military vigilance; Astraea was not only a general emblem for the golden age that the monarch was creating but, especially after Catherine's 1766 *Nakaz* (*Instruction*) to the Commission on Codification, represented the principle of law as a path to the good life.[137]

As early as her coronation, Elizabeth had been referred to as "the Minerva of our years." [138] And Astraea was associated (but not necessarily equated) with the monarch by 1745, when a school drama celebrating the birthday of Elizabeth depicted Astraea as returning "the golden age of Peter" to Russia because of the birth of his daughter.[139] By the early 1760's, the reign of Elizabeth was itself being referred to as the "age of Astraea," perhaps reflecting an identification between England's "Virgin Queen," Elizabeth I (who, as we noted in Chapter 1, was frequently called Astraea), and her unmarried Russian namesake.[140] For example, Aleksei Naryshkin's "Ode on the Death of Empress Elizabeth" calls Elizabeth's reign "the age of Astraea," which is paraphrastically defined as "that golden age." [141]

During the reign of Elizabeth, the goddess Diana was also identified with the monarch and occasionally linked with paradise. For example, Sumarokov's 1755 Birthday Ode describes Elizabeth as Diana pursuing wild beasts, much as the English monarch had been described some 150 years earlier: "With its fierce mouth open, a wild beast runs out of the bushes. Pursuing him is a *brave virgin, Diana*, or Peter's daughter. . . . We Russians are a happy people; *the golden ages have been restored by Elizabeth for our sake.*" [142] This passage probably is an allegory for Elizabeth's war against the Prussians (the "wild beasts" whom she pursues), and it portrays her as the "protectress" of her people's golden age, just as Lomonosov was to do in his 1761 Accession

Day Ode, where she is portrayed as "the Russian Diana" from whose arrows "the Western Titans fall."[143]

Diana, Minerva, and Astraea were all virgins. From medieval times, the three goddesses had been frequently linked with the Virgin Mary in Western Europe;[144] under Western influence, explicit connections were occasionally made in seventeenth- and eighteenth-century Russia as well.[145] Indeed, Elizabeth's "virginity" (i.e., unmarried state) contributed to a cult connecting her not only with the virgin Astraea but also with the virgin Mother of God, who would restore her people's happiness and lead them to paradise. In Lomonosov's 1748 Accession Day Ode, Elizabeth is even called "blessed among women" (*v zhenakh blagoslavenna*) and asked by the citizens of Moscow to restore the "golden time";[146] under her guidance, Petersburg (called by the pseudo-Greek name Petropolis) is said to be "imitating heaven."[147]

Ironically, this imagery of virginity was applied not only to the unmarried Elizabeth but later to Catherine the Great as well. Thus, female monarchs were associated by their *office* with Christ (see above) but by their sex with the Virgin Mary.[148] In this way a political theology was created in eighteenth-century Russia, uniting the monarch with the "holy family" of Christianity and hence linking her with the Christian vision of perfection—often using the names of classical goddesses!

Imagery of virgin goddesses (especially Astraea and Minerva) was in all probability used in the early reign of Catherine as a means of linking the none-too-virginal usurper with Elizabeth and the Romanov dynasty. Indeed, Lomonosov in his 1762 "Ode on the Accession of Catherine II" portrayed Catherine not only as Minerva but even as a "risen Elizabeth," who would bring about an ideal state:

Listen, all ends of the world, and know what God can do! *Elizabeth has risen for our sakes.* . . . It is she, or Catherine. For *Catherine is the unity of both!* Her energy and her dawning light will start a *golden age for the sciences* and will redeem her beloved Russian people from their indifference [caused by Peter III].
. . . .
Rejoice now sciences: *Minerva has ascended the throne.* . . . She will quiet all storms and with her generosity and zeal *will build a beautiful paradise* . . . for us.[149]

By portraying Catherine as a "risen Elizabeth" (just as Elizabeth had been portrayed as a "risen Peter the Great") and by praising the usurping monarch through the sort of paradisal imagery used to praise Elizabeth, Lomonosov depicted the "unity" of Catherine with the Romanov dynasty and thus justified her reign. There was thus most likely a political purpose in entitling Catherine's coronation celebration "Minerva Triumphant."

Catherine ultimately became more closely linked with Astraea and Minerva than Elizabeth had been; from her coronation to her death (and even afterward), Catherine's reign continued to be called "the age of Astraea."[150] As Rzhevskii's 1763 Birthday Ode proclaimed: "Astraea has now descended to us, the golden age has begun in Russia, and wisdom [*premudrost'*, one of the qualities of Minerva] has come to the throne as a result of the holy will of the Almighty." The classical goddesses Astraea and Minerva are thus portrayed as having been placed on the throne by the Judeo-Christian God![151]

In sum, by the mid-eighteenth century, much Russian literature and ceremony were based on a principle that Clifford Geertz has called "the doctrine of exemplary center," whereby the king, his court, and his capital "form at once an image of divine order . . . , reproduc[ing], albeit imperfectly, the world of the gods . . . , provid[ing] an ideal toward which life outside the court . . . ought properly to aspire, upon which it should seek to model itself."[152] The paradise myth strove to sanctify the secular state during this period, celebrating both implicitly and explicitly the "inherent sacredness of central authority," which Geertz has called one of the "master fictions" by which all political systems live.[153]

CHAPTER THREE

In the Re-beginning

*W*hen Prince Antiokh Kantemir announced that because of
the Petrine reforms "we suddenly have become a new people,"
he was voicing a theme that would echo throughout much "official" eighteenth-century literature and political propaganda—
the idea of a Russian cultural rebirth and of new beginnings for
Russia.[1] By portraying a particular event as a "new beginning"
or using imagery of birth, spring, or resurrection to describe
it, Russian poets were tapping the universal idea of perfection
in beginnings and thus idealizing and mythologizing the event,
making it "sacred" and distinguishing it from the profane world
of everyday life.[2] This same logic explains the attribution of perfection to man's first age in most mythologies (e.g., the biblical
Eden or the classical golden age). As Edward Said observed in
Beginnings:

[W]hat is first, because it *is* first, because it *begins,* is eminent. Most
utopian models derive their force from this logic. The beginning as first
point in a given continuity has exemplary strength equally in history,
in politics, and in intellectual discipline—and perhaps each of these do-
mains preserves the myth of a beginning utopia of some kind as a sign
of its distinct identity.[3]

This chapter explores the relationship between the paradise
myth and the theme of re-beginnings in the literature, histories,
and courtly festivals of eighteenth-century Russia, stressing the
iconographic strategies used to emphasize the renascence of a
paradisal Russia in this period.

Repeating the Cosmogony

As we have already observed, eighteenth-century Russian panegyric literature frequently took biblical passages and substituted
the name of the monarch for that of God, Christ, or the Mother of
God—a style befitting the Russian tsar's position as "the image
of God on earth." Thus, just as the monarch was described as
"the resurrection and the life," "the beginning and end of all
things," and "blessed . . . among women," so was he or she also
depicted in the image of the cosmogonic God of Genesis, who
created a paradisal world "in the beginning."

The theme of the tsar as creator ex nihilo appeared particularly frequently in literature praising Peter the Great. When State
Chancellor Gavriil Golovkin proclaimed in a 1721 speech celebrating the Treaty of Nystadt that through Peter the Russian
people "were created out of the darkness of ignorance [and
brought] into the theatre of glory of the entire world and, so to
speak, *from nonexistence* [*nebytiia*] *to existence* [*bytie*]," he was depicting the tsar as creator of his people.[4] In a similar vein, Peter's
contemporary apologist Petr Krekshin praised "our father, Peter
the Great, [who] led us from nonexistence to existence."[5] Although on the surface both Golovkin and Krekshin use the image
of Peter as parent[6] (he is called a "father" by Krekshin, and the
word *proizvesti* used in the past passive participle by Golovkin
often meant "to give birth to"),[7] their underlying meaning, presenting Peter in the image of the cosmogonic God who created
being from nothingness, is far more important (a point reflected
in the phrase "*our* father," with its clear transformation of the
Lord's Prayer). Any less "ambiguity" would have been blasphe-
mous, explicitly equating "the father of the fatherland" with "our
father who art in heaven."

As early as Trediakovskii, poets circumvented such blasphemy
by having a classical god praise Peter with biblical vocabulary, as
Minerva does in Trediakovskii's "Elegy on the Death of Peter the
Great," where she calls him the "new creator [*sotvoritel'*] of his
state," employing a word associated with the cosmogonic God of
Genesis.[8] Peter himself contributed to this myth by calling Petersburg "Paradise"—his creation of light out of darkness and dry

land out of swampy waters; his "cosmogony" was emphasized in Russian poetry from Trediakovskii through Pushkin.[9]

Russian literature of the mid-eighteenth century often portrayed God re-creating the universe and restoring time to its paradisal beginnings as a result of some event connected with the reigning monarch. This cosmogonic strategy most often used (or transformed) the words of Genesis 1—especially the words "let there be light" (*Da budet svet*); it appeared most often in odes dedicated to a monarch's accession, coronation, or birthday or in New Year's odes—in short, in works that actually *did* mark some new beginning or its anniversary. These odes resemble our contemporary New Year's celebrations, which "ring out the old and ring in the new," reflecting the general optimism of calendar rituals, where the beginning of a new period is frequently connected with hope for a better life and for an end to sorrow and suffering.[10]

One of the most important works to employ the cosmogonic strategy was M. V. Lomonosov's 1746 Accession Day Ode to Empress Elizabeth. This poem—about the rebirth of happiness in Russia resulting from Elizabeth's accession—translates history into mythology, portraying her 1741 nighttime coup (which overthrew Ivan VI and the entire "German party") through the biblical opposition between darkness and light and chaos and cosmos. Lomonosov has God appear and, seeing Russia "in gloomy darkness," state those world-forming words from Genesis: "*Da budet svet.*" Lomonosov's persona then continues, in imitation of the narrator of Genesis, "I byst! O tvari Obladatel'! / Ty paki sveta nam Sozdatel', / Chto vzvel na tron Elisavet." ("And there *was* light. O Ruler of all creation. / You are again the Creator of light for us, / Now that you have placed Elizabeth on the throne.")[11] Appropriately, the phrase *Sozdatel' sveta* ("the Creator of light") also meant "the Creator of the *world*," implying the re-creation of the world with the accession of Elizabeth to the throne.[12]

Lomonosov's cosmogonic formula in the 1746 Accession Day Ode became a virtual template for later Russian poets of the eighteenth century, as his poetic devices often did. Even G. R. Derzhavin, who in his later poetry frequently challenged or parodied panegyric commonplaces, transformed this cosmogonic tech-

nique in three of his poems to Catherine the Great. In "A Song to
Catherine II" (1779), Derzhavin uses Lomonosov's cosmogonic
formula to depict the messianic world that Catherine has created
for her subjects and for Europe: "Europe in its storms is obedient
to her. She said, 'Let there be peace,' and there is" (*Rekla: "da
budet mir"—i est'*).[13] In his 1782 "Felitsa," Derzhavin's persona
describes the title heroine (Catherine) as having the power of the
cosmogonic God: "For you alone, O Princess, it is fitting *to create
from darkness light*, dividing chaos into spheres with order." [14] And
in his "Representation of Felitsa" (1783), he invokes the painter
Raphael from the dead and instructs him to depict Catherine
negotiating an end to the War of Bavarian Succession through
the 1779 Treaty of Teschen: " 'Let there be peace,' she said [*"Da
budet tishina," skazala*] and peace would come to us at once"
(stanza 50).[15] Earlier in the poem, after a speech by Catherine
outlining some of her accomplishments (stanzas 12–15) Derzhavin frames one entire stanza (stanza 16) with her repetition of the
cosmogony, beginning *Rekla* ("She stated") and ending *i byl svet*
("and there was light").[16] The Raphael painting "commissioned"
by the persona is thus supposed to represent Catherine in the
image of the cosmogonic God.

  These cosmogonic metaphors and frames continued in Russian poetry at least through the early nineteenth century, when
N. M. Karamzin wrote to Alexander I on his coronation in 1801:
"Let there be under your sceptre a Russia [that is] the epitome
of goodness and happiness. And there will be. . . . [Y]ou are
the father of the fatherland, the second creator for your subjects.
God and virtue are with you." [17] The monarch was thus portrayed
as both the father of his fatherland and the image of God the
Father—a father and a creator of his subjects and, as a result, of
a paradisal world.[18]

Eternal Return and Resurrection

Despite the frequent use of Genesis to frame the Russian re-
creation of the world, the myth of Russian rebirth often owed
more to classical than to biblical sources. Indeed, the very idea
of a new cosmogony contradicted the Judeo-Christian theory
of history as linear and goal-directed (which allowed only one

world creation), reflecting instead the *classical* theory of history as cyclical—the idea that events regularly repeat themselves. This theory of "eternal return" or "eternal recurrence" assumed multiple creations of the world and multiple repetitions of events. Perhaps the most important conduit of this classical idea into Russia was Virgil's Fourth Eclogue, a work that prophesied the birth of a savior or messiah during the reign of the consul Pollio: "The great succession of ages is beginning again, the Virgin is returning now, and *the age of Saturn is beginning*; now a new race is being sent down from high heaven."

The Fourth Eclogue fit well into the scheme of courtly literature since it could be used to state or imply that in the reign of the monarch on the throne the golden age (the "age of Saturn") would return and a new cycle of time would begin; it fit particularly well into the literature praising female monarchs, who could (no matter what their marital status) be identified with Virgil's famous Virgin—Astraea. For example, in the program book for Moscow's 1763 New Year's fireworks, called "The Return of the Golden Age," a Latin inscription, "taken from Virgil's [fourth] eclogue," described contemporary Russia: *Iam Redit Et Virgo Redeunt Saturnia Regna* (translated as "Astraea is already descending, and the golden age is returning to us").[19]

The paradisal rebirth of eighteenth-century Russia was often linked with imagery of spring, as in Lomonosov's 1742 "Ode on the Arrival in St. Petersburg from Moscow of Empress Elizabeth": "Just as the *spring*, driving away the fierce frost of winter, gives life to frozen waters and *resurrects* the universe again, *renewing* nature for us and adorning the fields once again with flowers, so now the grace and love and radiant gaze of Peter's daughter enlivens us with *new life*."[20] Under the possible influence of old Russian works like Kiril Turovskii's famous twelfth-century sermon "For the First Week After Easter," where the image of spring had represented the rebirth of man through faith in Christ, eighteenth-century authors sometimes transformed Christian rebirth imagery to stress the idea of rebirth through the monarch.

By the mid-eighteenth century, the motif of "Russian spring" had already become sufficiently frequent that some works ostensibly devoted to spring hid panegyric allegories about the rebirth of the good life in Russia.[21] Indeed, V. K. Trediakovskii's 1756 "Spring's Warmth: An Ode" does not explicitly discuss Russia until the last stanza; on the surface the poem simply seems to be about *nature's* rebirth in the spring. But given its general context and the structural strategies of mid-eighteenth-century Russian poetry, the work can be viewed as a panegyric allegory using the controlling metaphor of spring to stand for a reborn Russia that is flowering like a garden. Although the subtitle "An Ode," the high style and archaisms typical of panegyric poetry, the brief references to Peter and the Neva, and the statement that "among us the golden age has arisen" provide a clue, the allegory is not made fully clear until the last stanza, which develops the metaphor of Russia as the "Northern Eden." This final stanza suggests that the reader reevaluate the entire poem and consider the possibility that from its very beginning the poem has been discussing Russia, using the imagery of the rebirth of nature and of the seasonal change from winter into spring to represent the reign of Empress Elizabeth, who has given new life to Russia and eliminated the political terror ("winter") of the "German party": "Ruddy spring has come, youth has risen in the fields, spring has brightened winter's darkness."[22]

Another frequent strategy depicted a "resurrected" Russia as a result of the deeds of Peter the Great or the current monarch, as in Feofan Prokopovich's 1725 "Funeral Oration for Peter the Great," which portrayed Peter as having "resurrected Russia from the dead."[23] During the reigns of Elizabeth and Peter III this image of a resurrected Russia was often accompanied by that of a resurrected Peter the Great, reflecting the Old Testament idea that a person achieves rebirth through his descendants (here his daughter and grandson);[24] in the reign of Peter III, the image of Peter the Great's resurrection also relied on onomastic play, implying that *a* Peter must be *the* Peter. As Ippolit Bogdanovich wrote in his 1762 Accession Ode to Peter III: "Again great Peter has risen."[25] Similarly, Lomonosov's 1761 "Ode to Peter Fedorovich on His Accession to the Throne" proclaims in the opening stanza: "Our tearful loss [i.e., the death of Elizabeth] more dear to us than treasures of gold, has now been doubly restored. We are happy a hundred times over: the Russian nation again greets Peter the Great."[26] The poem goes on to say that the "great eagle

[Russia] has been revived" and that "great Peter will live forever." This link between the resurrection of "great Peter" and
the revival of the "great eagle" is particularly apt since the symbol of Russia (the two-headed eagle) is combined with the Old
Testament symbolism of the eagle, which represents renewal (as
in Psalm 103: "Bless the Lord . . . Who satisfieth thy mouth
with good things; so that thy youth is renewed like the eagle's").
Images of paradisal renewal run throughout the poem, which
pictures Peter I's "resurrection" in his grandson resulting in the
creation of "heaven on earth" and "a joyful Russian Zion," whose
ruler is the "reincarnation of Samson, David, and Solomon."[27]

Occasionally, Peter the Great was depicted as a phoenix, the
never-dying bird of Egyptian, Greek, and Roman mythologies
that was forever reborn from its own ashes. As Lomonosov wrote
in his 1742 "Ode on the Arrival of Peter Fedorovich from Hol-
stein"—a poem that depicts the future Peter III (who had just
been declared successor to the throne by Empress Elizabeth) as
the resurrection of both Peter I and Elizabeth: "O goddess [Eliza-
beth], whose empire the seven seas can't embrace. . . . Your
hope has been realized, and joy has again been renewed. You
see *Great Peter, who has risen like a phoenix* now. Your dear sister
is alive in her darling son."[28] Since the phoenix had symbolized
both the resurrection of Christ and the return of the golden age,
its use was particularly appropriate.[29]

Associated with the themes of resurrection and eternal return
were the frequent depictions of great world heroes revived (often
in the person of the monarch) and of great world events repeated in contemporary Russia. Although, under the influence
of Byzantine rhetoric, Russian panegyric literature had for centuries praised grand princes as "new Constantines," "new Alex-
anders," and the like, during the eighteenth century not only
heroes but also events were "born again" in Russia. Throughout the century, adjectives like *novyi* ("new") and *vtoroi* ("second"), nouns like *vozvrashchenie* ("the return"), and adverbs like
paki ("again") and *vnov'* ("anew") multiplied to describe the rebirth of great historical or mythological civilizations, events, or
personalities in Russia. Thus, Russia was often described as the
"new Rome" or "new Athens"; its citizens were depicted through
such epithets as "the second Columbus," "the new Pindar," or

"the new Horace"; and courtly festivals were given such titles as *Fortuna Redux* ("The Return of Happiness") and *Vozvrashchenie zlatago veka* ("The Return of the Golden Age").[30]

This technique of "eternal recurrence" worked particularly well for propagandizing Catherine the Great's so-called Greek Project, which attempted to re-begin an Orthodox empire in Constantinople by conquering Turkish territory. For example, Bogdanovich's "An Ode Composed by a Shepherdess from the Fields of Ochakov on the Taking of Ochakov," written after the Russian victory over the Turks there in 1788, praises Catherine through the persona of a local shepherdess who calls herself "a remnant of the ancient Greeks" (i.e., one of the residents of this former Byzantine territory). Although on the surface this epithet might simply identify the shepherdess with the singing shepherds of Arcadia made famous by Theocritus or reflect her pastoral panegyric (sung on a "quiet shepherd's pipe"), it also implicitly justifies Catherine's Greek Project by identifying the captured Ochakov with "Greece"/Byzantium. This link is expanded by depicting a "rerunning" of Greek and Byzantine history and myth in the events of the contemporary period, signaled by the repetition of phrases like *ne paki li* ("Hasn't it recurred?") and *vnov'* ("anew"): "Isn't the roar of monsters *again* guarding the golden fleece within the walls? Hasn't the anger of Achilles *again* spread horror in the *new Troy*? Is the current of the Bosphorus *again* getting stirred up at the approach of the son of Igor? Or is the darkened East in the process of receiving the light from *Constantine*?"[31]

Through this strategy of eternal recurrence Bogdanovich revives characters from history and myth to encode some of the actors in the contemporary Greek Project: The "new Constantine," Catherine's second grandson (who had been named Constantine with the specific aim that he would become the head of his grandmother's Orthodox empire that was to include Constantinople), would restore the "light" (Orthodoxy/Christianity) to the "darkened East" (the former Byzantine territory dominated by the Islamic religion of the Ottoman empire);[32] the new "son of Igor" (a reference to Sviatoslav Igorevich, who in the tenth century invaded the Byzantine empire and almost achieved success) would again invade Constantinople; the new (Russian)

Achilles would help defeat the "new Troy" (Turkey); and the new Jason would bring the golden fleece home to the "new Greece" (Russia). History was to be repeated and corrected during Catherine's "golden age," which was to embody the perfection of the great historical civilizations.

By the latter part of the reign of Elizabeth and, especially, by the beginning of the reign of Catherine II, Russian strategies for expressing the idea of rebirth often resembled those of Western European Renaissance and seventeenth-century courts. At the courts of England's Elizabeth I (reigned 1558–1603) and France's Henry IV (reigned 1589–1610), for example, images of re-beginning—especially those of the golden age, Astraea, and the phoenix—had been used for propagandizing the ideal of a universal Christian empire.[33] At these and other courts of the sixteenth and seventeenth centuries, the image of the golden age frequently represented the idea of *renovatio*—the restoration of a universal Christian empire of peace and justice; Astraea often symbolized the idea that justice was the most important imperial virtue; and the phoenix represented the idea that this holy Christian empire would be immortal.[34] In short, by borrowing Renaissance courtly imagery of perfection, Russian writers of the eighteenth century were often proclaiming their country as the center of a sacred Christian empire—the moral and religious fulcrum for the world—much as had been done in fifteenth- and early-sixteenth-century Muscovy.[35] So it is fitting that the 1763 fireworks entitled "The Return of the Golden Age" had as its first allegorical plane a "Trajan's Column" erected in honor of Catherine and surrounded by many altars where "the blessed peoples of the Russian empire" could bring their sacrifices or tributes "in the old imperial manner."[36]

The New Rome

In stressing Russia's rebirth and its expansion into an empire of worldwide importance, eighteenth-century Russian writers often identified their nation with ancient imperial Rome—the archetype of empire in the Western mind—resurrecting, at least tacitly, the earlier idea of Moscow (Russia) as the "Third Rome."[37] In eighteenth-century literature, the glory-that-was-Rome often came to signify the glory-that-was-to-be-Russia. "Rome" (especially imperial Rome) became a historical displacement of the paradise myth—a variant on the strategy of eternal recurrence, portraying Russia as the latest (and last) emanation of the "eternal city" and the empire it represented. As Aleksandr Karin wrote in 1761, "ancient Rome has begun to flourish again among the Russians."[38]

As has frequently been noted, many of the political conceptions of Peter's empire came from ancient Rome.[39] His foundation of the Senate in 1711 clearly reflects the influence of the Roman body of that name. Peter's Senate rewarded him in kind after major victories over the Swedes by officially bestowing on him three Roman titles: *Imperator* ("Emperor"), *Pater Patriae* (*otets otechestva*, "Father of His Country"—the honorary title of the Roman emperor), and *Maximus* (*velikii*, "the Great").[40]

This Roman political symbolism is reflected as well in Falconet's famous statue of Peter the Great, *The Bronze Horseman* (1766–82), where it is implicitly linked with the paradise myth. Like many other monuments to absolutist kings, Falconet's equestrian monument to Peter imitated the statue of Marcus Aurelius on the Capitoline Hill in Rome, echoing the Roman iconography of the emperor on horseback, which had symbolized the "all-conquering lord of the earth" (*kosmokrator*) at least since the time of Julius Caesar.[41] Depicting Peter in Roman garb, in consonance with his title of *imperator*, Falconet's statue (which some Russians of the time even dubbed "Marcus Aurelius")[42] portrays the emperor using his horse to crush a snake—a symbol of the ignorance and backwardness that Peter's program of westernization and modernization was designed to destroy. Falconet combined this Roman equestrian tradition with the old Russian (especially Novgorodian) iconography of St. George (one of Russia's most popular patron saints), who was usually portrayed crushing a dragon in the form of a snake, symbolically representing the serpent that had caused the Fall from Eden.[43] Falconet's statue thus represented Russia's first emperor as a modern St. George, a patron of progress, who by destroying the serpent of backwardness would restore paradise to his people.[44]

Peter's city, St. Petersburg, was itself often linked with Rome. Not only did this new "city of St. Peter" emphasize the cult of its patron saint through its focal Cathedral of Sts. Peter and Paul, but even its coat of arms transformed that of Rome.[45] Petersburg was often dubbed the "Northern Rome," as in the anonymous 1759 "Speech in Praise of Emperor Peter the Great," which states that "Romulus's little town became the sovereign of the world, Peter's little hut has become the Northern Rome."[46] Similarly, Sumarokov wrote about "Petropolis" (as Petersburg was sometimes called in imitation of great classical cities) that it would become an "eternal city" and "be the Northern Rome."[47]

At first the Rome image carried relatively little distinct meaning in the Russian paradise myth, merging with other literary tropes to signify the reestablishment of the good life in Russia. This historical ideal, in other words, was simply *an* ideal—one of a number of interchangeable and functionally synonymous markers of perfection in a poetry that Sumarokov had described as "praise weaving."[48] Thus, Andrei Nartov in his 1756 poem "In Praise of Petersburg" sang the virtues of this "Northern Rome" and the Russia that it synecdochically represented: "You are a happy country, where Peter's daughter [Empress Elizabeth] lives, where the temple of science is open and its entrance is vast. *The golden ages have come again*, the fields are splendid, the *trees are bearing fruit*. What a great city you are. *You have become like Rome*."[49] Here the comparison of Russia to Rome is simply one undifferentiated trope in a paraphrastic series that achieves its panegyric aim through accumulation (rather than differentiation) of images. There is no clear distinction between the mythological ideal of the golden age, the garden ideal of fruit-laden trees and splendid fields, the Enlightenment ideal of the "temple of sciences," or the historical ideal of Rome; all are made virtually synonymous to rhetorically show what a "great city" Petersburg is and what a "happy country" is Russia.[50]

By the mid-eighteenth century, Roman history was sometimes mapped onto or equated with Russian history, providing not only a mythologized vision of Russia's past but also a glowing view of its imperial future. History, which Lomonosov called "the art by which Greek and Roman writers gave glory to their heroes,"[51] often functioned teleologically or panegyrically and gave many mid-century Russians an opportunity to proclaim the "glory" of their empire.[52] As Grigorii Kozitskii, a Latin teacher and future secretary to Catherine the Great, wrote in a 1759 article "On the Use of Mythology": "There is no history that is closer to our age than that of ancient Rome."[53] In his *Ancient Russian History* (1766), Lomonosov attempted to prove that anyone studying Russia's past will see "heroes and deeds that are fully comparable to those of the Greeks and the Romans."[54] He even argued that there is an "equation" between Russia's past and Rome's, caused by "a certain general similarity between the order of Russian and Roman events."[55] Lomonosov did note one major difference, however, between Russian and Roman history: while autocracy had been the cause of Rome's fall, it had led, he claimed, to Russia's strength.

While some writers were Romanizing ancient Russian history, others (including Mikhail Chulkov, Mikhail Popov, and Vasilii Levshin) were seeking an ancient Slavic mythology that could compare to the mythologies of Rome and Greece.[56] As Kozitskii had stated in the article "On the Use of Mythology," "mythology greatly aids history."[57] Like history, mythology helped create a glorious past that would pave the way for a glorious future and would justify comparisons to the great ancient empires of Greece and Rome. As Popov wrote in his "Short Description of Old Slavic Pagan Mythology": "Superstition and polytheism among the ancient Slavs were as widespread as among the Greeks and the Romans, and if our ancient times had had enough diligent writers, then we would have seen as many books as we have from [the Greeks and the Romans] on Slavic divinities, holidays, rituals, prophecies, divinations, auguries, and their other religious tendencies."[58]

A number of short stories and novels in the last third of the eighteenth century continued this invention of an idealized Russian history and mythology by depicting a glorious (but fictitious) past in which Russia had rivaled Rome (or, occasionally, Greece). For example, in *The Mocker*, M. D. Chulkov's 1766 collection of tales set in an imaginary ancient Russia, the first story tells of a Slavic paradise that rivaled Rome and Greece for power:

In the times of our ancient princes, even before the time of our great Kii, in the place where St. Petersburg now stands, there was a magnificent, famed, and most populous city named Vineta. In it lived *the Slavs, a brave and strong nation*. The leader of the city was named Nravoblag; he was a brave leader . . . *taking up arms against Rome and Greece*, and he subjugated many nations under his power. Prosperity and the wise legislation that he enacted . . . brought his territory into a flourishing condition. Happiness, reason, and strength gave him all that he desired, and he took comfort and was satisfied when he looked at the abundance and peace in his land, because the peace and prosperity of his subjects constituted his own well-being.[59]

This mythical Slavic city of Vineta (a name suggesting "guiltless"—the condition of man in paradise), under the leadership of Nravoblag ("Goodmoral"), was the first of several idealized Slavic empires of the past portrayed in eighteenth-century Russian literature as equal or superior to the civilizations of ancient Greece and Rome.[60] Such an empire represented not only a dream of Russia's past but a hope for its future—a flourishing empire of moral right and military might—and even entered the arsenal of the Slavophiles, who went as far as condemning the westernizing historian T. N. Granovskii for arguing that Vineta was mythical rather than real.[61]

A similar braggadocio was seen in discussions of the Russian language. For example, Trediakovskii in the preface to his *Tilemakhida* (1766)—a version of Fénelon's *Télémaque*—noted that "nature herself has given [the Russian language] all of the importance and imposing qualities of Latin," which he called "*rimskii iazyk*" (the *Roman* language) several times.[62] A similar idea echoed in Lomonosov's "Letter on Russian Versification" (c. 1739): "Benevolent nature has given Russia a sufficient abundance of words, as of everything else. . . . I cannot exaggerate my joy over the fact that *our Russian language is not inferior to Greek, Latin, and German* in its verve and heroic sound."[63] In such statements, "language" is metonymic for Russia as a whole—a trope strengthened by the fact that the word *iazyk* was still occasionally being used in its older meaning of nation or tribe.

The Russian interest in Rome as a historical and political surrogate was also reflected in the large number of translations of Roman history that appeared during the reign of Catherine the Great.[64] In addition, there were many translations of works about great Roman and Greek heroes, including several translations of Plutarch's very popular *Lives*, which established the desirable molds for the creation of Russian heroes.[65] By the 1760's the influence of these *Lives* could already be seen in original Russian works, which bore such Plutarchian titles as *Prikliucheniia Femistokla* (Fedor Emin's *Adventures of Themistocles*, 1763)[66] and *Numa, ili Protsvetaiushchii Rim* (Mikhail Kheraskov's *Numa; or, Flourishing Rome*, 1768). Gogol later parodied this Plutarchian vogue in *Dead Souls* (1842) when he named Manilov's son "Femistoklius," using a Latin ending on the Greek name to emphasize Manilov's pretensions.

By the 1760's, iconographic links between Russia and Rome (and, to a lesser extent, Greece) had become so frequent that allusions to these ancient empires frequently carried allegorical references to Russia. Indeed, clues that great *Russians*, especially Peter I or Catherine II, were being discussed were sometimes spread throughout works about (or referring to) Lycurgus, Pericles, Solon, Themistocles, Numa, or other great Greek or Roman heroes. For example, Kheraskov's *Numa*, which takes its basic plot from Plutarch's "Life of Numa," uses the well-established iconographic link between Rome and Russia to construct an allegory praising the Russian state and especially Peter I and Catherine II, who, like Numa, were establishing laws designed to make Russia into a "flourishing Rome" (see Chapter 6 below).

The Rome theme reached its apogee during the reign of Catherine the Great—one of the greatest periods of imperial expansion in Russian history—especially after the victories over the Turks in the last quarter of the century, which raised hopes for recapturing Constantinople (the "Second Rome").[67] Vasilii Maikov's 1775 Accession Day Ode declared in celebrating the "sweet peace" resulting from Catherine's signing of the 1774 Treaty of Kuchuk Kainarji, which ended the First Turkish War and gained some strategic territory for Russia:

If we look toward the East we will see your trophies [*trofei*: the spoils of war] there. If we look toward the North, there is *Eden in your territory*. If we turn our thoughts to the South the people there are marvelling at you. And when we turn our gaze toward the West, loud fame, flying there, voices the thought that the *Russian empire has spread out like ancient Rome*.[68]

This expansionism occasionally led to even more borrowings of Roman ideas and images to describe Catherine's "Holy Rus-

sian Empire," as in a 1770 allegorical ballet and pantomime entitled "Russia Victorious" where one scene portrayed the Russian
eagle tearing the Turkish moon to pieces.[69] Underneath this obvious allegorical display were the words: *Prishel, uvidel, pobedil*—
a Russian translation of Caesar's famous *Veni, vidi, vici;*[70] like
her Roman predecessor, Catherine was thus depicted as having
"come, seen, and conquered" for her paradisal empire.

Translation of Empire

Closely related to the theme and imagery of Rome in eighteenth-
century Russian literature was the structure of *translatio imperii*
("translation of empire"), which frequently was used in praising the Russian paradise. Unlike the Russia-Rome equation, the
translatio structure showed or implied a progression of great
world empires over the course of history, ultimately ending with
the current Russian empire (which was often depicted as eternal). As Trediakovskii wrote in the 1752 revision of his "Verses
Praising Russia": "And who in this whole wide world does not
now know your [Russia's] noble origin? After Rome, which was
trampled by Barbarians (and in Byzantium the dragon [Islam]
reigns), the eagle is soaring in your cities."[71]

The principle of *translatio* was articulated in Lomonosov's *Ancient Russian History* (1766), where he wrote that "the greatness
of one people begins when that of another people is waning;
the destruction of one gives birth to another."[72] This idea was
expanded in Mikhail Kheraskov's 1794 novel *Polydorus*:

Where there once were densely populated settlements, now there are
god-forsaken steppes. . . . And where there once were dark forests
where wild beasts dwelled . . . now people rejoice in magnificent cities,
rejoice at the laws of wise, meek, humanitarian rulers, and enjoy a flourishing existence. . . . Everything in this world has its morning, its noon,
its evening, and its night. . . . But morning will begin again, the day
will dawn, and there will be new peoples, new kingdoms. . . . There is
an incessant process of birth, and, finally, of death. [1:164–65]

This generalization is then explicitly applied to the Russia of
Catherine the Great in an apostrophe by the narrator: "My beloved homeland, you are a clear example of this process. You roar

with victories, you enjoy abundance and prosperity, and there is splendor in the peaceful embraces of your inhabitants." In short, by the reign of Catherine the Great the paradisal "empire" was frequently portrayed as "translated" to Russia.

Like many propagandists of the "eternal city," Russian writers often claimed that the process of *translatio* would stop now that it had reached their land.[73] As the narrator of Kheraskov's *Temple of Russian Prosperity* (1775) states: "There will not be a silver age in Russia after the golden. God helps Catherine in everything, and the mansion of our bliss will not collapse."[74] Similarly, in a 1786 poem written by a student named Ivan Vinogradov, depicting "in [Catherine's] laws a flourishing golden age," God appears (a device borrowed from Lomonosov) and states: "Know that I love the Russians. I shall bring to your feet all kingdoms that were holy in antiquity. Assyria and the New Rome [i.e., Constantinople/Turkey] and Persia, which was ruled by Cyrus, will all be combined into one and given to you by me for their happiness and will be ruled by you forever."[75] In other words, there will be no fourth Rome; the process of *translatio* will stop when the empire reaches Russia, where perfection will remain in timeless perpetuity.[76] Russia's emergence as the country most favored by God, the seat of a religious empire, was seen as history's ultimate goal.

One frequent variant of "translation of empire" was the topos of *translatio studii* ("transfer of learning"), which assumed that "the torch of civilization" passes from country to country during different periods. This topos in its Russian variant showed the progress of learning from Greece to Rome and ultimately to Russia. Assuming that their age had reached the summit of perfection, Russian writers celebrated their country as the place where the arts and sciences were flourishing and would continue to flourish. As Apollo says in the prologue to A. P. Sumarokov's 1759 allegorical ballet "New Laurels": "I see in Russia Helicon: the chains that had held back reason have now been broken there, and there the Muses dwell. . . . On these banks [St. Petersburg] has been erected ancient Rome, and ancient Athens is here. *Here the verbal arts are flourishing now.*"[77]

Occasionally during the eighteenth century, panegyric literature even expressed contemporary Russia's superiority to great ancient empires, portraying Russia's imperial expansion as more compassionate or as faster than that of the ancients and its emperors as superior to their early counterparts. In his 1756 "Inscription on the New Construction in Tsarskoe Selo," Lomonosov wrote: "Rome trod heavily on the kingdoms that it conquered. . . . Instead of this, you, O Monarch, are leading Russia with a gentle hand and without war."[78] And as he stated in his 1755 speech in memory of Peter the Great:

> With whom can I compare the Great Sovereign? I see in ancient and modern times possessors of the title "The Great." . . . However, in comparison to Peter they are small. . . . I will use no other examples except those from Rome. But *even Rome is inadequate.* What was accomplished in the 250 years from the first Punic War to Augustus by the Nepos, Scipios, Marcelli, Reguli, Metelli, Catos, and Sullas was done by Peter in the short period of his life.[79]

Such arguments were succinctly summarized by an allegorical Fate in a 1765 prologue written in Catherine's honor by students at the Kazan Gymnasium: "Every state has a prescribed time in which it rises to the highest degree of greatness and glory. *No other people has reached its height so fast as the Russians.*"[80] In sum, under Peter and his successors, time was perceived as compressed and progress portrayed as more rapid than in previous civilizations, foreshadowing the theme to be called "Time Forward" in Soviet literature.[81]

The Courtly Festival

One of the major focal points for the celebration of Russia's paradisal rebirth was the courtly festival—an amalgam of Russian school drama with the courtly festivals of the European Renaissance and Baroque and occasionally even the popular carnival or the Roman triumph. These festivals frequently presented a vision of wild nature overcome by human intellect, of chaos and vice defeated by order and virtue.[82]

The rebirth of Russia was celebrated by a number of different genres of courtly festival, all portraying happiness and harmony returning to earth with the accession of the monarch (who was often seen as a materialization of the Platonic idea of the

Good);[83] like their European predecessors, these festivals fused dance and drama, music and murals, architecture and allegory in the service of the state and in ritual homage to its rulers. The *masquerade* presented a procession of costumed and masked mummers celebrating the triumph of Virtue over Vice. Allegorical *fireworks* proclaimed this triumph through symbolic pyrotechnics and were often accompanied by *illuminations*—allegorical drawings painted onto large transparent cloths lit from behind by thousands of lamps of various colors.[84] Allegorical *ballets* provided support for the reigning ideology using symbolic motion and geometric groups (which were often accompanied by pantomime, songs, and either a spoken text or "titles" and lacked the leaps and pirouettes that we associate with ballet today).[85] And the allegorical *carousel* consisted largely of costumed horses and riders who (together with pages and musicians on foot) paraded before the courtly audience and formed various symbolic figures,[86] using the traditional symbol of horsemanship to represent man's control of wild nature and hence the sovereign's control of his people.[87] These allegorical festivals thrived at the Russian court for most of the eighteenth century—years after they had disappeared from the major courts of Western Europe. Indeed, while the European Enlightenment was reacting strongly against such affirmations of absolute power, Russia was still celebrating absolutism in the style of the Renaissance and Baroque.

Courtly festivals often became visual extensions of panegyric odes, celebrating through an "iconography of happiness" many of the same events that evoked odes: New Year's Day; a new tsar's accession; the reigning tsar's name day, accession day, or birthday; marriages or births within the tsar's family; and victories in war. Many courtly festivals asserted that Russia had regained the golden age with the help of its current tsar, creating an "image" for the monarch in much the way that is done in advertising products (and presidential candidates) today. Although frequently performed for a limited audience at court—the very audiences who were its "heroes" and were depicted in control of the world and of nature[88]—the courtly festival occasionally "went public" when fireworks were set off on the Neva, illuminations erected in public areas, or masquerades moved onto the streets, enveloping the people in celebration of the paradisal perfection that Russia had (at least in principle) attained.

In celebrating order and peace and in proclaiming Russia's harmony with heaven, these courtly festivals sometimes added elements of the (disorderly) popular carnival;[89] some masquerades were even staged on *maslenitsa* (Shrovetide—the Russian Mardi Gras) and used its carnival-like festivities to create a propagandistic "festival of state."[90] But unlike the true carnival, where people are liberated from authority, behavior is unfettered, hierarchy is suspended, and a fool is mockingly crowned king, the "courtly carnival" celebrated authority as sacred.[91]

In Russia, as throughout Europe, the courtly festival was frequently allegorical, based on sources like emblem books, mythological handbooks, and iconological dictionaries—typical tools of the Renaissance artist and poet, which became quite popular in the Russian eighteenth century.[92] Many Russian festivals included what they called "hieroglyphs" (symbolic visual images), reflecting the Neoplatonic idea (which entered Russia through the festivals of the European Renaissance and seventeenth century) that truth could be apprehended without the intervention of words.[93] These hieroglyphs became the language for a festival of magnificence[94] (albeit a language completely incomprehensible to the folk and needing extensive translation for even the educated, who could understand it completely only through explanatory program books). Such festivals often portrayed an allegorical battle between Good and Evil, frequently represented by two opposing "geniuses": a genius of good, who was usually associated with the reigning monarch; and an opposing evil genius, who was inevitably defeated during the course of the festival.

In both theme and structure the Russian courtly festival frequently emphasized change and progress, stressing Russia's rebirth and its metamorphosis from evil to good, darkness to light, sadness to joy, hell to paradise, and the iron age to the golden age. Festival titles often reflected this process: "Russia Rejoicing Again After Her Sadness" (which pictured Elizabeth as Astraea),[95] "Happy Russia" (a 1787 presentation for Catherine's silver jubilee, portraying the transformation of Russia during her reign), "The Island of Happiness" (a 1745 firework portraying Russia's happiness stemming from the Romanov family, who were portrayed as being eternal, like the never-dying phoenix), and "The Return of the Golden Age" (a New Year's fireworks presentation for 1763).[96] Coronation celebrations also stressed such transformations; for example, the 1730 coronation of Empress Anna began with the order that people remove their garb of mourning and replace it with bright clothing, thus changing night into day and darkness into light, symbolically repeating the cosmogony.[97]

Sometimes, courtly festivals even depicted the metamorphosis of nature itself, which was seen as yielding to the control of the monarch.[98] For example, M. M. Kheraskov's 1776 "Russia Rejoicing" represented Catherine's Russia by a "temple of happiness and hope" where day is driving out night, light expelling darkness, and spring displacing winter; it ascribed this metamorphosis of Russia to the goodness of Catherine, whose godlike powers make "everything possible" and even make "nature modify its laws."[99] Such scenes reflect the probable influence of Baconian science in Russia with its symbolic association of absolutism and scientific discovery.[100] Science is also seen as helping to transform Russia and eliminate its backwardness in a 1768 allegorical ballet entitled *Prejudice Overcome*. In this ballet, Ruthenia (the Russian people) is worried about the effects of smallpox until the Russian Minerva (Catherine), "for the well-being of her people," emerges from the Temple of Aesculapius (the Roman god of medicine)— which is opposed to the Temple of Ignorance—and agrees to be inoculated; Ruthenia immediately follows suit, and a "grand dance" of hope begins, celebrating the expulsion of Superstition and Ignorance.[101] Here, the Russian paradise is again linked with the willingness of the monarch to suffer for her people.

In celebrating the rebirth of happiness in Russia, several eighteenth-century Russian courtly festivals transformed the ancient Roman triumph—a procession honoring a military victor (called *Triumphator*) that traveled through the streets of Rome celebrating the defeat of a foreign power and the resultant "triumph" of the empire itself.[102] Given the equation of Russia with Rome, this use of a Roman model for celebrating Russia's renewal was quite fitting. The Roman triumph was recalled explicitly in a December 1742 program book for the unveiling of two arches of triumph celebrating Empress Elizabeth's return to St. Petersburg after her victory over the Swedes. The program portrayed Elizabeth in the image of Fortuna (Happiness) entering her winter home with a horn of plenty in one hand and a helm in the other; under the illustration in the program book was the Latin inscription *Fortuna Redux*—a motif that, the book noted, came from the Roman idea that the return of a victorious emperor to his city after a triumph signified "the return of happiness."[103] The second arch of this celebration portrayed the triumphant Elizabeth surrounded by her subject nations in their national costumes, with the inscription "Their languages are different but all in concord call her 'mother.'" This "triumph" was thus being used to further the ideology of empire, whose worldwide goal was indicated by the image of a globe.

The Roman triumph merged with the popular carnival to celebrate the rebirth of paradise in Russia in the most famous eighteenth-century courtly festival: the allegorical masquerade "Minerva Triumphant" staged for the 1763 coronation of Catherine II. Designed by the theatrical director Fedor Volkov, the masquerade was divided into fourteen sections containing two main divisions: a series of allegorical vices led by Momus the Mocker, followed by Bacchus, Discord, Deception, Ignorance, Bribery, the Perverted World, Arrogance, and Prodigality;[104] and a procession of virtues including the Golden Age, Parnassus and Peace, and Minerva and Virtue.[105] As Kheraskov's explanatory "Verses for the Grand Masquerade" declared: "O Vice, embarrassed, look upon these people [the Russians] with a worried glance: You will see in yourself an example of hell and in their dwelling [Russia] beautiful paradise."[106] In this masquerade, the "Victor" ("Triumphator") is Minerva/Catherine, who, like victorious Roman generals, rides in a chariot while the defeated vices march in front of her like captured prisoners in ancient Rome.

The division of this masquerade between vices and virtues recalls Ben Jonson's separation of some of his masques into two sections: an "antimasque" depicting a world of vice, disorder, and chaos where "preposterous" characters (often grotesque or comic denizens of hell) "do things contrary to the customs of [civilized] men"; and the main masque, depicting an ideal world (the world of the monarch and his or her court) that overcomes the vice and disorder of the antimasque.[107] In the "vice" section of the 1763 Russian masquerade appear such typical antimasque figures as troublemakers, savages, furies, devils, witches and wizards, and lame truth (on crutches)—figures functioning (as was typical for the antimasque) like vices in morality plays until the forces of virtue appear and triumph over them.[108]

The combination of the opposing worlds of carnival and court in "Minerva Triumphant" reflected the likelihood that this festival, staged during *maslenitsa*, [109] was meant to entertain the populace in order to gain their support for the usurping Catherine.[110] This carnival world dominated the entourage of Momus the Mocker, which included a number of figures from the Italian commedia dell'arte (which M. M. Bakhtin has observed "kept a close link with its carnival origin"):[111] Pantalone, the *dottore*, Arlecchino, and various other *zanni*.[112] These figures were accompanied by a "chorus of comic music," which included tambourines and cymbals—typical instruments to accompany the carnival.

The section of this masquerade most indebted to carnival was "The Perverted World" (*Prevratnyi svet*), which was based on the very essence of carnival—inversion, or the world inside out.[113] Volkov's design for this part of the procession featured four figures moving backwards, an open carriage drawn by footmen in which a horse was riding, dwarfs and giants, "a cradle in which an old man is in swaddling clothes and a baby boy is feeding him," "a pig with roses," and "an orchestra in which an ass is singing and a goat playing the fiddle" (a predecessor of Ivan Krylov's famous "Quartet"). This "perverted world"—the world of "vice"—was "conquered" in the second part of the masquerade by the triumphant "virtues," which were explicitly linked with the paradise myth.[114] As Sumarokov's "Chorus to the Golden Age" (one of a number of his choruses presenting the themes of individual sections of this masquerade) conventionally stated:

The blessed times have come and have illuminated Russia with the sacred light of truth. Listen, universe! Astraea is on earth, *Astraea has settled in the lands of the Russians, Astraea has ascended the throne.* Generous fate has said: "Come, you desired golden age, come to the Russians!"

The *streams of Russian rivers are flowing with milk and honey*, to the surprise of their neighbors.[115]

In contrast to this, Sumarokov's original chorus for the "Perverted World" section of the masquerade sharply challenged the official myth of Russia as paradise. The government's rejection of his original version (which will be discussed in Chapter 6 below) clearly revealed the official attitudes toward satire and irony—the genres that impugned the ideal world of the courtly triumph and its idyllic conception of Russia. The watered-down, "official" version printed in the program book describes the arrival "in our land" of a dog and a nightingale from abroad. Asked about their country, the dog replies: "Much there deserves contempt. I would be able to describe it if I dared sing satire. But I don't wish to sing. I shall only bark at vices. Nightingale, pay your dues, whistle us some foreign vices." The nightingale whistles (the word *svist*—"whistle"—appears in the program), and the dog barks, using only the word *kham* ("rabble"), which functions as a nonsense word through its repetition for five lines: *za morem kham, kham, kham, kham, kham, kham* ("Abroad there is rabble, rabble, rabble, rabble, rabble, rabble").[116] The stammering dog and the whistling nightingale (symbol of the poet) clearly fear the censor. Sumarokov's desire for specific satire foreshadows the position of Novikov in his 1769 debate with Catherine II on the nature of satire.[117]

With Sumarokov's original "Chorus to the Perverted World" begins the reaction against panegyric culture in Russia, marked by satiric thrusts at the official panegyric style and thus at the paradise myth (see Chapters 6 and 7). But panegyrics remained a mainstay at the Russian court until the end of the century, as is reflected in Prince M. M. Shcherbatov's comments in *On the Corruption of Morals in Russia* (1786–89): "Everywhere there roared praises of [Catherine the Great], in speeches, in compositions, and even in the ballets presented at the theatres, so that I myself once heard her say: 'they are flattering me to such an extent that they'll spoil me.' "[118] Despite the existence of an occasional stab, like that of Sumarokov's original "Chorus," these allegorical festivals continued to "spoil" the ruling class throughout the rest of the century, loudly proclaiming through the iconography of happiness the "virtues" of rulers and the "paradisal" land they ruled. Like panegyric culture in general, the courtly festival—originally designed to teach virtue and heroism by example—had become an apology for the status quo, a means of advertising, rather than advising, the monarch's political decisions. Momus the Mocker, the patron of satire, was thus expelled from court while Fortuna complacently ruled "paradise" in the elaborate style of European absolutist courts.[119]

CHAPTER FOUR

The Happy Garden State

*I*n his 1769 dissertation, *A Discussion of Natural Theology*, Dmitrii Anichkov wrote that paradise is usually conceived of as a "most beautiful garden filled with joy."[1] Such conventional conceptions of a paradisal garden became quite frequent in eighteenth-century Russian literature, where they often served as metaphors for the state and its rulers. As Sergei Domashnev wrote: "O country, country in the likeness of paradise, you are a garden of all the virtues."[2] This chapter examines the topos of Russia as a "happy garden state" and some of the unusual fruits and hybrids that it produced.

The Garden and Its Gardeners:
Planting the Russian Eden

As the image and likeness of God—the "planter" and "gardener" of Eden[3]—the Russian tsar was often portrayed as planting a new Eden in his territories. The explicit image of the tsar as gardener and of Russia as his garden became frequent only after the death of Peter the Great, who was often referred to as the "gardener" who "planted" modern Russia; in the process, Russia itself (and occasionally St. Petersburg) became "Peter's garden."[4] This image of Peter as planter is central to Trediakovskii's 1756 "Spring's Warmth," the last stanza of which declares: "Then what are these *gardens* established here, *planted by the great father* [Peter], where his daughter [Elizabeth] is now the leader, equally great, equally first, goddess among the peoples of the earth like Minerva? Shout out: '*They are the Northern Eden.*' "[5] Similarly,

A. P. Sumarokov's 1763 "Dithyramb" combines the motif of a Russian garden planted by Peter and the renewal theme: "I see Russia's luxurious cities and her pleasant gardens, like *Eden or Peter's garden*. New rivers that men have dug are flowing: the path through all of Russia is new. The hills pour out gold, the ocean splashes with gold."[6] In this poem, Sumarokov praises the newly crowned Catherine II for renewing "Peter's garden" and, implicitly, restoring the age of gold (symbolized by the omnipresence of "gold" in her country).

Like the image of the golden age, the convention of a Russian Eden became central to the panegyric poetry of the reign of Catherine, as in M. M. Kheraskov's 1763 Name Day Ode, which begins by portraying Russia as an icon of Eden: "In the likeness of the Garden of Eden, Russia is flowering in our days."[7] The poem goes on to depict all Russia as a "beautiful paradise . . . flowering in delightful peace" because "God loves the Russians" and has sent Catherine "to end the evil time [i.e., the reign of her husband, Peter III] and to begin an age of golden days."[8] Similarly, Sergei Domashnev's 1762 Accession Ode depicts Russia as "the Eden of the universe."[9]

In portraying their new Eden, Russian poets of the mid-eighteenth century often borrowed biblical phrases describing the changes to be made by the Lord in Zion from wilderness and desert to paradisal garden (e.g., Isa. 51:3). For example, Ermil Kostrov's 1781 Birthday Ode to Catherine transforms the cosmogonic structure (see Chapter 3) to praise the empress's construction of new cities in southern Russia:[10] "She speaks, and *the fruitless deserts are transformed into a garden*. . . . She looks at the fields, and the corn then ripens. Under her modest steps the meadows, which have been dressed in flowers, flow with streams of nectar."[11] The poem goes on to depict Russia as a place favored by nature because it is favored by God.

The garden was often a symbol of order and calm in Russian literature and festivals of the second half of the eighteenth century, as demonstrated in the 1750 Accession Day illumination for Empress Elizabeth designed by Jakob von Staehlin (the Professor of Rhetoric and Poetry at the Academy of Sciences). In Staehlin's original plans (written in German), the main focal points were a labyrinth (symbolizing the entangled political situation—*Biro-*

novshchina—out of which Elizabeth had led Russia) and a garden. But on the basis of an ambiguous line-for-line Russian translation, Lomonosov produced a poem for the program book that changed Staehlin's "labyrinth" (*vavilon*) to "Babylon" and thus depicted Elizabeth as leading God's chosen people out of their "Babylonian Captivity" into an Edenic garden of bliss: "From the woes of Babylon under your leadership we have come into *beautiful gardens of peace* and, placing columns in your praise, we are tasting the pleasant fruits of joy." [12]

In the eighteenth century, when Russia was frequently at war, the image of a quiet garden also celebrated peace, as in M. M. Kheraskov's 1775 *The Temple of Russian Prosperity*, written for the first anniversary of the Treaty of Kuchuk Kainarji, which had ended the six-year war with Turkey:

When in our fatherland, *peace is flowering like a garden* . . . , when the breath of the pleasant zephyr informs us of the victory of beloved peace, then the rivers, valleys and forests rejoice all around, and the voices, of the joyful Russian people can be heard. . . . O leave your fury, Mars, and sleep forever, war. For golden peace is sweeter to us than all the victories of war.[13]

As in many other works using the garden image, there is perfect unity here between man and nature; the garden is an emblem for man's "natural" condition of peace—the condition that had flourished along with nature in Eden.

During the relatively peaceful periods from 1748 (when Russia left the War of the Austrian Succession) to 1756 (when Russia intervened in the Seven Years' War) and from 1763 to 1768 (when Russia went to war with Turkey), the image of the quiet garden blossomed in Russian literature to celebrate peaceful times. Thus, Kheraskov's 1753 Accession Day Ode pictures Russia "counting her victories over her enemies" and becoming "like paradise in its peace," having received "a garland from the Almighty" and "flowering like a joyful garden in the gentle calm of cities" (i.e., being at peace when others are at war).[14] Similarly, a 1770 allegorical firework entitled "Russia Victorious" depicted "Russia-at-Peace" sitting in a garden until disturbed by war: "Russia was sitting . . . in a garden of her own bliss and looking at her children living in perfect peace . . . until Envy . . .

and restless Malice . . . succeeded in awakening the goddess Discord from her sleep." [15] Under the influence of school drama, the allegorical figures of Discord, Malice, and Envy are thus portrayed as beginning the Russian-Turkish War, disturbing Russia's paradisal garden. [16]

The "Pleasant Place"

Since Virgil's description of the "fortunate woodlands" of Elysium as *locos laetos et amoena virecta* ("lush spots, pleasant glades" —*Aeneid*, VI, 638), commonplace descriptions of beautiful nature came to be known in rhetorics as *locus amoenus* (the "pleasant place"). As used by Virgil the term referred to any beautiful place cultivated for the sake of pleasure, rather than for practical purposes. [17] But as the rhetoric of ideal landscapes developed, the term became relatively consistent, following at a minimum the six "charms of landscape" formulated by the fourth-century Greek rhetorician Libanius: "Causes of delight are springs and trees and gardens and soft breezes and flowers and bird voices." [18] By medieval times, this rhetoric of *locus amoenus* was used fairly frequently to describe paradise, which St. Boniface called *amoenitatis locus* ("place of pleasure"). [19]

The rhetoric of *locus amoenus* appeared in Russian literature as early as the thirteenth-century "Tale of the Destruction of the Russian Land," which, mourning the Tartar invasion of Russia, describes the Orthodox Russian land as a kind of paradise:

O brightly bright and beautifully adorned Russian land. You are wondrous with *your many beauties*: with your many *lakes*, you are wondrous, with your *rivers* and your locally renowned *springs*, your steep *mountains*, high *hills*, your many leafy *groves*, your wondrous *fields*, your diverse animals, innumerable *birds*, great cities, wondrous towns, your monastery *gardens*, your churches and awe-inspiring princes, your honest boyars, and many lords—you are filled with everything, O Russian land, O Orthodox [*pravovernaia*] Christian faith. [20]

This text (which gained new popularity in the growing Russian nationalism after the fall of Byzantium) expands the normal catalog of the *locus amoenus* to envelop not only nature but also the Orthodox Church and the leaders of the state, which together are depicted as making Russia a "lovely place." By the eighteenth century, this rhetoric was again frequently used to describe a paradisal Russia and the tsars who had created it.

During the eighteenth century, the rhetoric of the "pleasant place" was used particularly often in two kinds of literature in Russia: that praising the paradisal life of the country and that describing the ideal garden of love. In addition, the rhetoric was sometimes used in describing the *heavenly* paradise, reflecting the frequent equivalency between descriptions of heavenly and earthly paradises. For example, the Egyptian king Sezotris in P. I. L'vov's 1790 *The Temple of Truth* describes heaven as "a most beautiful garden" with "paradisal singing," "very sweet smells," "softly babbling brooks," and "growing flowers, one more beautiful than the other."[21]

Typical of the use of *locus amoenus* to describe country life was A. P. Sumarokov's 1759 essay "A Letter on the Beauty of Nature," which opposed the good life of rural isolation to the pretense and deception of the city. In praising the country, which he explicitly identified with the golden age, Sumarokov created a virtual catalog of the *locus amoenus*: green meadows; soft grasses; singing birds; cool, babbling brooks; the playing of reed-pipes; and the simplicity of shepherdesses' songs.[22] Other details frequently found in such Russian descriptions of rural isolation included thick forests (*dremuchie lesa*), clean air, flower-covered fields, and sweet smells.

Many Russian works praising the country contained a generalized satire on urban vice, creating a "rural ethic" bemoaning the loss of man's innocence and virtue with the growth of the city (and in the process prefiguring the structure of elegy— the genre mourning the passing of some ideal condition, such as love, virtue, innocence, or the person who had embodied it).[23] A number of these poems were based on or made use of Horace's Second Epode, *Beatus ille* ("Happy is he")—the source for many works in Russian with the equivalent *Blazhen tot*.[24] So important was this epode and its *locus amoenus* commonplaces to the conception of a rural paradise in Russian literature of the second half of the eighteenth century that its ironic last lines, which call this paradise into doubt as a daydream of an urban usurer, were sometimes omitted in translation.[25] Influenced by

Horace's epode, the poet A. Naryshkin wrote in a 1761 essay entitled "The Life of Isolation": "I consider *happy the man* who, being satisfied, enjoys the fresh air in his village, despising all the splendors of the city, leaving that other world-filled-with-flattery. *That man is happy* who spends his hours, days, and years in country life, without any anxiety, being healthy in body and calm in spirit."[26] Through the end of the century, works praising the rural paradise often contained a generalized satire "on vice" of the kind that also appeared in the satirical journals of 1769–74.[27] As Trediakovskii wrote in a 1757 essay entitled "On the Pleasantness and Absence of Vice in Country Life," which states that the life of the isolated country "is comparable in every respect to the primal condition of pre-Fall man" and "brings to our minds the picture of an earthly paradise":

Country life leads a man to fairness, to moderation, to temperance, to frankness, in a word *to all virtues*; it keeps a man in isolation from all the agitating and seething vices. . . . And, in reality, luxury, acquisitiveness, unfairness, imprudence, arrogance—uniting, perhaps inseparably, with extravagant riches and even pursuing them—usually frequent the large cities. The rigorous work-life of the country does not have such vices.[28]

The natural calm, simplicity, and honesty of the rural dweller (especially the shepherd and the farmer) thus frequently became synonymous with paradisal life, creating a pattern that would give rise to such major eighteenth-century Russian works as Kheraskov's *Numa* and Karamzin's "Poor Liza"—both of which are structured on the opposition between the ideal country and the vice-ridden city.[29]

In addition to praising the paradisal life of the country, the *locus amoenus* was used particularly frequently in eighteenth-century Russia to describe a place where love thrived—most often a garden.[30] One of the first important works to describe a paradisal garden of love in Russia was V. K. Trediakovskii's 1730 translation of Paul Tallemant's *Journey to the Island of Love*. The novel takes the form of two letters from Thyrsis to his friend Lycidas telling of his passion for Aminta, which develops on the allegorical Island of Love.[31] This island is frequently described through paradisal conventions—especially the *locus amoenus*:

Eternal spring keeps the *air clean* there, the sky shows its truly brightest
light to eyes, *flowers do not fade* in any season and new ones bloom with
every hour. Trees always have *ripe fruit, branches are always green*, and
the *fields are filled with flowers.* . . . Nature herself . . . attracted all the
singing birds there who through their sweet chirping sing of love in their
songs and of its play. . . . And through the *green grass small streams* flow
with a *pleasant sound.*[32]

This paradisal landscape at first provides a conventional backdrop for the pleasures of love. But as the novel goes on, the
island becomes less than ideal. In the tradition of Renaissance
poets from Petrarch to Spenser, this garden of love incites Thyrsis to seek sensual pleasure; ultimately, love's inconstancy causes
him great pain.[33] As will happen more often in Russian literature
written later in the century, what at first looked like paradise
turns out to be hell.

Mother Russia in the Garden of Love

Unlike Tallemant/Trediakovskii's island garden, the more typical garden of love in Russian literature of the eighteenth century
was closer to the Christian paradise of *spiritual* love, emphasizing
agape rather than eros; its "love object" was more often Mother
Russia than a sensuous Circe.[34]

   In epithalamiums (marriage odes) written to members of the
tsar's family, Russia itself often became the paradisal garden of
love, producing not the vicissitudes and lust of Tallemant/Tredia-
kovskii's island but constant, conjugal love resulting in "fruits"
(i.e., offspring) to gladden the royal family and the nation as
a whole.[35] These fruits were particularly important to Russia,
which wanted to avoid another Time of Troubles, when there
was no heir to the throne. For example, Lomonosov's 1745 "Ode
on the Wedding Day . . . of Grand Prince Peter and Catherine"
(the future Peter III and Catherine II) begins with an equation of
Russia and Eden ("where the first marriage was performed") because of these "most loving spouses."[36] This epithalamium goes
on to portray God expressing His happiness at the marriage by
ordering springs of water to flow in the "deserts and arid fields"
and the "dreaded Russian regiments" to replace their swords
and helmets with "green branches and flowers" (a variant of

the image of "swords into ploughshares"), making Russia into a paradisal Kingdom of Love (stanzas 2–3).

Repeating several times the idea of a re-beginning for Russia with a new Peter and Catherine (recalling Peter I and his wife Catherine I), Lomonosov varies the theme of Russia as a lovers' paradise by picturing in stanzas 5–10 an "imaginary Kingdom of Love,"[37] frequently described through the *locus amoenus*:

Fruits spotted with color and branches washed with honey suddenly manifest spring and summer. . . . Rapture delights all the senses. *Isn't it here that love reigns?* . . . The tender sigh of turtledoves, and the embraces of pure doves show the power of love. The trees wave their leaves and embrace each other with branches, and even in inanimate things I see the passion of love! Brooks follow brooks. First they chase each other and then they beckon, then they rush directly to each other and, uniting into one, they babble. [stanzas 6–7][38]

In this allegorical description, nature imitates the supposedly ideal love of Peter and Catherine—an example of what Lomonosov himself had called "the animation of inanimate things" in poetry.[39] Indeed, in this fairy-tale description of the Kingdom of Love, Lomonosov for many stanzas forgets the royal lovers themselves (perhaps reflecting his knowledge of their actual indifference to each other).[40]

When the focus finally moves from the Kingdom of Love to the couple, primary emphasis is placed on their potential progeny, expressed largely (stanzas 15–20) through the image of hoped-for growth from the "branch of Peter's root" and of "sweet fruits for us" from Catherine—hope that "the Russians' Renewer" (Peter I) "may live forever in his descendents" and that "Peter's First" (*Petrova Perventsa*: the first child of this newly married Peter) will soon be embraced by Empress Elizabeth (the would-be baby's great-aunt). In short, the great celebration of the wedding of Catherine and Peter was as much for the continuity of the kingdom as for the specific marriage—a celebration of Russia, which would live forever through its royal family as though it had eaten of the paradisal tree of life.

Although history cast Lomonosov's 1745 epithalamium in a very ironic light when in 1762 "Eve" (Catherine II) seized power and had her "Adam" (Peter III) arrested in a coup d'état in the

"Russian Eden," Lomonosov's rhetoric remained a model for later Russian epithalamiums. Among such poems was G. R. Derzhavin's 1773 ode "On the Marriage of Grand Prince Paul and Natalie," which also pictures Russia as a "temple of love, a paradise of bliss," where "storms have turned into zephyrs."[41] Before describing this Russian paradise of love, the persona presents a view of the heavens that open to him to reveal "what it is forbidden for a mortal to see": "There stands a woman [*zhena*, i.e., Russia] wrapped in byssus crowned with the crown of kings." Under the clear influence of the allegories of school drama, the woman is lifted by an eagle (symbol of Russia), holds a lion (the symbol of Sweden) "with her hand in a union" (referring to treaties with Denmark and Prussia that had successfully held off Sweden's planned invasion of Russia), and tramples on a moon (the symbol of Turkey, with whom Russia was still at war), stating to the Creator:

I [Russia] have been blessed that You [God] gave me to the hands of Peter [the Great] to support me and that you decreed that a woman who is like him [Catherine II] should be given to his grandson [Peter III] to represent You. Through You, the young hero [the future Paul I] is ripening, through You he is living, flowering, and maturing. . . . But who is after him? You . . . and he . . . are the only ones of your kind [*Odni*]. [stanza 8]

Russia therefore asks the Creator ("the tsar of tsars") to give Paul in marriage so that the line may continue and the tsar/phoenix (the only one of his kind) may attain eternal life.

Derzhavin's poem uses the popular idea of the marriage of Father Tsar and Mother Russia (*Batiushka Tsar'* and *Matushka Rus'*) to portray Russia as a "wife" to the tsar—a point suggested by the repeated ambiguity of the word *zhena* ("wife"/"woman") in stanzas 6–8. The "woman" is given "into the hands" of the tsar so that he can "support" or "hold" her and crown her with his "crown of kings"—a reference to the practice of using crowns in the Orthodox marriage ceremony;[42] she waits for the young Paul to "mature" or "ripen" for her. These verses thus celebrate not only the specific marriage of Tsarevich Paul (with its hopes for the continuation of the Romanov line) but also the "marriage" of Russia itself, reflecting the actual marriage rites of Russian tsars, where the bride often assumed the role of "Mother Russia," who mated with the autocrat to produce new fruits for Russia's people.[43]

Derzhavin's epithalamium goes on to describe a paradisal Kingdom of Love, picturing through the *locus amoenus* a land created by the joy that "we will always have the blood of Peter" (line 158)—a land of turtledoves, zephyrs, aromatic fields, sweet singing of birds, and crystal waters where "everything . . . is captivated with happiness, everything has been turned into bliss." As the narrator states (echoing Lomonosov in the last two sentences): "Here the malice of hell does not belch. . . . There is no hatred, no sedition, no murder. The weak and strong live side by side in harmony, and at every hour rejoice anew. The trees embrace each other, and under their bark show they have a heart. *No doubt, love dwells here*" (lines 188–210). This fairy-tale paradise is explicitly equated with Russia in the last stanza, when the poet states to Empress Catherine: "O Monarch, love has taken these young spouses into its settlement, and to this place the land ruled by you is similar as well" (lines 221–24). Although the poet ends by saying that "I am not beginning a panegyric," there could be no greater panegyric than this conventional vision of Russia as a paradise of love—a fertile "royal garden" of eternal fruits.[44]

Paradisal Flowers and Fruits

In addition to its royal fruits, which would guarantee the survival of the nation, the Russian garden also produced other flowers and fruits that had been linked with paradise in the Bible and patristic writings—especially the lily, the rose, and the grape.[45] The flower most often connected with the paradise myth in this period was the lily—the frequent symbol of purity and virginity associated with the Mother of God[46] and the Sister-Bride of the Song of Songs ("the lily among thorns"). From the late seventeenth century, both the tsar and his or her Russia were frequently linked with this lily of purity in panegyric verse.[47]

During the reign of Catherine the Great, the lily came to symbolize the Edenlike condition brought by the monarch, reflect-

ing the fact that the Russian word for "lily" (*krin*) provided a
suitable rhyme for Catherine's name (*Ekaterina*) and thus could
poetically link Russia's flowering to the monarch. From Kheraskov's 1762 Name Day Epistle to Catherine, "the lily of paradise"
(*raiskii krin*) was to become a favorite topos of the panegyric
ode: "For evil-doers, the monarch carries a sword in her hands;
for the virtuous she carries a branch more beautiful than the
lily of paradise. For tsars and for philosophers Catherine provides an example." [48] By the mid-1760's the lily had become so
firmly established in the paradise myth that it began appearing
independently of Catherine's name as a metaphor for the good
life brought by her. As Aleksandr Perepechin's 1765 Accession
Day Ode to Catherine II states: "Your power, O Monarch, has
a beauty like the summer days; Russia, its glory renewed, is
flowering like a lily of paradise. . . . We live in the midst of a
Garden of Eden." [49]

Among other flowers growing in the Russian Eden was the
rose, which V. K. Trediakovskii called "a flower of paradise." [50]
According to St. Ambrose, St. Basil, and a number of other
Church Fathers, the rose grew without thorns before the Fall—
a point emphasized in some Russian school texts of the late
seventeenth and eighteenth centuries (see the section The Transplanted "Image" in Chapter 2). Under the possible influence of
such teachings and of Renaissance literature like *Paradise Lost*
(where Milton described Eden as having "Flowers of all hue,
and without thorn the rose"—IV, 256), this rose without thorns
played a central role in two important eighteenth-century literary works: Catherine the Great's 1781 "The Tale of Prince Khlor"
and G. R. Derzhavin's 1782 "Felitsa." In Catherine's allegorical tale—one of the first children's tales printed in Russia[51]—a
young Eastern prince is abducted by a neighboring khan, who
tests the prince's reputed qualities by making him search for "a
rose without thorns, which does not prick." [52] In his search for
this paradisal flower, Khlor is aided by Felitsa ("Happiness"), the
beautiful daughter of the khan, and is accompanied by her son
Rassudok ("Reason"), who urges the young prince to stay "on
the straight and narrow path" and helps him discover a moun-
taintop where the rose without thorns grows. Khlor ultimately

learns that this rose is "nothing other than virtue" and is attainable only by overcoming the difficulties of a "very steep and rocky road."

The search for this rose without thorns is one of the main subjects of Derzhavin's 1782 poem "Felitsa," which takes its name and imagery from Catherine's tale. Derzhavin praises Catherine by associating her with the ideal princess of his title: "O godlike princess of the Kirghiz-Kazakh horde, whose incomparable wisdom revealed the true path for young Prince Khlor to ascend that high mountain where the rose without thorns grows, where virtue dwells. . . . It has captivated my mind and spirit. O give me advice on how to find it."[53] Throughout the work, Felitsa is associated with wisdom, reason, and virtue[54] and is portrayed as capable of leading her people to the paradise where the rose without thorns grows—a paradise that, like many, is located on a high mountain.[55] But, many of her courtiers lack the virtue needed to help their subjects find this rose without thorns. For example, in the second stanza, Derzhavin's persona (a mirza at Felitsa's court and hence a symbol of Catherine's degenerate courtiers) is depicted as being "too weak to follow" in Khlor's footsteps and abandons the search for virtue when he falls slave to his vices. Thus, unlike earlier panegyrists, Derzhavin does not depict the ideal monarch leading her citizens to paradise, but, instead, describes the way that "Felitsa's" courtiers corrupt the iconic principle. In contrast to the "godlike" nature of Felitsa, human nature is weak; only through positive examples of the *entire* court (not only of the monarch) can the people be reformed and given the strength to reach the rose without thorns and thus regain a paradise of virtue.

About five months after the appearance of Derzhavin's "Felitsa," an anonymous theatrical presentation entitled "A Festivity for the Rose" was staged for Accession Day, linking Catherine herself with the rose of true virtue and the restoration of paradise on earth. The work begins with a speech by a priest of Cybele— the "Great Mother" or "mother of the gods."[56] The priest states that "through the order of the wise queen [Cybele], a wondrous branch" of a rose tree was granted to Russia—a reference to Catherine, who is praised as "the rose that has shown us true virtue," the "heavenly branch [through which] the horrible spectres [presumably Peter III and his advisers] have disappeared";[57] this "rose" is in turn credited with creating "heaven on earth" in Russia (p. 5). Continuing this imagery, the priest says that "this blessed flower [Catherine] from the garden of the Monarch [God] . . . has given [her people] the joys of paradise" and "the ages of gold" (p. 7). Toward the end of the work, the priest, like a shaman, sends his spirit to look at the future of Russia and sees a "brilliant kingdom" there, where "violence and perfidy are falling" and "the race of mortals is renewed" (p. 8). The word "falling" here implies a reverse "Fall" in the future of Russia, a fall of vice, which is made explicit at the end of the work when a chorus celebrating this "news of paradisal joy" states that "the Mother of the Gods, the great mother Cybele, is sending to Russia *an Edenic state to reverse the Fall of man.*"[58]

Perhaps the most important fruit in Russia's paradisal garden was the grape, which had been associated with the promised land since biblical times.[59] These biblical associations were used in an 1801 ode on the coronation of Alexander I by students of the theological seminary in Belograd:

"Arise O cold North, come O warm South, and blow into my *beloved vineyard* [*vinograd*] and pour your aromas into it!" In this way the church once called when it awaited Christ's arrival in David's city, holy Zion. . . .

Our *Monarch in the image of Christ* is approaching the regal city of Moscow, and with a most gracious word calls his faithful subjects into Moscow; he calls those from the North and the South and from all the bounds of the Russian sphere, he calls the peoples to the temple of God.[60]

In addition to implying that Moscow is the new Zion and stating that the new monarch is "in the image of Christ," these verses implicitly compare Moscow to the "vineyard" of the Lord (the promised land) and the state to the church,[61] emphasizing that under Alexander the "golden-dewed rain" of the "first age" will return and make the Russians "flourish like a lily."

Under the probable influence of a popular Bogomil legend, the Edenic tree of knowledge was sometimes assumed in Russia during the second half of the seventeenth century to be a *grape vine* rather than the apple tree of Western legend.[62] Although

in original Russian tales of the seventeenth century, this Bogomil conception was often "transplanted" to the hop (since grape
vines were not known in Russia at that time),[63] the connection
of the grape vine with the tree of knowledge was revived in the
late eighteenth century when the grape began to be cultivated in
Russia.

Under the influence of the Enlightenment, this grape vine of
knowledge became a *positive* symbol in Russia, where it was seen
as providing the fruits that would *restore* mankind to paradise. It
even gave a title to one pedagogical journal—*Rastushchii vinograd*
(*The Growing Grape*, 1785–87)—which used the grape as a symbol
of science, knowledge, "cultivation," and the paradisal life that
they would bring to Russia. One poem in this journal, entitled
"Ode to the Planter of the Grape in the North," allegorically celebrated the sciences by focusing on the introduction of the vine
to Russia and praising Catherine the Great, under whom it was
introduced:

O incomparable naturalist, gifted with higher wisdom [*premudrost'iu*] by
the king of higher nature [God]! In your deep knowledge are hidden the
wondrous secrets of how to correct the capricious laws of crude nature
and how to transform countries where strong frosts rage into lands of
abundant crops and how to grow fruits amidst the ice. When it pleased
you, through your great wisdom . . . the *forests* where only cold had
reigned, where fright and horror dwelled, *became filled with fruits and
turned into a joyful garden.*[64]

Here the garden symbolizes the subjugation of irrational nature (represented by the forest) to human reason, of chaos to
cosmos. This conquest is credited to Catherine, reflecting the influence of Renaissance (especially Baconian) science, which saw
absolute monarchy (symbol of man's power over the universe)
as the source of all scientific discovery.[65] Indeed the poem portrays the "planter" (with a feminine ending, clearly referring to
Catherine) as having the magical powers once granted to Adam:

I am told that only a *magic power* . . . could create this transformation. . . .
What is she like, tell me, who has planted the grape amidst the ice? It
was, you know, a planter, Adam, . . . to [whom] . . . God entrusted the
keys to the secrets of nature. . . . In having command over nature, what
is there that one can't create [*sotvorit'*]? She says, "Let it be so," and it is
[*Rechet, da budet tak, i byst'*]. [pp. 3–4]

This thaumaturgist (Catherine) is thus praised as being like Adam, in the image of the cosmogonic God. The poem later calls her a "person versed in the laws" (*zakonnik*) of nature who can transform substances "with just a word from [her] lips": "[She] utters a word and things are in a new form. Everything is subject to [her] words" (p. 7).[66] In sum, this poem to the "planter of the grape in the North" transforms a specific event—the introduction of the grape vine to Russia—into a general allegory portraying the "gardener" (Catherine) as being granted the power by God to create a new Edenic garden, filled with grape vines (the new tree of knowledge) that will yield useful fruits of learning to the Russian people and "return the golden age to mortals" (p. 6).[67]

A number of works published in *Rastushchii vinograd* emphasize the "juice" resulting from this planting of a Russian vineyard. One work, for example, talks of the sciences as a "nectar" that is very useful to drink.[68] Another states the hope that the grape will soon "bear the fruits that Russia has been awaiting . . . and for the gathering of which it has been preparing its children."[69] The "growing grape" and the "juice" that it would yield thus propagandized the useful fruits of science and learning brought to Russia from other European countries and left to mature—fruits of one of the more unusual gardens in the Russian paradise myth, the "garden of sciences."[70]

The Garden of Sciences

In a 1786 poem entitled "The Flourishing Condition of Russia," the young poet Aleksei Fialkovskii declared: "But now, O Russia, . . . [y]ou are spending golden days. . . . You show in yourself an open *garden of all the sciences* in flourishing form. And now every day you are bringing your bliss to perfection."[71] This image of a blissful "garden of sciences" [*sad nauk*, i.e., a garden of all knowledge] became popular in Russia during the final third of the eighteenth century, reflecting a major change from the Eden of Genesis: in this Enlightenment garden, people are *encouraged* (rather than forbidden) to partake of the tree of knowledge and rewarded with a paradise of perpetual progress.

Since classical times, the garden has provided an image of "cultivation"—not only of flowers but also of knowledge in general.[72] The metaphor of the garden often became a general frame for collections of "pleasant and useful" moral teachings and poetry. Such garden metaphors began to appear in Russia by the seventeenth century[73] in works such as Simeon Polotskii's 1677–78 encyclopedic collection of poems *The Garden of Many Flowers*—a title that derives from the same roots as the English words "anthology" (etymologically a "flower-gathering") and "florilegium" (its Latin calque).[74] Polotskii in his introduction explained this title through further garden and floral metaphors:

There is a habit among creatures who are endowed with the light of reason by God . . . that if one should happen to be in rich gardens and enjoy the sweet aroma of various flowers . . . then he should . . . either plant seeds in his own domestic plot or should plant a root for general use and for the joy of all . . . who were not able to visit the distant gardens. . . . So I, the sinful slave of God, have by His divine grace been deemed worthy of seeing and visiting the richly flowering *gardens of foreign languages* and tasting the soul-enlivening pleasure coming from their *sweetest flowers most useful to the soul* and have put much effort . . . so that I might carry out from there the *transplanting of roots* and the *rerooting of seeds bearing flowers of divine fragrance* into the Slavonic language [Church Slavonic] of my home, the bulwark and protection of the Russian church.[75]

Such transplantation and rerooting helped prepare the ground for the creation of a paradisal "garden of sciences" in Russia.

Peter the Great was often depicted as the "gardener" who first planted the garden of sciences in Russia, as in one anonymous inscription (*nadpis'*) written for a statue of him unveiled in 1750: "He sowed, he grew, the arts, the sciences."[76] An allegorical Russia proclaims the paradisal results of his work in an anonymous 1786 poem entitled "An Ode: The Victory of Russia": "Everywhere the *sciences have been planted* and *gardens bearing their fruit* prophesy my blissful days. Woes are simply unknown to me."[77]

This allegorical vision of a garden of sciences underlies Dmitrii Levitskii's 1773 parade portrait of Prokopii Demidov—a wealthy donor to Moscow University and other schools. In this painting (Illustration 2), he is standing in front of a building, holding one hand on a watering can and pointing with the other to two potted plants. Despite one critic's observation that these plants reflect

Illustration 2. D. G. Levitskii, Portrait of P. A. Demidov (from I. E. Grabar', ed. *Istoriia russkogo iskusstva*. Moscow: Izdatel'stvo nauki, 1961, 7:51).

Demidov's "love for flowers,"[78] we can more plausibly interpret this painting against the background of the garden of sciences and see it as representing Demidov's support ("watering") of educational institutions that will help the young ("the plants") to "grow" and to "flourish." The likelihood of this interpretation is increased through a comparison with G. R. Derzhavin's 1777 poem "An Epistle to I. I. Shuvalov," written four years later; here, Shuvalov, the director of the Kazan Secondary School, is depicted as *"planting [nasazhdaia] the arts and fine taste"* and *"planting [sadia] schools"* "during the days of Minerva, in the days of Catherine," whose wise leadership will encourage him to "multiply . . . the gardens of [his] good deeds."[79] These images of the educator as "gardener" and his school as a "garden of sciences" (whose Edenic fruits would help Russia attain a golden age) became fairly frequent in the late eighteenth century.[80]

Under Catherine II, Russia was often referred to as "Minerva's garden," as in Kheraskov's 1767 ode on her codification of new laws, which pictures "wise Minerva" (Catherine) "planting gardens everywhere"—by implication gardens of science.[81] As Petr Kaisarov wrote in his 1795 "Ode: The Prosperity of Russia," which pictures eternity opening before the poet and showing him a "vision of the paradisal Russian countries" where inhabitants are enjoying the fruits of a golden age brought about through proper cultivation of sciences and education: "The descendents of the Russians are sitting there, filled with sweet rapture, and see *Russia in bloom and brilliance.* One thinks one is seeing a bright, holy *Eden, where the sciences are flowering like a garden"* (pp. 3–4). But perhaps no poem goes so far in its hyperbolic praise of Minerva's paradisal garden as Vasilii Tuzov's 1769 Birthday Ode to Catherine, which in its topoi-turvy exuberance describes rivers flowing with *science* and honey: "[V]alleys are flowering here more beautiful than the fields of Boeotia. *Pallas* [Minerva] *makes the sciences flow lavishly* in rivers and honey-filled streams."[82]

This image of a paradisal garden of sciences became the controlling metaphor of M. M. Kheraskov's 1761 epic poem *The Fruits of Learning (Plody nauk,* literally *The Fruits of the Sciences),* which redefined the golden age as the time when learning (*nauka* in its broadest sense) became known and allowed man to leave

the cave.[83] The introduction of learning is portrayed as a cosmogonic change from darkness to light, which is equated with the
change in Russia from a dark age (before Peter I) to a bright or
golden age under Peter and his successors.[84] The persona depicts the introduction of learning through the *locus amoenus*: "The
zephyrs began to blow more tenderly in the fields, the *chorus of
birds* on the branches sang out more tenderly, the *fruits* ripened
more rapidly and sweetly, and the heavens shone more brightly"
(p. 8). Imagery of planting, fruits, and flowering becomes a key
to the allegory by canto 3, which describes the flowering gardens
(implicitly gardens of science) and abundant harvests resulting
from the development of new agricultural techniques that allow
a seed to more quickly flower: "On plowed land fruits ripen more
quickly; through learning [*nauka*] minds flower and mature more
quickly." Thus, the "fruits of learning" of Kheraskov's allegorical title come from the same garden as the "plants" cultivated
by Demidov in Levitskii's painting;[85] these fruits (here, education) will help "cultivate" Russia more rapidly (or, to use Kheraskov's metaphor, enable it to increase its harvest like a field being
plowed by a machine) and allow it "to reestablish the golden
age" (p. 15).

Russians favoring the rapid growth of learning implied by the
garden of sciences often strongly criticized what they thought
was Jean-Jacques Rousseau's defense of the noble savage (as
opposed to civilization) in his *Discourse on the Arts and Sciences*
(translated into Russian in 1768, 1787, and 1792). Among Rousseau's Russian opponents was N. M. Karamzin, who attacked
Rousseau's discourse in a 1794 retort entitled "A Word About the
Sciences, the Arts, and Enlightenment," condemning Rousseau's
defense of the "savage" Spartans (who knew neither sciences
nor arts) over the cultivated Athenians and their "gardens of philosophy": "Even divine Socrates . . . , fighting for his Athens, was
fighting for the place of his happiness, of his pleasures, which
he savored in the gardens of philosophy in conversation with his
friends and wise men."[86] For Karamzin, as for many others at
the end of the century, the philosophical garden (a variant of the
"garden of sciences") was a place to cultivate the mind, to grow
the fruits that would create the good life (the thoughtful life).
But under the influence of their reading (or misreading) of Rous-

seau, Russians continued to debate whether the fruits of the garden of sciences actually benefited the human race. This debate was still going on when Pushkin was writing *Eugene Onegin*, in which a disagreement between Onegin and Lenskii strongly reflects Rousseau's influence: "Everything engendered arguments between them and led them to reflection: the social contracts of past tribes, *the fruits of science*, good and evil, prejudices age-old" (chapter 2, stanza 16). While most Russians continued to wish that their country would become a "garden of sciences," some feared the dangers of its fruits.

The Garden in the City: The Marriage of Nature and Art

The paradisal garden and the rhetoric of the "pleasant place" glorified not only Russia and its science but sometimes even cities—a paradoxical pattern that had many precedents in classical literature.[87] In such cases the *locus amoenus* served a general encomiastic function, moving beyond an appreciation of nature to praise man's "art" (i.e., his "improvement" of nature).[88]

One of the earliest Russian works to use this pattern was V. K. Trediakovskii's "Verses in Praise of Paris" (1727–28), which described the city as though it were a paradisal garden:[89]

Beautiful place: dear banks of the Seine, *the Elysian Fields are no better than you*. Home of all joys and of sweet peace, where there is *neither winter nor summer heat*.

Above you the sun rolls laughing through the sky, and nowhere does it shine better. A *pleasant zephyr* clothes the *flowers*, making them beautiful and fragrant for a long time.

Through you flow all the *cool waters*, strolling nymphs sing harmonious songs. Apollo and his muses play in a delightful way on the lyre, on the psaltery [*gusli*] and on flutes.

Beautiful place, dear banks of the Seine, where a village manner would not dare to exist: Because you nobly maintain all things in your bounds, you are a natural place [even] for gods and goddesses.

Your waters sweetly nourish the laurel. All types of people desire to live in you always, *you ooze milk, honey, and sweet joy*, such as truly never existed before.

Beautiful place, dear banks of the Seine: Who does not love you?

Such a person would be a bumpkin. And I can never forget you, as long as I exist on this earth.[90]

This poem illustrates how panegyric poetry may praise a city through the *locus amoenus*, thus associating it with paradisal nature. Indeed, if it were not announced that these are "verses praising Paris," if the river Seine were not mentioned, and if it were not for the derogatory comments about bumpkins and village manners, the reader would probably assume that this is a poem about a *country* place—especially given motifs like "sweet peace," "Elysian Fields," "pleasant zephyr," "fragrant flowers," "flowing waters," "strolling nymphs," "natural place," and "oozing milk and honey."[91] Paris is thus portrayed as an "urban Arcadia"—a garden paradise and a "natural" city.[92]

Beginning with the Renaissance debate as to whether untouched "nature" is better than man's interference with nature by "art," the idea of the paradisal place harmoniously blending nature with art has appeared frequently in Western literature.[93] In Russian culture of the eighteenth century as well, paradise was often depicted as a place integrating nature and art.[94] This ideal combination was reflected in the vogue for "winter gardens," which attempted to translate the paradisal motif of "eternal spring" at least partially into life by creating a magnificent garden scene indoors.[95] One of the more famous winter gardens of the eighteenth century was at Prince Potemkin's Tauride Palace in Petersburg, described here by Derzhavin:

At first glance one might hesitate and think that this [garden] is an act of enchantment . . . but coming closer, one will see live laurels, myrtles, and other trees of temperate climates, not only growing but also weighed down with flowers in some cases and fruits in others. . . . Everywhere *spring reigns* and *art is fighting with the delights of nature*. One's spirit swims in pleasure.[96]

"Eternal spring" was similarly perceived by a visitor to the winter garden at the Winter Palace, who noted that his "eyes were astounded . . . at the pleasant garden, where greenery, flowers, and the singing of birds had, it seemed, *transferred an Italian spring to the snowy north*."[97] This winter garden with its singing birds and fragrant herbs and flowers was explicitly designed to remind the viewer of Eden.[98]

Among works portraying a Russian paradise resulting from the marriage of nature and art were many poems to Tsarskoe Selo, the summer home of the tsars. Given the etymology of "paradise" (from the Old Persian word for a royal garden or park), this myth was particularly appropriate for such works. For example, Lomonosov's 1750 ode to Elizabeth "For the Royal Favor Shown to Him in the Town of Tsarskoe Selo" begins with imagery of pleasance ("What joy do I feel"), including the *locus amoenus*: "How tender is the wealth of Flora here. How the pleasance of the air is linked with the goddess of these beautiful heights" (Elizabeth, who has just been compared with Diana).[99] Part of Lomonosov's ode (stanzas 8–14) is spoken by a river nymph, allegorically representing the "Slavena" (actually, Slavianka)— the small stream near Tsarskoe Selo that Elizabeth wanted to connect by canal with the Neva River to allow boat transportation from St. Petersburg to her summer palace.[100] The nymph asks the "Sovereign of Russian waters" (the Neva, which is compared to the "wide Nile which flows from paradise")[101] to "take my small streams into yourself": "*A beauty equal to Eden* crowns my springs, where the Goddess [Elizabeth] plants her garden and where the *fields imitate heaven* and dot themselves with flowers. . . . *There nature luxuriates, awakened by* the *art* of hands" (stanza 7). This theme of the marriage of nature and art leads to descriptions of flowering sciences and presents the idea that just as man's arrangement of nature into gardens makes Tsarskoe Selo a "pleasant place," so can his arrangement of the world through science lead to the good life. Tsarskoe Selo is thus seen as a microcosm of Russia, a place where "Peter's daughter has shown favor to the sciences in a motherly way and with her generosity brought ecstasy." Indeed, although the poem on the surface is about beautiful nature, its actual theme concerns the benefits *science* ("art") can bring to man.[102]

In a similar way, Lomonosov's 1764 poem "To Tsarskoe Selo" praises both the town and Catherine II.[103] Beginning with the rhetoric of *locus amoenus*, Lomonosov once again describes a place combining nature and art (here using architecture as his example of art): "Your meadows, bushes, pleasant heights are an *example and model of Edenlike beauty*. . . . Is it not because everywhere there are pleasures in the gardens, and tender Zephyrs luxuriate among the flowers? Or that for your [Tsarskoe Selo's] sake the power of the glorious *arts* has reached its heights, expended all of its potential and skill [*khitrost'*]" (lines 1–8). This paradisal description is expanded in later lines to praise Catherine: "More than all of these, Catherine herself decorates this land. In her presence it is the golden age, and paradise is flowering" (lines 13–14). This image of a place that is pleasant precisely because of the presence of the monarch was to remain characteristic of poems to Tsarskoe Selo.[104]

A number of eighteenth-century poems to country estates use the same structure as the Tsarskoe Selo poems, focusing on an ideal landscape or scene to praise an idealized person. For example, the anonymous 1771 "Ode in Praise of Raifa, a Place Beautified by Nature"[105] uses the image of a paradisal garden to praise Raifa (a name that recalls the word *rai* ["paradise"]), the estate of Iakov Shubskii, and, through association, Shubskii himself. The persona wonders "whether this is the garden of Eden that I am seeing," stating that "the choice of nature is [so] completely delightful" that "I do not notice the hands of art." He notes that "the creator himself [*zizhditel' sam*]" (Shubskii) "has combined everything to perfection" (as in the garden of Eden). By citing the words "the creator himself" from Lomonosov's 1743 poem "Morning Meditation on the Majesty of God," the poet makes an implicit analogy between man-the-creator (the "gardener") and God, who both can blend nature into art to create a paradisal place.

The theme of creating paradise by reordering nature through art was sometimes associated with poetry as well. As Ippolit Bogdanovich wrote in his 1765 poem "A Perfect Bliss," the muses dwell in a place recalling the golden age, where "spring reigns constantly, where eternal day shines and the darkness of night is unknown."[106] Similar connections between poetry and paradise had been made by Western poets since the Renaissance, when under the influence of Neoplatonism poetry was portrayed as improving fallen nature and restoring the lost paradisal wholeness of man.[107] For example, Sir Philip Sidney in his "Apology for Poetry" combined imagery from Genesis, Plato, and Neoplatonic philosophers (especially Plotinus) to portray poetry as superior to the fallen nature that surrounds it, and the poet as superior to fallen man because he retains his "likeness to God":

> Only the poet, . . . lifted up with the vigor of his own invention, doth grow in effect another nature, in *making things either better than nature bringeth forth*, or, quite anew, forms such as never were in nature. . . . *Her [Nature's] world is brazen, the poets only deliver a golden.* . . . [T]he heavenly Maker [God] of that maker [the poet], having made man to his own likeness, set him beyond and over all the works of . . . nature: which in nothing he showeth so much as in poetry, when with the force of a divine breath, he bringeth things forth far surpassing her doing.[108]

This reordering of nature was sometimes linked with the creation of a paradise in the imagination. As Karamzin wrote to Dmitriev, "A poet has two lives, two worlds. If he is bored in the physical world then he escapes into the land of his imagination and there lives according to his tastes and passions *as a pious Mohammedan in a paradise with his houris*."[109] In effect, then, the poet was seen as being like the gardener (and the Gardener), improving nature through art.

The related image of an Edenic garden of poetry blossomed in Russia in the last decades of the eighteenth century and was sometimes identified with Russia itself.[110] As one 1777 student work stated, "the muses are dwelling in Russia" and "where the muses dwell there are golden days."[111] The poem goes on to observe that instead of Hippocrene the Muses now have the Neva and that from this "flowering [Russian] garden of the muses" sounds are emerging "that are giving joy to the city of God."

Although the quality of these student verses, like their adult models, often makes one wonder whether hubris grew in the Russian garden of poetry, the image of Russia as a garden of the muses became rather widespread, perhaps reflecting the Russians' own feeling that they were finally developing a national literature worthy of note. Indeed, by the last quarter of the century, this image became sufficiently common that works with "Parnassus" in their titles often referred allegorically to Russia. For example, V. I. Maikov's 1775 prologue on the recovery of Catherine II from smallpox, "Parnassus Triumphant," has the Parnassians sing of how happy they are at the recovery of "the heroine of these latest days, the cause of the general happiness, the Mother of her subjects." The work, whose title clearly alludes to the "Minerva Triumphant" pageant celebrating Catherine's coronation, proclaims Russia as "the country beloved by the Muses" and the Russian Parnassus as an Edenic garden growing "lilies of paradise" (its citizens), whose condition is improved by "art" (here, medicine, which has created the smallpox vaccination).[112] As we shall see in the next chapter, this idea of creating a new paradise by improving nature through art was extended by the brotherhood of Freemasonry to human nature as well.

CHAPTER FIVE

Paradise Within:
The Masonic Component of
the Paradise Myth

"Freemasonry is . . . the best, the only expression of
the best and the eternal sides of humanity . . .
[M]asonry is the teaching of Christianity freed
from the fetters of government and the church; the
teaching of equality, brotherhood, and love."
—Pierre Bezukhov, in Tolstoy's *War and Peace*

*I*n Russia, as throughout Europe, the Masonic movement attracted many of the most creative minds of the eighteenth century. Just as the brotherhood had embraced such Western European writers as Lessing, Goethe, Schiller, Swift, Diderot, Pope,
and Voltaire, so in Russia it included writers like Sumarokov,
Kheraskov, Novikov, Radishchev, Karamzin, Rzhevskii, Maikov,
Lukin, and Shcherbatov—all of whom participated to greatly dif-
fering extents.[1] Indeed, with the exception of Lomonosov, Fonvizin, and Derzhavin,[2] most of the major writers of the second
half of the eighteenth century were Masons, participating in a
movement that attempted to restore the moral perfection man
had once possessed in Eden—a perfection often represented by
paradisal imagery.[3]

Paradise and the Masonic Quest

For the Masons paradise, Eden, the golden age, Zion, and the
promised land were central, interchangeable metaphors for the
highest morality achievable by man—a moral state retrievable,

they contended, through their movement. The Masons often called their lodge a "restored paradise" and claimed that it enjoyed "a new golden age" or the "blessings of Eden."[4] As members of one lodge were told upon their initiation into the Fellow Craft degree (the second of three degrees of the "lower order" or "English" system of Freemasonry—the rationalist common denominator of the many Masonic systems), they were being led "to joyous Eden to spend [their] life in bliss";[5] some other initiates were told that their lodge was located "in the promised land."[6] As a symbol of this attempt to restore paradisal perfection, the Masons frequently asked candidates during initiation to relinquish all objects made from metal, in order to show them "that happy original condition" when people had no need for money or other valuables.[7] Here, as throughout Freemasonry, the original, paradisal condition of mankind was associated with the spiritual (as opposed to the material) side of life.

So important was the paradise myth to Freemasonry that Astraea was sometimes named in Masonic texts as "the protectress" of the Masons and represented as carrying the two main symbolic instruments of the brotherhood: the square and the compass.[8] There were even two eighteenth-century lodges named "Astraea" in Russia, and a Grand Lodge of Astraea was founded in 1814.[9] As Ivan P. Elagin, the first head of the Grand Russian Provincial Lodge, asserted in a 1786 manuscript, "our science [Freemasonry, which was frequently called a "science" in Masonic texts] was already discovered in Eden," and "the tree of life, which was once planted in paradise, has remained in the center of our temples [lodges]."[10]

According to Masonic doctrine, paradise could be restored by finding the "higher wisdom" (*premudrost'*) that man had possessed in paradise;[11] one eighteenth-century manuscript explicitly defined the goal of Freemasonry as "the obtaining of the knowledge lost by Adam."[12] As another Masonic article stated, "the cause of all human errors is ignorance, and the cause of all perfection knowledge."[13] The Masons sought this knowledge through the lodge, which they called "the temple of higher wisdom"; in their search for this hidden knowledge, those in "higher order" lodges (the antirationalist or mystical lodges with more than the three degrees of the rationalist, English system)[14] used many arcane sources, such as alchemical texts, the Jewish Cabala, and seventeenth-century mystical writings—all of which came to provide material for Masonic rituals and literary allegories. (See Appendix B.) Through these sources, higher order Masons sought to restore the Edenic time when "the book of nature was open to man's understanding, and he could understand all of its mysteries." [15]

"Higher wisdom" could only be obtained, the Masons argued, as man became more virtuous and came to "know himself." As the Mason proceeded along the road of self-perfection, higher wisdom was revealed gradually (in Masonic terms, by "degrees"—*stepeni*), often as a result of an apprenticeship or vow of "obedience" (*povinovenie*) to those having greater virtue and hence greater knowledge (i.e., to Masonic officers and to those who had already attained more advanced degrees). The number of degrees necessary to obtain total Masonic initiation varied from the three of the English lodges to the thirty-three or more degrees of some higher order lodges.

By perfecting themselves, the Masons hoped to restore perfection to the world. Implicit in this goal was a circular conception of time and history—an attempt to "return mankind to its natural, primal goodness" lost in the Fall.[16] Indeed, the many utopias described in Masonic fiction were often projections of the Masonic lodge—places where all were Masons in conduct and principle if not in name. The lodge itself was often portrayed as a sacred, paradisal space and referred to as a "temple" (*khram*) or a "cathedral" (*sobor*);[17] non-Masons were even called *profany* ("profane ones"). As one higher order song declared in portraying a candidate leaving the world of vice for the sacred lodge:

Leaving the corruptibility [*tlennost'*] of the world, leaving its vanity, you will penetrate to the ether, you will see its order, its beauty. Driving vices to hell, constantly proclaim VIVAT.

You will find perfection, having found the golden age; you will find harmony, bliss, and true peace. Driving vices to hell, constantly proclaim VIVAT.[18]

This song reflects the frequent opposition in higher order Masonry between the incorruptible world of God (and hence, implicitly, of Freemasonry) and the corruptible world of fallen man.[19] To attain this sacred world of Freemasonry, a candidate had to undergo a series of initiatory trials (*ispytaniia*) representing a ritual death; through proper instruction he could then be reborn to a new, paradisal life, and often assumed a new name to symbolize this re-beginning.[20]

Masonic rituals, literature, and songs often depicted the lodge as giving its members a life of internal bliss, frequently compared to a "paradise within"—a term reflecting the theological tradition that unfallen man enjoyed a threefold paradise: the external garden in Eden, a body fully attuned to its harmonious surroundings, and a paradise within his soul.[21] As one song declared: "Blessed is he who attends to suffering and gives aid to the poor, who dries the tears of orphans: he will find *paradise within himself.*"[22] Another song portrayed the Masons as "tasting the golden age" in providing help for the poor and stated that in practicing charity (both generosity and *caritas*) they had "tasted paradise already."[23] Some songs explicitly depicted God as the builder of this internal paradise.[24]

Higher order Masonry often portrayed the Masons as knights who would return morals to the age of chivalry—frequently equated with the golden age, when men acted for the good of others rather than self-interest.[25] One Russian song even equated the words "knight" and "Mason," redefining the golden age as a time when all were Masons: "When love in all its glory shone on all in the Golden Ages, and people lived in brotherhood, then all were Masons. But when the gloom of vice arose, placing a multitude of obstacles to truth, how valued and how high were placed the name 'knight' and 'Mason.'"[26] Other songs showed the Masons performing "useful exploits" (*podvigi polezny*)—a phrase often used for the brave deeds of knights. This association reflected not only the high standards of moral conduct in Freemasonry but also the fact that both Freemasonry and chivalry symbolically embodied a rite of passage "marking the transition from youthful innocence and ignorance to self-knowledge, maturity, and, in religious terms, salvation."[27] In Masonic ritual and literature this "salvation" was also referred to through the metaphor of paradise.

Masonic Codes:
The Symbols and Hieroglyphs of Paradise

As an emblem of his search for the higher wisdom once possessed by Adam in Eden, the Mason was gradually given access
to secret codes, symbols, and "hieroglyphs" (visual symbols),
which sometimes were assigned different meanings as he passed
through various degrees.[28] For the Masons, hieroglyphs represented a means of restoring the original, "adequate," nonverbal
language of paradise and thus returning the word of God to the
heart of man. Typical of the Masonic hieroglyphs was the very
sign of the organization (Figure 1)—a star of Solomon with the
letter "G" inside, interpreted differently in various degrees to
stand for "Gnosis" (the secret knowledge that was sacred to
the Masons), "God," "Geometry," "Generation," and so on. In
some interpretations, the two triangles composing the star were
said to represent the "inevitable struggle" between good and
evil and between spirit and flesh: the upward-pointing triangle
stood for the spiritual principle, or man before the Fall; and the
downward-pointing triangle for the material principle or man
after the Fall.[29] Similarly, an arc of sixty degrees surrounded by
a circle was said in Rosicrucian lodges to stand for "paradise on
earth in the bosom of the order, where the sun of higher wisdom
is always shining." [30]

   In addition to its hieroglyphs, Freemasonry used a number of
verbal symbols (some commonplace, some specifically Masonic)
to encode its basic doctrine.[31] As one Mason stated, "to destroy
our symbols means to destroy Freemasonry." [32] The most frequent symbolic system was that of architecture and building,
reflecting the supposed origin of Freemasonry in guilds formed
during the construction of the Temple of Solomon. Much Masonic ritual allegorized the description of this construction in
1 Kings 5:1–9:25, implying that the Mason was building a spiritual temple within himself, shaping "rough stone" (man in his
post-Fall state of ignorance) into a finished building (the Mason
who has passed through all the degrees of Masonic knowledge
and come to "know himself"). Among the central symbols of
Freemasonry were the "tools" that helped the Mason build this
spiritual temple and restore the paradisal condition to his soul:

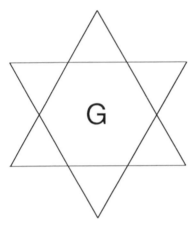

Figure 1. The Masonic Star.

squares, compasses, levels, and plumbs. In building this spiritual temple, the Mason was viewed as moving closer to the original "design" of the "Grand Architect of the Universe" (God), which man enjoyed in Eden before the Fall.

A second symbolic system depicted the Masonic activity as a journey, the person seeking Masonic perfection as a traveler, and Freemasonry as a "guide for the road" (*putevoditel'*). Truth was seen as being (like paradise) in the East, but to get there the traveler had to find his way out of a labyrinth, which represented his vices and passions; errors and falsehoods were depicted as "wanderings" from the correct path. Such imagery was parodied by Tolstoy in his ironic mocking of Masonry in *War and Peace*, where Pierre Bezukhov meets the Mason Bazdeev (who is referred to at first simply as a "traveler") while on a "journey"; Pierre's Masonic journey ultimately leads him not *out* of a labyrinth but *into* one (Tolstoy uses the image of a bog [*boloto*] from which Pierre cannot extract himself).[33]

A third system of imagery, the alchemical system (appearing mostly in works by higher order Masons), used gold ("the perfect metal") as the dominant metaphor for the Masonic quest,[34] depicting the movement as perfecting "base metals" (new candidates) by turning them into "gold" (full-fledged Masons). Just as the Masonic initiate had to be "reborn" to achieve true perfection, so did the symbolic gold of the Masons have to undergo a process whereby it was cast back into the earth, dissolved, and "by a path of rebirth" brought back to its original state of perfection. In this system, God and Christ were depicted as "Alchemists" (*Khimiki*). One Masonic document even called Jesus "the Alchemist who is rich in love" and portrayed him as the head of the Masonic order.[35]

Freemasonry also absorbed several more general symbolic conventions that were common as well in non-Masonic works. For example, a geometrical system associated the triangle with strength and the pyramid with rebirth and used both as symbols of perfection. A numerological system associated three and seven with perfection (seen especially in such distinctly Masonic images as "threefold light"—*troiakii svet*). And a visual system identified truth with light and sin or error with darkness; non-Masons were "blind men" in this system and Masons "saw the light" with the aid of the "All-Seeing Eye" (*Vsevidiashchee Oko*: God), who provided them with "a shining star as a guide" (the morning star) to show them the path to paradise; as one song stated, the "wonderful brilliance of the star will lead us to Zion," which implicitly was within the Mason.[36] Within this visual system, as within Masonic ritual as a whole, the Masons portrayed themselves as seeking the lost light of paradise, which would restore to man his likeness to God.

Paradise Unshrouded:
The Masonic View of Image and Likeness

The poets and writers of Russian higher order Masonry often used imagery of light to represent the "memory" of paradisal existence that lives within the soul.[37] Imagery of "inner light" (closely connected with the image of "paradise within") in Masonic songs, symbols, rituals, and literature of the late eighteenth century often reflected the influence of St. Augustine and the seventeenth-century thinkers whom he influenced (especially mystics like Boehme, Arndt, Weigel, Pordage, and Angelus Silesius)—all of whom were being translated by Russian higher order Masons during the last quarter of the eighteenth century.[38] According to Augustine, God, the "true light," "lighteth every man that cometh into the world"[39] through an "inner light" that always exists in the mind, even when not used: "We must find, in the rational or intellectual soul of man, *an image of its Creator. . . . [T]hat image always remains,* whether it be so faded that scarcely anything is left, whether it be obscured and defaced, or clear and fair."[40] Under the influence of such passages in Augustine and his successors, higher order Masons felt that the enlightened spirit could attain the inner paradise that still exists as a "spark" (*iskra*) within man's memory. Believing that "what was given by God can never be lost or destroyed," they saw this spark as covered by mist, enshrouded rather than lost, and thus felt that through proper preparation and searching, man could find the hidden light.[41]

This idea of a recoverable "spark" of paradise within all human beings was closely linked to the concept of recovering man's lost "image and likeness" to God (see Chapter 2). As one Russian manuscript circulating in the eighteenth century stated, the goal of Freemasonry was to bring man "to the primal source of all things and *to return his previous likeness to God lost in the Fall.*"[42] As the German Mason and Moscow University professor Johann G. Schwarz stated in his lectures on "three types of knowledge," men are given a "secret spring to lift them to the *perfect image of God* that was hidden in them by the Fall," a "small spark" of their pre-Fall state, when they were "temples of the living God" and "were perfect like God."[43] The Masons (especially the Rosicrucians to which Schwarz belonged) tried to ignite this "spark" in reconstructing the temple of perfection within man.[44]

Unlike the monarchical version of the paradise myth, the Masonic version saw the restoration of the divine image in man not as a political mission but as a moral one; if the monarchical version portrayed the tsar as the mediator in the road to perfection who through his suffering would remake himself in the image and likeness of God and then provide the perfect example for the remaking of his citizens, the Masons portrayed *themselves* in this exemplary role. As one Mason wrote, the goal of Freemasonry was twofold: "to correct ourselves and through our example to lead others outside our organization to a knowledge of virtue."[45] And Ivan Lopukhin argued in a work called *The Spiritual Knight* (1791): "[All suffering will stop on earth] when the Golden Age, which previously a small group of elect people [the "spiritual knights," i.e., the Masons] had attempted to restore within themselves, will spread everywhere and appear externally."[46] Through the help of these "spiritual knights," man would, Lopukhin believed, be restored to his original, paradisal state, where God made him "incorruptible and in His own image and likeness" (p. 29) and he was "through his rational soul like God himself" (p. 27).[47]

The Masonic goal of returning man to the image and likeness of God was integrally connected with the resurrection of Adam's lost paradisal knowledge. According to a legend used in one Illuminist lodge, the secret knowledge of the Freemasons began after the expiration of Adam's period of punishment, when God sent a ray of light that had earlier illuminated paradise— a light that, while not as bright and not emitting the exact light that had shined there, nevertheless enlightened the mind with knowledge not otherwise available to post-Fall man.[48] After being passed to the biblical patriarchs, Noah, Moses, and Jesse, and then preserved in the temples of ancient Egypt, this ray was ultimately transferred to Palestine by Adoniram ("Hiram Abif," the chief architect or "builder" of the Temple of Solomon);[49] through Adoniram this knowledge was transmitted to the Masons.

Among the lost Edenic knowledge sought by the Masons was the Adamic language—the original, privileged language of man that provided a key to the secrets of the universe and allowed full communication between man and God.[50] According to the Masons, with the Fall of man came a fall of language and a consequent inability to understand the word of God. One function of Freemasonry was to make the human word adequate as it was in paradise by remaking man in the image and likeness of God.

Together with a number of other Masonic conceptions, this Masonic idea of a privileged language of Adam provides a key to N. M. Karamzin's poem "Poetry" (written in 1787 while he was still a Mason). Karamzin depicts poetry as an Edenic language of "delight and love," originating in the spontaneous overflow of tender feelings of paradisal man at the "grandeur," "wisdom," and "good" of God and at his own bliss in Eden.[51] This harmonious language of poetry, according to Karamzin, fell with man from Eden but nevertheless retained some of its paradisal heritage. Having survived the flood, this "holy language of the heavens" became a source of comfort for an *elect clan* who preserved poetry and were enlightened by it." In addition to projecting onto the poet and the lover of poetry the term "elect," frequently used by the Masons to describe themselves, Karamzin applies to poetry the term "holy science" that the Masons had used for their order, and talks of poetry ("a song to GOD") as "resounding in the *temple of Solomon"*—a reference simultaneously to the psalms of the Old Testament being sung in Solomon's temple and, on a second level, to the spirit of Eden remaining in the ritual of Freemasonry ("Solomon's temple"). Karamzin thus transfers the Masonic idea of "paradise within the Elect" from Masonry to poetry; in so doing he reflects the new, inward direction in Russian literature, which was in part influenced by Freemasonry.[52]

The Paradise Myth in Masonic Fiction: The Works of M. M. Kheraskov

During the eighteenth century, many of the principles of Freemasonry outlined thus far were translated into fiction written by Masons. Masonic fiction (especially the novel and the epic) often was based on the initiatory trials of Masonic ritual. Thus, Ivan Elagin's description of Masonic initiation closely resembles the plot of much Masonic fiction: "[T]he roads leading to the temple of truth are dark, narrow, and like paths through swampy and thick forests that lead a traveler astray." The function of Masonic literature was that of Freemasonry itself: to help a brother find this "temple" (the Masonic lodge) by leading him "through the narrow and very difficult path to that which is very bright but invisible, to that which is everywhere but which is hidden from the eyes of mortals."[53] This "temple" was often identified with paradise.

During the period from 1782 to 1794, M. M. Kheraskov, Russia's most interesting and complex Masonic writer, wrote four works dealing directly or indirectly with the Masonic paradise quest: the Eastern tale *The Golden Wand* (1782); the epic *Vladimir Reborn* (1st ed., 1785); the novel *Cadmus and Harmonia* (1st ed., 1789); and its "sequel" *Polydorus: The Son of Cadmus and Harmonia*

(1st ed., 1794). All four works reflect the general beliefs dominating much Masonic literature: that paradise is within the self; that only the virtuous person can achieve it; and that this achievement requires significant self-knowledge, self-improvement, and self-sacrifice. Taken together, these works provide a concise overview of eighteenth-century Russian Masonic fiction in its various genres and allegorical strategies.[54]

Although *The Golden Wand* began Kheraskov's clear "Masonic period," traces of Masonic themes can already be found in *Numa* (1768), a work about a virtuous man who can rule others because he knows and can rule himself. Its epigraph, "Let all men remember that they are brothers," sounds vaguely Masonic; the comment from the "publisher" that this work may be a translation of an original written by someone living "in the East" (a frequent symbol of the Masonic lodge) hints at the author's links with Freemasonry.[55] The case for potential Masonic influence is bolstered even further by the fact that some higher order lodges of Freemasonry saw their organization as originating with Numa.[56] Although this, as well, may be coincidence, it is possible that Kheraskov was to some extent rewriting Plutarch's story of Numa Pompilius with a Masonic focus, perhaps hinting at affinities with the Masons even before his formal initiation. At the very least, *Numa* anticipates some of the concerns that develop far more clearly and fully in Kheraskov's Masonic works of the 1780's.

'The Golden Wand': An Eastern Tale

During the last third of the eighteenth century, the genre of the Eastern tale gained great popularity in Russia, reflecting the success of the first Russian translation of the *Arabian Nights* (1763–71) and of the genre that this collection had spawned in eighteenth-century Europe.[57] Given the use of the terms "the Orient" and "the East" for the Masonic lodge,[58] the Eastern tale occasionally provided an attractive frame for Masonic allegory; several tales even used "Arabia" as a symbol of the Masonic brotherhood and its values. One clear example was an anonymous 1789 work entitled "The New Year: An Eastern Scene" (published in Novikov's Masonic-oriented journal *Reading for Children*),[59] which uses the myth of "Arabia Felix" ("fertile Arabia"—a happy state in the Arabic world) for Masonic purposes.[60] Although it is stated that "the action takes place in happy Arabia,"[61] there is not a single mention of Arabia in the entire work. Instead, the work takes place in "the interior of a huge temple filled with people"— clearly a representation of the Masonic lodge.[62]

Kheraskov's Eastern tale *The Golden Wand* (1782), which bears the label "translated from the Arabic" to give it the proper "authenticity" and exoticism, is also a Masonic allegory.[63] The work, which concerns man's search for happiness, has two main plots: the story of the materialist courtier Albekir and his Masonic regeneration; and the story of Magoteosopher, which propagandizes the Masonic values that lead to the courtier's rebirth. The tale begins in the happy kingdom of Caliph Shah-Bah (a descendent of the famous storyteller Scheherazade of *Arabian Nights* fame)—a peaceful land of complete idleness, where the caliph can listen to stories and whittle wooden spoons all day and yet be loved by his flourishing subjects.[64] But happiness, as the narrator states, is a "fickle god" (p. 7); everything suddenly goes wrong in this kingdom, resulting in a plot against Albekir, who is forced to flee the court.

In his "journey," Albekir meets an old hermit, Magoteosopher (whose name combines "magus" and "theosopher" and thus probably represents the [higher order] Mason). The hermit's tale of his life is the typical Masonic allegory of man's birth into paradise and eventual loss of bliss because of the bestiality of unreformed human nature. In Magoteosopher's paradisal homeland, there were no courtiers, no huge and magnificent buildings, no lawsuits (pp. 35, 42); people lived simply and ate only milk and fruits, as in the golden age (p. 46). The laws of this land were simple—what Kheraskov ironically calls "an unnatural law," resulting from "grace sent down from heaven" (p. 47).[65] But this paradisal land was "turned to dust" by invading neighbors. Given human nature, in other words, any terrestrial paradise must be temporary.[66]

On being forced from his homeland, Magoteosopher is told by a voice to head for Egypt and to search for a person who can teach him to get light from a stone; this light-producing stone (*kamen'*) is, of course, the "foundation" of Freemasonry (*svobodno-kamen'shchichestvo*). Magoteosopher—man exiled from his earthly paradise—must learn the Masonic path to a better, internal paradise. He is shown the way by a veiled woman in white, who represents Virtue. To purify his soul, she leads him into a "great pyramid" (a frequent symbol of rebirth in Free- masonry), and he (in the fashion of the Masonic initiate) "obeys her in silence." The typical foundation for Masonic literature (especially higher order literature) has thus been laid: a basically good person who is not sufficiently pure in his soul wishes to recover man's "former light";[67] to do this he must come to "know himself" and then purify himself by undergoing initiatory trials.

Virtue leads Magoteosopher along a narrow and steep stair- case (recalling that of the Masonic lodge) and leaves him (as in Masonic ritual) "in a dark, frightening, and unknown building." On descending the twenty-seven stairs ($3 \times 3 \times 3$, reflecting the association of the number three with perfection in Freemasonry), he is accosted by three-headed snakes, lions, and tigers (repre- senting the bestiality in man). After being tortured with fire and water, he finally falls asleep; when awakened by divine singing he finds himself in "a certain marvelous country"—an exter- nal representation of the Masonic paradise within. In this place, where everything seems a hundred times better than anything he has previously experienced, he sees an unusual, transparent light. At this point, Virtue again appears (this time without a veil) and hands him a ring, which forces its wearer to "understand himself" and shows him "the secrets of nature"—the secrets of Freemasonry (p. 84).

Magoteosopher (who, like the lodge master in much Masonic literature, is often called an "elder" [starets]) attempts to teach this Masonic truth to Albekir. But the courtier does not under- stand his "learned speech" with its Masonic building metaphors. To help him comprehend, Magoteosopher gives him the "golden wand" of the title, which allows him to become invisible, to un- lock any door, and to reveal the true thoughts of anyone whom it touches. Using the wand, Albekir searches for true happiness but is unable to find it; as Magoteosopher tells him, "man can- not be truly blissful in this world" (p. 258, misnumbered as 158). He informs Albekir that "there will be a time when Higher Wis- dom [Premudrost', i.e., Masonic wisdom] will descend from the heavens and will enlighten minds and the human race." In the meantime, he gives Albekir a book that will help him be relatively happy (presumably a Masonic handbook), telling him: "Learn to understand it, and you will be happy; for even now there are people in the world who are happy"—a clear reference to the Masons (p. 259 [159]). Kheraskov is suggesting (in the fashion of the higher order Mason) that true happiness lies only within oneself and can be obtained only through correction of one's own morals.

Kheraskov's tale implicitly contrasts the immoral, foolish courtiers with the moral, sapient Masons. Although this contrast may simply reflect the opposition between flesh and spirit that runs throughout the tale,[68] it is possible that it also reflects a satiric backlash against the anti-Masonic policies and propaganda of Catherine's court in the early 1780's.[69] This contrast is emphasized when the reformed Albekir, after learning Masonic truth, returns to tell the caliph about the corruption in his kingdom. When he arrives at court, he sees that the kingdom is now in chaos, run by jesters as a result of the defeat of the caliph by the revenge-seeking Rusoslav.[70]

When Albekir tries to reform the court, the new sultan assumes that he is joking and appoints him to be his third jester. But like Albekir some jesters are fully serious. At one point there is an argument among them regarding the role of science. As one jester states: "Is it not the sciences that have invented death-dealing weapons, poisons, deceptions, slanders, ruinous policies and all of those things from which the human race is suffering and perishing? Were [these sciences] known to man in the golden times?" (pp. 217–18). This jester (who is criticized by his fellows) articulates higher order Masonic concerns about the harm resulting from science and its misapplication. Kheraskov has thus come full circle from his 1761 poem "The Fruits of Science" (where he had opposed Rousseau's position in the *Discourse on the Arts and Sciences* that the rebirth of the arts and sciences has not led to an improvement in morals) to a new point of view where paradise is defined as the time when science and technology were not yet known. Under the influence of higher order Freemasonry, Kheraskov implies that the road to hell is paved with good inventions; the only science useful for mankind is the "science of Solomon"—Freemasonry.

'Vladimir Reborn'

Kheraskov described *Vladimir Reborn* as being *not* the typical epic, where "battles, knightly feats, and marvels are sung," but an account of the "wanderings of an attentive man along the path of truth, on which he meets worldly seductions, is subjected to many temptations, falls into the gloom of doubt, fights with his innate passions, finally overcomes himself, finds the path of truth, and, after achieving enlightenment, is reborn."[71] These comments in effect describe the allegorical plot of much Masonic literature: the hero is a *spiritual* knight (a Mason), whose external actions become metaphors for the "battles" taking place in man's soul.

Kheraskov's skeletal plot for *Vladimir* comes from the Primary Chronicle.[72] But in retelling the tale of the tenth-century Christianizer of Russia, Kheraskov transforms Vladimir into a Mason; in Kheraskov's work Vladimir's battle against paganism and against his own sensuality becomes a typically Masonic struggle between good and evil and between spirit and flesh. Indeed, when God declares in canto 1 that it is time that the Russians were converted, there is a second, Masonic meaning: the "conversion" of Russia to the "true faith" propagated by Freemasonry (perhaps under Tsarevich Paul, who was thought by many Masons to have been initiated during his trip to Berlin in 1781–82).

History becomes the vehicle for allegory at several points in Kheraskov's work, especially in cantos 16–18, which describe Vladimir's attempts to capture the Byzantine city of Chersoneus and to marry Anna, the sister of Emperor Basil II of Byzantium. Kheraskov uses the classical *nomen omen* (a device where the etymology of a name provides a clue to the essence or destiny of a character) to tell of "Vladimir" ("the ruler of the world") and his quest for "Anna" ("Grace"),[73] who is attainable only by embracing the "true faith" ("Orthodoxy," but here Freemasonry as well—a link reflecting the identification made by Masons between their order and the "True Christianity").[74]

Vladimir Reborn repeats many of the basic patterns that dominate Kheraskov's Masonic works, stressing the idea that the true Mason, a devout Christian, can, after conquering his baser instincts, receive a foretaste of paradise on earth and then help others to achieve it.[75] Kheraskov's Vladimir undergoes some of the typical trials of Masonic initiation before he is "reborn"; only when he comes to know and "rule himself" can he rule his nation and lead it to the "true faith" and the paradise it offers.[76] But he is tempted many times before he is able to reach this paradise and attain "Anna"/Grace.

A number of Vladimir's positive actions are linked with a paradisal garden. For example, in canto 7 after he has turned to God, he dreams of a "heavenly garden," which materializes when he awakens. This garden, described through the *locus amoenus* and other paradisal topoi (pp. 87–88), is surrounded by gates with the inscription: "He whose heart is kindled with pure love and who wants to live in God may enter these gates. But the sinner should beware and not enter" (p. 89). This paradisal garden represents the Masonic lodge with its gates closed to sinners and serves as an emblem of "the paradisal existence of blissful men" granted to the true Mason/Christian. In this Masonic garden, the previously lecherous Vladimir comes to experience the joys of spiritual love (*caritas*).[77] As a result, he is told by his guide, Idolem (who functions like the master of a lodge), that he has gone "from corruptibility to incorruptibility" (pp. 92, 95)—the typical "journey" of the Masonic initiate. In this paradise of incorruptibility, Vladimir is taught the Masonic-Christian dogma that paradise is within us: "*A pure spirit transforms all places into paradise. . . .* He whom the Lord's hand leads to bliss . . . does not have to ascend to heaven; *he can taste the days of paradise while still on earth*" (p. 98).

Kheraskov's epic is dominated by an almost Manichean opposition between paradise and hell. As Vladimir is told by the "ancient philosopher Cyrus" (*Kir*[78]—who functions as another Masonic master): "Both good and evil and light and darkness are contained in us. *We are supposed to be in paradise, or swallowed up by hell*" (p. 109).[79] Cyrus tells Vladimir that to enjoy the kind of paradise he has been shown he "must repulse all that is connected with the flesh" and invites him into a prototype Masonic "temple" where he "will learn the truth and will come to know himself" (p. 99). Like the Masonic lodge, this temple has a "ladder" or "staircase" (*lestvitsa*) from which Vladimir falls several times in his attempt to ascend;[80] its priests teach a secret doctrine that is called a "holy science" (p. 99). But only toward the end of the work does Vladimir see the light.

At first Vladimir is blinded by this Masonic light, but, with the help of Cyrus, he becomes a "new Vladimir"—the "Vladimir Reborn" of the title—and the "Messiah is born in him": "[H]aving new hearing and new eyes he saw before him the open heavens, he saw the kingdom of the Messiah in Zion and the souls of the righteous in the bosom of Abraham" (p. 242). At this point he has a vision of a future, brilliant Russia "which will develop under the influence of the True Faith": "[S]uddenly the Russian kingdom, great and glorious, began to shine and became unconquerable." After he orders his subjects to follow his example, "hell became sealed with a holy seal and Russia was illuminated with grace [*blagodat'iu*]" (p. 245). Through the "True Faith" of Freemasonry, "Vladimir" has thus brought "Anna" to Russia.

'Cadmus and Harmonia'

On the surface, Kheraskov's novel *Cadmus and Harmonia* is a tale about the "builder" of Thebes and his wife, derived in part from Ovid's story in *Metamorphoses*. But the choice of these figures was far from coincidental; one Russian Masonic manuscript of the period even argued that the secrets later revealed in Freemasonry were brought to Greece by Cadmus and Inachus (*Imak*, the first king of Argos).[81] Like Ovid, Kheraskov recounts Cadmus's search for his sister Europa (Russian: *Evropa*), who had been abducted by Zeus, and his founding of the city of Thebes. But unlike Ovid, Kheraskov stresses Cadmus's moral falls: his seduction by an alluring siren, who leads him to debauchery and causes him to lose the Boeotian throne; his betrayal by an evil prince, whose handsome appearance he mistakes for virtuous essence; and his engulfment in the vice of Babylon. Cadmus achieves rebirth only at the end of the novel, when he learns to control his passions and sees that appearance often masks essence.

On several levels, Cadmus emerges as the Masonic Everyman. His Russian name, Kadm, resembles that of the biblical Adam, as Kheraskov himself acknowledged in his preface to the first edition.[82] Like every man, Cadmus is searching for harmony—in

Russian *garmoniia*, the name of Cadmus's wife, whom he meets, loses, and regains in the course of the novel.[83] Since *garmoniia* was frequently viewed as the goal of the Masonic quest and was also the name of a Masonic lodge founded by Kheraskov,[84] the allegory of Kheraskov's novel may be seen as the tale of the archetypal Mason, who like the Old Adam falls and loses *Garmoniia* but like the New Adam is resurrected and regains *Garmoniia* forever.

Kheraskov's allegory takes his Cadmus through the various stages of Masonic initiation. The chronological beginning of the novel (which plunges in medias res) occurs in a labyrinth— the Masonic symbol for the sinful life of the "profane" outside world. Like the Mason, Cadmus must try to escape from this labyrinth and find *Garmoniia* (both Harmonia and Harmony). His success results largely from fulfilling his vow "to be obedient" to Chiron (the wisest and most gentle of the centaurs in Greek mythology), who functions like the master of a Masonic lodge, helping his "candidate" to see and understand past vices while guiding him onto the Masonic path that will ultimately lead him to rebirth.[85] On emerging from the labyrinth, Cadmus finds himself dressed in white clothing—a symbol of purity sometimes worn by Masonic initiates. The novel thus allegorically illustrates the frequent precept that "the thread of the Sciences of Solomon [Freemasonry] . . . is the only way out of the labyrinth of fallen nature."[86]

Cadmus's path toward rebirth is emphasized by his change of name, reflecting the frequent acquisition of a new name during the process of Masonic initiation. After his first fall, he assumes the name "Admon," confirming the narrator's comment that "Cadmus is no longer in this world," that is, he has abandoned his sinful former self. In his quest for spiritual perfection, Cadmus ultimately goes to an Egyptian pyramid, where he undergoes a series of "trials." He enters the pyramid (which, as we noted, was often a symbol of rebirth in Freemasonry) by a winding staircase (the Masonic symbol of ascent to enlightenment and truth). Like the Masonic initiate, he is left alone in darkness for an extended period, giving him time to realize that many of his errors are caused by the "snake of pride" (2:124). Under the guidance of a priest of Isis, he comes to "know himself" and "feels as though he has been born again" (2:136). This symbolic rebirth makes Cadmus/Admon a full-fledged Mason; only at this point does he find *Garmoniia*.

Cadmus's new identity can be unraveled by juxtaposing his two Russian names—giving "Kadm Admon," a typically Masonic anagram for "Ad(a)m Kadmon," an important figure in the Jewish Cabala, which by the time of Kheraskov's novel had become a strong influence on higher order Masonry by way of Renaissance Christian Neoplatonism.[87] In the Cabala, Adam Kadmon was the first emanation of light from God, a purely spiritual prefiguration of the biblical Adam and, as spirit-without-flesh, the nearest form of man to God. Sometimes called the *Urmensch* or first principle in man, Adam Kadmon was used in Freemasonry to prove that man (*microtheos*) is potentially a perfect reflection of God (*macrotheos*).[88] Adam Kadmon—the Godlike man—thus became a symbol of the ideal Mason, who has returned to the image and likeness of his creator. This symbol was sufficiently important to Freemasonry that the star of Solomon—the symbol of the Masonic order—was sometimes embellished with the letters "A. K." on the base of the bottom-pointing triangle, as in the frontispiece (Figure 2)[89] to a book published in Russia five years before *Cadmus and Harmonia*; the Arabic numbers in the triangles indicate that a cabalistic interpretation was to be given.[90]

As we have observed, the final state of initiation in Masonic fiction often rewards the hero with a return to paradise. Cadmus finds this state when he finally finds *Evropa*. But this *Evropa* is not his long-lost sister: it is a paradisal land inhabited by a group of people called "Slavs." When Cadmus learns where he has landed, he kisses the ground and implores, "take me, O promised land" (2:253). Thus Cadmus fulfills a Masonic prophecy uttered by Zeus at the beginning of part 2 of the novel: "Man fell from the sphere that he inhabited during the Golden Age. But after many temptations he is again capable of returning to this state" (2:3). When Cadmus finds this Slavic promised land (Russia), he abandons his search for *Evropa* (here not Europa but Europe); nascent nationalism has merged with Freemasonry here. In sum, Cadmus has gone on a typical Masonic journey, allegorically following the path of the Masonic initiate from dark-

Figure 2. Modified Masonic Star (Cabalistic version). From frontispiece to Stanislaus Ely, *Bratskie uveshchaniia k nekotorym brat'iam sv[o]b[od]nym k[a]m[e]n['']shch[i]k[a]m*. Moscow, 1784.

ness to light and from moral death to rebirth, harmony, and paradise.[91]

'Polydorus'

Cadmus and Harmonia was so successful that Kheraskov decided to continue it, writing a sequel under the title of *Polydorus: Son of Cadmus and Harmonia* (1794). Even more than its parent novel, *Polydorus* emphasizes the Masonic opposition between appearance and essence. Within the novel, those seeking paradise find deception until they come to "know themselves" and obtain Masonic knowledge. Much of *Polydorus* concerns the title hero's quest for Teandra, a goddess who will reveal the secrets of life to those who can reach her "Kingdom of Higher Wisdom" (a typical name for the prototype Masonic lodge).

As in many of Kheraskov's works, one level of allegory in *Polydorus* is reflected in names. For Kheraskov, man is *Polidor* (Greek: the possessor of "Many Gifts"); but to reap the benefit of these gifts, he must overcome external obstacles and perfect his internal self. When he does this, he can reach "Teandra"—the ideal combination of god (Greek: *theos*) and man (Greek root: *andr-*), that is, the latent, godlike perfection that the Masons sought to restore to man.[92] But Teandra wears a veil, making it hard to know whether a person has found the real Teandra or an imposter.

Among the obstacles that Polydorus must overcome in this novel is a false paradise, recalling the paradisal traps of the European Renaissance epic.[93] This pseudo-paradise is the realm of the "false Teandra"—a "pretender" to the throne of virtue; she traps Polydorus in a place that is depicted using many of the same topoi (including the *locus amoenus*) frequently used to describe the earthly paradise in eighteenth-century Russian literature. As Kheraskov writes, "everything there was rejoicing, everything breathed cheerfulness—everything seemed to be laughing."[94] But the word "seemed" is significant, stressing the opposition between appearance and reality. Indeed, the reader soon suspects that the description of this scene as "captivating" may be more literal than figurative. The first hint comes when the narrator notes: "Polydorus no longer doubted that he was on the island of Teandra, where his heart would rest content. Poor Polydorus: he had forgotten that chastity never lives in such luxury" (3:66). Since there is no clear indication of what is "true" or "false," the temptation of Polydorus becomes for a time the temptation of the reader. The narrator, reliable while Polydorus is perceptive, suddenly becomes a trickster. But by the end of book 9, he announces the truth: "Readers, and especially my female readers: Undoubtedly, there are some of you who would like to come to this delightful island. But remember that all that glitters isn't gold" (3:91).[95]

The island of the false Teandra is called "Anafa," suggesting the Russian word *anafema* ("damnation," "curse"); the true Teandra lives on the island of "Khriza," suggesting the Greek word *khruzoz* (Russian transliteration: *khrizos*) meaning "gold"—the internal gold brought to the true Mason.[96] The kingdom of the false Teandra is described through the metaphor of a labyrinth (the labyrinth of fallen nature); here the false Teandra tries to initiate Polydorus into a cult of her own beauty—a cult of surface appearance rather than virtuous essence. After pledging him to obey her laws, she has him don vestments that are gold rather than white—symbolizing the substitution of luxury for purity and chastity. The result is a parody of the Masonic initiation ceremony (accompanied by mock Masonic songs). Only later is Polydorus initiated in the proper Masonic way, led by an "elder," who requires him to pass through a whirlpool of flame and climb a high mountain (Olympus). At the summit is a "temple of higher wisdom" dedicated to Teandra, where Polydorus meets the *true* goddess. Here Polydorus, like the Mason, is reborn. Having found Teandra, he decides not to return to the mortal earth and sacrifices his life. At this point, Teandra tells him: "your mission is complete" (3:451). Polydorus thus fulfills the important Masonic doctrine that "death, only death is the beginning of life"; he has finally found the permanent paradise, but this paradise is accessible only through death.

As in *Cadmus and Harmonia*, Kheraskov includes a vision of a Russian paradise. Just before his death, Polydorus is told a prophecy by Teandra, who states that she once lived on earth under the name Astraea. Being prescient, she tells Polydorus that in the future an "anointed woman" will call her and she will help this monarch write a "wise mandate" (*mudryi nakaz*) (3:444). This monarch, who will rule "in a Northern region" where "the golden days will shine," is, of course, Catherine the Great, who was still being praised for her *Nakaz* to the Commission on Codification. As Teandra says, "the glory of her and of my kingdom [i.e., Russia] will continue until the end of time" (3:444). Thus, Russia will become the paradisal "kingdom of Teandra"— a pattern typical of many Russian panegyric "eutopias" to be discussed in the next chapter.

In sum, Kheraskov's Masonic works, written during a period when allegory was one of the more important constructive devices of Russian literature, reflect the development in Russia (under the influence of a broader European pattern) of a *Masonic* allegory in which the myth of an earthly paradise (often representing the Masonic lodge) plays a central role. Although this earthly paradise is at best "preparatory" for another, higher paradise—which is attainable only after death—it represents the best life available on this earth, a life of internal perfection where the principles of Freemasonry bring a person to taste some of the joys of paradise that had disappeared from the earth with the Fall of man.

CHAPTER SIX

The Rise of
the Russian Utopia

"[I]n the land where we live . . . we always see the
perfect religion, the perfect political system, the perfect
and most accomplished way of doing everything."
    —Montaigne, "On Cannibals"

In a 1930 propaganda play entitled *Utopia*, three Soviet writers
described the launching of a ship by that name—an obvious
symbol (like that of the Promised Land in Mayakovsky's *Mystery-
Bouffe* [1918 and 1921]) for the newly founded Soviet Union.[1] At
first glance, such symbolism may appear to be the fleeting result
of excitement generated by the 1917 revolution. But on closer in-
spection, this use of "utopia" for propaganda has extensive roots
in Russian literature and culture. As we observed in Chapter 2,
from earliest Christian times there was a curious blur in Russia between paradise and the contemporary status quo; by the
Muscovite period, the Russians had so developed the philosophy that "whatever *is* is right" that works praising the status quo
often portrayed contemporary Russia as an ideal state.

During the reign of Catherine the Great, paradisal praise of
the monarch resounded everywhere. In the words of Prince
M. M. Shcherbatov, Catherine was "fond of glory and osten-
tation, [loving] flattery and servility."[2] Catherine's vanity was
reflected throughout the literature of her age, when flattery infil-
trated many genres that would seem to be diametrically opposed
to panegyric literature, including the literary utopia.

The first Russian prose utopias often contradicted the standards of Plato and More. In the dichotomy suggested by Karl

Mannheim, many of these works were more "ideological" than "utopian."[3] As the genre of the novel developed in Russia beginning in the 1760's, descriptions of ideal lands sometimes contained the satire of More's *Utopia* but more often embodied the mythologized visions of Russia found in contemporary panegyric poetry. As a result, the "good place" (the *eu-topos* of More's pun) in eighteenth-century Russian literature was often *not* More's "no place" (*u-topos*) but contemporary Russia, represented by surrogates ranging from an island to the moon, which usually had essentially the same legal structure, political system, and leadership as did Russia in the age of Catherine the Great. Therefore, one must, I believe, speak of two different genres of utopian literature in Russia during the last third of the eighteenth century: the panegyric "*eutopia*" (which asserts that the "good place" exists here and now and deserves praise) and the more typical satiric *utopia*.[4]

Despite the comment of one early-twentieth-century Russian critic that there was "a particular interest in utopias in the eighteenth century," both the panegyric eutopia and the satiric utopia have received relatively little critical attention.[5] This chapter attempts to partially fill that gap by examining the following eighteenth-century Russian novels or tales depicting at some point a society enjoying the good life:[6]

M. D. Chulkov. "The Dream of Kidal," in *The Mocker; or, Slavic Tales* (1789 edition).
F. A. Emin. *The Adventures of Themistocles* (1763).
———. *Fickle Fate; or, The Adventures of Miramond* (1763).
M. M. Kheraskov. *Numa; or, Flourishing Rome* (1768).
———. *Cadmus and Harmonia* (1789).
———. *Polydorus: The Son of Cadmus and Harmonia* (1794).
V. A. Levshin. "The Adventures of Balamir," in his *Russian Tales* (1783).
———. *The Latest Journey* (1784).
P. Iu. L'vov. *The Russian Pamela* (1789).
N. N. "A Letter from Saturn" (1772).
M. M. Shcherbatov. *A Journey to the Land of Ophir* (1783–84).
A. P. Sumarokov. "The Happy Society: A Dream" (1759).
———. "Another Chorus to the Perverted World" (1763).[7]

Works that simply propose *projects* for a better Russian future, like A. N. Radishchev's *Journey from Petersburg to Moscow* (1790)

with its two "projects for the future" in the Khotilov and Vydro-
pusk chapters, will be excluded from consideration here because
they do not depict an ideal society or use the paradisal or utopian
conventions outlined in Chapter 1, emphasizing instead "how
far removed we still are from the ideal of social happiness."[8]

The Panegyric "Eutopia"

In a 1799 speech entitled "The True Happiness of Russia," a
teacher named Petr Gilarovskii stated: "O divine student of the
most wise Socrates [i.e., Plato]: *the happy society* that you once
imagined now *exists in reality. It is Russia*. In it the philosopher rules and the ruler philosophizes."[9] Like Gilarovskii, many
writers in eighteenth-century Russia were, in effect, modifying
the traditional Western concept of utopia (the idea that the "good
place" is "no place") to argue that an ideal state had actually
come into existence in contemporary Russia. This practice had
historical precedents in Muscovite ideology—a point made explicitly by N. M. Karamzin in his 1811 *Memoir on Ancient and
Modern Russia*: "[O]ur ancestors, while assimilating many advan-
tages which were to be found in foreign customs, never lost the
*conviction that an Orthodox Russian was the most perfect citizen and
Holy Rus the foremost state in the world*. Let this be called a delu-
sion. Yet how much it did to strengthen patriotism and the moral
fiber of the country!"[10]

When the animus against secular prose fiction disappeared
in Russia by the mid-eighteenth century,[11] the patriotic assumptions later articulated by Karamzin were embodied in an unusual fictional hybrid resulting from mating the panegyric ode
with the prose utopia.[12] The resulting "panegyric eutopia" was
in part made possible by the rhetorical structure of the traditional utopia, which is actually *panegyric*, praising some "good
place" (*eu-topos*) for its good government and good life, using a
guidelike narrator who in his enthusiasm resembles the persona
of the panegyric ode.[13] In the eutopia, as in the ode, the picture
of the good life is closer to what Frank and Fritzie Manuel call
the "religious paradise" ("brought into being by a transcendent
God . . . [and] dependent upon his will alone") than to what they
call the "modern utopia" (a "man-made paradise on earth" that

usurps the omnipotence of God and represents a "Promethean act of defiance of the existing order of the world").[14]

Although there were no full-length eutopian novels in Russian literature of this period, the eutopian episode became an important building-block for travel, adventure, and philosophical novels and literary dreams, often depicting an ideal tsar who is like a father or mother to his or her people and creates a paradisal life for them through education, just laws, support of Orthodoxy, and restoration of peace both at home and in Europe. Such panegyric eutopias sprouted seeds that were to blossom into "Official Nationality" and Slavophilism in the nineteenth century. While some eutopias occasionally challenged individual policies of the monarch on the throne, made suggestions for change, or even functioned as "red herrings" (criticizing the government while praising its head, much as Derzhavin was to do in "Felitsa"), most rested on solid support for the Russian autocratic system with its idea of a tsar placed on the throne by God.[15]

During the first part of Catherine's reign, several specific projects received wide support from Russian intellectuals and provided a basis for the panegyric eutopia, as they had for the panegyric ode: her project for the codification of laws and her *Instruction* (*Nakaz*) to the Commission on Codification; the educational projects of her reign, which significantly increased the number of schools and established education for girls for the first time; and the attempt to recruit foreign immigrants to Russia to settle the Volga region. Indeed, at points Catherine's early projects actually attempted to justify (at least to the intellectuals) the ideology that her age was golden. Even in the July 6, 1762, manifesto issued on her accession (written by Nikita Panin), Catherine sketched plans for a eutopian Russia: "My general aim is to create happiness without all the whimsicality, eccentricity, and tyranny which destroys it."[16] She pledged "to enact such ordinances that the government of my beloved country would function strongly within its borders" and provide for "good order in everything."[17] In short, it is probable that many writers of panegyric eutopias in the 1760's and 1770's were not simply seeking rewards from Catherine but were quite happy to be living under her enlightened rule.[18]

One of the earliest Russian panegyric eutopias appeared in the conclusion to Fedor Emin's 1763 novel *Fickle Fate; or, The Adventures of Miramond*, which brings the hero's friend Feridat to an ideal land called the "Kingdom of Delights and True Belief." On the throne is "Jupiter's Daughter," who is surrounded by "a multitude of geniuses," two of whom are superior to the others. The first genius is in charge of education and the sciences, and the second of military matters.[19] Emin describes this "happy kingdom" as a Parnassian garden, "where the joyous muses sang every day [and] the hardworking bee of Parnassus, gathering the sweetness from the various flowers, made honey and poured it into all the joyous hearts" (3:348). But the flourishing condition of this kingdom is threatened by the death of Jupiter's daughter and her succession by a monarch who drives the geniuses from the court and brings "dark days" to the kingdom. These days of gloom are soon brought to an end, however, when the evil monarch is replaced by another representative of the Good:

Suddenly Parnassus was illuminated with a most pleasant light; exclamations of joy were heard everywhere. *Pallas ascended Parnassus, and with her exalted wisdom there returned the golden age.* As they soared through the excellent air, eagles carried in their mouths inscriptions with the words, "Long and happily live *our Goddess, whose beauty and wisdom have created a new paradise for us.*" [3:350–51]

Using commonplaces from contemporary panegyric poetry, Emin constructs an allegory about eighteenth-century Russian history: The Kingdom of Delights and True Belief[20] is Russia; Jupiter is Peter the Great (king of the "gods"); his daughter (Astraea) is Elizabeth I; the monarch who brought gloom is Peter III; the goddess who restores the golden age is his wife, Catherine II, who toppled him. The first genius in charge of education is probably Ivan Shuvalov (founder of Moscow University) and the second his cousin Petr Shuvalov, Elizabeth's field marshal.[21]

The organizing metaphors of Emin's allegory also come from contemporary panegyric poetry: the reign of Peter III is a time of darkness and the accession of Catherine the restoration of light; Catherine is Minerva (Pallas), who through her wisdom has restored the golden age; and Russia is a Parnassian garden.[22]

Indeed, this eutopian section (written by the same writer whose 1767–69 *Russian History* was subtitled "Containing the Lives of All the Rulers of Russia from the Very Beginning, All the Great Acts Worthy of Eternal Memory by Peter the Great, . . . and *A Description of the Golden Age in the North during the Reign of Catherine the Great*") is so strongly panegyric that David Budgen has cleverly suggested that it be viewed as Emin's contribution to the 1763 "Minerva Triumphant" pageant.[23] This prototype of Catherine's kingdom is so attractive that Feridat (who the foreign Emin later acknowledged was to some extent a representation of himself)[24] decides to remain there, just as Cadmus would later remain in the ideal Land of the Slavs in Kheraskov's *Cadmus and Harmonia*.

The image of an ideal Russia with great appeal to foreigners was itself probably rooted in panegyric poetry, where it was used to praise an aspect of contemporary foreign policy.[25] As a 1761 panegyric ode by Aleksei Rzhevskii stated in depicting a "golden age" under Elizabeth: "How happily we live because of you. If only the world recognized this through our glory, then envying our peace *everyone would wish to live in Russia*."[26] This idea was expanded in Aleksei Naryshkin's 1762 ode to Peter III, announcing that all who, like Diogenes, seek honest men, should flock to Russia: "Come together now in Russia, *come to us and be amazed, seeing our happy age*."[27] Such poems praised a number of actual attempts made during the 1760's to attract foreigners to Russia. Under the influence of similar immigration policies in Austria, Spain, and Prussia, Catherine issued a vague order inviting foreigners to settle in Russia as early as December 1762. As she stated upon her accession: "We need population, not devastation."[28]

Although the initial results of such policies were not very positive (since many of the new settlers had no experience in agricultural labor), they were described in distinctly paradisal terms in works like Vasilii Maikov's 1767 "Ode on . . . the Selection of Delegates for Composing the New Code of Laws of 1767," which focuses in stanzas 10 and 11 on the recruiting of foreigners:

In your territory, there is more usefulness than in the rivers flowing from Eden, your soul is more peaceful than a zephyr, giving us a peaceful age. Having heard of the mildness of this nature, *people from distant countries have been flowing to your vast territory*. . . . There are ears of *corn* that yellow in fields *where previously thorns had grown;* there people care about their work and have brought the arts [of agriculture] there. Where previously beasts had dwelled and birds of prey had flown, where the land had been wild, now peoples are settled there and nymphs rejoice in the groves at seeing such beautiful fields.[29]

As Vasilii Sankovskii wrote in his 1764 Accession Day Ode to Catherine: "We shall soon see the times when Russia will be filled with foreigners, leaving their own cities, flowing to Russia to seek our joys for themselves. . . . [W]ith the passage of time, our golden age will be extolled by the muses."[30] This theme of the future appeal of Russia to foreigners was extended even further by N. M. Karamzin in his 1787 poem "Poetry," which depicts a Russian Parnassus to which foreigners will come to seek poetic light: "The gloom of night [the time when Russia had no excellent poets] has disappeared; already the light of Aurora is shining in ***, and *soon all people will come to the North to light their lanterns*, as in fables Prometheus came to fiery Phoebus to warm and light a cold, dark world."[31]

During the last third of the eighteenth century, panegyrics to Russia were sometimes projected onto ideal prototypes located on faraway islands or even on another planet, like Saturn or the moon. One such panegyric eutopia was the first part of the 1772 "Letter from Saturn" signed "N. N."—probably from the Latin *Non Nominatus* ("not named"), which was already beginning to appear in Russian literature as an emblem of anonymity.[32] This first letter from "one of [the narrator's] friends who went to the planet of Saturn"[33] expresses amazement at the politics of the planet. On the eastern side of Saturn, he notes, lives a gang of "proud brigands" who consider themselves the rulers of other parts of the planet and have taken as their coat of arms "the second light of the heaven, that is, the moon, not understanding that it has often been subjected to eclipses and changes" (pp. 41–42)—a reference to Turkey, with whom Russia had been at war since 1768. This nation, according to the narrator, is united in friendship with another people, whose coat of arms is the lily and who are characterized by their "craftiness, envy, . . . and similar pride"—clearly France, which was financially supporting

Turkey against Russia during the first Russo-Turkish war. This second nation is jealous of a third nation located in the North, "which at the beginning of the current century began to be enlightened through the help of a great man who ruled it; and now in its glory, its sciences, and its arts, it is not inferior to any other nation." This third nation, which has an eagle as its symbol, is, of course, Russia, and its "great man" Peter the Great. This country is described as a eutopia, "governed by a woman who is respected for her wisdom not only by her subjects but by all people who are able to discern worthiness" (p. 42). In addition to "gathering her subjects and ordering them to make laws for themselves" (the Commission on Codification), she has also done a great deal for popular education and set up schools. As a result, she has succeeded in establishing a "happy state" (p. 43).

This ruler, called "the Northern Minerva," wants to make her neighbors happy as well and to free them from the "vile superstition" to which they had been subjected (pp. 43–44). But although she has placed on their throne a "person capable of making them happy," the people have "rebelled against their own happiness" (p. 44). This unwilling neighbor is Poland under Stanislaw Poniatowski—the former lover of Catherine who was placed by her on the Polish throne in 1764. The "vile superstition" is Catholicism, and the rebellion reflects the Polish protests against the granting of political rights to Protestant and Orthodox minorities there; the attempted suppression of those rebellions by Russia resulted in the "Eastern brigands" (i.e., Turkey) declaring war against Russia on the pretext of defending Polish liberties.[34] As a result of this war, "the moon [Turkey] is already getting pale," and "the lily [France] is . . . withering while the eagle [Russia] is soaring"; Russia's subjects are "enjoying under [Catherine's] shade, despite the war, that golden age sung by ancient poets" (p. 44). As the work progresses, the narrator depicts the cause of Russia as messianic, designed for the "general good" of all nations and the destruction of "the scoundrels of the human race" who have snatched the happiness from "innocent people" (p. 46); he predicts that "the human race will see in [Catherine] its savior" (p. 46). The work thus projects Russian jingoistic propaganda of the First Turkish War onto the genre of the literary eutopia.[35]

A slightly more complex example of the panegyric eutopia appears in Vasilii Levshin's "The Adventures of Balamir" in his 1783 *Russian Tales*. Having inherited the throne of a people called the Whins (*Uiny*) whose capital city was on the site of what is now Kiev, Balamir tries to create an ideal kingdom and "happiness for his subjects," but does so out of vanity.[36] When he asks his friend Alavir whether there is any better country in the world, he is chided for his pride and told that "a monarch who is doing a great deal never should think that he has done enough" (p. 7). Alavir reminds him that although he has established "peace, plenty, and good courts" in his state, there is still much that needs improvement, and tells him of Milosveta, queen of the Dulebs, who rules a country even better than his own.

Although Balamir hesitates to believe that a woman can rule better than he, he decides to visit her capital. There he sees a city without luxury, where the nobles provide examples of moral conduct that commoners imitate. The hotels (which seem like castles) are free. Everywhere Balamir hears praises of Milosveta's virtues; people talk of her "almost as a deity who has been sent to earth for the happiness of this country" and mention that her laws, generosity, and wisdom are "almost superhuman" (p. 14).[37]

Milosveta shares a number of characteristics with Catherine the Great. She is female and foreign and, like Catherine in the official propaganda, has inherited a country on the verge of ruin and turned it into an ideal kingdom. On the surface, then, this looks like the typical panegyric eutopia. But it is likely that Balamir represents another side of Catherine—the talented but vain ruler—and thus the advice of Alavir is probably meant as a warning to Catherine to avoid complaisance. In addition, the "city without luxury" is quite unlike the luxury-loving Petersburg, and the nobles, who provide positive examples for the lower class, are quite unlike their real-life counterparts. Thus even the panegyric eutopia sometimes combined advice, warnings, and satire with its praise.

From Eunomia to Eutopia

In the years following Catherine II's accession and especially her 1766 *Nakaz* (*Instruction*) to the Commission on Codification,

much Russian literature portrayed good laws (*eunomia*) as the
key to the good life, reflecting a point made by Kheraskov in
Numa (1768) that "the true happiness of mankind depends upon
reasonable laws." [38] To some extent this literature reflected an implicit image in the *Nakaz* itself of a paradisal Russia where law
is king.[39] As article 520 stated: "God forbid that after this legislation is finished any nation on earth should be more just and
consequently should flourish more than Russia." [40] Article 521
continued: "[T]his work ought to produce no other effect than
to . . . *render the people of Russia the most happy . . . of any people
on earth.*" And article 2 depicted the aim of the codification as
bringing Russia to "the very summit of happiness, glory, safety,
and tranquility." As has occurred more than once in Russian history, the government was providing writers with a text for their
eutopias.

Five classical and biblical characters often figured in Russian
visions of a paradise or utopia based on law: Numa, Lycurgus, Astraea, Moses, and Themis (the Greek personification of
law, order, and justice); all five were frequently identified with
Catherine after her *Nakaz*.[41] For example, Ermil Kostrov's 1780
Birthday Ode pictured the monarch as a new Moses bringing
laws to God's chosen people and depicted her being carried
away to Sinai, where God, "presenting a marvelous view of
paradise . . . writes the laws of justice for her." [42] The image of
Catherine as Themis was particularly frequent in the *visual* arts,
ranging from Dmitrii Levitskii's 1783 "Portrait of Catherine as
the Giver of Laws" (which depicts her in the temple of Themis,
with whom she is visually identified)[43] to Mikhail Kozlovskii's
sculptural portrait of Catherine as Themis sitting in a chair and
holding the scales of justice. And as we have already observed,
images of Numa and Lycurgus recurred in works influenced by
Plutarch, and the image of Astraea was omnipresent.

Under the influence of Catherine's legislative projects, the
theme of law and the character of the lawgiver became frequent
components of Russian utopian and eutopian fiction. Even before the *Nakaz*, Catherine's interest in codification (which was
announced upon her accession) was reflected in Fedor Emin's
1763 *The Adventures of Themistocles*, which depicts a utopian king-

dom of Thrace (*Frakiia*) where law and justice reign supreme. Given the dedication of this novel to Catherine (with its proclamation that she is restoring the golden age), it is not coincidental that this ideal land based on law, where "justice dwells," is ruled by a woman.[44] To warn of the consequences of injustice, Emin implicitly contrasts this eunomic Thrace to a dystopian Caria, where the verdicts of the senate and of other judicial bodies favor "whoever put[s] money in their hands" (p. 34), where "merit is measured by money" (p. 43), and where officials use their spurs more often on their citizens than on their horses. This Caria probably represents another side of Russia and its great corruption, implicitly suggesting to Catherine that she needs to eliminate the rampant bribery and cruelty in the bureaucracy and other areas of government.[45]

The concern with law in Russian utopian and eutopian fiction is reflected in Kheraskov's three novels—*Numa*, *Cadmus and Harmonia*, and *Polydorus*; all in one way or another involve a search for law. Kheraskov's first novel, *Numa*, published only two years after Catherine's *Nakaz*, presents the most obvious example of this search, using ancient Rome as a surrogate for modern Russia (the "Third Rome") and Numa as a surrogate for Russia's "lawgivers"—Catherine II and Peter I.[46] Based largely on Plutarch's "Life of Numa" (and its companion "Life of Lycurgus"),[47] *Numa* tells of a simple farmer who is invited to become emperor of Rome and gets the warring Romans to emulate his natural values by turning their swords into his plowshares.[48] In the novel, which Kheraskov himself called a "utopia,"[49] Numa establishes laws "based upon nature" with the help of the divine nymph Egeria. As Egeria tells Numa, the final result of this "codification" will be "truth triumphant, virtue rejoicing, and vices driven out" (p. 46)—phrasing purposefully recalling descriptions of the 1763 "Minerva Triumphant" pageant on which Kheraskov had worked.

Similarities between eighteenth-century Russia and Numa's Rome are suggested throughout the novel. Already in the preface, Kheraskov, using the persona of "the Publisher," includes some verses that initially focus on Lycurgus and Numa but then make an abrupt transition to praise Peter and Catherine and their skill as lawgivers:

Greater than all kings was the *lawgiver Peter*. He worked, he kept a vigil, he awakened Russia. *He showed Russia new heavens and a new earth.* . . . He glorified his subjects and became immortal himself. . . .

After him, Catherine appeared in our land, flowering in our eyes more beautiful than a lily of paradise. . . . In her we recognize the perfection of blessings eternal. She has found the paths to the temple of happiness.

For her there will be a crown of immortal fame. *For her kingdom there will be a golden age.* The world is now rejoicing about our happiness, and she is called an example for all kings. . . . Peter gave the Russians their bodies, Catherine gave them a soul. [preface, n. pag.][50]

In changing the focus from Greek and Roman to Russian rulers, Kheraskov is implicitly comparing the great Spartan lawgiver and his Roman successor (and Plutarchian "double") with the two eighteenth-century leaders who have established a eutopian Russia based on law; his statement that Numa "put the science of ruling into action" reflects his optimism at Catherine's convening of the Commission on Codification. Indeed, as the "Publisher" states, "truth, virtue and justice . . . are now beginning to triumph in Russia. May heaven grant the completion of this" (preface, n. pag.).

Like Numa's Rome, contemporary Russia is implicitly compared at the end of the novel to the *Republic* of Plato: "Rome for a long time had not seen such a golden time as it enjoyed under Numa. It is now possible to say with divine Plato that *happy are the peoples among whom a philosopher is king or the king becomes a philosopher.*" This quote probably reflects Catherine's attempt to cultivate the image of a "philosopher-tsar," in part through her friendship and correspondence with Enlightenment *philosophes* like Voltaire and Diderot. In sum, Kheraskov places great hope in the future development of Russia under the leadership of an intelligent monarch who rules by law.

Despite his stress on law in *Numa*, Kheraskov emphasizes the need for a strong monarchy. The very reason that Numa is called to govern Rome is that "Rome [had been] perishing from various authorities without having a single leader" and was like "a body without a head" (p. 18). Government by nobles (like that of the "two hundred tyrants" between Romulus and Numa) is criticized by Kheraskov throughout the work, reflecting his opposition to contemporary proposals for such rule. But Kheraskov's work is not without warnings or advice for Catherine. In the preface he implicitly warns her that "the happy condition for society" was brought about by Numa "not by vanity and not by favoritism" but only by "a love for truth and a desire for the good of the human race." And although he states that "true happiness for mankind flows from prudent laws," he stresses that these laws "demand fulfillment" (p. 147).[51] Nevertheless, Kheraskov's advice and criticism in *Numa* are relatively mild and often little more daring than Catherine's own statements in the *Nakaz*.[52]

Kheraskov's two other novels allegorize the search for law to portray a leader who learns that to rule his nation he must first learn to rule himself—an idea combining the contemporary concern with law and the important Masonic precept of self-knowledge and self-control. Like *Numa*, *Cadmus and Harmonia* and *Polydorus* are about a process of "codification": the establishment of a set of "laws"—external and internal, social and personal—by which both society and the individual can find harmony. The goal of all three Kheraskov novels is to sufficiently codify these laws to attain the ideal kingdom. In the first two novels, this harmony is found in a prototype of Russia; even in the third novel, as we observed in Chapter 5, there is a link with Catherine's Russia, reflecting the importance of the panegyric tradition to all three Kheraskov novels.[53]

The Patriarchal (E)utopia

Like many writers of pre-Enlightenment utopian fiction in the West, eighteenth-century Russian authors often assumed that the earthly good life could be achieved only through patriarchy—the rule of a strong, authoritative leader who acts as a parent to his (or her) people. Although etymologically and historically patriarchy had been linked with a male ruler (identified with the omnipotent father), eighteenth-century Russians often continued to use patriarchal vocabulary to refer to the tsar even when she was female: writers spoke favorably of the "patriarchal [*not* the matriarchal] system" that Catherine represented as tsar, while referring to her as "mother of the Russians."[54]

Patriarchy reflected a pessimistic view of uncontrolled human nature; it saw autocratic government as the only way to protect citizens from Hobbes's "state of nature," where life was "solitary, poor, nasty, brutish, and short."[55] Implicit in patriarchy was the assumption that human beings are unruly children who will destroy others and possibly themselves unless an omnipotent parent watches over and restrains them.[56] Exemplifying this patriarchal mentality, Peter the Great once stated about the Russians:

Our people are like children who would never of their own accord decide to learn. . . . But later, when they have finished their studies, they are grateful for having been made to go through them. This is evident today: *has not everything been achieved through constraint*? Yet now one hears gratitude for much that has already borne fruit.[57]

From the patriarchal point of view, human beings are subjects rather than citizens—too morally weak to rule themselves.

Given the authoritarian implications of patriarchy (especially the inability to question the patriarch-parent), most Enlightenment thinkers strongly opposed it. As Sir William Blackstone wrote in his 1765–69 *Commentaries on the Laws of England* (which, ironically, came to replace Montesquieu's *Spirit of the Laws* as Catherine the Great's bedside reading during the mid-1770's), the laws of nature require that "the empire of the father . . . give place to the empire of reason."[58] From the Enlightenment onward, many Western utopias repeated this opposition between "reason" and patriarchy. In Russia, however, the support of patriarchy remained constant through the mid-nineteenth century.

Given the importance of the family in Russian culture and the frequently used image of "Father Tsar" ruling "Mother Russia," it is not surprising that when the first Russian eutopias and utopias appeared in the last third of the eighteenth century, many depicted the ideal society organized into family units or extended families ruled by an elder wielding beneficent, tradition-based authority over his clan.[59] In so doing, these works often affirmed the kind of patriarchal extended families praised by the Slavophiles more than seventy-five years later as "typical" of the Slavs and their peasant communes.[60]

In the Russian eutopia, patriarchy often reflected a fear of chaos and revolution—a view that had been used to justify a centralized, autocratic government in Russia since the Muscovite period. As Emin wrote in his *Russian History* (1767–69), monarchical governments are superior to republican governments "because *even in republics fathers are superior to children, as masters are to servants*. If the children and servants were equal to their fathers and masters, then there would be many insurrections." [61] So just as the eutopian scenes in Kheraskov's 1794 novel *Polydorus* reiterate that "a good tsar . . . is a good father of his family" (2:62), the anti-utopian scenes there reflect the chaos resulting from challenges to such patriarchal rule. Similarly, in the first pages of *Cadmus and Harmonia*, Kheraskov states that the good tsar is "a wise father" and "friend of his people" who forms "a single family" from his happy subjects (1:2–4).[62] So common were comments like this in Russian eutopian and utopian scenes of the eighteenth century (which almost all stressed the beneficent aspect of patriarchy rather than its authoritarian aspect) that the critic Vladimir Sipovskii identified what he called a "patriarchal structure"—defined through such commonplace phrases as "the father of his subjects," "the guard and servant of the people," "a friend of the people," and a ruler who is so concerned about the happiness of his subjects that he "forgets himself" and lives for their sakes.[63] This benign patriarch was often portrayed as the opposite of the tyrant.[64]

Eighteenth-century eutopian and utopian scenes sometimes translated these patriarchal topoi from state to estate, portraying harmony resulting from landowners acting like "fathers" to their peasants. In Pavel L'vov's "Rosa and Liubim" (1790), for example, an ideal landowner prevents the peasant Liubim from being taken away from his fiancée, Rosa, when the village elder tries to conscript him. The landowner, Rassudin ("Reason"), even gives Rosa a dowry and Liubim ("Beloved") a cottage to enable them to marry. This patriarchy on the estate is taken to reflect the ideal patriarchy of Russia as a whole. Liubim's father, who has been abroad, declares about Russia: "There is no land better than our tsardom. . . . We have everything. *Our sovereigns are like fathers to us*. Wherever a merciful sovereign sits on the throne like God, it is paradise." [65]

The patriarchal model even figured in some works written

by "opposition" figures like Nikolai Novikov, who sketched an ideal government combining patriarchal monarchs and nobles. In Novikov's works the "kind landowner" who is a "father" to his peasants creates happiness for them and, in turn (through their increased productivity), for Russia as a whole. As Novikov wrote in some 1770 New Year's wishes to the peasants of Russia: "May your landlords be your fathers and you their children. I wish you bodily strength, health and hard work. Having this, you will be happy. And your happiness leads to the well-being of the entire state."[66]

Novikov's criticism of contemporary agriculture and politics often emphasized their lack of patriarchy. For example, the village of Razorennaia ("Ruined") in his "Fragment of a Journey to *** by I*** T***" represents an anti-utopia where a "tyrant" drives his serfs to "poverty and slavery" with his cruelty and receives poor harvests as a result.[67] Similarly, in his "prescriptions" for a number of social ills, Novikov's persona tells the landowner Bezrassud ("Unreason"), who feels that "peasants are not people but simply peasants," to "think how true human beings— human beings who are gentlemen, *gentlemen who are fathers of their children and not tyrants of their slaves* as you are—must abhor you."[68] Consistent with Novikov's patriarchal ideal, these "true human beings" had been called earlier in the article "landowner-fathers," whose peasants "enjoy perfect calm and do not envy the happiness of anyone on earth" (p. 135). As Andrzej Walicki has observed, Novikov's "patriarchal utopia" was "an idealized picture of certain aspects of the social relationships prevailing in pre-Petrine Russia."[69]

During the last ten to fifteen years of the eighteenth century, patriarchy was frequently equated by conservatives with "Russianness," opposing the avalanche of foreign influences that they felt were overwhelming native traditions. As N. M. Karamzin wrote in his 1792 story "Natalia the Boyar's Daughter": "*Who among us does not love those times when Russians were Russians*, when they dressed in their own national clothing, walked with their own gait, lived according to their own customs, spoke their own language according to their heart, i.e., spoke as they thought. I, at least, love those times."[70] In this story—which A. G. Cross has called an "attempt to make old Rus the homespun counterpart of Arcadia"—Karamzin sharply contrasts those ideal "*patri-archal times*" with the westernizing present;[71] in those times Russians "brought up their children as *nature* brings up grass and flowers," and the result was excellent "even though they did not at that time read either Locke on education or Rousseau's *Emile*" (8:23–24). As in this work the ideal Russian state, based on patriarchy and native values, was often linked with "nature."

Nature Versus Nurture: Russians on the Moon

As the eutopian and utopian scene developed in Russian literature of the 1780's, paeans to Russia often included satire against westernizing influences. In such scenes, the opposition between Russia (or the Slavic lands) and the West was often represented through a contrast between "nature" (man and the world as God created them in Eden) and "nurture" (man and the world as changed by education and the various sciences and arts).[72] In many Russian works, both utopian and nonutopian, of the last two decades of the eighteenth century, "nature" was linked with Russia before Peter the Great and "nurture" with the European culture artificially imposed on Russia from the time of Peter.

Russians before Peter (or those wishing to cling to the pre-Petrine traditions) were sometimes depicted as "noble savages" during this period. Prince M. M. Shcherbatov in his 1786–87 essay *On the Corruption of Morals in Russia* explicitly compared the simple morals of pre-Petrine Russians with those of nomadic "wild peoples" whose "virtues [were] *instilled by nature* into the human heart."[73] In other works, "nature" symbolized such supposedly Slavic (pre-Petrine) values as simplicity, peacefulness, a strong family or communal orientation (as opposed to the individualism of the West), and patriarchy. This glorification of Slavic values and of Orthodoxy and the related contrast between an innocent and peaceful Russia and a debauched, ever-feuding West prefigure frequent themes in Russian literature from Dostoevsky to Solzhenitsyn, including many works of the nineteenth-century Slavophiles.[74] Indeed, the fear of science as a threat to Slavic values, which appeared regularly in nineteenth-century Russian literature, was also developed in the "pre-Slavophile"

utopias of the eighteenth century, implicitly opposing government propaganda about science as the path to the good life.[75]

Among works with utopian scenes expressing a preference
for Slavic "nature" over Western "nurture" were Levshin's *The
Latest Journey* (1784), L'vov's *Russian Pamela* (1789), and Chulkov's "Dream of Kidal" (1789). In all three, the surrogate for an
ideal Russia is placed far from other civilizations to stress its uncorrupted state: Chulkov's and Levshin's works take place on the
moon,[76] and the utopian section of L'vov's work takes place on
an isolated island. All three express the sentiment articulated by
L'vov in the preface to his novel: "[In Russia] morals . . . are still
not corrupted, and prejudice does not reign there as it does in
other places."[77] In all three works, simplicity is seen as positive;[78]
progress is the least important product for these surrogates of
Russia.

Like the Europeans of Michel de Montaigne's essay "On Cannibals" (1580; Russian translation 1762), the Europeans of L'vov's
Russian Pamela at first assume that the inhabitants of the utopian
island on which they land after a shipwreck are cannibals because of their strange dress (see translation in Appendix C); but
like Montaigne's cannibals, the noble savages of L'vov's island
have a civilization that is superior to that of Europe. In this utopian "island of prosperity," which is governed by a patriarchal
system that corresponds to their natural way of life, all citizens
live under a single roof and have regular access to their governor,
who "is as concerned for their peace as a loving father would be
for the welfare of his children." This "father of fathers" is advised
by counselors who have no thought of personal gain and are not
afraid to contradict him when necessary. On this island, there are
no rich or poor, and all laws are based on two basic principles:
the worship of God and brotherly love. All citizens, including
the governor (who is, significantly, called "tsar" at this point),
obey all laws. As a result, L'vov's narrator notes, the kingdom's
inhabitants have "preserved on the island their golden age," and
every citizen is virtuous, responsible, and moral (2:128). The narrator concludes: "[W]e call these unenlightened islanders . . .
savages only because they do not know how to delude with
flattering sweetness, to speak with eloquent rhetoric, because
they do not know luxury and they dress poorly" (2:130). The

superiority of these "savages" to the Europeans is reflected in their governor's amazement "at European prejudice, arrogance, and, most of all, wars" and, ultimately, in his request that the travelers stop their narration about their barbaric customs—a request recalling that of the King of Brobdingnag after hearing Gulliver recite his "panegyrics" to England in Swift's *Gulliver's Travels* (which had been translated into Russian in 1772 and was reprinted in 1780).

Within the context of L'vov's *Russian Pamela*, these "cannibals" symbolize the Russian peasants, who still live according to the uncorrupted, natural traditions of their native land.[79] As the author argues in his preface:

We have so many tender hearts, great souls, and such noble sensitivity among the people of the lower classes: there are Pamelas, New Héloïses, and similar types. . . . [I]n England, France, Germany, and other countries where these characters are so well known . . . they are met more seldom than in Russia. . . . Through this novel, I wanted to show to all who put foreign countries above their native land that it contains virtuous heroes, worthy of respect and astonishment. [1:i–ii]

L'vov thus implies through this utopian island that by following native habits and religion and avoiding European "prejudices," the Russians can retain their paradisal state. But L'vov's utopian section also can be read as a satire on the absolutist pretensions of the Russian tsars, who acted as though they were above the laws; on the distance of the tsars from the people and the difficulty of gaining access to the tsar (characterized by the Russian proverb that "it is high to heaven and far to the tsar"); on flattering courtiers who worked more for their personal interest than for that of their subjects; on the excessive luxury at court and in the capital; and on the great disparity in Russia between the conditions of the rich and the poor. His solution to these problems was to return to the values of the pre-Petrine past, which still exist in the Russian countryside—the only place where (according to his heroine's father, Phillip) one can still find the golden age.

In stressing this "primitivist" theme, Chulkov's and Levshin's lunar utopias attack modern science.[80] On Chulkov's moon, there is "no science except that by which each person tries to teach himself to be virtuous and to subject his passions to his reason";[81]

Levshin's moonmen see science as a Pandora's box and have rejected it in favor of farming and shepherding.[82] Unlike their Russian contemporaries at the Academy of Sciences and at court, Chulkov's moonmen are interested only in learning "who created the universe, what gratitude [they] should pay him for this, how to glorify him, and how to ask forgiveness for [their] sins" (5:39); they believe that the path to paradise lies in religion and tradition.

In rejecting "nurture" in favor of "nature," both lunar utopias return to the mentality of earlier Orthodox precepts like the following: "He who enjoys geometry is impious before God: to study astronomy and the books of Greece is a sin of the soul; through his reason the believer can easily be led astray; love simplicity more than wisdom; don't search for what is above your reach."[83] Despite challenges to such views in eighteenth-century Russia, this obscurantism continued (albeit somewhat muted) in certain conservative circles and helped delay the appearance of science fiction in Russian literature until the 1820's.[84]

Both Levshin and Chulkov depict a moon dominated by Edenic innocence, which Levshin's hero, Narsim, opposes to modernization, formal laws, and systems of bureaucracy—a clear rebuff to the Europeanizing tendencies of Peter the Great and his followers. As one of Levshin's characters states, "through the efforts of our family heads, our character is still in that same state of innocence as it was in the first man" (14:5). On Chulkov's moon, this primal innocence is reflected in the landscape, where vipers, crocodiles, tigers, lions, and other wild beasts live in harmony with man in a veritable "peaceable kingdom." As in many utopias, Chulkov's moonmen live and eat together, hold all property in common, and obey only the laws of nature. Through such primitivism[85] both Chulkov and Levshin proclaim the potential of Russia to become a millennial paradise by following its own national traditions rather than those of Western Europe.

Both lunar utopias depict a moon that at first looks like the earth; but the heroes soon conclude that the two places are as different as paradise is from hell. To emphasize this theme, Levshin has one of his moonmen illegally travel to earth, where he observes such problems as envy, malice, pride, violence, flattery, and godlessness. On his return, he explicitly proclaims that he has "broken free from hell" (14:10–11). In explaining the earth's decline, he gives a capsule history of that planet from its golden age (which resembles the current state on the moon) to the present, emphasizing that increased population there has caused an insufficiency of resources, the displacement of the weak by the strong, and the beginning of private property.[86] Unlike the earth, Levshin's moon has no monks or soldiers, no temples, no sovereigns.[87] Like many utopias since Lycurgus's Sparta, it has no written laws, since the few laws are all simple and clear enough to remember. To ensure equality, there are no ranks on this utopian moon; although a movement had appeared to establish ranks and other distinctions among the people, the movement was quelled and its instigators exiled to the dark side of the moon—a clear criticism of Peter the Great's Table of Ranks. To emphasize this criticism, the hero of Chulkov's work is told that he has been brought to this utopian moon "in order to resolve some kind of disorder among your people" (5:49). Levshin's appellation of his lunar people as "the Lunatics" thus reflects irony; for his "Lunatics" are the only sane people in the universe and thus, by implication, the non-Lunatics (i.e., Western Europeans and westernizing Russians) are insane for their overreliance on science and their stress on progress instead of tradition.[88]

On traveling through this lunar land, Narsim reaches a large city located on a river, with magnificent buildings, wide streets, and bridges connecting its various parts. In this surrogate for St. Petersburg, Narsim observes that many courts lie vacant for half a year, there are no poor people, all cripples are cared for like children in a special home, and all vagrants are sent to work for their food and clothing (16:51). These comments reflect the typical wish-dreams of the satiric utopia: dreams of a humane society with social and economic equality and no disputes among its citizens. It is possible that the conservative Levshin's placement of these details in a prototype of St. Petersburg implies that in the true, Slavic paradise (unlike the westernized St. Petersburg) a society of this type could be achieved.

Despite Levshin's satire, he nevertheless uses many techniques of the panegyric eutopia, especially in the last part of the work. For example, his moon is divided into two parts: a bright side (representing Russia) and a dark (i.e., nonenlightened) side that is inhabited by a people named "Turks"—a "former band of brigands . . . frightful to all mankind, both because of their ignorance and also because of the strange foundations of their faith, which allows them to kill all those who are not of the same opinion as they" (16:38). As in the typical panegyric eutopia, the monarch of the bright side of this moon resembles the Catherine of panegyric poetry: "Just one word from her will create peace between hostile countries and will resolve what otherwise was unresolvable without bloodshed" (16:52). Despite her peacemaking tendencies, the Turks have pushed this monarch to war, but she has forced them "to beg for peace at any cost" (16:39)—an exaggerated reference to the Treaty of Kuchuk Kainarji that settled the first Russian-Turkish war in 1774. As Levshin's returned hero states: "They were lucky that they were dealing with the greatest, the wisest, and bravest of mortals, who, besides, is also the most humane" (16:39). This monarch, who is compared with "Wisdom herself," has studied the laws of other lands and seen that the fiercer the punishments the fiercer the crimes. Under her rule, "millions of subjects [have been brought] to the summit of prosperity" and "everywhere there was mercy, which not only her subjects but also foreigners enjoyed" (16:38, 52).[89] In short, the last part of this lunar utopia depicts the best of all possible Russias led by the best of all possible Catherines—a monarch who is "more than human" and is so admired by foreign monarchs that they leave their thrones and come to her country "to see her and to learn" (16:53).

Such praise of Catherine may reflect Levshin's nationalism, patriotism, and support for the "holy war" against Turkey; but it is more likely a means of sugarcoating his criticism of Russia's westernization and hence a decoy to the censor. In sum, the descriptions of the utopian island in L'vov's *Russian Pamela* and of the utopian moon in Levshin's *Latest Journey* and in Chulkov's "Dream of Kidal" anticipate a number of important themes that will appear in nineteenth- and twentieth-century Russian literature, including the future downfall of the West because of its individualism and its overreliance on science and the future salvation of the world through the traditional spiritual and religious values of Russia and the Slavs.[90]

Satire and Utopia

In his article "Russian Satire in the Age of Catherine the Great," the nineteenth-century critic Nikolai Dobroliubov wrote that "our [Russian] literature began with satire, continued with satire, and to this time still rests on satire."[91] Although this book, it is hoped, has provided some balance to Dobroliubov's exaggeration, the fact remains that satire was one of the major genres of the eighteenth century, numbering among its practitioners such central figures as Kantemir, Fonvizin, Sumarokov, Novikov, Kapnist, Radishchev, and Krylov.

Despite the frequent panegyric function of the Russian paradise myth, the myth had been used in some satires for a long time. Indeed, one of the earliest uses of the golden age image in Russia was in a philippic by the sixteenth-century diplomat Fedor Karpov, who headed the Foreign Office under Ivan IV: "In truth, the golden age has come; for gold one can buy oneself rank; love consults with gold; one can obtain friendship for money, but the poor man is needed by nobody."[92]

When used in eighteenth-century Russian satire the paradise myth most frequently portrayed an ideal past contrasted with an unpleasant present, as in Prince A. D. Kantemir's *Satire 1*, "Against the Defamers of Learning" (1729, published in Russia only in 1762): "[T]hat time in which wisdom reigned above all else and alone assigned the crowns, when she alone was the means to the greatest advancement has not continued to our days. *The golden age has not reached our time.* . . . Pride, laziness, wealth, all have overcome wisdom, and ignorance has gained the upper hand over learning" (lines 157–62).[93] Similarly, Fedor Volkov's unpublished song "Let us begin to sing an old song, brothers, about how people lived in the first age," probably written during the reign of Peter III (whom Volkov helped to topple), describes a golden age with no private property, serfdom, ranks, money, or weapons—a time when all were free and equal. But, as the author laments, "those golden ages have passed."[94] Were it not for the ideological importance of the golden age myth in the Russia of the late 1750's and early 1760's, Volkov's simple song might seem like a trifling reminder of Ovid. But against the backdrop of the ideology that the golden age was being restored by the Russian tsars, this song, with its strong contrast between "then" (the time of the golden age) and "now" (when people have lost their goodness and happiness) appears as an early challenge to Russia's dystopian life of serfdom, rank, and class.

The ideology of Russia as paradise was so strong in Catherine's reign that even the satirical journals of 1769–74 used the paradise myth very little and contained no satiric utopias.[95] Indeed, in Novikov's last two satirical journals, the myth was even used *panegyrically* in odes published at the end of a volume, probably implying that the time for renewal of the journal's publication permit was at hand;[96] during those years of war and civic unrest (culminating in the Pugachev rebellion of 1774), even a satirist had to prove his "loyalty."[97]

One of the few eighteenth-century satiric utopias to be published on completion[98] was A. P. Sumarokov's short work "The Happy Society: A Dream" (1759). This work criticizes the late reign of Elizabeth, often using the negative formula (see Chapter 1). Several historians have suggested that the work contains ideas similar to those being discussed by Catherine and Nikita Panin for the governance of Russia, implying that there *may* even have been an element of future-oriented panegyric in this satire.[99]

Unlike the Russia of 1759, Sumarokov's "happy society" is governed not by the monarch's favorites but by a meritocracy. Its ruler does not enjoy absolute power but governs with the aid of a state council, which is responsible for enacting laws, appointing judges, serving as the ultimate court of appeals, and supervising the military council. The ruler himself is wise and benevolent, recognizing excellence in others, living for the good of his people, and enjoying their "love, fear, and respect."[100] This happy society has few laws (which all of its people know by heart) and a fair, dispassionate, and rapid system of courts, where judges who accept even a minimal bribe are not only removed from office but lose their entire fortune; there is no parasitism; clergy are supported by the state and give good, moral advice that reflects their exemplary (and simple) lifestyle; and no ranks or offices are inherited, so the child of a peasant has as much chance to become a government official as the child of a nabob. The basic principle by which this society operates is a version of the golden rule: "Don't wish for others what you don't want for yourself" (p. 355). But the satire uses such kid gloves in its implicit criticism of contemporary Russia (and does not even criticize such problems as serfdom) that it was even reprinted several times.

Several utopian works written in the eighteenth century depict a debauched Russia in much more vivid terms. The liveliest is Sumarokov's original "Chorus to the Perverted World" (1763) written for the "Minerva Triumphant" festivities but rejected for the program book, where it was replaced by the tamer, "official" version discussed in Chapter 3. First published posthumously in 1781 under the title "Another Chorus to the Perverted World," this original version is one of the few masterpieces of eighteenth-century Russian irony. The work begins like the official chorus except that a tomtit—not a dog and nightingale—arrives from the other world. From the first line of the tomtit's remarks, "Everything is perverted there," the reader is lured to expect a negative place. But irony results from the fact that the "vices" of this perverted world are actually virtues, making it seem like paradise and the "ideal" society (Russia) seem like hell by contrast. Since each of the paradisal "vices" provides a paraphrastic expansion of the first line, each increases the irony. This satiric and ironic use of the paradise myth was so inconsistent with the myth's established panegyric function in Russia that it is clear why the original work was not published in the festival program.

In the "perverted" society originally described by Sumarokov (which embodies many of the themes that were to occupy Russian satirists from Maikov and Kapnist to Gogol), government funtionaries live quite simply ("They do not ride in coaches-and-six, their wives do not wear diamonds");[101] flattery goes unrewarded. Clerks there are honest and refuse all bribes, and there are no tax farmers;[102] high officials are not arrogant ("They do not bend their neck backwards"). Landowners do not beat the skin from peasants and do not sell them like cattle; people are judged by their work, not by their birth, and thus "a working peasant is better than an idling gentleman." All children of the nobility (not just boys) are given an education. The natives of this "perverted" land do not hold their language in contempt and do not travel around the world imitating foreign customs. This "perverted" society—a utopia created by the negation of Russian vices—thus becomes an all-embracing critique of the Russian "paradise." [103] The rejection of this critique (and its replacement by five lines of nonsense language in the official version) proved that satire was still premature in this panegyric culture.

Some of the sharpest political satire in the eighteenth-century Russian utopia appears in an unfinished 1783–84 work by the historian Mikhail Shcherbatov entitled A Journey to the Land of Ophir, which was sufficiently caustic to remain unpublished until 1896. Shcherbatov's work—Russia's first novel-length utopia— contains more specific details than any of its predecessors about food, clothing, laws, housing, language, and other aspects of the ideal Ophir [104]—a cold country in the Antarctic where the climate, vegetation, and wildlife "are exactly like those of North- ern European countries." [105] Its main city is Peregab, a port on a major river near the border of another country (with which it has fought a war) in an area that had once been swamps and weeds. Founded by King Perega, who introduced into his backward country an orderly system of government and a knowledge of science and military tactics, Peregab replaced the city of Kvamo (located on a river of the same name) as capital.

Shcherbatov uses such names and details to make it clear that Ophir is a surrogate for Russia and that Perega represents Peter, Peregab Petersburg, Kvamo Moscow (for which it is an anagram, with the letter "s" in Moskva eliminated), and the neighboring country of the Dysvy (an anagram for svydy) Sweden. [106] But un- like the Russia that it parallels (whose vices Shcherbatov was soon to enumerate in his 1786–87 essay On the Corruption of Morals in Russia), this "corrective" utopia of Ophir has a "wise system of government":

[T]he sovereign's power is conceived with the utility of the populace [in mind]; high-ranking noblemen [vel'mozhi] have the right to express their thoughts to the monarch with appropriate boldness; flattery has been thrown out of the king's court, and truth has unrestricted access; the laws are made with the general agreement of the populace, and through constant observation and correction are brought to optimum perfection; judges are few but so are legal proceedings . . . ; high-ranking officials are not luxury-loving or pleasure-seeking but are skillful and industrious and have the praiseworthy ambition of making the people who are subject to them happy; [and] the rest of the populace is industrious and virtuous and honors virtue first, law second, and only after that the tsar and the nobles. [pp. 751–52][107]

Shcherbatov's utopia strongly condemns the panegyric flattery dominating his contemporary Russia. In Ophir the populace is forbidden from praising the emperor or showing any public signs of satisfaction with his reign. To avoid presenting to the emperor the idea that he is a god ruling paradise, the Ophirians have introduced measures to "humanize" him from birth until death and limit his power.[108] In the hereditary Ophirian monarchy the rooms of the monarch's children are decorated with slogans like those from a mirror of princes:[109]

The populace does not exist for the kings, but the kings for the populace because before there were kings there was the populace.

Flattery is the most cruel poison for rulers.

The king must himself be the first to obey the laws of his country, for by just these laws he is king.

When the king's morals are good, the morals of his subjects will be good [since] all like to imitate him. [pp. 979–80]

To encourage rulers to perform good deeds, the Ophirians do not automatically guarantee them an honorable place in history, and have even established a policy of delaying monuments to rulers until thirty years after their death, when an evaluative commission decides whether there will be any monument at all, the size of this monument, and the wording to appear on it; bad deeds of monarchs are inscribed on the graves of their victims. As the shipwrecked narrator, Mr. S., is told, "we judge our rulers more severely than our private citizens" (p. 1024).

To avoid tyranny, the Ophirians deny the monarch a bodyguard; to show him the real condition of his country, they refuse to repair problems in towns he is to visit until after his departure (in marked contrast to the Russian practice).[110] In short, the utopian Ophir described by Shcherbatov (unlike the dystopian Russia he soon was to depict in *On the Corruption of Morals*) is a simple, "natural" land. As Mr. S. notes: "[A]ll that I saw and heard here brought me to a state of amazement. . . . Here I saw simple nature and common sense leading them to such a high level . . . that they surpass even the most learned European peoples in all spheres" (p. 969). But this "natural" simplicity has been attained only by rebelling against the unnatural reforms of Emperor Perega (Peter the Great) and his successors.[111]

Much of Shcherbatov's novel, like much of his historical writing, analyzes the results—both positive and negative—of Perega/Peter's reign. Indeed, his novel is one of the first in Russian literature to indict Peregab/St. Petersburg as an "unnatural" city, prefiguring works by such later writers as Pushkin, Gogol, Dostoevsky, and Bely. On the one hand, Perega led his people out of ignorance, created an Academy of Sciences, and built in Peregab "something supernatural" (p. 792). But he placed the city too far from all other parts of his empire (making Ophirian leaders lose sight of the actual conditions of their country) and too close to the country's enemies. Thousands of people were killed in its construction (which is said to have done "violence unto nature"), and the treasury was bankrupted. Finally, the people revolted against their leaders and their unnatural customs. Under the leadership of Sabakola, the capital was moved back to Kvamo, wealth redistributed from the court to the public, and Peregab made into a manufacturing center. The utopia resulting from such purges of luxury and the consequent elimination of the "corruption of morals" in Ophir presents a model for Russian emulation.[112]

Shcherbatov's postrevolutionary Ophir has become an aristocracy dominated by the hereditary nobility, who through their Senate enact legislation and supervise administration and the courts. To compensate them for their services, the state supports them financially, so that they may fully use their talents without worry of economic ruin.[113] The emperor plays a much more minor role than the Russian tsar and is strictly limited by law. As might be expected from a nobility-based utopia, serfdom is continued; but it is made more efficient by the creation of a military class, which eliminates the necessity of providing peasant recruits for the army.[114]

In Ophir, the preservation of law, order, and the rights of citizens is guaranteed by the police force, which is composed of the most virtuous people in the state and regulates not only social conduct but also public health and individual morality. The most virtuous policemen are chosen as priests and perform religious functions (in the deistic Temple of God,[115] which all citizens must attend) and judicial functions (serving as judges and enforcers of the laws, which are few and simple enough to be known by every schoolchild). These police (who to some extent resemble the Guardians of Plato's *Republic*) are at the center of an authoritarian state that regulates almost every aspect of individual conduct, including the dress, food, drink, and even plates of its people, which are all determined by rank to prevent the return of unbridled luxury. This brave new world has been justly called "the blueprint of a society in a straightjacket" and the model of a well-ordered police state dreamed up by "an enlightened Prussian bureaucrat." [116]

Like many utopias, Shcherbatov's work is structured on the opposition between "moral" (Ophirians) and "immoral" (foreigners, who are called "French" here but of course represent the Russians). Unlike the "French," the Ophirians have no alcoholic beverages. Indeed, under the influence of alcohol one of the French sailors starts a fight that ends in the death of a Peregabian, motivating a complete description of the judicial system. In contrast to contemporary Russia, justice moves swiftly in Ophir; as soon as the Ophirians hear of the fight, judges convene and start the judicial procedure. In passing sentence, the judges condemn not the sailor but the customs of his country, which encourage the imbibing of poisonous substances that "corrupt reason."

In contrast to the panegyric eutopias discussed above, Shcherbatov's utopia contains many criticisms of the person and policies of Catherine the Great. Not only does Ophir's powerful aristocratic Senate directly oppose the practice of Catherine's government (which Shcherbatov had elsewhere described as "absolutely despotic, [uniting] the legislative and executive power in the monarch" and thus decreasing the power of hereditary nobles despite the 1785 Charter of the Nobility), but its court (which allows no flattery) directly contradicts that of the vain Catherine.[117] And to ensure that no foreign-born person could assume the throne (as the German-born Catherine had done), the Ophirians introduce legislation requiring the heir to the throne to marry an Ophirian citizen.

As a result of the cultural (and censorial) conservatism engendered by the Pugachev rebellion of 1774, such clearly satiric works could not be published. Instead, there flourished in Russia panegyric and semipanegyric eutopias and eutopian scenes, which praised Catherine while occasionally satirizing the abuses of her courtiers and administrators and which affirmed traditional Slavic values while criticizing the westernizing reforms of Peter the Great.

The French Revolution and the Downfall of Utopia

After the French Revolution, both the Russian censorship and many Russian authors reacted strongly against literary dreams of an ideal world, which, they argued, could be particularly dangerous if people tried to achieve them on earth through revolution. The French Revolution figures prominently in the only eighteenth-century Russian novel with utopian scenes published after 1789: Kheraskov's *Polydorus*. In this work, Polydorus visits a decidedly dystopian prototype of France: the "floating island" of Terzit—a name that recalls both the word *terzat'* ("to tear to pieces") and the name *Tersit* (the Russian name of Thersites, the quarrelsome, loud-mouthed troublemaker who goads Odysseus in book 2 of the *Iliad*).[118] Once a paradisal kingdom under King Iland (whose people regarded him "like a father" [1:80]), the island has been plunged into turmoil over the past years as the result of a revolution. Old men (symbol of wisdom in many of the patriarchal and Masonic utopias of the eighteenth century) decry the disorder, turbulence, and violence that have been perpetrated by youthful revolutionaries in the name of "liberty." The people, says Kheraskov's monarchist persona, "were everywhere like a flock wandering without a shepherd" (1:176). Polydorus helps the old men restore order, stating that "equality is a monster that gives birth to itself and in unbound fury tears itself to pieces" (1:272). Thus Kheraskov criticizes the French Revolution and its cries of "liberty" and "equality."

In a 1791 review of the first Russian translation of More's *Utopia*, N. M. Karamzin similarly opposed any disruptive means of achieving utopia. In this article, Karamzin argued that descriptions of an "ideal or imagined republic" like Plato's have many ideas that "contradict each other" and "could anyway never be put into action."[119] His equation of the words "ideal" and "imagined" reflected his distrust of utopian thought and his belief that an ideal republic could exist only in fantasy.

The reasons for Karamzin's opposition to utopia are made clearer in the section of his *Letters of a Russian Traveler* labeled "Paris, April 1790,"[120] where he explicitly speaks of Thomas More in the context of the French Revolution, which he calls a "tragedy."[121] Discussing More's work, Karamzin implies that it inspires the bad citizen who loves "les te-te-troubles" (the reason a stuttering Marquis gives Karamzin for his revolutionary activity), rather than encouraging the citizen who loves virtue and order. Karamzin connects revolution with man's attempt to quickly realize utopia:

Every civil society . . . is sacred for good citizens, and one must be amazed at the wondrous harmony, organization, and order even in the most imperfect of them. "Utopia" will always be a dream of the good heart or may even be realized some day through the imperceptible passage of time, by means of slow . . . accomplishments of reason, of enlightenment, of education, and of good morals. When mankind will comprehend that virtue is essential for its own happiness, then the golden age will begin, and in every state man will rejoice at the peaceful well-being of life. But every violent shock is destructive. [1:382]

For Karamzin, the attempt to create utopia through revolution was an oversimplification of social problems and of history: "Simple minds think that everything is easy; wise men know the danger of any change and live quietly" (1:382). For him, revolution represented man's attempt to usurp the power of God and challenge divine Providence: "Let us hand ourselves over, my friends, to the power of Providence. Providence, of course, has its plan; in its hand are the hearts of rulers—and that is sufficient" (1:382).

Karamzin's opposition to revolutionary utopias and utopian revolutions (which at points anticipates views to be expressed by Dostoevsky in *The Possessed*) is linked to his justification of monarchy. Although he explicitly justifies only the French monarchy, he implicitly justifies the Russian monarchy as well, warning Russians of the danger of a "utopian" revolution: "Under the peaceful shadow [of the French monarchy] have grown the arts and sciences; social life has been beautified with the flowers of pleasure, the poor man has found his bread, the rich man has enjoyed his abundance. But impudent people have raised their axe to the holy tree" (1:383). This "holy tree" symbolizes monarchy, which Karamzin connects with heaven and opposes to anarchy, "the worst form of government" (1:383).

Given Karamzin's promonarchic opinions, it is not surprising that at the same time he was condemning More's *Utopia* he was praising Kheraskov's *Cadmus and Harmonia*,[122] underscoring that for eighteenth-century Russians there was a major distinction between what I have called the "paradise myth" or the "panegyric eutopia" and the general Western traditions of utopia. Noting that at the end of Kheraskov's novel Cadmus finds *"Evropa"*—"not his sister but the land of that name"—and, following the will of the gods, "remains there forever to live in peace among the Slavic people," Karamzin applauds his decision. For Karamzin, the paradise myth in *Cadmus and Harmonia* provided a positive underpinning for the nationalistic and autocratic system he supported; but Western "utopian visions" were essentially negative—a destruction of tradition in the name of reform.

After the death of Catherine II and the accession of her son Paul, the Russian censorship became even more opposed to any vision of utopia and was particularly insistent that if an author was to depict an earthly paradise it must be in Russia or some clearly defined allegorical surrogate with no major political differences. A case in point may be found in the censors' actions regarding Karamzin's own ecstatic descriptions of Switzerland in his *Letters of a Russian Traveler*. For Karamzin Switzerland was indeed a paradisal land, and in the first edition of his travel narrative he expressed his ecstasy: "So I am already in Switzerland, in the land of picturesque nature, in the *land of freedom and happiness*. It seems that the air here has something invigorating about it. My breathing has become easier and more free."[123] Attuned to Aesopian language, the censors insisted that Karamzin change the first part of this description in his 1797 edition of the *Letters* to avoid any political "ambiguity." Instead of "the land of freedom and happiness," Switzerland in this edition became "the land of *peace* and happiness." Through such required changes, the censors made the government view quite clear: a vote for utopia (a land of "freedom") was a vote against Russia. Such conservative views and governmental strictures combined with widespread disillusionment at the results of the French Revolution to virtually eliminate utopias from Russian literature from the 1790's until the second third of the nineteenth century.[124]

CHAPTER SEVEN

Epilogue:
Toward the Iron Age

> God attributes to place
> No sanctity, if none be thither brought
> By men who there frequent, or therein dwell.
> —Milton, *Paradise Lost*

Nothing more clearly demonstrates the importance of a literary pattern than rebellion against it during times of stylistic, generic, or cultural transition. With the declining importance of panegyric literature among the major figures of Russian literature in the last three decades of the eighteenth century—caused by numerous factors, including the deaths of Lomonosov and Trediakovskii, the abandonment of panegyric literature by Sumarokov, the growing conservatism of Catherine the Great's government after the Pugachev rebellion of 1774 and especially after the French Revolution of 1789, the consequent dimming of hopes for the major political changes promised by Catherine, and ultimately the death of Catherine and the accession of her repressive and far less competent son Paul—the paradise myth was often parodied and negated as "outmoded" or relegated to hack writers. As the century ended, the dominant pessimism of European preromantic currents replaced the optimism of Renaissance and neoclassic styles in which the paradise myth had flourished. This chapter examines the changing views toward the paradise myth in literature of the last decades of the eighteenth century and beginning of the nineteenth and the accompanying transition from golden age to iron age imagery.

Paradise Lost: The Early Russian Elegy

When the elegy began replacing the panegyric ode as the dominant genre in Russian literature during the last quarter of the
eighteenth century, the death knell started to sound for the paradise myth, which the ode had used so often.[1] Structurally, the
elegy (the very name of which comes from a Greek word meaning "mourning") was diametrically opposed to the ode, contrasting the "bad Now" to some "good Then," where the panegyric
ode had contrasted the "*good* Now" to a "*bad* Then." Although
the elegy began to appear in Russia during the last part of the
reign of Elizabeth and the short reign of Peter III, the accession
of "Astraea" to the throne in 1762 temporarily slowed the elegiac
direction in Russian literature. However, from the last decades
of Catherine's reign through the first decades of the nineteenth
century, the elegy became extremely popular, ultimately attract-
ing such major poets as Zhukovskii, Batiushkov, Baratynskii,
Pushkin, and Lermontov.

The transition from panegyric to elegiac literature was frequently accompanied by a movement from paradisal to infernal
imagery, reflecting the emphasis of the elegy on man's loss of joy
or virtue and the debasement of life. Models for this transition
were provided by the many translations of European elegies in
the Moscow University journals of the early 1760's. For example,
the anonymous "Elegy on the Life of Man" (translated 1760)
mourned the disappearance of the "age of our forefathers"—the
Eden of Adam and Eve or the golden age:

Happy was the age of our forefathers, who served as an example of innocence for us, who led their lives happily and had no cunning, who lived
on earth without a moan. The land in those times of decency bore its
fruits abundantly for all, like a generous mother. It was not necessary
to plough the fields for sowing, since the land itself enriched the fields
with fruit. *But that age has passed*; debauched man has become frivolous,
haughty, violent, evil, and extravagant. He struggles all his life, like a
ship at sea.[2]

As frequently occurs in the elegy, motifs of the paradise myth
are translated into the past tense here to stress the loss of the
good times resulting from man's moral decline.

While literature using the paradise myth often pictured a happy world, elegiac poetry depicted a world devoid of joy. As one elegy published in 1760 began: "Our age is filled with vanity. Nowhere do we see happiness in it."[3] Similarly, the persona of Vasilii Sankovskii's poem "The Unhappy Man" stated: "No matter where I turn, no matter where I look, I cannot find happiness for myself anywhere."[4] This second example reflects the elegiac tendency to center on the sad individual (paving the way for the appearance of sentimentalism and preromanticism later in the century), unlike literature using the paradise myth, which usually concerns the happy *society*.

Among the conventions of the elegy was that of the lovers' lost paradise, which often used the paradise myth to describe the joy once felt by the persona or character when with his beloved—a joy obliterated by her betrayal, departure, or death; such combinations of past joy and present sadness had typified the elegy since its first appearances in classical Greece and Rome. In Kheraskov's "The Death of Clarisa" (1760), for example, the *locus amoenus* portrays the paradise of love felt by the persona when with his beloved: "The gay voice of birds, the babbling of clear waters, a pleasant breeze—that was our type of music. Green meadows, flowers, forests, caves—all presented *examples of the golden age* for us."[5] But this paradise is turned to hell by the death of Clarisa, and the persona mourns: "O hell! O heavens! Where is the tenderness of old? Where is life? Where is beauty?"

Under the influence of the elegy, the contemporary period was frequently dubbed an iron age, as in G. R. Derzhavin's 1794 poem "To the Lyre": "Are these the iron ages now? Have people become hard-hearted?"[6] Contrasting the good times of the past, when people were captivated by poetry, with the iron age of the present, when "all souls are colder than ice" and people "seek only gold and silver and remember only themselves," this poem (a probable source of Baratynskii's famous poem "The Last Poet") identifies one exception to this pattern: Platon Aleksandrovich Zubov (for whose name day the work was written)—"a lover of harmony," who recalls the denizens of the golden age and thus is "a true favorite of Astraea."[7] The satiric and elegiac levels of this poem (which contradict the official ideology of Catherine's reign as a *golden* age) are softened by the panegyric

to Catherine's latest favorite—a technique recalling the combination of praise and blame in other works of Derzhavin like
"Felitsa."

In contrast with the paradise myth, which frequently portrayed man as made for eternal life, the elegy stressed the omnipresence of an ever-hungry death. Indeed, in Ivan Dmitriev's
poem "A True Story" (1792), death even turns Eden into a cemetery: "Plague and death entered the magnificent city, and at that
very instant *the garden of Eden changed.* The place where yesterday
the god of Pathos [Eros] used to gambol with the nymphs turned
into a deep, stinking grave, a cemetery. It was an awful sight."[8]
The imagery used by Dmitriev (which would have been virtually
impossible in Russian literature some thirty years earlier, when
"Eden" would have been taken for Russia) reflects the new concern with death, sadness, and mourning. Under the influence of
preromantic currents like Ossianism (with its graveyard scenes
and sad, pale moons) and sentimentalism (with its emblematic
tears), a new emphasis on gloom, doom, and tomb helped sign
the death warrant for the paradise myth and its superficial optimism.

Along with the elegy, the genre of the epitaph occasionally
appeared in literature of the late eighteenth century, reflecting
the general pessimism of the period. For example, the 1782 epitaph "For Truth" states: "The most dear flower of the youthful
days of Astraea has faded. She has ended her life, leaving this
world. But she resides through her soul in the sky. And her body
clothes the spirit of the just."[9] This epitaph for the *dead* Astraea
(here decidedly *not* Catherine) implicitly mourns the death of the
golden age and, with it, of truth, implying that this is the iron
age, when Astraea has left the unjust earth.

The pessimism of the elegy is well illustrated by Derzhavin's
1810 poem "Nadezhda" ("Hope")—a title that in the mid-eighteenth century would likely have been accompanied by a vision
of an earthly paradise. Typical of the late eighteenth and early
nineteenth centuries, Derzhavin's poem is about the *death* of
hope (here both the death of his niece Nadezhda [Hope] L'vova
and the death of hope for joy on earth): "*Stupid mortals dream of
some kind of golden days* [but] their vanities are innumerable."[10]
Playing on the ambiguity of "Hope," the poet states that Hope

beckons him "to her ocean," that is, to death and that "immortal Hope is the Promiser of bliss." But bliss is not of this world. The poet reminds the dead Hope's husband that although he has lost Hope, his Hope is alive and he will see her: "The voice of Hope is the voice of God, . . . the joy of the coming good." This "coming good" is the paradise after death; the golden age on earth is dead.

Demythologizing Paradise

By the late eighteenth century, the potential existence of any earthly paradise was often challenged as a lie or poetic fiction—a distinct impossibility given human nature and fate. Foreign attacks on the golden age had appeared in Russia as early as the elegies translated in *Poleznoe uveselenie* in the early 1760's. Kheraskov's translation of Jean-Baptiste Gresset's pastoral elegy called "The Age of Shepherds," for example, used the title phrase as a synonym for the "golden age": "O age, which in the first times was called the golden life, what a cruel fate that you remain only in poems." [11] Although the poem describes an ideal time when all were happy, equal, and prosperous, when "there were no vices or vanity, and passion did not ruin nature," when it was unnecessary to have any laws, and when poetry was born from the sweet singing generated by games, the last two stanzas raise questions of the type that were to haunt original Russian literature later in the century: "Am I not describing a dream? *Did this age really exist?* I know no witnesses who would affirm its existence. All of these tales are idle, and envy of our ancestors is all in vain. *People have always been unhappy* and their life always poor" (p. 16). Such attacks on ideal times and places as nothing but the daydreams of poets marked the demythologization of paradise, which was to continue in Russia through the first decades of the nineteenth century. [12]

One of the views frequently articulated in Russian literature at the end of the eighteenth century and the beginning of the nineteenth was that the earthly paradise—and, indeed, any long-term happiness—was an illusion, a false dream. The poetry of Derzhavin, for example, often suggests that the only happiness one can attain is the result of "seizing the moment" (carpe diem);

since death lurks around the corner, all that man can do is "eat, drink, and be merry"—themes reflecting the influence of Anacreon and Horace, whose works had been quite popular for much of the eighteenth century in Russia.[13]

Unlike works using the paradise myth, Derzhavin's poetry often stresses that any happiness will not last for long. For example, "To My First Neighbor" (1780) describes what at first looks like the epitome of the "good life" of wine, women, and song in the feasts put on by the persona's neighbor; it narrates his neighbor's dream of being "happy forever," of "heaven itself . . . scattering the flowers of happiness" around him, "the Fates . . . not mowing down [his] days," and "a rain of gold" flowing to him (stanza 4).[14] But the persona warns his "neighbor" (man in general) that constant happiness is not the human lot: "Blessed is he who can be happy without interruption in this life. But only the rare sailor succeeds in sailing the seas without problems" (stanza 5). Using the convention of the stormy sea of life, Derzhavin thus challenges the possibility of a permanent paradisal life. For Derzhavin, change is life's essence: "Inconstancy is the lot of mortals. . . . Those boring hours will come—they will—when the Graces will stop patting your corpulent cheeks. . . . Maybe fate will no longer coddle you or the favorable wind blow toward your sail" (lines 51, 55–57, 61–64). As a result, Derzhavin urges his "neighbor" to seize the moment: "As long as [your] golden hours flow and evil sorrows have not arrived, eat, drink, and be merry, neighbor. We can live on earth only a short time" (lines 65–69).[15] Derzhavin thus challenges the optimism of the paradise myth with an Anacreontic vision suggesting that one enjoy any pleasure he can get, since this too will disappear with time— which in Derzhavin's work brings not progress, perfection, or paradise on earth, but the scourge of death.

Like most visions of paradise, the notion of a pastoral or rural paradise was also challenged in late-eighteenth-century literature; the works of the 1790's by N. M. Karamzin provide many examples of such challenges. In 1798 Karamzin translated Christian Weise's work called *The Arcadian Monument*—a one-act "rural drama" whose title refers to a funerary monument and thus to the theme of *Et in Arcadia ego* ("Even I [death] am in Arcadia").[16] Returning to Arcadia with her fiancé, Lysias, in search of "happiness, freedom, and peace," the shepherdess Daphne (who had been abducted from Arcadia as a child and been brought up by another former Arcadian) expects to find the paradisal land described by her guardian: "There everyone is gay and calm, there all are faithful and tender in love. . . . There is no hatred, perfidy, or malice there. *The golden time is flowing*."[17] But she finds an Arcadia where sadness and death dominate, as they do anywhere else. Indeed, her father, Palemon (who is weeping at her tomb on the fifteenth anniversary of her disappearance and does not recognize her) says that she has been imagining "an illusory happiness" (18:138) and that people "consider lost that which mankind in reality never possessed," that is, the paradisal good life of the golden age or Arcadia.[18] He tells her that the only true paradise is in heaven after death: "There we will dwell in blissful countries where good rules without evil, where . . . [there is] no woe, evil, or grief. And where the soul, being in eternal peace, is always satisfied and gay" (18:137).

This idea that the earthly paradise is an illusion also underlies Karamzin's "Poor Liza" (1792), a story clearly influenced by Weise's play. In Karamzin's work, the only place where "all will be happy" is also the heavenly paradise, where Liza's mother says that she will finally stop crying.[19] Many of the peasant Liza's problems are connected with the urban nobleman Erast's foolish search for a pastoral paradise, which he imagines through the literary commonplaces of *locus amoenus*:

[Erast] used to read novels and idylls, had a rather lively imagination, and often transferred himself mentally to those times (existent or non-existent) in which, *if one can believe the poets*, all people strolled through the meadows without a care, bathed in pure springs, kissed like turtle-doves, relaxed under rosebushes and myrtle trees, and spent all their days in happy idleness. [1:610][20]

Like Don Quixote in Cervantes's novel (which had appeared in a new Russian translation the previous year),[21] the city dweller Erast reads himself into an imaginary world, which contradicts the real life of the country—described by the narrator as sad, dull, and tedious (e.g., 1:605–6). Erast's love for Liza results from this reading. He pictures her as one of the ideal shepherdesses of pastoral literature who leads a life of "nature" (*natura*);

he calls her a "shepherdess" (e.g., 1:614), although she is *not* one (she makes her living selling flowers and fruits in Moscow). He dreams of living with her "inseparably in the village and in the thick forests *as in paradise*" (1:615).

Karamzin accentuates Erast's mania for the pastoral by ironically giving him a name that had been used for shepherds in both Fontenelle's "Fifth Eclogue" (translated into Russian by Sumarokov) and Sumarokov's own eclogue "Daphna."[22] But Erast's idyllic dreams are obliterated after he makes love to Liza, destroying his illusion about the "innocent soul" of his "shepherdess." Like the snake in Eden, Erast corrupts "paradise," leading to Liza's suicide. Paradise on earth (and, indeed, the idea of a union of the social classes) is thus dismissed as a dangerous dream, an illusion never to be found in life.

As if writing an epilogue to "Poor Liza," Karamzin the following year articulated his views on Arcadia in an essay entitled "A Word About the Sciences, Arts, and Enlightenment":

[T]his ever-flourishing country under a happy, bright sky, populated by simple, genial shepherds who love each other like tender brothers, do not know envy or malice, live in blissful harmony, obey only the impulses of their own hearts, and blissfully live in the embraces of love and friendship, is something delightful for the imagination of sensitive people. But let us be honest and acknowledge that *this happy country is nothing other than a pleasant dream, a delightful daydream [mechta]* of this very imagination. At least no one has yet shown us historically that it ever existed. The Arcadia of Greece is not that fantastic Arcadia by which the ancient and modern poets have been delighting our heart and soul.[23]

Such oppositions between the conventions of the literary Arcadia and the real life of the country were to continue in nineteenth-century Russian literature, which often focused more sharply than the eighteenth century had done on the economic and social problems of the real village. For example, in his punning epigraph to chapter 2 of *Eugene Onegin*, Pushkin concisely hints at the opposition between the ideal and the real: "O rus . . . (Hor.); O Rus'!" (" 'O rustic country' . . . [Horace]; O Russia!"). In this chapter, which focuses on "the village where Eugene was bored," Pushkin challenges the ideal country of Horace's *Satire* II, 6 (the source of his epigraph) by depicting what at first looks like "a delightful little corner, where a friend of innocent pleasures would bless heaven" (stanza 2). In reality, however, this pastoral paradise turns out to be a provincial backwater, where Eugene is viewed as a "most dangerous eccentric" and a "freemason" (*farmazon*—a "nihilist") (stanzas 4–5); even in delightful nature, *human* nature is incompatible with paradise. In sum, by the beginning of the nineteenth century, many of Russia's better poets had abandoned Arcadia, leaving it to the likes of their enraptured, conventional peers who, like Pushkin's Lenskii, still "believe in the perfection of the world" (chapter 2, stanza 15).[24]

Paradise Parodied

Literature is a perpetual dialogue, where development and change often occur through parody and other forms of rebellion against dominant genres, styles, authors, and directions.[25] The nineteenth century emerged out of its eighteenth-century cocoon through just such rebellions, including parody of the conventions of the paradise myth.[26] As Iakov Kniazhnin wrote in his verse "Letter to E. R. Dashkova on the Event of the Opening of the Academy of Sciences" (1783): "I know that insolent odes, which have already gone out of mode, are very able to annoy. They were always comparing Catherine to a lily of paradise, striving madly for a rhyme."[27]

Transitions in styles are often accompanied by a change in the meaning of key words. By the end of the eighteenth century, even the word *paradiz* had changed its meaning (reflecting, ironically, the success of Peter's westernizing reforms that had caused him to found his *paradiz* of St. Petersburg in the first place). No longer did it denote an ideal place but rather the "galley" or highest balcony in a theater (French: *paradis*), the place with the cheapest seats; the Russian word *raiok* (literally, "little paradise") developed simultaneously as a calque with the same meaning. Thus the narrator of Ivan Krylov's "Speech in Praise of Ermalafid" (1793) accuses the title author (a poetaster whose name suggests Greek words meaning "Verbose Nonsense" or "Windbag") of writing comedies that amuse not those sitting in the orchestra but those sitting in "paradise," that is, the hoi polloi.[28]

In Krylov's prose a number of paradisal conventions are sharply parodied. For example, in the Eastern tale "Kaib" (1792), a disguised Caliph Kaib escapes from his court to seek *true* happiness, despite the reiterations of panegyric poets that there was "paradisal happiness" at his court. In one incident Kaib takes refuge from a storm in the home of a poet writing an ode to a courtier who has "neither intelligence nor virtue." "Such people are horribly difficult as subjects of panegyric poetry," the poet notes (1:415).[29] When asked by Kaib why he engages in such lies, the poet cites Aristotle's statement that literature should discuss heroes not as they are but as they should be.

Disabused about the sincerity of the ode, Kaib continues his literary odyssey: "Having long read idylls and eclogues, he wanted to enjoy the golden age reigning in the villages. He had long wanted to witness the tenderness of shepherds and shepherdesses. . . . [A]s he had often said: 'If I had not been caliph, I would have liked to be a shepherd' " (1:417). Krylov parodies this pastoral paradise by having Kaib meet a shepherd who is not "the happy mortal who is enjoying a golden age near his flock" but "a soiled, filthy creature, burnt by the sun and spattered with dirt" (1:417). On learning that this is "the happy shepherd," Kaib remarks, "Oh, you must play the reed pipe splendidly," only to be told that the shepherd is too poor and hungry to enjoy singing and playing: "The man who wants to die from hunger and to freeze from cold would burst with envy at looking at us" (1:418).

In a number of parodies written at the end of the eighteenth century and the beginning of the nineteenth, the golden age is associated with ignorance. For example, in Krylov's "Speech in Praise of the Science of Killing Time" (1793)—a parody of the panegyric speech—the narrator declares to his audience: "[Philosophers] would look at you and acknowledge that man can avoid thinking if only he has an agile tongue, and that we, having the gift of not thinking, are at least as happy as people of the golden age" (1:427). Karamzin in his 1802 "Hymn to Fools" takes this idea one step further, declaring that for fools it is always a golden age:

Not that person is happy who is smarter than all others. Oh no. He is often sadder than others. But that person who, being a fool, considers

himself wise. It is him that I praise. A hundredfold blessed and happy
is he in his folly. . . . *How the world is perfect for fools.* . . .
    Let us open the chronicle of all times. When was man happy? Only
when, not able to think, he lived without reason by means of his stom-
ach. *For fools Astraea is always here and the golden age has not yet passed.*
[Karamzin, 1966, pp. 286–89]

The first lines of this hymn parody Horace's Second Epode, ne-
gating the Horatian *Beatus ille* to become *"ne blazhen tot"* ("not
happy is he").

Parodies of eighteenth-century paradisal conventions appeared well into the nineteenth century. In the works of Gogol,
for example, some typical commonplaces of eighteenth-century
panegyric poets appear in the speeches of rogues and swindlers.
In part 1 of *Dead Souls* (1842), some of Chichikov's mischief is in
part made possible by his use of eighteenth-century formulas of
flattery, including those of the paradise myth. When he arrives
in the provincial town, Chichikov's tactics are described through
words and phrases like *"pol'stit'"* ("to flatter"), *"skazal chto-to
ochen' lestnoe"* ("he said something very flattering"), and hints
that governments like this are *"dostoiny pokhvaly"* ("worthy of
praise"). Later, Chichikov describes Russia's vast size to Sobakevich "with great praise" and says that it is larger than the Roman
empire and a source of amazement to foreigners—typical formulas of the eighteenth-century ode used by Chichikov to convince
Sobakevich that Russia is too large to burden government offices
with frequent inquiry about the number of serfs who have died.[30]
Of course, one might simply ignore these phrases as typical of
the unctuous flatterer; but given the rhetoric of paradise that
sometimes accompanies such panegyrics, it is likely that Gogol
was at points intentionally parodying eighteenth-century panegyric formulas on which he (like most authors of the first half of
the nineteenth century) had been raised.[31] For example, Chichikov says to the provincial governor that "one enters your guber-
niia as one enters paradise, the roads everywhere are like velvet"
(5:17).[32] Chichikov later encourages Manilov to sell him dead
serfs by stating that if he could live with or near him, the two
could walk in the shade and philosophize (even though Manilov has not read beyond page 14 of a book for two years), and

it would be a "paradisal life" (5:53)—a probable parody of the image of a garden of philosophy.

In a somewhat different vein, Gogol parodies the paradise myth in part 2 of the novel to challenge the westernizing conceptions that had kept Russia from achieving its messianic potential. In the description of Colonel Koshkarev's estate—a would-be utopia set up along a foreign bureaucratic model (much as Peter I had reorganized his Russia)—Gogol has the colonel use the "Here I have" formula of the paradise myth (which, as noted in Chapter 1, was often used for mock utopias) to describe his estate with its various committees, officers, and commissions. Koshkarev uses the myth to explain his mad ideas for creating the ideal estate in Russia: "[I]f only you dress half of the Russian peasants in German pants, the sciences will be elevated, trade will grow, and *a golden age will begin in Russia*" (5:439). These crazy foreign schemes of Koshkarev are opposed to the ideas of Kostanzhoglo, an active type who eschews theory in favor of practice. (He does not even have a study—a symbol of paperwork and theory.) Unlike Koshkarev's "ideal" organization (which results in constant failure and allows his peasants to rob him), Kostanzhoglo's estate (described with the "There he has" structure and the negative formula but, significantly, *without* the imagery of paradise) is successful because he keeps the muzhiks at work on the soil.[33]

Gogol's parody of the eighteenth-century paradise myth continues in *The Gamblers* (1842), where the swindler Glov (who uses the language of the *raisonneur* from eighteenth-century drama) says about Uteshitel'nyi ("Comforting"—another swindler who is in cahoots with him and also speaks like a moralizer): "Well, if we had more such men in Russia who would judge so wisely, then, my God, what would it be like: *it would simply be a golden age, sir, an age of Astraea*" (4:314). In sum, by the early nineteenth century, the paradise myth, once the language for praising tsars, became the language of fools, madmen, and cheats; literary parody was erecting a gravestone for the paradise myth and its conventions.

Enlightening Paradise

Literature using the paradise myth in eighteenth-century Russia was largely opposed to the Enlightenment flourishing in contemporary Western Europe—a movement characterized by its challenge to absolute monarchy, its pursuit of individualism and intellectual independence (the polar opposite of patriarchy), its critical spirit, and its philosophy of equal rights for all classes.[34] Although both Russian writers using the paradise myth and Western Enlightenment philosophes believed that man is capable of leading the good life on earth, they differed considerably as to the means by which this good life could be achieved. For philosophes like Kant, Diderot, Voltaire, and Montesquieu, the earthly good life could be attained by "the freeing of men's minds from the bonds of ignorance and superstition, and of their bodies from the arbitrary oppression of the constituted social authorities."[35] For most Russian users of the paradise myth, on the other hand, the good life could be attained through service of those very same "social authorities" whom the Enlightenment criticized.[36] Thus, it is not surprising that most of the true Enlightenment writers of eighteenth-century Russia—like Novikov, Radishchev, Fonvizin, and Kniazhnin—did not use the myth very frequently in their works; when they did use its conventions they usually negated or parodied them.

By the last two decades of the eighteenth century and the early years of the nineteenth, Russia, under the influence of the Enlightenment, had begun to change from a centripetal, court-centered culture (epitomized by the ideal tsar) to a more centrifugal culture (epitomized by the individualist—frequently an artist or poet who accepts no earthly gods). From this period, challenges to the conventions of the paradise myth frequently extended beyond literature to question the political orthodoxy and status quo that the myth had supported, including autocracy itself. During this time, the Enlightenment spirit of individualism and independence, which had appeared only sporadically in earlier Russian culture, began to flourish among the major figures of Russian literature, resulting in challenges to some of the more authoritarian conventions of the paradise myth such as that of the political icon, which had depicted the monarch as being in the image and likeness of God. In late-eighteenth- and early-nineteenth-century Russian literature, the poet was often depicted as an "iconoclast"—the breaker, rather than the maker, of the political icon.

Literary challenges to "sacred authority" are reflected in some of the most famous poems of the late eighteenth and early nineteenth centuries, including Derzhavin's "Felitsa" (1782) and "The Mirza's Vision" (1783), Radishchev's "Liberty" (1783), and Pushkin's "The Monument" (1836). Given the first words of Derzhavin's "Felitsa"—*Bogopodobnaia tsarevna* ("O godlike princess") —one would expect a typical poem in the iconic tradition.[37] And in many ways the depiction of Felitsa actually *is* typical. Felitsa (Catherine II) is portrayed through many of the conventions of the ideal monarch developed in Russian literature since the time of Simeon Polotskii: her very name suggests the Latin *felicitas* ("happiness"), and the words *schast'e* ("happiness") and *schastlivyi* ("happy") are among the most frequently repeated words of the poem; she is called "a gentle angel, an angel of peace" (line 175), a "heavenly branch" (line 242); and she carries a "scepter sent down from heaven" (line 177). Like the ideal monarchs of panegyric poetry of the mid-eighteenth century, she has, as we observed in Chapter 3, the ability (in the image of the God of Genesis) to "turn darkness into light" (line 122) and chaos into cosmos. But the iconic convention implies that the ideal monarch will be an example for his or her kingdom, a model capable of reforming mankind in his or her own "image and likeness." And it is just here that Derzhavin's iconoclasm begins. In the poem his persona—a profligate, hedonistic, late-rising courtier with no concern for his duties or his subjects—is in direct contrast (*un*likeness) to the ideal monarch Felitsa. If Felitsa is in the image of God, the courtier is in the image of fallen man, and his conduct is *bezobrazno*—directly opposed to that of the godlike monarch. And the people, instead of being like the monarch, are like her *courtier*, who confesses: "Thus, Felitsa, I am debauched but all the world resembles me" (lines 101–2). In short, Derzhavin's depiction of a courtier whose conduct is so unlike that of the ideal monarch, represents the first step in the demythologization of the court. The mimetic ethic was being destroyed.

This demythologization continues in his 1783 poem "The

Mirza's Vision."[38] Felitsa appears to the persona-mirza in a dream and reminds him that tsars are "also people" (*liudi te zhe*—p. 112) and thus go astray at times and need to be corrected (an idea echoing Locke's statement in the *Second Treatise on Civil Government* that "absolute monarchs are but men").[39] In effect, then, Felitsa herself is presented as abandoning the idea that tsars are God's image on earth, implying that poets are sent by the gods to improve the monarch; no longer was the poet a "slave" to the tsar.[40] Derzhavin had stated a similar thought in his 1779 ode "On the Birth of a Royal Child," where he had given the following "advice" to the newborn Grand Prince Alexander: "Be a *person* on the throne" (*Bud' na trone chelovek*) (Derzhavin, 1957, p. 89). This challenge to the apotheosis of the monarch clearly influenced Karamzin's 1801 Coronation Ode to Alexander I, where an exchange takes place between Clio, the muse of history, and a poet. When in his excitement at Alexander's coronation, the poet conventionally proclaims, "Astraea is with us, or the age of Saturn has arisen," Clio corrects him, transforming Derzhavin's famous line: "You have a person on the throne."[41]

At approximately the same time as Derzhavin challenged the conventions of the political icon, A. N. Radishchev launched a full-fledged assault on them. His ode "Liberty" sharply satirizes the idea of the tsar as an image of God on earth, reminding readers that divine kingship was not just a rhetorical convention but also a tool of absolutist ideology. For Radishchev, *law* is the true king and liberty its viceroy. In arguing this, Radishchev overturns the conventions of seventeenth- and eighteenth-century courtly literature, substituting the words "law" (*zakon*) and "liberty" (*vol'nost'*) in places where earlier rhetoric would have placed the word *tsar'*.[42] In his poem, only law, not the tsar, is "the image of God on earth" (*obraz bozhii na zemli*, line 60);[43] only liberty, not the tsar, will "change the darkness of slavery into light" (line 7). Radishchev sees the ideology of divine kingship as a sinister product of the "symphony" of church and state, which "in union oppress society" (line 97)— a reaction against that same union praised so strongly by Ushakov in his "icon" *The Planting of the Tree of the Russian State* more than one hundred years earlier. By challenging the conventions of divine kingship, Radishchev was challenging the whole structure of autocracy, arguing that the tsar is not God's icon but a usurper of His power, a perverter of His principles who needs to be bound with a constitution.

By the early nineteenth century, then, the culture gap with Western Europe had narrowed; medieval and Renaissance ideas of divine kingship were giving way to Enlightenment ideals. As Pushkin wrote in his 1818 poem "To N. Ia. Pliuskova": "On my noble, modest lyre, I did not praise earthly gods, and in the free strength of my pride I did not burn incense to them with the censer of flattery" because "I was not born to amuse tsars" (lines 1–4, 7).[44] This implicit equation of the panegyric poet with the court jester was typical of the reaction against the iconic conventions in the late eighteenth and early nineteenth centuries. Indeed, Pushkin lambasted eighteenth-century Russian poets for their "incomprehensible . . . baseness" in "extolling the virtues" of monarchs like Catherine II, who, he felt, was not a goddess but "Tartuffe in a skirt and crown."[45]

The theme of the poet as an iconoclast who "does not bend his proud head at the feet of popular idols"[46] runs throughout the works of Pushkin and is well exemplified in his poem "The Monument." This free adaptation of Horace's *Ode* III, 30, strongly influenced by Derzhavin's 1795 poem "The Monument" (which had claimed poetic immortality for its author because "for the first time [he] dared . . . to tell the truth to tsars with a smile"),[47] describes Pushkin's works as "a monument *not made by hands*" (*pamiatnik nerukotvornyi*)—immediately recalling the "icon not made by hands" (*ikona nerukotvornaia*).[48] In using this term from the vocabulary of the icon, Pushkin adds a religious dimension to the basic architectonic metaphor of Derzhavin and Horace, implying divine consecration of the poet's art—a consecration that, as we have seen, had previously been limited to kings. Pushkin even states that his own poetic "monument" rises higher than the monument to Alexander I in Palace Square, implying clearly that the long-term role of the poet is more "monumental" than that of the ruler. The poem strongly supports the ideal of the iconoclastic poet, who praises freedom in a "cruel age" (*zhestokii vek*, i.e., an *iron* age) and pleads for "mercy for the fallen" (i.e., for political opponents of absolutism like the Decembrists).[49] Thus Pushkin praises in himself those very same qualities that in an 1837 article he was to praise in John Milton: iconoclasm and defense of the people—qualities incompatible with the absolutist idea of the tsar as God's earthly icon.[50] At least through Mandel'shtam, many of Russia's greatest poets continued to see themselves as iconoclasts[51] and to view the poet—not the tsar—as holding the key to paradise.[52]

With the new iconoclasm there developed a new Rome theme to challenge the autocratic myth of Russia as Rome restored and the official paradise myth of which it had become part. Under the influence of the Enlightenment (and, later, of the French Revolution), *republican* Rome became a symbol of freedom under the law, guaranteed rights, and monarchical obligation to provide justice (as opposed to *imperial* Rome, which remained linked with autocracy).[53] As Matvei Dmitriev-Mamonov, a mid-eighteenth-century publicist who often referred to himself as "a citizen of Rome," wrote: "A citizen of Rome is more noble than the crowned heads."[54] Similarly, Aleksandr Radishchev in his "Historical Song" stated that "one word, and the spirit of old was reborn in the heart of all Romans: 'Rome is free.' "[55] Free (republican) Rome represented a dream of a free Russia governed by law.

If in the "official" Rome myth the heroes were most frequently autocrats, the heroes of the republican version were opponents of tyranny, like Cato the Younger (Cato Uticensis, famed for his leadership in the civil war against Julius Caesar and his suicide to avoid falling into Caesar's hands)[56] or Cincinnatus (the farmer who was "dictator" of Rome for sixteen days and then returned to his farm after saving his country). As Sergei Glinka wrote in his memoirs of the first years of the nineteenth century: "The voice of the virtues of ancient republican Rome, the voice of the Cincinnatuses and Catos, echoed loudly in the passionate young hearts of the cadets. . . . Ancient Rome became my idol too. I didn't know under what government I was living, but *I knew that liberty was the soul of the Romans.*"[57]

Along with republican Rome, free Novgorod and its popular assembly (*veche*) became symbols of historical perfection among those favoring a free Russia. As the Decembrist P. I. Pestel' declared in explaining why he had come to believe that a republican constitution was preferable to an autocratic form of government:

"I remembered the blissful times of Greece, when it consisted of republics, and its pitiful position afterwards. I compared the great glory of Rome during the days of the Republic with its lamentable lot under the rule of the emperors. The history of Novgorod the Great also confirmed my belief in the republican way of thinking."[58] There were even Novgorod variants of Cato such as *Marfa Posadnitsa* (Marfa Boretskaia—whom Karamzin called "the Cato of her republic"[59]—the widow of the *posadnik/* mayor of Novgorod and leader of the opposition to Ivan III's attempt to eliminate its republican government and subject it to the autocracy of Moscow) and Vadim of Novgorod (the leader of a revolt against the Varangian ruler Riurik, whom the Russians had "invited" to rule them).[60]

By the first third of the nineteenth century, the idea that Russia was an anti-Rome (i.e., that the essence of Russia was opposed to that of the Roman Republic) began to appear in Russian satiric literature. Perhaps the best-known work of this type was A. S. Pushkin's lyric "To the Portrait of Chaadaev" (1820): "Through the highest will of the heavens, he was born in the fetters of the tsarist service. In Rome he would have been a Brutus, in Athens a Pericles, but here he is a hussar officer."[61] In this poem, fettered Russia is distinctly opposed to free (republican) Rome and democratic Greece. Chaadaev is identified with the tyrannicide Brutus (who killed Julius Caesar in an attempt to restore the republic) and with Pericles (leader of democratic Athens); but his fate in Russia is limited to being in the tsarist service. Unlike the free periods of Rome and Greece, according to Pushkin, contemporary Russia squelches freedom-loving heroes and limits the individual to the point where he cannot develop himself or serve the people, no matter what his abilities. In the literature of nineteenth-century liberals, Russia was definitely *not* an ideal land. Instead, it was what an anonymous Decembrist poet called a land of "dirt, villainy, stench, and cockroaches, . . . which many fools call the 'Holy Motherland' "[62] or what Mikhail Lermontov dubbed "unwashed Russia, a land of masters and of slaves."[63] What had once been called paradise was frequently being called hell!

The Iron Age and Early-
Nineteenth-Century Russian Poetry

In the first chapter of his unfinished poem *Vozmezdie* (*Retribu-tion*, begun 1910), Aleksandr Blok called the nineteenth century "the iron age," comparing the century (with its industrialization and dominant iron of machines, railroads, and factories) to the last (and worst) age of mankind decried by classical poets like Hesiod and Ovid: "O nineteenth century, of iron, in truth you were a cruel time. [Man] lived weak-willed: it was not he [that played a role] but the machines and cities."[64] In these lines Blok was developing a frequent theme in Russian poetry of the early nineteenth century, when the period that has gone down in his-tory as the "golden age of Russian poetry" was portrayed as the "iron age" of Russian society—the polar opposite of the paradise discussed in this book. This concluding section briefly exam-ines some works condemning Russia's contemporary iron age, focusing on poems of Baratynskii, Del'vig, and Pushkin.[65]

Blok's description of the nineteenth century as "iron" was in part indebted to the first line of Evgenii Baratynskii's 1835 poem "The Last Poet" (which in turn alludes to Derzhavin's 1794 lyric "To the Lyre" discussed earlier in this chapter). Baratynskii's work begins with a scrambled image of the contemporary period as the iron age: *Vek shestvuet putem svoim zheleznym* ("Our age moves along its iron path").[66] In this current iron age, according to Baratynskii, "the youthful dreams of poetry have disappeared with the light of enlightenment, and the generations devoted to industrial cares do not bother with it;[67] people are concerned with "profits" and occupied with "the necessary and the useful." Thus, the iron age is connected with industrialization, science, and the materialism that they have engendered and is directly opposed to poetry (which is implicitly associated with the van-ished golden age, as was often to happen in the early nineteenth century). Even in the "original paradise of the muses" (i.e., Greece, which had just been liberated from the Turkish yoke) the "sounds of the lyre" are no longer heard because people are only concerned with sciences and trade.

Like many elegies of the time, Baratynskii's poem depicts "the winter of the ever more decrepit [*driakhleiushchego*] world," which implicitly opposes the "spring" of poetry.[68] But when suddenly "Parnassus begins to flower" and a poet emerges, this winter is stilled and nature is reborn.[69] In singing of "love and beauty and the emptiness and vanity of the sciences," the poet tells his contemporaries that things were better "in the days of ignorance"; but they laugh at his dreamy ways and continue to be concerned only about their profits in this "world cold with luxury," which "tints its lifeless skeleton with silver and gold." In this iron age of materialism, there is no room for poetry; the golden age is dead.

Typical of the "death" of the golden age in the poetry of the early nineteenth century is Anton Del'vig's idyll "The End of the Golden Age" (1828). The first line "No, I am not in Arcadia"[70] applies not only to the persona (a "Traveler" who has journeyed from city to country in expectation of seeing the good life) but perhaps to Russia in general, where any remaining hopes of seeing and living in an ideal world were shattered by the brutal crushing of the Decembrist revolt of 1825. In asking an "Arcadian shepherd" how he learned to sing his "mournful song so repulsive to the gods, who send [him] joy," the Traveler is told that such happy times are gone: "Yes, we were happy once. I still remember that bright time! But happiness, we later learned, is only a guest on this earth." The Traveler has been fruitlessly searching for this "guest" "in wondrous Colchis [where Jason found the golden fleece], in the lands of the Atlantans [i.e., Atlantis] and the Hyperboreans [the paradisal land beyond the North where there was perpetual sunshine],[71] and even at the edge of the world" (p. 198). Happiness, in short, has left the earth. Grief has come to Arcadia as a result of the city dweller Meletius's corruption of the shepherdess Amarilla, which has brought unhappiness to Arcadia as a whole and led Amarilla to drown herself (undoubtedly after reading Karamzin's "Poor Liza"). The shepherd informs the Traveler that he should search for happiness and joy elsewhere, but warns him that "it is possible that they no longer exist in this world." The idyll, once the domain of happy shepherds, has been absorbed by the elegy, portraying shepherds who recall their happiness but who have it no more. Arcadia has thus gone the way of the vanishing golden age; happiness and joy are dead in the contemporary iron age.

In 1829 Del'vig sent Pushkin a copy of his collected verse.

In response, Pushkin sent him a bronze sphinx, with the four-line verse "Kto na snegakh vozrastil Feokritovy nezhnye rozy?" ("Who has grown the tender roses of Theocritus in the snow?"). Phrased in the form of a riddle, the verse continues, "Who in the age of iron, tell me, has divined the golden age?" The answer to the riddle, which the persona asks "resourceful Oedipus" (who had guessed the answer to the Sphinx's riddle in ancient Thebes), is Del'vig himself, "a young Slav, Greek in spirit, and a German by heritage."[72] Pushkin here is playing on the contrast between the golden and the iron ages. The age of iron refers to the current age of Nicholas the First, the epoch of pessimism that historians have referred to as "frozen Russia." However, the golden age is used here *not* in its eighteenth-century meanings (which as I have been arguing had become "outmoded") but as a metaphor for classical culture and for poetry in general (as it was in Baratynskii's "Last Poet").[73] Del'vig, in continuing Theocritus's tradition, was growing his "roses" (pastoral poems, idylls) "in the snows" (in Russia) and in so doing was overcoming the stagnation of Nicholas's "iron age." As was to occur often in late Pushkin, there is an implicit opposition here between poetry and autocracy.[74]

The impossibility of a golden age in an era of autocracy is one of the implicit subjects of Pushkin's "Bronze Horseman" (1833), which overturns many of the eighteenth-century themes and patterns discussed in this book, portraying Peter the Great creating *not* a golden age but an age of bronze, the forerunner of the (contemporary) iron age.[75] In "The Bronze Horseman," Pushkin strongly challenges the panegyric culture that had depicted Peter as Russia's god. The poem shows autocracy (even creative autocracy like Peter's) as an enemy of Russia's people, and it can be read on one level as an "anti-ode" to a pretender-god, an iconoclastic rebellion against absolute monarchy.[76]

The poem appears to begin with a depiction of Peter in the image of the cosmogonic God of Genesis. An unnamed *"he"* (whom one *assumes* to be Peter, given the fact that the work takes the title of Falconet's famous statue) is shown planning St. Petersburg, which is said to be his "creation" (*tvoren'e*—a word sometimes used at this time for the creation of the world).[77] Like the cosmogonic God of Genesis, Peter is described through syntax where the verb comes first and a pronoun-subject follows: *stoial on* ("stood he"—line 2), *dumal on* ("thought he"—line 11). And like Him, Peter is depicted as transforming darkness into light (the "dark forests" of the Bay of Finland "unknown to the sun's rays" into the light of Petersburg with its "bright" Admiralty needle—lines 23, 9, 53–54) and chaos into cosmos ("a bog of swamps" into the "austere, orderly appearance" of Petersburg—lines 23, 44).[78] But what at first looks like another panegyric to Peter and Petersburg is so contradicted by the rest of the poem, which depicts not cosmos but chaos in Petersburg (symbolized by the archetypal image of chaos—the flood), that it is possible that Pushkin's use of the unnamed "he" implies an identification of Peter not with God but with the devil, who by tradition was left unnamed and who challenged the good works of God. This ambiguity between good and evil, God and devil remains throughout the poem, which wavers between admiration for Peter and Petersburg and contempt for the autocratic system that allowed Peter to build his *paradiz* at so great a cost in human lives.[79]

Describing the Petersburg flood as resulting from "God's anger" (line 200), the poem portrays a contest between "nature" (God's creation) and "art" (man's creation). In this battle, Peter does not see the truth later recognized by Tsar Alexander: "It's not for tsars to control the elements of God" (lines 206–7).[80] Unlike the paradise often portrayed in eighteenth-century panegyric poetry, Pushkin depicts the hell created for Petersburg citizens like Parasha (who loses her life) and Eugene (who loses his mind and, eventually, his life) as a result of Peter's "creation." In short, the Petersburg flood represents divine retribution for Peter's hubris, a "mockery by heaven of earth" (line 250).

The implicit analogy between the Petersburg flood and the great Flood of the Bible is bolstered by eighteenth- and early-nineteenth-century figural interpretations, which linked the Flood with man's "bronze age" (*mednyi vek*). For example, Nikolai Kurganov's popular *Pis'movnik* (a handbook for self-education in language and literature published in eleven editions between 1769 and 1837) stated: "The bronze age [represents] the corruption and evil of mankind, which reached such a level that God destroyed everyone except Noah and his family in the Flood."[81]

As in the classical bronze age, Peter's project results in a state of war between man and nature, tsar and people—as opposed to the perpetual peace of the golden age.[82] Pushkin's "Bronze Horseman" thus depicts Peter as creating not a *golden* age but an age of *bronze* for Russia's "little men" like Eugene, who are threatened by the autocrat's "*iron* bridle" throughout their "unhappy li[ves]" (lines 421, 375).[83]

By the beginning of the nineteenth century motifs of a "paradise lost" and of an iron or bronze age had thus come to replace those of paradise in Russian literature. Pushkin in "The History of the Village of Goriukhino" (1830) succinctly summarized the attitude of the early nineteenth century to the paradise and golden age myths in a section ironically entitled "The Fabled Times": "The thought of a golden age is inherent in all peoples and shows only that people are never satisfied with the present and, having in their experience little hope for the future, decorate the irretrievable past with all the flowers of their imagination" (Pushkin, 1962, 6:191). For Pushkin, as for most major authors of the early nineteenth century, the golden age was no longer a symbol of satisfaction with the status quo; life was grief-filled (hence, perhaps, the emphasis on "Goriukhino," from *gore* ["grief"]), and man dreamed of escaping to the "irretrievable past."

But although the paradise myth was temporarily gone from the mainstream of Russian literature, visions of paradise and utopia nevertheless remained very much alive in Russian culture. During the second quarter of the nineteenth century, they surfaced in areas ranging from Decembrism (where some participants dreamed of founding a Platonic republic on Sakhalin Island)[84] to Slavophilism (which revived many of the ideas and images discussed in this book) and beyond. As N. V. Gogol wrote in section 10 of his *Selected Passages from Correspondence with Friends* (1847): "Our poets have begun to understand the higher meaning of the monarch, having sensed that he inevitably must in the end make his entire self into pure love, and in this way it will be visible to everyone why *the monarch is the image of God*, as our entire land recognizes, for the time being through their feelings" (Gogol', 1937, 8:255). Here, as in the eighteenth century, the conception of the iconic monarch is tied to a vision of paradise—a

vision of an ideal Russian community based on the imitation of
the monarch's selfless charity (*caritas*), a "harmonious orchestra"
of loving beings led by a loving tsar:

Loving everything in his kingdom, down to each individual of every
class and rank, and summoning everything that is in it into his own
body, as it were, worrying about everyone, grieving, sobbing, praying
day and night for his suffering people, the monarch will acquire that all-
powerful voice of love, which itself alone can reach ailing humanity, . . .
which alone can bring reconciliation to all classes *and turn his state into a*
harmonious orchestra. Only that people will be fully healed whose monarch can grasp *his highest significance—to be the image on earth of the one*
who is love. [8:256]

As I have been arguing, this vision of a Christlike emperor of love
had many precedents in earlier Russian culture. Like some other
aspects of the Slavophile ideology, the ideal of the tsar as God's
"image and likeness" reflected a link posited by Orthodoxy between heaven and earth embodying what one religious historian
has called the "dynamic manifestations of man's spiritual power
to redeem creation . . . aimed at demonstrating that men, animals, and plants, and the whole cosmos could be rescued from
their present state of degradation and restored to their proper
'Image.' "[85] As nineteenth- and twentieth-century Russian literature and twentieth-century Russian political events testify, the
paradise myth did not die at the end of the eighteenth century.
Instead, as Renato Pogiolli succinctly stated in the 1950's: "[T]he
Russian people have preserved, in this iron age, for so many
years of blood, sweat, and tears, the mythical vision of a golden
age, of a land of milk and honey where the soul lives blissfully, at
peace with itself and the world."[86] Although today this mythical
vision is largely eclipsed,[87] it is likely, given historical and cultural patterns in Russia, that this tenacious myth of an earthly
paradise will someday return. If it does, not only the future but
also the past will determine the form that it will take.

Appendixes

Definitional Details of
the Paradise Myth

The most frequent definitional components of the paradise myth found in classical, biblical, and patristic texts are schematically outlined here.[1] Details marked with an asterisk have been the most productive for defining ideal times and places.

Hesiod, *Works and Days* (lines 109–20)

Golden race of men
The reign of Cronus
Men living like gods
No sorrow or grief
Merry life
*No evil
Frequent feasts
No problems in aging (old age easily borne)
Death coming like sleep
*Abundant food without work (no tilling of the fields)
*Life of ease
*Peace reigning in the world (no wars)
Men rich in flocks
Men loved by the gods

Ovid, *Metamorphoses* (I, 89–112)

No judges
*No laws
No fears
*No crime
Complete safety for all

No foreign travel or trade
*No wars (hence no trenches, trumpets, horns, helmets, swords, or
    soldiers)
*Eternal spring
*Placid zephyrs (gentle west winds)
Flowers born without seeds
Rivers of milk and rivers of nectar
Yellow honey flowing from the oaks
*Reign of Saturn
No need of shelter (hence no rain or snow, no inclement weather) (men
    living outdoors)
*All goods held in common (no private property)
*Astraea (the virgin goddess of justice) living on earth among men
Men eating wild fruit and acorns[2]

Other Classical Details

*Philosopher-king (Plato, *Republic*, V, 473c)
*Elysian Fields (Homer, *Odyssey*, IV, 561–68)
Islands of the Blessed (Hesiod, *Works and Days*, 167–69)
Fortunate Islands (Virgil, *Aeneid*, VI, 638–41)
Land of the Hyperboreans (Pindar, "Pythian X")
Reign of Numa (Calpurnius Siculus, *Eclogue* I, and Plutarch, "Life
    of Numa")
Garden of Alcinous (*Odyssey*, VII, 112–34)
Garden of the Hesperides (Hesiod, *Theogony*, 215–17)
*Sweet smells (Diodorus Siculus, *Library of History*)
Arabia Felix (Diodorus Siculus, *Library of History*)

Eden Tale (Genesis 2–3)

Trees that were delightful to see and good to eat
*Adam and Eve
*Tree of life
*Untouched forbidden fruit
*River watering the garden and branching into four streams on leaving
    the garden
*No clothes (nakedness without shame)
Innocence
*Tree of knowledge of good and evil
Located in the East

Book of Isaiah (2:2–4, 11:1–9, 35:1–10, 51:3)

*Wolf lying with the lamb
 Leopard lying with the kid
 Ox, wolf, and lion grazing side by side
*Child herding wild animals
*Friendship between man and beast and between formerly hostile
   beasts
 Holy mountain (Zion)
 No poisonous snakes
 No injury or killing among men or beasts
*Swords beaten into ploughshares
*Spears beaten into pruning hooks
*No wars
 The blind able to see
 The deaf able to hear
 The lame able to leap like deer
 Dumb tongues speaking out for joy
*Brooks appearing in the desert and streams in the steppes
 Blossoming deserts (deserts like gardens)
*Messianic kingdom of Zion
 People living lives of joy and gladness
 No sorrow or sighing

New Jerusalem (Rev. 21:1–22:5)

*New heaven and a new earth
*New Jerusalem
*Heaven descending to earth (heaven on earth)
*God dwelling with men
 No death
 No sorrow, tears, or pain
 All things made new
 Fountain of the water of life
 City of gold
 City like clear glass
 Gates of pearl
 No night
*No more time
 River of water of life
 Healing leaves from the tree of life
 No more curse (ending of consequences of the Fall)

Other Biblical and Patristic Motifs

*Promised land (Gen. 12:7, 15:18; Exod. 32:13, etc.)

*Pure, clean air (St. John of Damascus, *De fide orthodoxi*; Pseudo-Basil, *De paradiso*, etc.)

  Rose without thorns (St. Ambrose, *Hexameron*; St. Basil, *Hexameron*, etc.)

*Garden enclosed (*hortus conclusus*) (Song of Songs 4:12)

*Land flowing with milk and honey (Exod. 3:8, 17; Lev. 20:24; Jer. 11:5; Ezek. 20:6; etc.)

Freemasonry and Seventeenth-Century European Mysticism: John Pordage's
Fifth Tract on Paradise

A number of seventeenth-century European mystical works about external and internal paradises strongly influenced European and Russian higher order Masonry and helped the movement focus its ritual and rhetoric on recovering the paradise lost by Adam. In Russia, one of the most popular of these was *The Fifth Tract on Paradise* by John Pordage (Rus: Pordech or Pordedzh, 1607–81), published in 1787 but circulating as well in many manuscript copies.[3] Pordage's tract contains lengthy descriptions of paradise, embodying the entire spectrum of the paradise myth from Eden to the New Jerusalem and using many of the patterns and images outlined in Chapter 1 and Appendix A. Although Pordage (a follower of Jakob Boehme and the leader of a mystical sect called "Philadelphians")[4] focuses primarily on paradise after death, his tract reflects the frequent similarities in descriptions of heavenly and earthly paradises. The paradise Pordage describes as awaiting the good soul restores that perfect existence lost by Adam in the Fall—the existence the Masons hoped to achieve in *this* life through the improvement of morals.

Pordage assumes that the various paradises described in the Bible compose "a single paradisal sphere," no matter what name is given to it; this land, says Pordage, was figuratively referred to in the Bible as the "promised land" and the "new heaven and new earth."[5] This ideal place (often compared to a garden of joys or an enclosed garden) has "no dragon, snake, dissembler, devil, or unclean person" (p. 1), no night or winter (p. 3), no sorrow, and no death (because the tree of life and the river of life are there) (p. 4); its inhabitants sing songs of praise (pp. 4–5) because they have been victorious over evil. Pordage's paradise is characterized by its marvelous colors, smells, and trees (where a picked piece of fruit grows back immediately—p. 3). The land is full of silver and gold of a peculiarly pure kind, which is transparent—the kind described in Revelation 21:18 as "like glass" (pp. 36–37). The place is filled with wonders for all the senses, with an infinite variety of "marvels" to satisfy its happy inhabitants (including marvelous smells and colors and beautiful music). Every joy in this paradise is available without work, and the inhabitants can eat or drink milk and honey (which flow in streams), wine (which also flows in streams), manna ("the bread of heaven," which is everywhere), and the living waters of life (pp. 58–62).

Among elements in Pordage's work that probably influenced European Freemasonry were the series of degrees an inhabitant had to pass through before ascending to the kingdom of Mount Zion (p. 63); a new degree attained is marked by a change of dwelling place. Even an inhabitant's robe reflects the degrees achieved; although all robes are white, the lower the degree the less the robe shines, but the closer that an inhabitant comes to Mount Zion (the "heart of glory" from which all good things of paradise flow), the more radiant the robe. At the entrance to Pordage's paradise is a "temple of higher wisdom" (*khram premudrosti*—words also used for the Masonic lodge) where the worthy receive instruction from "angels and other famous figures"; here, the laws of paradise are taught (pp. 70–71). The path from this temple to Mount Zion is very narrow and almost impassable, with an abyss of fire on one side and an abyss of water on the other, but once people pass the gates of paradise, all that remains to do is to go through a "valley of wells," where there are fountains depicting the "wonders of God's new creations"; in this "very pleasant place" people gradually acquire a single ageless appearance (mature but not old—like that of Adam and Eve in Eden or Christ when he left the desert to be baptized, pp. 72, 76–77).

Pordage argues that before the Fall people were like "little gods," having both male and female sexes in themselves and thus possessing the potential of creating their own descendents by simply stating the cosmogonic word *FIAT* (*da budet*: "Let there be"), like God; but the only person that Adam created by himself was Christ, "the first-born of all creatures, the son of man," who walked with Adam in the Garden of Eden (pp. 89–101, 105–6). In Pordage's version, as later in higher order Masonry, Adam had a twofold paradise before the Fall: an external paradise in nature and an internal paradise within himself (p. 143). After the Fall God took back the external paradise but did not destroy the internal paradise, which remained "separated from the external world . . . and hidden within each person's own self" (p. 157). According to Pordage, through Sophia (divine knowledge—*premudrost'*) and through Christ, this internal paradise can be restored again. When this knowledge becomes common to all men, "all the world will be paradise," wrote Pordage, prefiguring a common Masonic ideal (p. 157).

Utopian Section of Pavel L'vov's
The Russian Pamela

"Finally the dawn appeared, and before our eyes was an island not too far away. Our rapture at this sight was indescribable. Approaching the shores, we saw a crowd of strangely dressed people who were tossing some very long hooks at us in order to snare our boat. At this point our joy again changed to great grief. We took these islanders, from their haste and dress, for famished cannibals, and, bearing down upon the oars, we tried to get away from these shores; but, having noticed this, they made friendly signs to us and raised their hands to the sky to let us know that they vowed not to harm us. Finally, after a great deal of convincing, we approached the shore and came upon a situation that we had not at all anticipated; for, as soon as we had reached land, they met us with a branch decorated with many layers of fragrant flowers as a sign of friendship. They received us ever so gracefully, gave us some fragrant herbs for relaxation, lit a fire so that our clothes could dry, and brought us a multitude of skins, which served as their clothes; for food they brought us various fruits. They tried to calm us. After this, they led us to their lodgings, which, while not magnificent, were adequately constructed. Everyone lived under one roof: people were not separated by barriers or fences; there were no doorkeepers, no guards; in short, their whole city consisted of one very long house, and this one good and friendly dwelling made their many families into one single family.

"In the middle of their dwelling rose two high and spacious buildings, built in such a way that each could hold all of the inhabitants. One of these buildings was their temple and the other was the residence of the governor, which was decorated without splendor, with cleanliness and simplicity. Their governor lived in spacious quarters or, more properly, in a large structure, not so that he could expand his immoderate wants, not for luxury, not to be waited on by many servants. No, he lived there in order to gather his citizens together for conversations with him about their interests, to tell them about his new ideas for their benefit, to listen to their candid and just opinions, to hear the complaints and assertions of each person. All of this made him just and made the people conscientious and not quarrelsome. Criminals were punished more with disgrace than with corporal punishment.

"The officials surrounding the governor were not cunning yes-men, base schemers, enemies who flatter, sycophants who abuse others, or cunning extortioners. Rather, they were benign, philosophic men; serious, but not proud; just, but not out of personal interest; exacting, but not tyrannical; devoted, but not meek. They loved the governor without any thought of gain, and they were virtuous without pretense. The governor loved them so much that he was concerned for their calm as a loving father would be for the welfare of his children. His subjects thus found in him a most amiable friend, a friend whom they looked upon as their respected father, and a father whom they regarded as their revered ruler. Thus, this system of rule preserved their golden age on the island. In short, every citizen was that type of person whom we refer to as a philosopher. It follows that a philosopher is a person who is not guilty of prejudice, who is a sound thinker, who is virtuous, and who does nothing to upset his conscience. We marvel at a person if he is the sort who fulfills all of his responsibilities well and who guards all the rights that holy truth and nature prescribe. What blindness to marvel at our equals if they are perfect.

"I never saw a single rich man or even a single poor one there, because among them there is no such thing as a mighty plunderer or a helpless pauper. The ruler, using his wisdom and keeping the general well-being of the people in mind, can weigh the condition of his citizens equitably, since there are no thieves of his wisdom who would dare to tell him a lie in the form of the truth. His confidence in wise and ardent advisers repels the brigands of his mercy and his thoughts, and as a result there exists a common prosperity. It is surprising to hear of the ruin of a person there or even to hear of a distressed or alienated person. On this island there are no servile, self-willed officials, who, promising to fulfill the requests of a petitioner, do not what is necessary for the petitioner but what is profitable for themselves.

"What captivating places there are on this island! Leaf-shaded trees cover the high mountains; the summits of these mountains stretch to the clouds, spreading most fragrant aromas from the flowers and fruits growing there. There are lush valleys filled with flowers, and hills covered with healthful plants and with fruit-bearing bushes. The land is fertile; cattle of various breeds wander through the rich pastures; the meadows are adorned with magnificent groves, the dales irrigated by vast rivers, which, bearing their trickling streams, flow along cliffs formed from shells by nature herself and get lost in the forests of oak, inhabited by rare species of birds, whose many-colored wings are as beautiful as their sweet songs, which produce surprising harmony.

"The habits of these people were simple, without the least bit of prejudice or eccentricity; they were based on tranquility, on freedom of thought, and on goodwill. Their warm hospitality was reflected on all occasions. Worship of God and brotherly love were their principal laws; faith was respected, and all scoffers at religious faith were exiled from the temple of the sun, despised by all, and deprived of all aid. Parasites were excluded from their society and driven from the city. In their society the bad was surprising and not the good; this was the case because the good was common among them, and the bad occurred very, very rarely. Use of weapons never entered their minds. Even the minor laws were followed to the letter, in emulation of the monarch himself, who obeyed all of the ordinances of his predecessors; the best laws were in imitation of his virtue. His main concern was to serve as an example of piety for all of his people.

"Old people, wise people, those who work hard, and those who discover more effective means of work were distinguished, honored, and respected above all others. Young people were meek, and parental supervision preserved them from violence and indolence; the fathers cared for their sons, and the mothers for their daughters. In case of parental injustice, of undeserved persecution of their children, the ruler, like a father of fathers, would step in and examine the situation. Disobedience on the part of children was punished by disgrace and hatred from all of the people; hard work was singled out and rewarded. Aid to one's neighbor was a prime responsibility there.

"This is the way that these unenlightened islanders, who live in happiness, philosophize—these islanders whom we call savages only because they do not know how to delude with flattering sweetness or to speak with eloquent rhetoric, because they do not know luxury and dress poorly."[6]

Reference Matter

Notes

All notes are keyed to the Selected Bibliography at the end of the book; in cases of multivolume editions only the year of publication of the first volume is given. The following abbreviations are used in these notes:

GBL—Archives of the Lenin Library, Moscow
GPB—Archives of the Saltykov-Shchedrin Public Library, Leningrad
IRLI—Archives of the Institute of Russian Literature (*Pushkinskii dom*), Leningrad

KSXVIII—Card-index for *Slovar' russkogo iazyka XVIII veka.* USSR Academy of Sciences, Institute of Linguistics, Russian Language Division, Dictionary Section, Leningrad

Preface

1. For the latter view, see Serman, *Russkii klassitsizm*, especially pp. 43ff.

2. As early as the memoirs of Giles Fletcher (ambassador to Russia under England's Elizabeth I), foreign writers have observed this tendency toward consent in Russia. Fletcher noted that the *Zemskii sobor* would be asked to automatically agree to any law proposed by the tsar and would do so "without any great pausing" (quoted in Szamuely, p. 35). As I was completing this preface, Nobel laureate Andrei Sakharov had just raised a similar point in condemning the "aggressively obedient majority" in the new Soviet Congress of People's Deputies. One member was quoted as saying that after his election as a deputy he expected that he would just "vote yes, of course, as is customary" (Victor Astaf'ev, quoted in Kennan Institute Meeting Report for October 26, 1989). Cf. old Russian proverbs like "No one is against God and the tsar" (Dal', *Poslovitsy*, 1:189).

3. For a brief overview of the topos of the poet as slave, see Sazonova, "Ot russkogo panegirika," p. 123. Sazonova links this motif to the old Russian hagiographical topos of the author as simpleton (*khudoumnyi*). Although I find this hypothesis stimulating, I believe that it understates the absolutist politics behind the image of poet as "slave."

4. On the concept of topoi and their importance in the study of literature, see Curtius.

5. On some early nineteenth-century predecessors of Slavophilism that are direct outgrowths of subjects discussed in this book, see Al'tshuller, *Predtechi*.

6. For a discussion of the relationship of socialist realism to the eighteenth century, see Tertz [Siniavskii], pp. 195–201, 207–8, who argues that the Soviet style should be called "socialist *classicism*."

7. On the concepts of monologic and dialogic literature, see the works of M. M. Bakhtin, for example "Slovo v romane" in *Voprosy literatury i estetiki*, pp. 72–233. See also Clark and Holquist. On challenges to this monologic world in Russian literature from the last third of the eighteenth century, see Chapter 7 below.

8. To cite one example connected with the theme of this book, the iconography of Catherine II's court—dominated by the image of Catherine as Astraea, the virgin (*sic*) goddess of the golden age—bears much more similarity to that of the court of England's Elizabeth I (who was also frequently called Astraea) than to that of contemporary Western European courts.

Chapter One

1. Peter I, *Pis'ma i bumagi*, 4:207, 368; 10:57; etc.

2. Although for Peter *paradiz* was a Western word, it actually derives from an Old Persian word signifying the enclosed garden or royal park of the Persian king (Giamatti, p. 11).

3. Some old Russian princes, like Andrei Bogoliubskii, had called their out-of-town residences *Rai*. Others, like Daniil Galitskii and Vladimir Volynskii, named the town where such residences were located *Rai*. For the old Russian background, see Likhachev, p. 47.

4. Already in classical times, descriptions of such after-death paradises as Elysium and the Land of the Blessed had become virtually identical to those of the golden age; Hesiod's Land of the Blessed in *Works and Days* (lines 156ff), Homer's Elysium in *Odyssey* (IV, 561–68), Virgil's Elysium in *Aeneid* (VI, 637–94), and Horace's Islands of the Blessed (which he also calls the "Fortunate Isles") in *Epode* XVI all use motifs that also appear in the golden age myth. On the general amalgamation of myths of perfect times and places in the classical period, see Giamatti, p. 17.

5. On the role of an amalgamated paradise or golden age myth in the European Renaissance, see H. Levin, St. Clair, and Duncan. Where Levin's use of the term "golden age myth" stresses secular elements in the Renaissance, my use of the broader term "paradise myth" emphasizes the survival of many religious elements in secularized eighteenth-century Russia.

6. Quoted in H. Levin, p. 36. By the eighteenth century in Russia, earlier Orthodox objections to this kind of amalgamation of classical and biblical myth had been largely eliminated.

7. This interchangeability perhaps reflects the influence of the typological reading of the Bible, which viewed these myths as prefigurations of the heavenly paradise and New Jerusalem, implicitly manifesting the designs of God. On the typological reading of the Bible, see Bercovitch, chapter 2.

8. The classical motif of the garden of the Hesperides became much more closely associated with paradise in the Renaissance than it had been in classical texts. As Sir Walter Raleigh wrote in his 1614 *History of the World*, paradise was "transported out of Asia into Africa and made the Garden of the Hesperides" (quoted in Duncan, p. 27). Duncan observes that the Hesperides was "Milton's favorite golden age site" (p. 33).

9. This amalgamation and interchangeability were aided by the fact that there is no canonical description in the Bible of a place labeled "paradise." Although conceptions of a paradisal "Garden of God" (presumably Eden) occur several times in the Old Testament, paradise is mentioned by name only three times in the Bible (Luke 23:43; 2 Cor. 12:4; Rev. 2:7). Of these, only the description of the paradisal New Jerusalem in Revelation involves a description of the "good life" and even this uses some terms borrowed from Genesis.

10. For a more specific description, see Curtius, pp. 192–97.

11. This same cult of detail has occurred in all genres using the myth, including the literary utopia, which Barthes argues was dominated by an "imagination of detail" (p. 105).

12. Compare Tynianov's observation that "every speech context has an assimilative power that forces a word to have only certain functions and colors them with the tone of the activity in which they participate" ("Meaning," p. 144).

13. Adjectives (like "paradisal," "golden," "ideal," "pleasant," or "perfect") were also frequently assimilators, indicating nouns representing perfection.

14. The term "negative formula" is taken from Patch, p. 12, where it is used in a slightly different way. This formula (like the other formulas of the myth) is still used in literature and political texts today.

15. This latter detail reflects the idea that foreign travel could corrupt

perfection through bad examples and thus could taint morals.

16. In Horace's *Epode* XVI, for example, the paradisal Islands of the Blessed are contrasted with Rome in the civil-war period. The islands are described through both positive and negative conventions of the paradise myth: a place where "the vine ripens, unpruned, its clusters into wine, . . . and fields unplowed their wealth on man bestow," where "herds and flocks unbidden bring their milky offering" with "no wolf around the sheepfold striding"; Rome, on the other hand, is described as their opposite—a hell destined to be abandoned to "mountain wolf" and "barbarian" as a result of the civil war (DeVere translation in Horace, pp. 118–20).

17. Motifs that might contradict the definitional vocabulary or the assimilated motifs of any period or work must be negated if irony is to be avoided. So if a ruler is praised with the statement that he has re-created the golden age, the qualifying statement "however poverty remains" cannot appear without vitiating the myth. The word "hell" is naturally excluded from the paradise myth, just as "bronze age" or "iron age" can only appear as foils.

18. As Barbara Herrnstein Smith has argued, "repetition is the fundamental principle of thematic generation" in paratactic structures (p. 98). Works using the paradise myth often relied heavily on enumeration of paradisal tropes as the deep structure (although the surface form of the work does not always reveal this).

19. See, for example, the description in book 7 of Homer's *Odyssey* of the garden of Alcinous, which, according to Justin Martyr, "preserves the likeness of Paradise" (Duncan, p. 25). To emphasize the paradisal qualities of this garden, Homer not only lists details that suggest a paradisal place (abundant fruit all year and hence no winter, the presence of the zephyr, perpetual perfection of the fruit) but also uses repetition to create an atmosphere of abundance.

20. See Chapter 4 below for more on these paradisal flowers.

21. The courtly paradise myth of the European Renaissance exerted both direct and indirect influences on its eighteenth-century Russian counterpart. Indirect influences came through seventeenth- and eighteenth-century courts that had themselves been influenced by the Renaissance, ranging from that of Louis XIV (whom some commentators consider the apogee of the Renaissance monarch) to those of small German principalities whose citizens came to Russia under Peter the Great and his successors.

22. Quoted in St. Clair, p. 59.

23. Quoted in St. Clair, p. 59. For another example, see Joachim du Bellay's 1547 "Salutation" on the accession of Henry II, which portrays

the king as slaying the monster Ignorance and restoring the golden age —a theme that would be repeated occasionally in eighteenth-century Russian literature, especially in works connected with Peter the Great.

24. Virgil, 1:561–63. The "god" referred to is Augustus's father (or actually adoptive father), Julius Caesar, who was deified after death. The "fields where Saturn once reigned" connote Rome, where, according to tradition, Saturn had fled after being overthrown at the end of the golden age (see Virgil, *Georgics*, Book II, and *Aeneid*, Book VIII).

25. This variant of the messianic pattern is also used in jeremiads, like H. G. Wells's *Time Machine*, which describes the hell that will result if class oppositions continue. The source of the "I saw" pattern used by the Time Traveler to describe the future is almost certainly Revelation.

26. Quoted in Patch, p. 139.

27. The positive or negative value ascribed to these adverbs has tended to reflect the genre of a literary work. Panegyric odes to reigning monarchs have usually identified paradise with "here" or "now," and hell with "there" or "then." But most utopian novels have associated "here" (the place in which the author was writing and his audience reading) with hell, and "there" (the perfect society described by his traveler) with paradise. Thomas More's *Utopia* is (at least on the surface) structured on just such an opposition between a flawed "here" (the England described in part 1) and a perfect "there" (the land of Utopia, as described in part 2 by the returned traveler, Raphael Hythloday).

28. Cf. Sebastian's reply to Gonzalo's statement in *The Tempest* that he would be king on an island with "no sovereignty": "The latter end of his commonwealth forgets the beginning" (II, i, 161–63).

29. In the words of the narrator of Zamiatin's anti-utopian novel *My* (*We*, 1924), the inhabitant of paradise or utopia is "not one but one of." Even the imagery used in the paradise myth often falls into the category that Northrop Frye has called "apocalyptic," describing a "world of total metaphor in which everything is potentially identifiable with everything else, as though it were inside a single infinite body" (*Anatomy*, p. 136).

30. On the repetition of the cosmogony, see Eliade, *The Sacred and the Profane*, pp. 29–36.

31. This connection of paradise with light is seen as early as Sumerian mythology, where the earthly paradise was called the *"bright* land of Dilmun" and linked with the sun god. See J. Armstrong, p. 10. The importance of solar imagery in the paradise myth and utopias is reflected in titles like Campanella's *City of the Sun* and perhaps even in the central role in the myth of the color gold, traditionally associated with the sun.

32. Medieval maps often explicitly represented paradise in the East

and hell in the West. Two exceptions to this East-West opposition were the Islands of the Blessed (usually assumed to be in the West in the Atlantic Ocean) and the Garden of the Hesperides (the name "Hesperides" deriving from the Greek word meaning "West").

33. A somewhat less frequent theme associated with paradisal beginnings was the fountain of youth (an outgrowth of the rivers of Eden, according to some legends), which attempted to return time to the beginning and freeze it there.

34. Frank and Fritzie Manuel have noted that paradises have often reflected a longing for the womb and used such maternal symbols as islands, gardens, and valleys. They quote, for example, the gnostic Simon Magus, who argued that the Garden of Eden was but an allegory for the womb ("Sketch," pp. 87, 98–99). Jung has also argued for a close connection between paradise symbols and the mother archetype, observing, for example, that "mothers in a figurative sense" (including the Mother of God and Sophia) frequently appear in works connected with "the goal of our longing for redemption, such as Paradise, the Kingdom of God, the Heavenly Jerusalem" (Jung, p. 333). On the role of the mother archetype in Russian paradisal literature, see the sections Christian into Classical in Chapter 2 and Mother Russia in the Garden of Love in Chapter 4.

35. One apparent exception to this generalization occurs in the anti-utopia, where plots frequently depict a rebellious individual or group trying to destroy a state that pretends to be paradisal; these individuals are themselves most frequently destroyed.

36. On sacred space, see Eliade, *The Sacred and the Profane*, chapter 1. In works using the paradise myth, space has often been interchangeable with time; little or no distinction has been made between a paradisal place separated from the existing world by time and one separated by space, just as there have been few thematic distinctions between the golden age (man's first time) and Eden (man's first place).

37. Height was often associated with paradise (reflecting closeness to heaven and God), as in Dante's *Purgatorio*, where the earthly paradise is located on a high mountain.

38. Even the literary utopia has been fundamentally panegyric in its rhetoric, praising the good system of government by embodying it in an ideal place. Although the utopia has usually *functioned* satirically, its primary rhetorical thrust has been panegyric, praising the "good place" (*eu*-topia); satire has resulted when the praised "good place" is juxtaposed with the society of the author, which by comparison becomes a "bad place" (*dys*-topia). On these points, see Chapter 6 below.

39. By inserting specific criticism into this rhetorical language, an

author can also use the paradise myth as a subtle vehicle for suggestion or satire; criticism is softened by being submerged in a sea of synonyms of the "perfect."

40. The negative formula provides both a literary and a political structuring principle for this description of paradise in the second half of the poem: Charles is described as the negation of Cromwell and his rule associated with the absence of the "bad" and the "sad."

41. Poetry and poetic creativity have often been explicitly associated with paradise. See, for example, the sections The Garden in the City in Chapter 4, Paradise Unshrouded in Chapter 5, and The Iron Age and Early Nineteenth-Century Russian Poetry in Chapter 7.

42. The process of assimilation of Charles's name into the paradise myth in Herrick's text may be summarized thus: Line 7 begins with the image of a golden age, which is equated in line 8 with Charles's reign by parallel syntax. Through their parallelism to lines 7–8, lines 9–10 equate a transformed definitional phrase of the paradise myth ("smooth and unperplext seasons"—a variation on the theme of "eternal spring" or "no summer or winter") with a historical specific (the time of Maria, Charles's wife). As the sentence continues, poetic creativity is implicitly linked with this returned golden age and thus assimilated into the myth—one of the good events opposing the "bad" season of Cromwell when the "sad" poet is unable to create. Finally, the three topoi dealing with poetic creativity ("Curles half drown'd in Tyrian Dewes," "Head with Roses crown'd," "Knock at a Starre with my exalted Head"—the latter a direct quote from Horace, *Ode* I, 1, regarding poetic creativity) also become components of the myth as synonyms of an already assimilated activity.

43. Given the panegyric and propagandistic role of the paradise myth, it is not surprising that the myth today often figures in advertising—the modern equivalent of the panegyric ode.

44. For example, William Blake expressed his belief in a spiritual England by linking it to the Garden of the Hesperides, the Island of Atlantis, the New Jerusalem, and Eden (Frye, *Fearful Symmetry*, p. 371).

Chapter Two

1. Kantorowicz, p. 87. Kantorowicz portrays political theology as a frequent structuring device for political ideas in Western Europe since the Middle Ages.

2. Ladner, *Idea*, chapter 3.

3. Ladner, *Idea*, pp. 63, 82.

4. Irenaeus, *Adversus haereses*, V, 20, 2, quoted in Ladner, *Idea*, p. 70.

5. Origen, *Selecta in Genesim*, quoted in Ladner, *Idea*, p. 70; Eusebius, 2:267 (a new Russian translation of Eusebius was published in 1786); Ephraem, "Sixth Hymn on Paradise," quoted in Ladner, *Idea*, p. 70.

6. Quoted in Ouspensky, p. 28. Ouspensky also mentions St. Simeon of Thessalonica's description of the consecrated church as "a mysterious heaven."

7. Ouspensky, chapter 1; Ladner, *Idea*, chapter 3; Salaville, pp. 123ff.

8. Ladner, *Idea*, pp. 69, 292, 292n. The term "spiritual paradise" itself came from Eastern Church Fathers (e.g., Clement of Alexandria). See Ladner, p. 70.

9. Quoted in Ladner, *Idea*, p. 291. This hymn is attributed to St. Germanus. Similar imagery exists in the liturgies for the Easter season. On the relationship of the crushing of a serpent with the return to paradise, see also the discussion of Falconet's *Bronze Horseman* in Chapter 3 below.

10. Ladner, *Idea*, p. 292.

11. *Povest' vremennykh let*, in Dmitriev and Likhachev, eds., p. 68. Among the themes of the eighteenth-century paradise myth prefigured in this chronicle description were a stress on the inadequacy of the language of post-Fall man for describing the joys and beauties of paradise (a theme used particularly often in the Masonic variant of the myth) and on God dwelling in paradise with men (a theme recalling the classical myth of the golden age, when Astraea and other gods dwelled on earth with mortals).

12. It is probable that the influence of the Church Fathers on the image of heaven on earth in the Russian Chronicle came not only directly but also through the intermediary of prayers in the Orthodox liturgy. On the related idea that through baptism one becomes part of the Kingdom of God, the heavenly Jerusalem, or Mount Zion, see Bulgakov, "Le ciel sur la terre." Bulgakov argues (on the basis of Heb. 12:22–24) that in the church there is no distance between "that which is terrestrial and that which is celestial, . . . all are together, all are one, heaven on earth and earth sanctified" (p. 57). Since paradise is a symbolic representation of the holy, the capstone of the religious quest, several definitions of the church by Bulgakov and earlier theologians (as being beyond space, beyond time, indescribable in words, eternal) are closely related to the archetype of paradise described in this book.

13. On the idea of the church as a "provisional paradise" in Christian theology, see Williams, pp. 27ff. As Ouspensky has observed (p. 22), "The new Israel—the church . . . brings the presence and the promise of the Kingdom of God to the fallen world."

14. On the idea of heaven and earth as a single world, see, for example, Simon, p. 126, and Bulgakov, "Le ciel sur la terre." The descent of

heaven to earth was emphasized through representations in the cupola of Christ as ruler of the universe—Pantocrator—or of Christ in judgment.

15. Meyendorff, *Byzantine Theology*, pp. 214–15.

16. Meyendorff, *Byzantine Theology*, pp. 214–15; Bulgakov, *The Orthodox Church*, p. 183.

17. Runciman, *Byzantine Theocracy*, pp. 1–2. The Byzantine ideal of a universal Christian empire was reinforced in eighteenth-century Russia by European imperialist theories of the sixteenth and seventeenth centuries, which themselves had been influenced by Byzantine ideas. See Yates, *Astraea*, p. 1, and the material on *renovatio* in the section on eternal return in Chapter 3 below.

18. Fedotov, p. 208. This implicit relationship between Christ (the so-called icon not made by hands—*nerukotvornaia ikona*—who was himself sometimes called a "king") and the Byzantine emperor was made explicit in Byzantine thought when the latter was portrayed as *christomimetes*, the "imitator of Christ" on earth, and given such titles as the "Image of Christ," the "Figure and Image of Christ and God," and even "Second God by Grace." Christ and the Emperor literally became two sides of the same coin in Byzantium, and monuments to emperors were inscribed *Christos Basileus* ("Christ the Emperor") and icons created showing Christ in the imperial garb. See Kantorowicz, pp. 46–48 and 88–89; Ladner, "Concept of the Image," p. 22; Guerdan, pp. 17–18, 28, 103; and Hussey, p. 86. This relationship between ruler and Christ was already foreshadowed in the Old Testament, where kings are called "anointed ones" (*christi* in the Septuagint) and prefigure the advent of Christ, "the Anointed of Eternity."

19. On the opposition between *obraz* and *bezobrazie* in Russian literature, see the following works by Robert L. Jackson: *Dostoevsky's Quest for Form*, p. 58; "The Triple Vision," p. 228; "'Matryona's Home': The Making of a Russian Icon," p. 69; and *The Art of Dostoevsky*, pp. 18–19 and pp. 304–6. Quotes are from Jackson.

20. On the renewed Byzantinization of Russian culture during this period, see Zhivov and Uspenskii, p. 93; on the sacralization of the tsar, see esp. pp. 72–121. I am grateful to Professor Uspenskii for giving me this valuable work, which unfortunately was received only after submission of the present book.

21. Eusebius, "Oration," p. 5. On Eusebius, see Baynes, pp. 168–72; Ladner, *Idea*, p. 109; and Ladner, "Concept of the Image," p. 21.

22. On the role of Agapetus in Russia, see the excellent articles by Ševčenko listed in the Selected Bibliography. Translations of Agapetus into Russian were published in 1766 (with only 56 of the 72 chapters,

according to the subtitle) and 1771 (when two translations were published, one by Vasilii Ruban, dedicated to Catherine the Great, and one
by Stepan Pisarev, dedicated to Pavel Petrovich). See *Svodnyi katalog* 1:23
(items 57–58) and supplement, p. 63 (item 363). As of 1975, no copies
of the 1766 edition could be found in the libraries of the Soviet Union,
and there is some question as to whether this volume actually was published; but judging from some of the early Russian utopias discussed in
Chapter 6 below (especially Kheraskov's *Numa*), Agapetus's work—the
most popular mirror of princes in Russia—was probably known during
the 1760's. While it is of course possible that authors knew the work in
the original or in translation, or were reading some other work in this
genre, the probability of a 1766 Moscow edition as stated in the *Svodnyi
katalog* is great. On the role of the mirror of princes in the creation of
a utopian genre in Russian literature, see Chapter 6, note 15 and the
section "Satire and Utopia."

23. Agapit, p. 3. Future translations will be from this edition.

24. For example, Agapetus's chapter 21 states: "In the essence of his
body, the tsar is on a level with any other man, but *in the authority of his
office he is similar to God*, the ruler of all. . . . [A]s a mortal he must not
extol himself too highly. For although he is respected as the image of
God (*obrazom Bozhiim*), he is, however, mixed with earthly dust as well."

25. Quote is from Bolshakoff, p. 52, and is included in a description of
the Josephite [Possessor] legacy in Russian culture, which provided an
underpinning for the paradise myth in later Russia, just as it supported
virtually all aspects of the autocratic status quo.

26. Pipes, *Russia Under the Old Regime*, pp. 232–33.

27. There had been strong Byzantine influences on Bulgarian culture since the first Bulgarian empire of the ninth and tenth centuries,
especially during the reigns of Boris, his son Symeon, and grandson
Peter. According to Steven Runciman, Symeon's cultural policies attempted "to translate Byzantium into Slavonic terms" ("Byzantium and
the Slavs," p. 351). See also Wolff, p. 192; Dvornik, pp. 372ff; B. Meyendorff and Baynes, pp. 383f.

28. The Byzantine theory of the emperor as the man chosen and enlightened by God was already being used in church descriptions of
Muscovite Prince Basil II not long after the fall of Byzantium; by 1492
the Moscow metropolitan, Zosima, was calling the grand prince "the
sovereign and autocrat of all Russia, the new Tsar Constantine of the
new city of Constantinople—Moscow." Rulers of rival Russian cities
were praised in similar ways. Under the influence of Byzantium, the
Monk Foma praised Boris Aleksandrovich, Prince of Tver (d. 1461),
as God-chosen, the image of God, a new Moses, and a "ruler ad-

mired throughout the world" (Ševčenko, "Neglected Source," p. 87). Byzantine-derived epithets of this sort would recur in conjunction with the ideology of Russia as the realm of a new golden age in the eighteenth century.

29. The term "perfected theocracy" comes from Masaryk, 1:41. On this tendency of Russia to see itself as a realized utopia, see also Szamuely, p. 61.

30. On the ideology of *translatio imperii* and the Third Rome theory, see Stremooukhoff, p. 85, and Treadgold, pp. 20–21. For fuller bibliographical references on the Third Rome and its sources, see also Wolff, p. 196n.

31. Curtius, pp. 28–29. Among the biblical justifications for the theory of translation of empire were Ecclesiastes 10:8 (which stated that "because of unrighteous dealings, injuries, and riches got by deceit, the kingdom is transferred from one people to another") and Daniel 2:31ff and 7:3ff (which described King Nebuchadnezzar's allegorical dream of a statue ["image"] composed of gold, silver, brass, iron, and clay representing successive kingdoms that would rule over the earth until ultimately God would "set up a kingdom that will never be destroyed").

32. This 1439 council was later depicted by the Orthodox Church as the main "heresy" for which God toppled Byzantium and translated his favor to Russia.

33. "Slovo izbrano . . . na latynu," in Andrei Popov, p. 360. See also pp. 392 and 395 for similar imagery.

34. Quoted in Voyce, pp. 25–26. This tale, with its false genealogy of the Vladimir princes (who, it claimed, were descended from Caesar Augustus and the Byzantine emperors), was used by Ivan IV to justify his claim of being the head of all Orthodox Christians (Terras, p. 420). For more on such false genealogies and their relationship with the theory of translation of empire, see Wieczynski, 30:48.

35. Although the specific role of Filofei's writings in the development of Russian messianism is debatable, the general idea of Russia as Third Rome did remain a strong component in Russian nationalist and messianic writings. For example, the first Russian patriarch, Job, insisted on including the wording of Moscow as Third Rome in the 1589 foundation charter of the Moscow Patriarchate (Dvornik, p. 387n; Wolff, p. 190). And in the preface to his 1680–81 florilegium called *Vertograd* (*The Garden*) Timofei Kamenevich-Rvovskii said that his work was written "in our great and glorious Slavo-Russian state of the Third Rome, the kingdom of Muscovy" (quoted in Sazonova, "Myslennyi sad," p. 91). Indeed, as late as the Napoleonic invasion of 1812, the image of Russia as Third Rome was still being used in literature, as in the anonymous "Sti-

khi o Frantsii": "The hypocrite Napoleon, after gathering a large force, went from summer to winter into the Third Rome" (quoted in Cooper, p. 180).

36. Cherniavsky's translation, *Tsar and People*, p. 38. The argument for Moscow as Third Rome is also stated or implied in several other documents, including a letter of about 1524 from Filofei to Deacon Munekhin of Pskov, in which he accents the idea that "our Roman Empire remains indestructible." See Malinin, appendix, p. 42, and Stremooukhoff, p. 95. For an excellent summary on the various ideas and controversies on the Third Rome, see Goldfrank. See also the extended version of the "Povest' o belom klobuke" ("Tale of the White Mitre"), where Pope Sylvester prophesies to the patriarch of Constantinople in a dream: "But in the Third Rome, which will stand in the land of Russia, the grace of the Holy Ghost will shine forth; and know, then, that all Christian men in the end will enter into the Russian kingdom for Orthodoxy's sake" (quoted, with changes, from Soloviev, p. 19). In this tale, translation of empire was also justified by "translation of regalia"—an argument that Russia was connected with the previous two Romes because the archbishop of Novgorod wore a mitre supposedly given by Pope Sylvester to Emperor Constantine of the "Second Rome."

37. On the addition of the "apple" to the Muscovite imperial regalia, see Medlin, p. 145. On the symbolism of the apple, see Comito, pp. 8–9, and Hall, *Dictionary*, p. 30.

38. Stuart, "Flowering," p. 97; Maschkowzew, p. 110. On the connection of the Mother of God to paradise, see the section The Spiritual Paradise later in this chapter.

39. Stuart, "Flowering," p. 97.

40. Cf. Florovsky's point that only considerably after Filofei did official publicists reinterpret Filofei's apocalyptic scheme in a panegyric sense (p. 12). His Third Rome theory was then transformed, according to Florovsky, into a distinctive theory of "semi-official chiliasm."

41. Of course, secularization had had much earlier roots in Russia—perhaps as early as around 1500 when Ivan III seized church lands in Novgorod.

42. Medlin, pp. 165–69.

43. Quoted in Szamuely, p. 105.

44. From the 1619 granting of the title of "Grand Sovereign" to Patriarch Filaret through the self-imposed exile of Patriarch Nikon in 1658, there had been, in effect, two tsars in Russia. To counteract such "competition," Peter not only appointed no new patriarch after the death of Patriarch Adrian in 1700 but "usurped" rituals and imagery previously used by the patriarch; for example, Peter was led on a donkey

into Moscow, just as newly initiated patriarchs had previously been led in imitation of Christ's entry into Jerusalem.

45. Pascal, *Avvakum et les débuts du Raskol*, quoted in Pipes, *Russia Under the Old Regime*, p. 239. Pipes has argued that as the state destroyed the independence of the church during the eighteenth century, the state developed a secular ideology that "sought to realize on this earth the paradise that Christianity had promised to provide in the next" (p. 245).

46. Quoted in Freeze, p. 13.

47. Cherniavsky, *Tsar and People*, pp. 33–36.

48. Polotskii, p. 206. Although the word *myslennyi* had other meanings during the seventeenth and eighteenth centuries, Polotskii's parataxis (where he equates *myslennyi Edem* with *dukhovnyi rai*) makes the meaning here unquestionable. See also Akademiia nauk SSSR, *Slovar' russkogo iazyka XI–XVII vv.*, 9:332.

49. Panchenko, p. 106. Published at the patriarch's own Iver Monastery, this 1659 book included the first heraldic verse in Russian literature—written in honor of an imaginary coat of arms of Patriarch Nikon.

50. "Privetstvo 10" from *Rifmologion*, in Polotskii, p. 144.

51. On Alexis and secularization, see Medlin, p. 214.

52. This image is mentioned, for example, in the discussion of Lazar' Baranovich's 1674 manuscript *The Trumpets of Preached Words* in Sazonova, "Myslennyi sad," p. 78.

53. Sazonova, pp. 71, 78, 86.

54. In the eighty years between Polotskii's *Garden of Many Flowers* and Lomonosov's 1759 Name Day Ode, the word *mysl'* was in the process of changing meanings from "spirit" to "thought." So the phrase *rai myslei* could also have meant "paradise of our *thoughts*." However, given the "heavenly" context of Lomonosov's ode, I have retained the word "spirits" in my translation.

55. Text in Vengerov, 1:319.

56. The paradise myth was often used in eighteenth-century "praise weaving" (*pletenie pokhval*)—a term probably coined by A. P. Sumarokov to link contemporary panegyric poetry with the old Russian style of *pletenie sloves*. See, for example, his "Congratulatory Odes on the First Day of the New Year," in Sumarokov, 1957, pp. 49–53.

57. From archival sources quoted in Pokotilova, p. 73. On the general influence of Polotskii on Lomonosov, see Sazonova, "Ot russkogo panegirika," and Pokotilova. In Polotskii's poetry, the paradise myth was extensively used for the first time in connection with all aspects of the tsar's person and surroundings, reflecting the movement of the state in a more secular direction. For example, Polotskii's 1671 "Privetstvo" to Tsar Alexis on his move to Kolomenskoe praises the beauty of the tsar's

new home by comparing it with the palace of Solomon and by stating that "the paradise that was planted by God in the beginning was hardly brighter in its decoration" (Buslaev, p. 330). Elsewhere, Polotskii wrote: "I now dare to call this house heaven since I went into it to be with the Tsar" (quoted from archival materials in Pokotilova, p. 73). This comparison of the tsar's home to paradise is particularly interesting since it represents the converse of a frequent Byzantine image comparing paradise to the court of a monarch—an image that reflected the glitter and luxury at the Byzantine court.

58. Lomonosov, 1950, 8:749. This poem refers to the fact that the Ural Mountains were supposed to provide a base for Falconet's statue of Peter the Great to be erected in Petersburg (Morozov notes to Lomonosov, 1965, p. 526). In effect, Peter is depicted here as transfigured (shining like an "immortal") through his statue—a theme that we shall explore later in this chapter.

Accession Day odes were written every year to commemorate the day on which the reigning monarch came to the throne (as opposed to Accession odes, which were written only once, for the monarch's formal accession to the throne). In a year when a tsar died, like 1761, there were often both an Accession Day ode to one monarch (before his or her death) and an Accession ode to the new monarch.

59. Lomonosov, 1950, 8:756. Pokotilova notes the influence on Lomonosov of Polotskii's lines describing the "bright stars of the Russian heaven" (p. 72).

60. Although some critics might argue that these images are simply mechanical topoi, it is significant that such tropes became frequent in Russian culture during just this period of secularization and renewed nationalism.

61. Ushakov's "icon" (which was commissioned by Tsar Alexis not long after the Church Council of 1666 had demoted Nikon) thus stressed the unity between church and state and the continuity between Russia's present and its past (and hence between the new Romanov tsars and the earlier "gatherers of the Russian lands").

62. On the cosmic tree, see Eliade, *Patterns*, pp. 298–300. Ushakov's tree has likely roots in two other traditions in world art: the tree of life (which also was represented as a cosmic tree) and the tree of Jesse (which also contained medallion portraits).

63. The motif of the rose without thorns (which symbolized paradise) was fairly common in patristic writings. For a fairly complete list of Church Fathers who used this image, see Corcoran, p. 21, n.17. On the rose without thorns in eighteenth-century Russian literature (including Derzhavin's famous "Felitsa"), see the section Paradisal Flowers and Fruits in Chapter 4 below. On the grape, see Mathew, p. 39, who notes

that vine tendrils were quite frequent in Byzantine art, symbolizing the "True Vine" onto which the Christian is grafted through participating in Christ. Cf. the third repetition of the Trisagion in the Orthodox liturgy of St. John Chrysostom: "Look down from heaven, O God, and behold and visit this *vine* which thou hast *planted* with thy right hand, and establish it" (text in Orthodox Eastern Church, *Service Book*, pp. 86–87). I am grateful to Professor Ronald Vroon for this quote.

64. Pypin, "Lomonosov i ego sovremenniki," pp. 313–14.

65. For another treatment of this theme of sacred kingship in Russian cultural history, see Zhivov and Uspenskii.

66. Polotskii's proclamation to Tsar Alexis is quoted in Pokotilova, p. 74.

67. See, for example, the discussion of Lomonosov's 1759 Name Day Ode to Tsar Elizabeth in the section on the spiritual paradise above. As we noted, the poet calls Elizabeth "the clear *image* of the cloudless heavens" (*"nebes bezmrachnykh obraz iasnyi"*—Lomonosov, 1950, 8:648). Lomonosov's lines are in turn alluded to as late as the opening stanza of Derzhavin's 1805 poem "The Voice of St. Petersburg Society," which addresses Tsar Alexander I through the language of earthly images, mirrors, and reflections of heaven (Derzhavin, 1864, 2:574).

68. Lomonosov, 1950, 8:82–102.

69. Compare the frequent tendency in the late fifteenth century to call Russia's enemies "pagan," "godless," "damned," or "cursed" (Malinin, pp. 147, 357).

70. For the text and context of this June 8, 1680, ukase, see Zhivov and Uspenskii, p. 75. On the eighteenth-century depiction of the monarch as the earthly representative of God the Father, see the sections on repeating the cosmogony in Chapter 3 and on the patriarchal utopia in Chapter 6 below.

71. In many eighteenth-century Russian panegyric poems, female monarchs were given attributes not only of Christ but of the Mother of God as well. On this, see the section The Virgin Goddesses of Paradise below.

72. See D. G. Levitskii's own description of his 1783 allegorical portrait of Catherine II as the Giver of Laws, which portrays the temple of the goddess of Justice, where "her imperial majesty . . . is burning poppies on an altar and *sacrificing her own peace for the peace of all*" (quoted in Chegodaeva, p. 78). As Marc Raeff has observed: "The tsar's lot is to be pitied, and his command obeyed in a spirit of compassion and forgiveness. This is why the ruler is seen as a Christ-like figure, for like Christ he has accepted the burden of power . . . to help men to the good life" ("In the Imperial Manner," pp. 235, 237).

73. Uspenskii, "Historia," p. 68. Uspenskii notes that on the surface

the word "christs" was used in its etymological sense of "anointed ones" but that the identification with Jesus was completely intentional.

74. Zhivov and Uspenskii, pp. 109ff; Uspenskii, "Historia," p. 68.

75. Quoted in Cherniavsky, *Tsar and People*, p. 86n.

76. Petrov, "Na zakliuchenie s Ottomanskoiu portoiu mira" in Vengerov, 1:368. Later, the poem uses the iconic convention, stating that Catherine is "the image of the all-powerful Deity" (1:369). Several additional examples of this use of biblical citation to equate the monarch with Christ are given in Cooper, pp. 93ff.

77. Uspenskii, "Historia," p. 69.

78. The image of the tsar as "earthly god" was so essential to the courtly etiquette of the last part of the seventeenth century that even evil kings depicted in literature were called by this epithet (Robinson, *Bor'ba idei*, chapter 2, esp. p. 157). Polotskii in his *Rifmologion* wrote that "in books every king (*tsar'*) is called an earthly god" (quoted in Robinson, p. 143).

The epithet *bogopodobnyi* ("godlike") was applied particularly frequently to Catherine the Great during her rule. For example, Ippolit Bogdanovich in a 1783 article on contemporary poetry notes how fortunate Russian writers are "to be supported now by the godlike Catherine" (*Sobesednik liubitelei rossiiskogo slova* 2 [1783]:140–41). See also the discussion of Derzhavin's "Felitsa" in the section Enlightening Paradise in Chapter 7 below. For a powerful satire on the idea of the tsar as the Russian God, see P. A. Viazemskii's poem "Russkii Bog" ("The Russian God," 1818).

79. Lomonosov, 1950, 8:611. Lomonosov also wrote: "If someone like you [Peter] had appeared in ancient times, would the people have called you the great father of the fatherland? No, they would have called you a god" (8:611). This speech calls attention to the transformed survival of ancient ruler cults in the panegyric culture of eighteenth-century Russia. On this, see Christian into Classical later in this chapter; on later criticism of such ruler cults, see the section Enlightening Paradise in Chapter 7 below.

80. *Sobesednik liubitelei rossiiskogo slova* 2 (1783):102.

81. Quoted in Cherniavsky, *Tsar and People*, p. 78.

82. It is likely that the Byzantine practice of icon painting was influenced by the Hellenistic cult of the emperor's portrait or "image" in the Greece of Alexander the Great and his successors. See Mathew, pp. 96–99. The usage of large, formal, iconlike portraits of political leaders during holidays and other festivals in the Soviet Union to some extent recapitulates this history of the icon and particularly its political heritage.

83. Cherniavsky sees the reign of Peter the Great as the turning point from medieval political theory to "early modern absolutism" (*Tsar and People*, pp. 93, 99). However, it is likely that elements of medieval theory and "modern" absolutism coexisted in Russian ideologies from the reigns of Alexis to Catherine II.

84. *Rifmologion*, quoted in Robinson, *Bor'ba idei*, p. 84. The specific "example" of this mimetic ethic given in Polotskii's poem is that of the French king Francis I (reigned 1515–47).

85. This basic principle was well articulated by Simeon Polotskii in his poem "Nachal'nik" ("The Leader") in *Vertograd mnogotsvetnyi*: "That country is happy and happy the city where a good leader is installed, but woe to the city and the country that an immoral leader rules. Where the leadership is bad, God's anger is there; where the leadership is good, His grace is there." The relationship between a tsar and his people, like that between the good tsar and God, was thus seen as being "iconic." See Polotskii, p. 13.

86. L'vov, *Khram istiny*, p. 46.

87. Lomonosov, 1950, 8:96, 99.

88. Stuart, *Ikons*, pp. 33, 176. See also the sections Paradise Unshrouded and The Paradise Myth in Masonic Fiction (especially parts dealing with the myth of Adam Kadmon in Freemasonry) in Chapter 5 below.

89. Ouspensky, p. 40.

90. This presence of the divine light in the transfigured world is celebrated in the liturgy of the feast of the Transfiguration, when the church anticipates the light of Christ's second coming: "Today on Tabor, in the manifestation of Thy Light, O Word, Thou unaltered Light from the Light of the unbegotten Father, we have seen the Father as Light and the spirit as Light, guiding with Light the whole of creation" (quoted in Meyendorff, *Byzantine Theology*, p. 219).

91. Quoted and translated in Hippisley, *Style*, p. 18. The idea of the tsar as the "light of all Russia" occurs as early as Polotskii's *Rifmologion* (Robinson, *Bor'ba idei*, p. 78). Such imagery of light used for the tsar had earlier been used for saints in hagiographies. For example, in the "Life of Saints Boris and Gleb" in the Primary Chronicle, the two saints are said to be "shining forever like beacons" and appearing "amid bright rays enlightening . . . the whole land of Rus." Elsewhere, they are said to be "brightly irradiate with the luminance of God" and "illumined forever with light divine." As a result, they "enlighten the souls of the faithful" (*Russian Primary Chronicle*, p. 129).

On another level this image may also have implied that the tsar was a lighthouse for the ship that was Russia (of which he was also "helmsman"). For examples of the helmsman/ship, light/lighthouse system of imagery, see Robinson, *Bor'ba idei*, p. 78.

92. Robinson, *Bor'ba idei*, p. 75. The Russian word *svetlyi* ("bright") was etymologically linked with the word *sviatyi* ("holy"). On this, see Cherniavsky, *Tsar and People*, chapter 4, and Soloviev.

93. On the comparison of the tsar's throne to Mount Tabor, see Zhivov and Uspenskii, p. 116.

94. Text in Vengerov, 1:368; sections of this poem are also quoted in Cooper, p. 93. Sometimes poems depicting Catherine as the giver of laws used the image of light shining from her to refer *not* to Christ but to Moses descending from Sinai with the Ten Commandments, emitting light and thus prefiguring the transfigured Christ. See Zhivov and Uspenskii, p. 116n, and the section From Eunomia to Eutopia in Chapter 6 below.

95. Text in Vengerov, 1:primechaniia i dopolneniia, p. 72.

96. In old Russian literature, solar attributes were often used to designate the good in words like *svetozarnoe* ("shining," "radiant"), *zlatozarnoe* ("golden-dawned"), and *presvetloe* ("very radiant") (Adrianova-Perets, pp. 25–36).

97. In still other poems, light is associated with celebration—especially with the "shining" of fireworks to mark a victory; so "Shining Russia" may simply be "Russia Victorious." On such fireworks and their connection with the paradise myth, see Chapter 3 below.

98. On the equation "tsar-sun" and its link with the absolutist tradition, see Grebeniuk, pp. 190ff, and Sazonova, "Ot russkogo panegirika," p. 112. Just as the tsar was the sun, his wife was often the moon in seventeenth-century panegyrics. But by the time of the Russian-Turkish conflicts of the eighteenth century, the moon (which came to represent Turkey because of the half-moon on its coat of arms) was more often negative than positive. See Chapter 6 below.

During the seventeenth century, the image of Christ as a "spiritual sun" (*myslennoe solntse*) was sometimes used in Russia (Grebeniuk, p. 190). Grebeniuk notes that this image was also used for Tsar Alexis.

99. The idea of one's nation as a land sacred to God or the gods recurs in literature from the Old Testament to Pliny, Virgil, Ronsard, and many American writers of the seventeenth and, especially, eighteenth centuries. Thus, when Pliny wrote in his *Natural History*, "This is Italy, sacred to the gods" (III, xx, 138), he was using a formula that would often be applied by poets to their homelands. Such nationalism was at the root of the paradise myth in eighteenth-century Russia. Indeed, as Sazonova has observed, the word "Russia" was included in a semiotic

field formed by "joy," "happiness," and "glory" during this period ("Ot russkogo panegirika," p. 120).

100. For the old Russian and seventeenth-century background of Russia as the new Israel, see Efimov. On Menshikov, see Uspenskii, "Historia," p. 69.

101. Trediakovskii, 1963, pp. 60–61. This work is a pastoral love poem to Russia, written from Paris. The persona begins his poem "on a flute" and calls Russia not only his mother but also his "dear"; in the manner of coronation ceremonies, he wishes her long life through the traditional *vivat*, repeated four times in the penultimate stanza.

102. For example, Feofan Prokopovich, in his "Speech on the Day of Saint and Prince Vladimir," wrote that Vladimir was the "founder of the spiritual Zion in our land" and called Kiev "the Second Jerusalem" (p. 477). In his 1705 tragicomedy *Vladimir*, Prokopovich had the apostle Andrew appear at the end of the play and address Kiev as a "city of God." On Kiev as the second Jerusalem, see Stupperich; on Moscow as the "New Israel," see Efimov.

103. Lomonosov, 1950, 8:649–50.

104. Lomonosov, 1950, 8:219.

105. *Poleznoe uveselenie*, May 1760, pp. 165–72.

106. Lomonosov, 1950, 8:772–81.

107. Kheraskov, *Oda na den' vozshestviia na prestol e.i.v. Ekateriny Vtoroi*, n. pag. Compare Ermil Kostrov's 1780 Birthday Ode to Catherine, which pictures her as born to "set up just courts and to carry out the promise [obet] of the Most High" and then portrays her being carried away to Mount Sinai, where God, "presenting a marvelous view of paradise, . . . writes the laws of justice for her" (text in Vengerov, 1:317–18). This poem depicts miraculous signs appearing in Russia at Catherine's birth, including rains of silver and gold and the appearance of "sweet honey" and "drops of milk," foreshadowing the golden age that Catherine would bring.

108. The image of the monarch as Moses can be traced back at least to Byzantine literature. In Byzantium, the emperor was called, among other things, the "giver of law" or "the animate and living law" (Hussey, pp. 92–93).

109. Kostrov, "Oda Ekaterine II na otkrytie gubernii v stolichnom grade Moskve," in Vengerov, 1:322. On these reforms, see Madariaga, chapter 18, esp. pp. 281–82 and 287–91. The "shining face" refers to Moses' shining on receiving the Ten Commandments, which, as we noted, anticipates the transfiguration of Christ. Kostrov also depicts Catherine as being like Moses descending from Mount Sinai with the

laws for God's chosen people in the 1778 Coronation Day Ode to Catherine (in Vengerov, 1:314).

110. Compare the statement by an allegorical, paradisal Russia in the anonymous "Conversation Between Fall, Spring, and Russia," honoring Alexander I on his 1801 coronation: "Great God, having a particular good will toward me, as he once had toward the House of King David, [has been] ceaselessly serving as a benefactor to the House of Peter the Great" (*Torzhestvennye pesni*, p. 33). Spring goes on to state that in the future she will bring to Russia "as many pleasures as were present in the paradise that God planted" (p. 35), including streams of "milk and honey, *as in the promised land*" (p. 36).

111. Lomonosov, 1950, 8:759, stanza 22. In the Old Testament, Zion was both a metonymic reference to Jerusalem (Mount Zion being one of the hills on which Jerusalem was built) and a metaphor for the earthly city of God. See Psalm 48.

112. The question of the audience for panegyric and other propagandistic literature has still not been adequately treated. However, in a state where a relatively small proportion of the population was literate, it stands to reason that the masses would not have been moved by most propagandistic allegories, with the exception of fireworks, illuminations, and those masquerades that spread from the court onto the street (see the section on courtly spectacles in Chapter 3 below).

113. Often the names of classical gods were substituted for the name of God, as we shall see below. To some extent, the use of mythological references for a monarch was typical of Baroque poetics. But as Zhivov and Uspenskii note, the Russian usage of classical mythology for sacralization of the monarch went far beyond typical Baroque conventions (pp. 124–25).

114. Medlin and Patrinelis, p. 160.

115. Cracraft, p. 81. On the Jesuit influences on the Kievan Academy and, through it, on the eighteenth-century Russian educational system, see Okenfus, and Sydorenko, chapter 5. The resulting paradox has been well stated by John Meyendorff: "A church with a Greek Byzantine tradition and a Slavonic liturgy was sponsoring schools where teaching was given in Latin according to western Roman Catholic standards and books" ("The Church," p. 318).

116. In rhetoric and poetics courses, as Feofan Prokopovich noted, students "wrote verse to the point of nausea." By the end of their rhetoric course, students became so well versed in the minutiae of mythology that they often sprinkled both their poetry and prose with extraneous mythological references—a practice reflected in much eighteenth-century literature. Indeed, Belinskii later commented that the poetry

of M. V. Lomonosov "grew out of the barbarous scholastic rhetorics of the church schools of the seventeenth century" ("Russkaia literatura v 1841 godu," in Belinskii, 5:524). Despite Belinskii's attempt to discredit Lomonosov, whose work he dubbed "so-called poetry," he did state a partial truth that many later critics have disregarded.

117. Dashkova, p. 146. In addition to von Staehlin, other members of the Academy of Sciences who helped to bring the allegorical and mythological culture of the West to Russia were: Christian Goldbach, Professor of Mathematics; G. F. W. Juncker, Professor of Moral Philosophy and Rhetoric; Christian Crusius, Professor of Classics and the History of Literature; K. F. Moderach, Professor of History; and J. W. Paus, a translator. On the role of these foreigners in the creation of allegorical masquerades and fireworks in Russia, see Röhling, pp. 94–100. Many of the mythological allegories created by members of the Academy had roots in European Renaissance and Baroque culture but reflected, as well, the more immediate influences of the German principalities in which many members had been raised.

118. This line is from a panegyric poem to Petr Mohyla entitled "Evkhristion . . . Petru Mogile" (quoted in Sobolevskii, p. 3). Even stranger combinations of Christian and mythological imagery (like "Herculean" or "Olympian" Christs) had occurred during the Renaissance in Western Europe. See Seznec, "Myth," 3:291. In the second third of the seventeenth century in Russia mythological references became so popular that even sermons and other religious writings occasionally used them. For example, Silvester Kossov in his 1635 *Paterik* (a collection of writings of Church Fathers, hagiographies, sermons, and other religious genres) compared the saints of the Kievan Monastery of the Caves to Saturn, Jupiter, and Mars (Askochenskii, 1:135, 332; Freeze, p. 93).

119. *Revnost' pravoslaviia*, in Demin et al., *P'esy shkol'nykh teatrov Moskvy*, p. 208. As allegorical references became more common, Peter was frequently identified with Hercules (representing his victory over the "lion" of Sweden), Mars (reflecting his victories at war), Neptune (reflecting his interest in the sea, and thus his navy and merchant marine), and Jupiter (representing his status as "king of the gods"). See Riasanovsky, *The Image of Peter the Great*, pp. 11–12.

120. Many of the motifs studied earlier in this chapter were repeated in Russian school dramas. For example, the 1704 drama *The Zeal of Orthodoxy* depicts the war between Russia and Sweden as a holy war between Orthodoxy and Protestantism, capsulized in the opposition between the "Orthodox Mars" (Peter the Great) and the "Bellona of another faith," who promises that she will "incite hell against the Orthodox" (*Revnost'*

pravoslaviia, in Demin et al., p. 208.) The war takes on a biblical dimension when Russia is identified with the Word of God and is aided by Jesus Navin (the Biblical Joshua), and Sweden is linked with Babylon. When Jesus Navin makes the sun stand still against the Swedes (cf. Josh. 10:13–14), the drama makes an implicit analogy between Russia and Israel, implying that the Russians are God's chosen people, destined to defeat the enemies of God (part 3, scene 7).

121. O. A. Derzhavina, introduction to Robinson et al., *Pervye p'esy russkogo teatra*, pp. 18–19. The plays in Kiev were performed during monthly readings, and the best works were presented to the public during the so-called May recreations—a festival lasting for several days (Sydorenko, pp. 120–21).

122. Quoted by V. V. Kuskov in his commentary to the school drama *Revnost' pravoslaviia* in Demin et al., p. 498.

123. On the opposition between Absolute Good and Absolute Evil as a fundamental allegorical pattern, see Fletcher, *Allegory*, pp. 222–28.

124. Like the medieval mystery play and the Jesuit school drama, Ukrainian and, later, Russian school drama often presented characters that were allegorized qualities, myths, places, or even institutions. For example, Russian school drama of the early eighteenth century included such allegorical figures as Faith, the Orthodox Church, Russia, the Russian Mars, the Iron Age, and the Golden Age. See, for example, the index of characters in school dramas in Demin et al., pp. 569–76.

125. Cf. such proverbs as *Gosudar'—bat'ka, zemlia—mat'ka* ("The tsar is our father, the land our mother"—Dal', *Poslovitsy*, 1:189). On the marriage of Father Tsar and Mother Russia and the role of wedding imagery in the coronation ceremony, see Hubbs, pp. 188–90.

126. Iosif Turoboiskii, *Preslavnoe torzhestvo svoboditelia Livonii*, in Derzhavina and Grebeniuk, *Panegiricheskaia literatura petrovskogo vremeni*, p. 179.

127. Dmitrii Rostovskii, *Rozhdestvenskaia drama*, in Derzhavina et al., *Russkaia dramaturgiia poslednei chetverti XVII i nachala XVIII veka*, p. 220.

128. Literary works from the high Middle Ages onward often equated classical and biblical myths. For example, in the anonymous fourteenth-century *Ovid moralisé* (which saw all Christian morality prefigured in Ovid), Christ was identified with Actaeon, the hunter changed into a stag and devoured by his own dogs; Ceres looking for Proserpine was identified with the church searching for the faithful. Such equations still occurred in school dramas and in manuals of poetics and rhetoric written or translated in eighteenth-century Russia (which were often extremely influential in shaping the paradise myth). See, for example, Sofronova, esp. pp. 67–71.

129. Since it was impossible, for religious reasons, to say that the monarch was God (although sometimes, as we noted, he was called *a* christ, in the etymological sense of "anointed one"), the possibility of associating him or her with a classical deity provided an escape from potential religious heresy. As Feofan Prokopovich wrote in a handbook for students of the Kievan Academy, where he taught poetics: "We should not and cannot say that a subject is greater than God's creation, or that he himself is God. But suffice it to say that he is similar to God (*podobnym Bogu*) or just slightly lower than Him" (quoted in L. N. Maikov, p. 98). On the use of classical imagery to express religious content, see Zhivov and Uspenskii, pp. 121ff, which I read only after I had completed this chapter.

130. "Faeton i Ikho," from *Orel Rossiiskii*. Text reprinted in part in Eremin, "Poeticheskii stil' Simeona Polotskogo," p. 143. Eremin notes that this poem is written in a Baroque style called *carmen echicum*, containing a rhetorical question and an answer to it (an "echo") (p. 142).

131. Lacombe de Prezel, p. 13. According to this article, the deification of emperors was often depicted on medals, which portrayed the emperor's head "in a laurel wreath and often with a covering with the inscription: '*Divus*,' i.e., deified."

132. Lomonosov, 1950, 8:109. This edition capitalizes the word "God" (implying not a classical god but the Judeo-Christian deity); the 1965 Biblioteka poeta edition does not. Given the English article, it is impossible to adequately translate what I assume is purposeful ambiguity between Christian ("God") and classical (a "god") here. Since these lines are recited by classical deities, the text on the surface implies an equation of Peter with a classical deity; but since the poem describes Peter as coming from "on high" and taking on flesh, an equation with Christ also seems likely.

133. Both the Hellenistic Greeks and the imperial Romans found that the worship of a deified emperor brought greater strength to the state. Since Augustus's attempt to create a religion of state, in which the state itself was the object of veneration and its emperor viewed as descended from the gods, the deification of the emperor and his state was often accompanied by the ideology that the emperor was to restore the golden age. On apotheosis and art in service of the state, see Hall, *History*, pp. 35–51. On the Russian "deification of state," see Cherniavsky, *Tsar and People*, p. 111. For a literary example, see "Deklamatsiia ko dniu rozhdeniia Elizavety Petrovny" (probably written by Mikhail Tikhorskii), in Eleonskaia et al., *P'esy stolichnykh i provintsial'nkyh teatrov*, pp. 510–13.

134. Quoted in Derzhavin, 1864, 1:394n.

135. See, for example, Lomonosov's September 10, 1750, ode to Eliza-

beth for "the Monarch's Very Great Mercy," where he addresses her as
"goddess" in a context of paradisal imagery (Lomonosov, 1950, 8:394–
403). A. P. Sumarokov in a 1759 allegorical ballet for Empress Elizabeth's
name day even represented St. Petersburg as a place where gods and
mortals mingle—a place recalling the golden age when the gods still
dwelled on earth: "The gods, who have descended from Olympus, . . .
converse, rejoicing at the name and blessed Kingdom of Her Imperial
Majesty" (*Novye lavry*, p. 2).

136. See, for example, Sumarokov's 1762 Name Day Ode to Catherine
(Sumarokov, 1957, pp. 66–68): "What more could Russia want? Minerva
is on her throne, mercy reigns above her! Astraea has descended from
heaven and in her beautiful former state has returned again to earth"
(1774 revised version).

137. From 1766 onward, Astraea was sometimes equated (especially
in the visual arts) with her mother, Themis—the personification of law
and order in the universe. Indeed, Catherine's reign was referred to as
both the "age of Themis" and the "age of Astraea" by some contemporaries. As Minerva says to Catherine in V. Prostoserdov's 1785 poem "A
Dream," where an ideal state seen in a dream turns out to be the real
Russia: "Nourishing your charges with generosity, you are renewing
the age of Themis" (*Pokoiashchiisia trudoliubets* 4 [1785]:233). The image
of Catherine as Themis continued until her death; as late as 1796 the
sculptor M. I. Kozlovskii produced a sculptural portrait of Catherine as
Themis sitting in a chair and holding the scales of justice.

138. Lomonosov's translation (8:74) of G. F. W. Juncker's April 29,
1742, poem written (in German) for the coronation celebration at the
Academy of Sciences.

139. [Mikhail Tikhorskii?], "Deklamatsiia ko dniu rozhdeniia Elizavety Petrovny," in Eleonskaia et al., pp. 510–13.

140. See, for example, G. F. W. Juncker's 1742 verse statement to Russia's Empress Elizabeth that she was "similar in everything to Britain's
Elizabeth" (Lomonosov, 1950, 8:76).

141. A. Naryshkin, "Oda na konchinu . . . Elizavety Petrovny" (*Poleznoe uveselenie*, Feb. 1762). Naryshkin's ode ends with an elegiac comment associating Elizabeth's death with the end of the golden age: "The
golden lights, the lantern of the Russian nation, had faded." But as
Rzhevskii's "Ode on the Accession of Petr Fedorovich" in the March
1762 issue of *Poleznoe uveselenie* shows, the motif of the golden age was
far from dimmed: "Russia's happiness is coming to my thoughts. I want
to sing the golden age. . . . The golden ages are flowering, the happiness
of our days has come" (p. 10). By the early 1760's, the golden age image
had thus become a staple of Russian political mythology.

142. Sumarokov, 1957, pp. 63–66. Quote is from stanzas 12–13. See also Wilson, who views the image of Diana applied to England's Elizabeth I as a patriotic focus for a renewed cult of chivalry centering on the protection of the Virgin (Elizabeth).

143. Lomonosov, 1950, 8:794, lines 191–94.

144. See, for example, Seznec, *Survival*, pp. 105, 266. On attempts to Christianize Astraea, see Yates, *Astraea*, p. 35. In courtly literature at the time of England's "Virgin Queen," the connection between Astraea (Elizabeth) and the Virgin Mary even reached the point where one poet, John Dowland, suggested that her subjects sing "Vivat Eliza" for "Ave Maria" (Yates, p. 78).

145. In seventeenth-century Russia, the "Queen of Heaven" (as the Mother of God was sometimes called) was occasionally identified with "the queen of sciences . . . Minerva." See, for example, the 1632 "Evkhristion" to Petr Mohyla quoted in Sobolevskii, p. 3. Minerva was often associated as well with Sophia—the incarnation of "higher wisdom" (*premudrost'*), who was also sometimes equated with the Mother of God. See, for example, Lacombe de Prezel, pp. 182, 242.

146. Lomonosov, 1950, 8:225. The reference to female tsars as "blessed among women" (Luke 1:28) was fairly frequent in eighteenth-century Russia. For example, Kostrov uses these words in his 1779 Birthday Ode to Catherine II (text in Vengerov, 1:316–17). The image was also used in panegyric references to Peter the Great's mother, implicitly making her the mother of Christ (Zhivov and Uspenskii, pp. 123–24). Among other characteristics of the Mother of God used to praise female monarchs were her "radiant gaze" and "gentle [*krotkie*] eyes." For example, in Lomonosov's 1742 Arrival Ode, the "radiant gaze" of Elizabeth is said to awaken the Russians with "new life" (lines 319–20).

147. Lomonosov, 1950, 8:224.

148. Throughout the history of the paradise myth, virginity has played an important role. For example, in the writings of the Church Fathers, virginity (considered as a spiritual rather than a physical state) was sometimes explicitly connected with a return to paradise. St. Gregory of Nyssa thus defined virginity as "the restoration to its original condition of the divine image in man" (quoted in Ladner, *Idea*, pp. 76–77).

149. Lomonosov, 1950, 8:772, 780–81 (lines 1–10, 231–50). As one of the founders of Moscow University, Lomonosov had an interest in encouraging Catherine to become a new Minerva and to create a "golden age for the sciences" by "everywhere strengthen[ing] learning" and "building beautiful temples" to the sciences (i.e., more educational institutions).

150. The image of Catherine's reign as "the age of Astraea" was even frequent in the reign of her grandson, Alexander I, who was viewed by many contemporaries as likely to move the direction of the government away from that of his father toward that of his grandmother. Many poems celebrating Alexander's accession and early years repeated imagery from panegyric poetry of the time of Catherine, including imagery of the paradise myth. For example, N. M. Karamzin's 1801 poem "To His Imperial Highness Alexander I" encouraged the new emperor to follow policies of Catherine II and used motifs typical of many odes to her: "in your very first word you are promising [the return of] *Catherine's golden age*, the days of happiness, glee, and glory, when wise statutes kept our internal peace and brought us praise from the outside" (Karamzin, 1966, p. 261). Overjoyed at the death of the repressive Paul, Karamzin (who had not joined the chorus praising Catherine during her lifetime) used "Catherine's golden age" not as a panegyric commonplace but a sign of hope for the rule of law in Russia. For a perceptive analysis of this poem, see Cross, *Karamzin*, chapter 7.

151. Rzhevskii, 1763. See also, for example, V. Sankovskii's 1764 Accession Day Ode to Catherine II, which attributes the golden age in Russia to God, who has placed Catherine on the throne: "A hundred times blessed is God, that he has cut off grief and given us the golden age with Catherine." The poem ends with the metaphorical identification of Catherine with the two major virginal goddesses of paradise (and, implicitly, with the Mother of God): "And the muses sing . . . : 'Live on, O mother of Russia, Minerva and Astraea'" (*Dobroe namerenie* [June 1764]: 249).

152. Geertz, *Islam Observed*, p. 36.

153. Geertz, "Centers, Kings, and Charisma," pp. 151, 171.

Chapter Three

1. Kantemir, satire 2, line 284, quoted in Lotman and Uspenskii, "Myth-Name-Culture," p. 17. Cf. their comment that the Petrine period is marked by a "profound belief in the complete and absolute rebirth of the country, a belief that naturally stresses the magical role of Peter the Great."

2. On the relationship between beginnings and the sacred, see Eliade, *The Sacred and the Profane*, pp. 26–34, and his *Patterns in Comparative Religion*, chapter 11.

3. Said, *Beginnings*, p. 32; emphasis his.

4. "Reliatsiia . . . v 22 den' oktiabria 1721 goda . . . ," quoted in Derzhavina and Grebeniuk, *Panegiricheskaia literatura petrovskogo vremeni*, pp.

29–30. It is interesting to contrast this view to Jean-Jacques Rousseau's in *The Social Contract* (1762), which depicts Peter as a "copyist" who had "no true genius, which is creative and makes everything from nothing" (p. 90 [book 2, chapter 8]).

5. "Kratkoe opisanie blazhennykh del . . . Petra Velikogo," quoted in Cherniavsky, *Tsar and People*, p. 85.

6. The image of Peter as parent became particularly frequent after the 1721 Treaty of Nystadt, when he was officially declared *otets otechestva* ("the father of his country"). Throughout the eighteenth century, female tsars were also called the "mothers" of their country. This image of the tsar as parent continued in Russian literature through at least the time of the Slavophiles. See, for example, Karamzin's 1801 poem "On the Joyous Coronation of Alexander I," which purposefully repeats imagery from panegyric poetry of the time of Peter the Great, stressing the idea that a monarch deserves the title of "first" not because of his name but because of his accomplishments: "[Y]ou are the *father of your country*, the second creator for your subjects, God and virtue are with you. Work hard . . . give us laws and you will be the First in your deeds" (Karamzin, 1966, pp. 265–70, stanza 17). See also Tolstoy's *War and Peace* (in a section set in 1812), when one member of the gentry urges his fellows to sacrifice everything "for the sake of *our father the Tsar*" (III, iii, 22 [book 9, chapter 22]).

7. The image of Russia as newly born was to continue throughout the eighteenth century and was often seen as a source of superiority to the dying countries of Europe. As Denis Fonvizin wrote in a January 25, 1778, letter from France: "If here [in Western Europe], they began to live earlier than we did, then at least we, as we are beginning to live, can give ourselves the form [of life] we want and avoid those embarrassments and evils which have root here. *Nous commençons et ils finissent*. I think that he who has been born is a bit more fortunate than he who is dying" (Fonvizin, 2:493). See Gleason, "Image of the West," p. 110.

8. Trediakovskii, 1963, p. 58. As we noted in Chapter 2, Lomonosov uses a similar device in his 1743 Name Day Ode to Grand Prince Peter, where Mars calls Peter Russia's "God." See also Zhivov and Uspenskii, pp. 124ff, which I read only after completing this chapter.

9. See, for example, Trediakovskii's poem "Pokhvala izherskoi zemle, i tsarstvuiushchemu gradu Sanktpeterburgu," which states that Petersburg, "where it was desolate, became Paradise" (Trediakovskii, 1849, 1:289). The capital letter on "Paradise" refers specifically to Peter's own title for his city. This poem, which begins with the words *Priiatnii breg* ("Pleasant shore"), was one probable source for the introduction to Pushkin's "Bronze Horseman" (which begins with Peter standing on "a

shore of desolate waves" and, like Trediakovskii's work, is based on the opposition of "then" and "now"). On the parody of such cosmogony in Pushkin's poem, see Chapter 7 below.

10. What are often assumed to be simplistic conventions of flattery, like the cosmogonic strategies discussed here, frequently arose from transformed myths or rituals. So while a "primitive" people like the Fijians *literally* called their coronation ceremony "the creation of the world," more sophisticated civilizations—like that at the eighteenth-century Russian court and its European counterparts—transformed the same idea into a metaphorical image or convention to praise the monarch at his coronation or some other event in his life and to emphasize the idea of this time as "sacred." On the symbolic repetition of the cosmogony, see Eliade, *The Myth of the Eternal Return*, esp. chapters 2–3.

11. Lomonosov, 1950, 8:140, and commentary on p. 919. Lomonosov discusses these lines from Genesis in his 1743 *Ritorika* and states that the Church Slavonic words *"i reche Bog: da budet svet, i byst' svet"* sound incomparably better than everyday Russian speech. On God as a "character" in the odes of Lomonosov, see Serman, *Poeticheskii stil' Lomonosova*, pp. 73–75.

12. In repeating the cosmogony by placing Elizabeth on the throne, God replaces chaos (represented by thunder, whirlwinds, floods, and even a fierce giant whose jaws "smoke with fury like Mount Etna") by cosmos, and darkness by light (Lomonosov, 1950, 8:140–42). For an interesting discussion of the general usage and context of the word *svet* ("world"/"light"), see Serman, *Poeticheskii stil' Lomonosova*, pp. 117ff. For an earlier example of this cosmogonic imagery in a panegyric ode, see G. F. W. Juncker's 1734 Accession Day verses to Empress Anna, which addressed a personified Russia: "And God's Providence, gloriously exalting you [Russia], was as follows: 'LET THERE BE LIGHT.' And so began the day when she was born" (Iunker, *Kratkoe opisanie onago feierverka*, n. pag.). This poem (which sounds more natural in the parallel German text than in the Russian) reflects the likelihood that the cosmogonic strategy was itself a clone or "rebirth" of a foreign model brought to Russia by Germans in the Academy of Sciences, who opened Russia's window to Western rhetoric.

13. Derzhavin, 1864, 3:334–36. Derzhavin also describes the messianic kingdom that has arisen in Russia under Catherine's reign, using paradisal imagery from several biblical sources: "Her cities are arising from ashes, . . . rivers are flowing through dry land, gardens are flowering in deserts, and man has risen from the dead."

14. Derzhavin, 1957, p. 100. Derzhavin wrote that the image of "dividing chaos into spheres" referred to the division of the empire into provinces (*gubernii*) (p. 376).

15. Derzhavin, 1957, p. 144.

16. Derzhavin, 1957, p. 136. The accomplishments mentioned in this composite speech include Catherine's attempt to eliminate the word "slave" as a synonym for the word "subject" and her toleration of more poetic freedom. Derzhavin is, typically, far more selective in his praise of Catherine than was Lomonosov. It is interesting to notice as well that Derzhavin uses *Russian* words instead of the Church Slavonic used by Lomonosov for the phrase "and there was light."

17. Karamzin, 1966, p. 269.

18. Given the connection of the cosmogonic theme with the ideology of absolutism, it is not surprising that the motif of a thaumaturgic tsar repeating the cosmogony virtually disappeared from literature after the Decembrist revolt. When the cosmogonic myth *does* appear in the work of a major poet after the second decade of the nineteenth century, there is frequently a problem, as in A. S. Pushkin's 1833 poem *Mednyi vsadnik* ("The Bronze Horseman"), which subtly parodies many of the traditions of the eighteenth-century ode in rejecting even enlightened absolutism. See Chapter 7 below.

19. *Vozvrashchenie zlatago veka*, n. pag.

20. Lomonosov, 1950, 8:96. The description of the "virgin" Elizabeth here resembles that of the Mother of God, who was often described by her "love" and "radiant gaze," which give "new life" to the Christian. On such secularization of sacred patterns, see Chapter 2, especially the section The Virgin Goddesses.

21. This relationship between the theme of spring and the rebirth of Russia is quite consistent until the 1770's, when the axes of Russian literature began to change, and many poets quite purposefully broke these patterns. For example, V. V. Kapnist's 1772 "Ode to Fortune" begins: "Pleasant spring has returned." In the mid-eighteenth century, a poem with this beginning would most likely have been a panegyric to Russia. But under the influence of preromantic currents, this work is a discussion of the way that love and friendship can enliven unhappy human life, like the flowers of spring (Kapnist, 1973, pp. 92–99). See also Kheraskov's 1783 poem "April," which begins as an ode to spring but ends as an elegy on man's loss of innocence (Kheraskov, 1961, pp. 136–37).

22. Trediakovskii, 1963, pp. 356, 357, 358, 362. For more background on this poem, see the section The Garden and Its Gardeners in Chapter 4 below.

23. "Slovo na pogrebenie . . . Petra Velikogo." Text in Derzhavina and Grebeniuk, *Panegiricheskaia literatura petrovskogo vremeni*, p. 279. Once again, we see here an ambiguity between earthly and heavenly father.

24. Edwin Lewis, "Resurrection," in Miller and Miller, p. 612.

25. *Poleznoe uveselenie*, Jan. 1762, p. 4.

26. Lomonosov, 1950, 8:752.

27. Lomonosov, 1950, 8:754, 756–57, 759.

28. Lomonosov, 1950, 8:62. On the use of the image of resurrection of a dead monarch for justifying succession to the throne, see the section The Virgin Goddesses in Chapter 2 above.

29. Ladner, *Idea*, p. 140; Yates, *Astraea*, p. 38.

30. On the "new Rome" and "new Athens," see the next two sections; on courtly festivals, see the last section of this chapter.

31. Vengerov, *Russkaia poeziia*, 1:596. The poem begins with a justification of Catherine's imperial policies, calling her "the monarch of vast countries . . . whom God has placed much higher than the thrones [of others]."

32. Constantine was even given a Greek nurse in connection with the Greek Project (Madariaga, pp. 383–84). According to Nicholas Riasanovsky, at Constantine's birth Catherine had medals struck with a reproduction of Constantinople's Cathedral of St. Sophia (*History of Russia*, p. 294). Another example of Greek Project propaganda was a 1791 courtly entertainment based on Catherine's own play *Nachal'noe upravlenie Olega* ("Under the Leadership of Oleg"), using Oleg's attack on Constantinople in the late ninth and early tenth centuries as a metaphor for Catherine's desire to conquer Constantinople and restore an Orthodox empire there. The ballet program makes it clear that the praise for Oleg also represents praise for "the successor of his deeds" (a phrase that pointedly uses the feminine form *naslednitsa*)—Catherine. See Krasovskaia, pp. 53–54.

33. On these images at the court of England's Elizabeth I, see Yates, *Astraea*, pp. 29–87; at the court of Henry IV, see Yates, pp. 208–14, and Vivanti. This "culture gap" of more than a century and a half justifies Weidlé's assertion that the cultural patterns of the reign of Peter the Great and his immediate successors derive *not* from contemporary Western Europe but from sixteenth-century Italy and seventeenth-century France (p. 34). To some extent this gap may be accounted for by the fact that many Russian borrowings came not directly from France, Italy, or England but through Germans from principalities that had belatedly experienced what has been called the "second Romanizing of Europe."

34. Yates, *Astraea*, p. 65; Vivanti, p. 188; and Kantorowicz, pp. 386–401. Cf. Yates's discussion of the relationship between the Elizabethan and the medieval traditions of sacred world empire (*Astraea*, pp. 38–39).

35. A somewhat similar proclamation of world empire was the "manifest destiny" idea in nineteenth-century America. As the journalist J. D. B. De Bow wrote in 1850: "We have a destiny to perform, a 'mani-

fest destiny' over all Mexico, over South America, over the West Indies and Canada. . . . The eagle of the [American] republic shall poise itself over the field of Waterloo, after tracing its flight among the gorges of the Himalaya or the Ural mountains, and a successor to [George] Washington ascend the chair of universal empire" (quoted in Thompson, p. xv).

36. *Vozvrashchenie zlatago veka,* n. pag. Connections between rebirth and the imperial idea in Russia can already be seen in literature celebrating Peter's 1709 victory at Poltava (which Lomonosov later called an "augury of empire," 8:584); the connection became more frequent in the late reign of Elizabeth and especially during the reign of Catherine II. Throughout eighteenth-century Russian literature, imagery of re-beginning often appears in the context of the imagery of a world empire (especially images like "the seven seas," "vast territories," and "the entire world").

37. During the eighteenth century, Russia was identified not only with imperial Rome but also with Christian Rome (representing God's favor). Only later in the century did references recur to republican Rome (representing freedom), reflecting a major challenge to the paradise myth and the autocratic traditions that it often represented in eighteenth-century Russia (see Chapter 7). The idea of a "New Rome" also occurred in American thought of the eighteenth century. See Tuveson, chapter 4, esp. pp. 94–97.

38. A. Karin, "Pis'mo," *Poleznoe uveselenie,* Mar. 1761, p. 110.

39. See, for example, Weidlé, p. 43.

40. In awarding Peter these last two titles, the Senate explicitly compared its actions with that of "the Roman Senate, [which awarded] such titles publicly for notable deeds" (quoted in Shubinskii, p. 42).

41. Jansen, pp. 149, 445, 449. In imperial Rome, equestrian statues were reserved only for the emperor, signifying his control over the "reins" of his empire. Falconet's statue probably had some more modern intermediaries such as Bernini's equestrian statue of Louis XIV.

42. Billington, p. 236. In consonance with the "Roman vogue," Falconet's *Bronze Horseman* even included a *Latin* inscription, *Petro Primo Catherina Secunda* (with a Russian translation *Petru Pervomu Ekaterina Vtoraia* ["To Peter I, Catherine II"]), implicitly depicting Catherine (who had commissioned the statue) as the direct successor to Peter (as "the second" is to "the first"). On the idea of Peter as *first,* see Uspenskii, "Historia," p. 70, and note 6 above.

43. In Old Russian, the words for dragon and snake were the same (*zmii, zmei*).

44. In traditional Christian iconography, the dragon/serpent often

represented paganism, and St. George stood for Christianity. Since the Christian church was, as we noted in Chapter 2, often represented as "paradise," St. George was restoring mankind to "paradise" by destroying the "serpent." There is even an explicit link in the Orthodox liturgy between the return to paradise and the crushing of a serpent. See the eighth-century hymn from the Christmas vespers quoted in the section Heaven on Earth in Chapter 2.

45. Lotman and Uspenskii, "Echoes," pp. 57–58. This article argues that much of the Rome symbolism of St. Petersburg was intended to emphasize the idea of the new capital replacing Moscow, the original site of the "Third Rome."

46. *Trudoliubivaia pchela*, Oct. 1759, p. 588.

47. Sumarokov, "Slovo 5-oe: na otkrytie Imperatorskoi Akademii Khudozhestv," quoted in Antsiferov, *Dusha Peterburga*, p. 52. In this work, Sumarokov predicted that Petersburg would be eternal as long as "the throne is not transferred from [it]."

48. See Sumarokov, 1957, pp. 49–53.

49. *Ezhemesiachnye sochineniia*, Dec. 1756, p. 551.

50. A similar paraphrastic technique is used in many panegyric poems of the mid-eighteenth century. For example, Aleksandr Karin's verse "Pis'mo" states that Peter the Great was "planting gardens of science on the Neva [see Chapter 4], so that the Russians, tasting its useful fruits, could show the world that ancient Rome has begun to blossom again among the Russians." It is clear that the Roman, the "scientific," and the garden motifs here stand simply for a generalized ideal land.

51. *Drevniaia rossiiskaia istoriia*, in Lomonosov, 1950, 6:170.

52. Some of the attempts to find glory in the Russian and Slavic past were so outlandish that one wonders whether the historian Vasilii Tatishchev may have been correct after all in his claim that the Slavs were descended from an ancient tribe called the *alazons*, whose name he took to be derived from a Greek word meaning "glory"—missing its connotation of "pretender," "imposter," "deceiver," or "braggart."

53. *Trudoliubivaia pchela*, Jan. 1759, p. 16. To some extent this idealization of classical antiquity reflects the influence of Western neoclassicism. On the various stages and degrees of Russian interest in classical antiquity, see Segel, "Classicism and Classical Antiquity."

54. Lomonosov, 1950, 6:170.

55. Lomonosov, 1950, 6:170–71; Rogger, pp. 215–16. On the basis of this equation, Lomonosov borrowed the periodization of Roman history for his *Ancient Russian History*, noting similarities between the first Roman kings and the early Russian princes, between the democratic

period in Roman history and the division of the Russian lands into principalities and free cities, and between the rule of the Caesars and that
of the Moscow autocrats.

56. On the invention of a Slavic mythology and its relationship to
national consciousness, see Rogger, pp. 167–71.

57. *Trudoliubivaia pchela*, Jan. 1759, p. 16.

58. M. I. Popov, *Dosugi*, 1:177. Similar ideas are found in the journal
I to i sio, Nov. 1769, week 46, and in Lomonosov, 1950, 6:170.

59. Chulkov, part 1, evening 1. References to Kii (one of three brothers
who founded Kiev, after whom the city was named), like references
to the apostle Andrew (brother of St. Peter, who had visited the site
of the future Kiev and predicted a great future for Russia), reflect the
importance of the Primary Chronicle to literature and history written in
eighteenth-century Russia. On St. Andrew, see Lotman and Uspenskii,
"Echoes," p. 58.

60. Among other idealized Slavic kingdoms is one in Kheraskov's
Kadm i Garmoniia (1789), which so impresses the Greeks Cadmus and
Harmonia that they decide to remain there forever. See Chapter 6 below.

61. Riasanovsky, *Russia and the West*, p. 89.

62. Trediakovskii, 1849, 2:lxiii.

63. Silbajoris, pp. 73–74.

64. Between 1762 and 1796 there were translations of at least nine
different Roman histories, beginning with Trediakovskii's translations
of Charles Rollin's sixteen-volume history and of four volumes of Jean-
Baptiste Crevier's twelve-volume work. Most translations focused on
the imperial period, though some covered the broad range of history
from "legendary times" to the reign of Charles V or Francis II. For a full
listing of works concerning ancient Roman and Greek history published
in eighteenth-century Russia, see *Svodnyi katalog*, 5:129. The catalog
has nineteen listings under "ancient Roman history" and twelve under
"ancient Greek history." At least two poets—Trediakovskii and Bogdanovich—translated Roman histories. There were also several original
Russian works on Roman history.

65. On the translations of Plutarch into Russian in the eighteenth
century, see *Svodnyi katalog*, 2:432.

66. Although Emin's work appeared two years before the first Russian
translation of Plutarch, it is unlikely that his choice of Themistocles was
totally separate from the decision to include this life as one of eight (out
of Plutarch's fifty) in the Russian translation. Indeed Emin was teaching
foreign languages at the Cadet Corps at the time that the translation of
Plutarch (from the French) was being prepared there and was "inten-

sively involved with [its] circle of translators" (V. P. Stepanov, "Fedor Aleksandrovich Emin," in *Kratkaia literaturnaia entsiklopediia*, 7:892–93).

67. On the imperial expansion in Catherine's reign, see Raeff, "In the Imperial Manner."

68. *Sobranie novostei*, Dec. 1775, pp. 33f.

69. The struggle between the Russian eagle and the Turkish moon (the figures in their respective coats of arms) is frequently seen in Russian literature of the last third of the century.

70. *Torzhestvuiushchaia Rossiia*, n. pag.

71. Trediakovskii, 1849, 1:400. I assume that Trediakovskii was using the word "dragon" (*zmii*) in its frequently used Old Russian metaphorical sense of an enemy of Christianity. Cf. the Kievan cycle of *byliny*, where Christian Kiev is frequently threatened by dragons/snakes (pagans). See also note 44 above.

72. Lomonosov, 1950, 6:170.

73. Cf. the Venerable Bede's assertion that "when Rome falls, . . . the world will also fall" (quoted in Thompson, p. xiii).

74. Kheraskov, *Khram rossiiskogo blagodenstviia*, n. pag.

75. *Rastushchii vinograd*, Jan. 1786, pp. 3–4.

76. Cf. Vasilii Sankovskii's 1762 "Ode to Tsarevich Pavel Petrovich," which begins: "This day gives birth to gladness and gives hope to all, that God is watching Russia and that through eternity Russia will never fall." See also Filofei's statement (Chapter 2) that the Third Rome "will not fall to others."

77. Sumarokov, *Novye lavry*, n. pag. Lomonosov similarly depicts new Virgils and Horaces arising in Russia as a result of the reforms introduced by Peter the Great and Elizabeth: "How can there not be Virgils and Horaces at this time? Elizaveta Augusta is ruling. . . . Great Moscow has been encouraged by the singing of the new Parnassus" ("Predislovie o pol'ze knig tserkovnykh v rossiiskom iazyke," Lomonosov, 1950, 7:592).

78. Lomonosov, 1950, 8:614. Similar hyperbolic comparisons showing the superiority of contemporary Russia to ancient Rome are found in Trediakovskii's "Ode Celebrating the Surrender of the City of Gdansk" (1734), which presents Tsar Anna as being "more august than Augustus" (*Anna Avgusta avgusteisha*, Trediakovskii, 1963, p. 134). It is possible that Trediakovskii may also have been referring to the Polish king Augustus III, whom the Russians supported against Stanislaw Lesczynski during the War of Polish Succession. See Strochkov notes to Trediakovskii, 1963, p. 486.

79. Lomonosov, 1950, 8:611. "Cato" refers to M. Porcius Cato ("Cato the Censor" or "Cato Major"), as distinguished from the republican Cato to be discussed in Chapter 7 below.

Under the influence of Lomonosov and others, the topoi of *trans-latio imperii* and Russia's superiority to Rome and Greece appeared frequently in school poetry and drama. For example, a 1777 ode by students in the Tver Seminary portrayed the Russian paradise as superior to Athens: "Be ashamed, O ancient Athens, before the realm of Catherine. . . . In Catherine's empire, the earthly dale is like paradise in bliss, beauty, and glory, having wisdom on its throne" ("Oda" in *Raznye sochineniia Tverskia seminarii*, p. 13).

80. *Prolog v den' rozhdeniia e.i.v., predstavlennyi v gimnaziiakh blagorod-nymi uchenikami*, n. pag. The idea that Russia was superior to the great empires of the ancient world probably reflected not only panegyric hyperbole but also the influence of a great European debate called the "quarrel between the ancients and the moderns," which was related to the broad question as to whether, given the huge contribution of the Greeks and Romans, progress is still possible in any realm of human endeavor. On this debate in its Russian context, see Rosenberg, who argues that the quarrel centered on "how to imitate the ancients while articulating one's sense of national dignity and distinctiveness" (p. 197).

81. See, for example, Valentin Kataev's novel *Time Forward*, which in part was inspired by Vladimir Mayakovsky's poem "The March of the Shock Brigades," with its vows to "fulfill the five year plan in four years, [to] rush it forward . . ." (Helen Segall, "Kataev, Valentin," in Terras, p. 218; Maiakovskii, 10:163–64).

82. Orgel, *Illusion*, pp. 54–55, 72; Strong, esp. p. 17.

83. Cf. Strong, p. 52.

84. Peter the Great had a particular fascination for fireworks. Jakob von Staehlin, the Professor of Rhetoric and Poetry at the Academy of Sciences, wrote that despite Peter's tendency toward frugality, the one area where he seemed to be "wanting in economy" was in fireworks, which he felt would accustom his subjects "to the more serious fire of musketry and cannon" (Staehlin, pp. 317–18). On fireworks, see Rovinskii, pp. 175–311; Alekseeva; Maggs; Vasil'ev; and Röhling.

85. Krasovskaia observes that the practice of using titles to explain the meaning of difficult ballet passages survived as late as the mid-nineteenth century (p. 29).

86. *Novyi entsiklopedicheskii slovar'*, 21:151–52.

87. On the symbolism of horsemanship, see Orgel, *Illusion*, pp. 54–55, 75. See also the discussion of Falconet's *Bronze Horseman* earlier in this chapter.

88. Orgel, *Illusion*, p. 55.

89. It is likely that carnival elements were added to Russian festivals to make them more palatable for the masses, who were obviously not interested in their complex symbols and allegories.

90. Peter throughout his reign combined festival, carnival, and theater to propagandize his projects and programs. Even his carnivalistic
crowning of an "All Fools' Pope" and creation of the "Most Drunken
Synod of Fools and Jesters" were revelry with a cause, condemning the
excesses and immorality of the church and thus implying the need to
place it under the control of the secular state. See Kliuchevskii, *Peter
the Great*, p. 46, and Bakhtin, *Rabelais*, pp. 270–71. On *maslenitsa*, see
Massie, pp. 366–69.

91. The details on carnival are from Bakhtin, *Problems of Dostoevsky's
Poetics*, pp. 101–4. On carnival as the destruction of a reigning ideology, see the works of Bakhtin, especially chapter 4 of *Problems*, where
he notes that the courtly masquerade "killed the spirit of carnival while
preserving and observing some of its external forms and symbols; the
worlds of officialdom and the carnival are mutually exclusive" (p. 107).
For another aspect of carnival in the eighteenth century, see Smirnov,
"Zabolotskii i Derzhavin."

92. Although only one emblem book was published in Russian translation during the eighteenth century (Daniel de La Feville's *Symbola et
Emblemata*, which was printed in 1705 for Peter the Great, for whom it
became a bedside book), copies of the more important European Renaissance emblem books and iconological handbooks (including those of
Horus Apollo, Alciato, Ripa, and Caussin) were in the personal libraries
of many Russian poets of the seventeenth and eighteenth centuries. The
influence of such books is reflected in the frequent use of terms like
"symbols and emblems" and "iconological descriptions" in the program
books of eighteenth-century Russian courtly festivals and in the very
structure of these program books (a combination of drawings, poems,
and mottos corresponding roughly to the figure, poem, and motto of
the emblem book). See Maggs, pp. 31–33; Hippisley, "Emblem," esp.
p. 170; Čiževskij, pp. 323–24, 348; Morozov, "Emblematika barokko"
and "Lomonosov i barokko," pp. 94–95.

93. See, for example, the description of "various hieroglyphic figures
and carvings" in Iunker, *Opisanie*, p. 6. As Inigo Jones was quoted in
Ben Jonson's *Discoveries* (1628): "The concepts of the mind are pictures
of things, and the tongue is the interpreter of these pictures" (quoted
in Orgel, "The Poetics of Spectacle," p. 371). Words were thus twice
removed from reality. See Strong, pp. 52, 56, 58, and 255ff.

94. As at Renaissance and Baroque courts, Russian courtly art sought
to display splendor and magnificence, which were thought to reflect
the virtues of the reigning monarch. This cult of magnificence had been
justified in Renaissance Europe by references to St. Thomas Aquinas
(who claimed that magnificence was a virtue) and to Aristotle (Strong,
p. 72).

95. On this ballet, see Krasovskaia, p. 41.

96. This 1763 fireworks display used many motifs that we have already encountered. As the program book stated, the display depicted "a part of the terrestrial paradise, where people live together in vice-lessness, calm, and harmony under the shadows of fruit-bearing trees; beasts that are now wild but were then harmless live together, the wolf with the sheep, the lion with the goat, and the eagle with the dove. Astraea, the goddess of justice and truth, descends in a cloud from the heavens in order to be among the blessed people of that golden age" (*Vozvrashchenie zlatago veka*, n. pag.). This "paradise" was, of course, Russia, and "Astraea" the newly coronated Catherine II. The program book went on to link the age of Catherine with the great ages of world civilization (including the reigns of Osiris in Egypt, Lycurgus in Greece, and Augustus Caesar, Titus, Trajan, Marcus Aurelius, and Marc Antony in Rome) and to state explicitly that the ages of Peter the Great, Eliza-beth, and Catherine II in Russia have been examples of "golden ages." This same ideology dominated a July 29, 1772, masquerade held by L. A. Naryshkin in honor of Catherine II, where Astraea was depicted as holding the traditional scales of justice in one hand and a horn of plenty in the other; below her played happy shepherds, while Discord and Quarrels made their escape (Pyliaev, p. 150).

97. During this coronation festival, the golden age motif of food and drink without labor was suggested by giving the people free food and filling the fountains with wine for them to drink. See *Opisanie korona-tsii . . . Anny Ioannovny*, p. 71.

98. On the role of transformed nature in the English Renaissance masque, see Orgel, *Illusion*, pp. 54–55.

99. Kheraskov, *Veseliashchaiasia Rossiia*, p. 1. The main theme of a courtly festival was sometimes portrayed through an allegorical "temple" (*khram*), which bore such names as the "temple of perfect bliss" or the "temple of virtues of the monarch."

100. Orgel has argued that the courtly festival embodied the essence of Baconian science (as reflected in Sir Francis Bacon's *Great Instauration*) by showing the monarch's powers to include "dominion over the sea-sons, the raising of storms at will, [and] the acceleration of germination and harvest." The courtly festival thus became a ritual in which society "affirm[ed] its wisdom and assert[ed] . . . control over its world and its destiny" (*Illusion*, p. 55). For more on Baconian science in eighteenth-century Russia, see the section "Paradisal Flowers and Fruits" in Chap-ter 4 below.

101. Krasovskaia, pp. 48–50; M. Smith, *Art of the Dance*, p. 10. On Catherine's risky decision to be inoculated against smallpox, see Clen-denning. See also the 1768 commemorative medal by T. Ivanov portray-

ing Catherine II and her son Paul receiving Russia and her children in front of a temple (presumably the temple of science or medicine) with a dead monster (smallpox) lying on its step. Sotheby catalog no. 0943 (London, 1980), item 275. I am grateful to Mr. Robert Dimsdale for providing me with a copy of this material.

102. Hall, *History*, pp. 43–45, 235–38; Yates, *Astraea*, p. 112.

103. *Opisanie oboikh triumfal'nykh vorot*, n. pag. In their self-comparison with Rome, eighteenth-century Russians often imitated Roman festivals and even the Roman "religion of state." For example, the program booklet for a 1736 fireworks honoring the birthday of Empress Anna described the Roman celebrations of the emperor's birthday and then went on to apply those descriptions to Russia. In the main plane of this fireworks display, Russia was depicted as a woman making a sacrifice for the empress before an altar, and along the sides of the display were twelve smaller planes with "the very same speeches that grateful Rome pronounced on Augustus's birthday" (*Iz"iasnenie*, 1736, n. pag.).

104. *Torzhestvuiushchaia Minerva*, pp. 116–23. These vices, representing hell, were followed by two gods, Vulcan and Jupiter (representing the gamut of gods from workman to king). Neither Kheraskov in his explanatory verses nor Sumarokov in his choruses written for the celebration (and also included in the program booklet) mentions these two gods, who seem to serve only as lines of demarcation between vices and virtues.

105. In the allegorical parade that comprised this masquerade, each vice and virtue had its own entourage. In Volkov's "Description of the Grand Masquerade," each section of the procession is announced by a "symbol" (*znak*) and an "inscription" (*nadpis'*)—terms reflecting, once again, the influence of the emblem book on the courtly festival. For example, the symbol of Bacchus is "a goat's head and clusters of grapes" and the inscription is "laughter and shamelessness"; included in his entourage are dancing satyrs and bacchantes with bunches of grapes on sticks and with tambourines, satyrs riding on pigs and goats, Bacchus's carriage drawn by tigers, a drunken Silenus riding on an ass and supported by satyrs (*Torzhestvuiushchaia Minerva*, pp. 117–18).

106. All quotes from the program book to this masquerade (including the explanatory verses by Kheraskov and Sumarokov) come from *Torzhestvuiushchaia Minerva* in Stepan Shevyrev's 1850 reprint.

107. Orgel, *Illusion*, pp. 40, 61, 72; Adams, "The Staging of Jonson's Plays and Masques," in Jonson, pp. 330, 315. See especially Jonson's *Masque of Queens* (1609) and *Neptune's Triumph for the Return of Albion* (1623).

108. Adams, in Jonson, p. 316.

109. *Torzhestvuiushchaia Minerva*, p. 111. See also Derzhavin's comment in his *Zapiski* about this "marvelous popular masquerade held on *maslenitsa* of that winter" (quoted in Smirnov, p. 155).

110. According to A. T. Bolotov, the folk were singing tunes from this masquerade for several years afterward (Vlasto, "Heraskov," p. 7).

111. Bakhtin, *Rabelais*, p. 34.

112. In the Italian comedy Pantalone was an old miser (although here he is described as an "empty braggart" and thus perhaps confused with the *capitano* or braggart figure); the *dottore* was a "stupid pedant"; Arlecchino was a quick-witted and unscrupulous servant (although he is depicted here more as a clown); and the *zanni* were comic servants.

113. On the world inside out as an essential aspect of the medieval carnival, see Bakhtin, *Rabelais*, pp. 11, 81.

114. Among the virtues was the Golden Age, followed by a chorus of shepherds with flutes and of twelve shepherdesses; a chorus of singing children carrying olive branches; twenty-four golden hours; and a coach for the Golden Age, in which Astraea was riding. Unlike the parade of vices, this allegorical entourage of virtues (which would have had far less appeal for the masses) was small. Description of the virtues was left more to the poets.

115. This and Sumarokov's other choruses are reprinted in Sumarokov, 1957, pp. 276–83.

116. Segel has observed that this series of barks conveys the image of "muzzling of the satirist." Noting that the word *"kham"* in Russian also meant people of the lower classes (especially peasants), he suggests that Sumarokov may have thus implied the true source of "barking" in this work (*The Literature of Eighteenth-Century Russia*, 1:242).

117. In this debate, Catherine argued for a satire on generalized vice and Novikov for a satire on specific vices and social problems. On this debate, see Berkov, *Satiricheskie zhurnaly N. I. Novikova*.

118. Quoted in Krasovskaia, p. 52.

119. Catherine herself was apparently bored by the "unbearable allegories" of these festivals. In one letter, she wrote: "A plan for the festivities has been drawn up and it is just the same as always: a temple of Janus, a temple of Bacchus, and a temple of who knows what devil. All these foolish, unbearable allegories . . . with an extraordinary effort to create something senseless" (*Russkii arkhiv*, 1878, book 3, no. 9, p. 16).

Chapter Four

1. D. S. Anichkov, *Rassuzhdenie iz natural'noi bogoslovii* (Moscow, 1769), p. 16. Cited in KSXVIII. Cf. the origin of "paradise" in the Old Persian word signifying the royal park or garden of the Persian king (Giamatti, p. 11).

2. Domashnev, *Oda . . . Ekaterine Alekseevne . . . na vseradostnoe vosshestvie na prestol*, n. pag.

3. Although the image of a gardener is never used *explicitly* for God in either the New or Old Testament, God is called a "Gardener" in a number of patristic works (e.g., St. Basil's *In hexaemeron*) and, under their influence, in some medieval and Renaissance literature (e.g., Dante's *Paradiso*). Gardens in both testaments are often linked with Eden. It is thus not coincidental that when Mary Magdalene sees the resurrected Jesus, she supposes him "to be the gardener" (John 20:15), since Christ had planted the seeds that would lead men to the new Eden; or that Christ is apprehended in a garden (John 18); or that he is buried in a garden in Gethsemene (Comito, p. 142).

4. In the late seventeenth century, the Russia of Tsar Alexis was occasionally *implicitly* called a garden, as in *The Play of Artaxerxes*. See Robinson, *Pervye p'esy russkogo teatra*, p. 30.

5. Trediakovskii, 1963, p. 362. In this poem, as in a number of other works depicting the happy garden state, the Roman goddesses Flora (goddess of flowers and of spring) and Pomona (goddess of fruit trees and wife of Vertumnus, god of gardens and orchards) and the god Zephyrus (the West wind, described as a god since Homer) contribute to Russia's springlike rebirth. Here, as elsewhere, there is frequently an overlap between the themes of the garden and those of spring and of rebirth.

6. Sumarokov, *Difiramv*, n. pag.

7. Quotes are from the version published in the journal *Svobodyne chasy* for Nov. 1763.

8. Not long before, Kheraskov had written some very similar lines about the golden days of this very same Peter III.

9. Domashnev, *Oda*, n. pag.

10. G. S. Tatishcheva, notes to Makogonenko, Serman et al., 1972, 2:507.

11. Makogonenko, Serman, et al., 1972, 2:146. The image of fields full of ripening corn is quite frequent in the eighteenth-century Russian paradise myth.

12. Lomonosov, 8:291, 970–71n. During the eighteenth century, the word *vavilon* meant both "Babylon" and "labyrinth."

13. Kheraskov, *Khram rossiiskogo blagodenstviia*, n. pag.

14. Kheraskov, *Oda . . . Elizavete Petrovne*, n. pag.

15. *Torzhestvuiushchaia Rossiia*, n. pag. It may seem strange that works with titles like "Russia Victorious" appeared four years before the Treaty of Kuchuk Kainarji ended the war with Turkey. Such false optimism was sparked by several Russian naval victories of 1770, especially the one at Chesme, which, Madariaga writes, "ranks with Lepanto and Trafalgar as a naval battle which marked the course of history and created a national myth." There was also an anonymous 1770 allegorical ballet entitled "Russia Victorious" where Envy tries to convince the allegorical Overjoyed Russia that these victories are not real. But Jupiter proclaims his support for Russia and sends Envy to the "depths of hell." As a result, the people celebrate with joyful dances (*Torzhestvuiushchaia Rossiia*, n. pag.).

16. On Envy as a character in school drama, see Chapter 2 above. Karlinsky mentions that Envy was an ally of Lucifer in school drama, a borrowing from the Invidia of Jesuit school plays (p. 17).

17. Curtius, p. 192.

18. Quoted with changes from Curtius, p. 197.

19. Curtius, p. 200n.

20. Text in Dmitriev and Likhachev, p. 326.

21. L'vov, *Khram istiny*, pp. 40–41. Other works in eighteenth-century Russia describing the heavenly paradise in such terms include Bogdanovich's *Dushen'ka* (book 2) and, to a lesser extent, Kheraskov's *Vladimir vozrozhdennyi* (canto 7).

22. *Trudoliubivaia pchela*, 1759, p. 313. This addition of a pastoral element is typical in such eighteenth-century catalogs of ideal nature.

23. On the use of the *locus amoenus* in classical literature to praise ideal country life and oppose urban vices, see Rosenmeyer, pp. 206ff. The eighteenth-century Russian opposition of the ideal country and the corrupting city anticipated in a simplified way a major concern of such nineteenth-century writers as Turgenev and Tolstoy. Pushkin in *Eugene Onegin* introduced an ironic dimension to this opposition (see Chapter 7).

24. The influence of Horace's *Beatus ille* can be felt in Russian literature as early as Kantemir's *Satire* 6, "Ob istinnom blazhenstve" ("On True Happiness," 1738), which begins with the line *"Tot v sei zhizni lish' blazhen, kto svoim dovolen"* ("Happy is he alone who is satisfied with his lot in this life"); as L. V. Pumpianskii has observed, this Horatian formula "was repeated frequently by virtually every Russian poet of the eighteenth century" ("Kantemir," 3:206). Kantemir goes on to praise the man who "knows how to live in quiet [*v tishine*, i.e., in the country],

free from the vain thoughts that torment others, . . . separated from the noises" (i.e., from the city). Another important source of the "rural paradise" was Virgil's Second Georgic, which idealized the life of the happy farmer in the rural land where Astraea had lived before leaving the world. On other classical sources of the "happy man" and his ideal country setting, see Røstvig, pp. 24–47.

25. The last lines reveal that the praise of country life is uttered not by the poet or his persona but by a usurer named Alphaeus, who has been dreaming of leaving the city to take up farming and even calls in his money to do so, only to decide at the last minute to lend it out again. Among Russian translations omitting the last lines of Horace's epode was Trediakovskii's version under the title "Strofy pokhval'nye poselianskomu zhitiiu" ("Verses in Praise of Country Life") (Trediakovskii, 1963, pp. 192–95), which do not even mention Alphaeus. Trediakovskii himself wrote that his version is free and does not follow Horace exactly but that it corresponds with "the usage of the present times."

26. *Poleznoe uveselenie*, Jan. 1761, p. 22.

27. On the concept of the generalized satire "on vice" (*na porok*), see Berkov, introduction to *Satiricheskie zhurnaly N. I. Novikova*.

28. Quotes are from *Ezhemesiachnye sochineniia*, July 1757, pp. 66f. and 73. Trediakovskii's article was reprinted twice (in 1781 and 1782) as an addendum to the Russian translation of Giulio Cesare Croce's work called *The Italian Aesop; or, The Satiric Tale of Berthold*.

29. On the clash of country and city cultures in "Poor Liza," see Chapter 7 below; on *Numa*, see Chapter 6. See also the excellent article by A. G. Cross, "Karamzin's Versions of the Idyll," pp. 85–87. Cf. Karamzin's statement in a 1795 essay on the idyll that "innocent pastoral love must be free from all the vices which are produced by the corruption of the city" (quoted in Cross, p. 87).

30. As early as the Greek romances, love was portrayed as dwelling in a garden, and many Latin and later writers placed love episodes (whether physical or spiritual) in a garden, grove, or other "beautiful place," often depicted as a transformation of Eden. Servius, a Latin grammarian of the late fourth or early fifth century A.D., had noted in his commentaries on the *Aeneid* the connections between the words *amoenus* ("lovely," "pleasant") and *amor* ("love") (Curtius, p. 192). Comito has argued that this identification of the "lovely place" and "a place for loving" reflected the particular potency of Roman garden gods like Priapus, Flora, Pomona, and Venus, who were all protectors of gardens (p. 89).

31. These typically pastoral names reflect the tendency of much love literature from classical times through the Renaissance to border on

the pastoral. Fontenelle argued that the pastoral is a marriage of idleness and love, and the Renaissance critic Scaliger went so far as stating that the shepherds of the pastoral were so concerned with love because of their leisure, scanty dress, adequate food, and proximity to animals (Rosenmeyer, pp. 77, 201). The hero-narrator of Tallemant's novel receives his name from the Thyrsis's of Theocritus's *Idyll* I and Virgil's *Eclogue* VII; the name of the heroine, Aminta, recalls that of the shepherdess-heroine of Torquato Tasso's pastoral drama of that name; Thyrsis's correspondent, Lycidas, has the name of a shepherd in Virgil's *Eclogue* IX. Even two of the minor female characters introduced briefly in the second part—Phyllis and Sylvia—have the names of pastoral wenches. On Trediakovskii/Tallemant's *Voyage* and the Russian pastoral tradition, see Klein, whose work was received only after the final submission of this book; on the broad tradition of the pastoral name Thyrsis in Russian literature, see my article "Who Is Firs?"

32. Trediakovskii, 1963, pp. 112–13. See also the paradisal description of the place called *Malye prislugi* (original French: *Petits Soins*): "Everything is smiling there. . . . Everything there is pleasant. . . . All vices have been exiled from there, and the gloomy man turns gay. The miser freely strews his treasure, and the silent man speaks adequately. The stupid man appears intelligent, and the sweet muses sing with a loud voice" (p. 104). But this ecstasy is only temporary.

33. Giamatti argues that in the Renaissance the paradisal garden often turns out to be a dangerous and deceptive place "in which man's will is softened, his moral fiber unraveled, and his soul ensnared" (p. 126). See Ariosto's description of the pseudo-paradisal island of Alcina in *Orlando furioso* (canto VI, stanzas 20ff), "where love and lust have built their habitation, where time well spent is counted as a shame."

34. See, for example, such poems as Trediakovskii's "Verses in Praise of Russia" (1728), a love poem sung to Russia (called "my dear") on a pastoral flute, and Lomonosov's "A Conversation with Anacreon" (1761), where the persona in a verbal agon with Anacreon asks a master-painter to portray not the sensuous beloved whom Anacreon requests (in "To a Maiden") but "my beloved Mother"—Russia itself. See Trediakovskii, 1963, pp. 60–61, and Lomonosov, 1950, 8:766.

35. Since the time of Catullus, many epithalamiums were set in a garden of love. On the classical tradition of the epithalamium, see Giamatti, pp. 48n, 49–50, who notes that beginning with Statius, gardens or natural enclosures have often been associated with physical love in the epithalamium. Trediakovskii in his 1752 "Second Treatise on Versification" lists Catullus I, 56 and Statius, *Silvae*, I, 2 among the classic examples of the epithalamium. See text in Silbajoris, p. 124.

36. All citations are from Lomonosov, 1950, 8:127–36.

37. Quote is from section 294 of Lomonosov's 1748 *Rhetoric*, in Lomonosov, 1950, 7:353–55.

38. Although the narrator says that this vision is of "another country" (i.e., the Kingdom of Love), there is a clear analogy with Russia because of the royal marriage. Indeed this paradisal vision flows into a description of the young spouses in stanza 11 with no demarcation.

39. See section 313 of Lomonosov's 1748 *Rhetoric*, where this example is used (Lomonosov, 1950, 7:369–70).

40. Lomonosov, 1950, 8:916n.

41. Derzhavin, 1864, 3:259–68.

42. This point is further supported by the fact that later, in line 130, Derzhavin uses the word *uvenchat'* ("to crown," "to betroth") specifically to indicate the crown of marriage, when Natalie says to Paul that "The crown [*korona*] does not betroth us [*uvenchaet*] as much as the fact that you love me."

43. Hubbs, p. 189. Hubbs notes that the language of a sacred wedding was also used in the coronation rites of Muscovite tsars from the fifteenth through the seventeenth centuries, where the tsar was "united" with Mother Russia (p. 188). This idea of the king as bridegroom to his country had been quite widespread in medieval Europe as well (where the monarch was frequently given a symbolic wedding ring upon his coronation). One source for such imagery was probably the marriage of Christ and the church in the New Testament. See Cherniavsky, *Tsar and People*, p. 84; Kantorowicz, *The King's Two Bodies*, p. 212.

44. Five years after the wedding of Paul, Derzhavin himself was "crowned" in marriage to Ekaterina Iakovlevna Bastidon. In consonance with the emergence of an "authorial personality" in poetry, Derzhavin transferred the rhetoric of *locus amoenus* from state to spouse in a 1778 poem entitled "To My Fiancée." Somewhat like Thomas Campion in "Cherry Ripe" (see Chapter 1), Derzhavin describes the "lilies on the hills of [his fiancée's] breast, the modest zephyrs given to [her] disposition, the valleys on [her] cheeks, [her] smiles like early dawn and like the spring, the honeycombs on the roses of [her] lips that emit a fine aroma," concluding "I see in [her] the bliss of paradise" (lines 9–12, 20 in Derzhavin, 1864, 1:58–60).

45. All three flowers and fruits had been associated with Christ or the Mother of God in the Bible or in the writings of the Church Fathers. For example, St. John of Damascus, whose works were well known in eighteenth-century Russia, called the Mother of God a "spiritual Eden," a "lily of the field," and "a rose without thorns" (Sermon II on the Assumption). Christ, who himself had been called a "spiritual Eden" (for example, in Karion Istomin's poem "Eden"), was often associated with

the grape. As St. Augustine wrote, "Jesus is the grape of the Promised Land, the bunch that has been put under the wine-press" (Hall, *Dictionary*, p. 330).

46. Hall, *Dictionary*, pp. 146, 330. A link between the lily and the Mother of God was implied in one of the anonymous 1762 student "Songs to Her Imperial Majesty" written on Catherine's visit to the seminary at the Trinity-Sergius Monastery: "This earthly paradise was discovered as a result of your arrival, O Mother of the Russians. . . . [B]ecause of you there have now arisen the golden times—the happiness of all Russians, peace, flowers more beautiful than the lily" (*Kanty*, n. pag.). The implicit association between the "Mother of the Russians" and the Mother of God was not coincidental in this seminary song, which localizes the paradise myth by implying that Catherine's visit to the seminary has made it paradise.

47. The Russian tsar had been associated with the lily at least since Karion Istomin's 1683 collection *The Book of Instruction*, which contains the panegyric lines addressed to eleven-year-old Tsar Peter I: "O Tsar Peter, O most gentle child, O most fair lily of the Russian kingdom" (verse 8, quoted in Eremin, "Sillabicheskaia poeziia," p. 358). As early as Lomonosov's 1739 "Ode to Empress Anna on the Victory over the Turks and the Tartars and on the Taking of Khotin," the image of Russia as a lily also began to appear: "Russia, like a beautiful lily, is flowering under the sceptre of Anna" (Lomonosov, 1950, 8:29).

48. Kheraskov, *Epistola*, n. pag.

49. Perepechin, n. pag.

50. "Oda v pokhvalu tsvetu roze," Trediakovskii, 1963, p. 403.

51. Gukovskii, "Ekaterina II," p. 375.

52. All quotes are from the Russian text in Manning.

53. Derzhavin, 1957, p. 97. Future references will be to this edition, pp. 97–104.

54. In the poem's original publication in the journal *Sobesednik liubitelei rossiiskogo slova* for 1783 (part 1, p. 6), Derzhavin explained the name "Felitsa" in his work as standing for "higher wisdom" (*premudrost'*—a word associated often with Catherine/Minerva) and her son for "virtue." On other aspects of "Felitsa," see Chapters 3 and 7.

55. See, for example, the Novgorod Chronicle for 1347, which includes a letter from the Novgorod archbishop, Vasilii Kalik, to Bishop Fedor of Tver stating that some Novgorodians had sighted paradise on a high mountain (Buslaev, pp. 165ff).

56. It is possible that the Great Mother was known in Russia through Virgil's *Aeneid*, where Cybele is mentioned by name and called the "mother of the gods."

57. *Teatral'noe predstavlenie, prazdnestvo Roze*, p. 2.

58. In the printed version of this work, an engraving follows this conclusion, portraying a large vase filled with rose branches and a naked man holding a branch. In the background is a city (presumably St. Petersburg) with buildings recalling Peter's ministries and the Academy of Sciences. The implication is that Russia is to become the new Eden and its citizens new Adams (represented in pre-Fall nudity), all as a result of the support of the "Great Mother" for Russia's paradisal rose.

59. See Lacombe de Prezel's *Ikonologicheskii leksikon*, which states that a bunch of grapes often signifies "abundance, joy, and a land filled with good wine" and that a bunch carried by two men was often used as a "symbol of the promised land" (p. 49). In the Bible, God's chosen people are compared to a vine (*vinograd*) that He brought out of Egypt but that brought forth bitter fruit (Ps. 80:8; Isa. 5:1); in the New Testament Christ is the "true vine" who would redeem the fruit (John 15:1) (see Chapter 2 above).

60. *Torzhestvo Belogradskikh muz*, pp. 7–8.

61. The phrase "God's vineyard" had been used to refer to the Russian church at least since Kiril Turovskii's "Sermon on the Blind and the Lame" (twelfth century). Compare the sermon of Simeon Polotskii explaining the various meanings of "A Certain Householder planted a vineyard" (Matt. 21:33): "He planted a vineyard, which according to its first, literal sense is the house of Israel. . . . The second is the spiritual, allegorical sense, according to which the vineyard is the Christian church. . . . The third is the moral sense, according to which God's vineyard is the soul of each one of us" (quoted in Hippisley, *Style*, p. 14). On *Russia* as a God-planted vineyard, see also Billington, p. 149.

62. Skripil', p. 287.

63. Skripil', p. 288. Such associations of the Fall with the grape and the hop reflected a clear attempt to link alcohol with the devil.

64. *Rastushchii vinograd*, Dec. 1785, pp. 1–2.

65. Cf. Francis Bacon's statement in *The Great Instauration*: "Of the sciences with regard to nature, it is the glory of God to conceal a thing, but it is the glory of the King to find a thing out" (quoted in Orgel, *Illusion*, p. 55). See also comments on Baconian science and the courtly festival in Chapter 3 above.

66. The anonymous poem ends with some astrological imagery, stating that the planter "has on her forehead 36 large stars like a crown, . . . her belt contains six zodiacal signs" (p. 8). Footnotes explain that there are 36 "possessions" (*vladenii*) in "the Russian empire [which] extends almost 180 degrees [and] constitutes half the zodiac" (p. 8n).

67. Since writing these pages I have read B. E. Raikov's introduction to the pedagogical writings of V. F. Zuev, which concurs that "by the

word 'grape' is understood the fruits of science and enlightenment that had been planted in Russia" (Zuev, p. 18).

68. *Rastushchii vinograd*, Aug. 1785, p. 49.

69. *Rastushchii vinograd*, Mar. 1786, p. 88.

70. By the word "science," I am implying not only the natural sciences but all branches of learning (as embodied in the Russian word *nauka* and the German word *Wissenschaft*).

71. *Rastushchii vinograd*, Jan. 1786, p. 7.

72. Cf. Plato's use of the metaphors of garden and gardener to represent both his ideal state and the philosopher-king who will bring it about externally (on the level of the state) and also within us: "[A]ll our words and actions should tend towards giving the man within us complete mastery over the whole human creature, and letting him take the many-headed beast under his care and tame its wildness, *like the gardener* who trains his cherished plants while he checks the growth of weeds" (*Republic*, IX, 588–89).

73. As early as 1632, members of the Kievan Academy dedicated a poem called "Eucharistirion" to their founder, Petr Mohyla, where Minerva shows him two "gardens of knowledge" (*sad umeetnosti*)— Helicon and Parnassus (Sobolevskii, p. 3). Although in Greek mythology, these "gardens" were both *mountains* sacred to Apollo and the muses, the Russians persisted in using the image of a garden instead of a mountain—perhaps reflecting the frequent interchangeability of garden and mountain as locations of the earthly paradise.

74. In his personal library Polotskii had such florilegia of Latin writings as Meffert's *The Garden of the Queen* (Virgin Mary), Martiantius's *The Shepherds' Garden*, and an encyclopedic collection entitled *Philosophical Commonplaces; or, A Florilegium of Objects and Matter*. See Eremin, "Sillabicheskaia poeziia," p. 343.

75. Text and commentary in Drage and Vickery, pp. 3–4, 186–88.

76. *Ezhemesiachnye sochineniia*, July 1756, p. 65.

77. *Rastushchii vinograd*, June 1786, p. 2.

78. Chegodaeva, p. 52.

79. Derzhavin, 1864, 1:50–52. These positive results are later expressed in Derzhavin's poem through the metaphor (recalling that of Polotskii at the beginning of this section) of Shuvalov as a bee, who gathers the honey from the flowers of the world and returns to fill the Russian air with a "sweet-smelling aroma" (1:56).

80. This usage was sufficiently frequent that the 1891 Academy of Sciences Dictionary edited by Iakov Grot defined *vertograd nauk* as "a metaphor for an educational institution" (quoted in Sazonova, "Myslennyi sad," p. 100n).

81. Kheraskov, *Oda . . . Ekaterine Aleekseevne na ustanovliaemye vnov'* *premudrye zakony*, n. pag. On Catherine as Minerva, see Chapter 2 above. One variant of the garden of sciences image is that of fields or orchards of sciences/learning, used, for example, in Vasilii Sankovskii's verses to Catherine II on her 1763 name day, which picture Russia as an Edenic field producing "fruits of knowledge" that will never fail as long as "Minerva will be on the throne" (Sankovskii, *Stikhi na den'* *tezoimenitstva . . . Ekateriny II*," n. pag.). In this edition, an engraving shows a woman in the middle of a garden filled with trees—probably representing Catherine and the Russian Eden.

82. Tuzov, n. pag. Not surprisingly, this seems to be the only work of Tuzov's that was ever published.

83. Kheraskov, *Plody nauk*, canto 1.

84. This "scientific cosmogony" is attributed to Peter the Great, who is depicted as "resurrecting" Russia. As the narrator says, "wherever I see usefulness [*pol'za*—meaning the sciences throughout this work], there I see Peter" (p. 8). Unlike Kheraskov, I. F. Bogdanovich in *Suguboe blazhenstvo* ("A Perfect Bliss," 1765) and its shorter second edition entitled *Blazhenstvo narodov* ("The Happiness of Nations," 1773) sees the first age of man as a golden age of equality and communal property, an age without poverty and wealth. Such disagreements about the relative values of the "state of nature" and civilization occurred frequently in seventeenth- and eighteenth-century Europe, sparked by the famous debate between Locke and Hobbes.

85. This similarity is not surprising in that Kheraskov was also connected with Moscow University, where he served as procurator.

86. Karamzin, 1964, 2:134–35.

87. Rosenmeyer has noted that in classical Greek literature "there is more overt appreciation of the charms of flowers, fields, and streams in choral songs and philosophical discourses praising a *city* or political idea than there is in early pastoral poetry" (p. 106). The commonplaces of what was later to be called *locus amoenus*, for example, glorified the city of Athens in the famous choral ode of Sophocles' *Oedipus at Colonus*, where the city is described in terms of green glades, trilling nightingales, bowers of fruit and berries, clusters of flowers, and never-dying trees—a place inhabited by gods and nymphs with streams that run like "perpetual lovers" throughout the land.

88. The very idea of a garden is an extension of *city* culture, an attempt to impose human patterns of organization onto nature (Rosenmeyer, p. 195). Indeed, the word *gorod* ("city") in Russian is etymologically linked with the Latin word *hortus* ("garden")—both originally being used to denote enclosed places. See Preobrazhenskii, p. 149.

89. This eighteenth-century tendency to idealize France as a paradise

is remembered today more through its satirical treatment in works like Fonvizin's comedy *The Brigadier* (1769).

90. Trediakovskii, 1963, p. 76.

91. Most of these motifs were components of the golden age myth or other variants of the paradise myth (see Appendix A). Indeed, the golden age ideal was decidedly rural (probably reflecting the fact that it was the product of city dwellers, for whom ideal existence was far from a city).

92. It is possible that such usage of garden imagery to praise cities may to some extent have reflected the contemporary ideal of *rus in urbe* ("the country in the city"), bringing elements of the country to the city through gardens and parks.

93. On this debate, see Tayler.

94. The depiction of a conflict between nature and art in eighteenth- and early-nineteenth-century Russian literature was occasionally a means of portraying a place as an anti-utopia. See, for example, the comments on Petersburg in Shcherbatov's *Journey to the Land of Ophir* in Chapter 6 below.

95. Compare Lomonosov's statement regarding landscape art depicting spring scenes: "During the winter, we delight in the vision of greening forests, flowing streams, grazing herds, and laboring farmers" (quoted in Svirin, p. 328).

96. Derzhavin, 1864, 1:385–86; Svirin, pp. 331–32. As Derzhavin wrote in another description of this garden: "[N]ature, art, and magic itself, so to speak, by means of inanimate and immobile objects, bring such amazement" (1:409–10).

97. Quoted in Svirin, p. 331.

98. Likhachev, p. 35.

99. All quotes are from Lomonosov, 8:394–403. In the eighteenth century, Tsarskoe Selo was still known as "Sarskoe Selo"—a name coming from the promontory there called Saari-mois (Morozov notes to Lomonosov, 1965, p. 523). Given the relative elevation of this town, and the presence of "gods" and "goddesses" (the royal family), Lomonosov compares it hyperbolically in stanza 1 to Mount Olympus.

100. Lomonosov, 1950, 8:985n.

101. According to legend, the Nile was the modern name of one of the four rivers originating in Eden.

102. T. A. Krasotkina and G. P. Blok, notes to Lomonosov, 1950, 8:984. In effect, the very idea of attempting to connect two rivers through a canal—one of the subjects of this poem—represents an attempt to improve nature through "art" and thus fits well into the general scheme of the poem.

103. Lomonosov, 1950, 8:806.

104. The technique of praising a person through praise of place usually operates, as here, through a connective—either a preposition (like *pri* ["in the presence of"] or *blagodaria* [because of]) or a verb—creating an underlying structure indicating that a person has brought the good life to a place (the "messianic pattern" of Chapter 1). Almost parodying this "gilt by association" is I. P. Bogdanovich's "Stikhi k muzam na Tsarskoe selo" (1790's), which describes the town as a place where "the elements are obedient to Catherine . . . and strive to surpass the norm of nature." The poem ends: "With all of these wonders inaccessible to the mind, my Muse, having shown me the delights of these gardens, . . . ultimately forgot the intention of these verses and wants everywhere to sing the deeds of Catherine." Thus the ideal place, where nature and art combine, is seen as being so perfect that it makes the poet forget his purpose (the praise of Catherine—which is remembered only as an afterthought) and hence saves him the servile task of rhetorical praise (text in Bogdanovich, pp. 181–82).

105. *Oda pripisannaia v pokhvalu Raify*, n. pag.

106. Text in Vengerov, 1:579. By the end of the eighteenth century, poetry was occasionally depicted as beginning in Eden and sometimes linked with the lost language of Adam (see Chapter 5). As an anonymous 1785 article in *The Growing Grape* argued, poetry came into existence in Eden soon after the creation of the world: "And poetry was the first language of man because it is the most noble language, born from ecstasy and inspiration" (*Rastushchii vinograd*, May 1785, pp. 51–52).

107. Tillyard, p. 22.

108. Text in Hazard Adams, pp. 157–58.

109. Quoted in Nebel, p. 174.

110. The comparison of poetry to a garden appeared in criticism as well. For example, Karamzin's 1791 review of a production of *Le Cid* implicitly compares it to a "regular" (French) garden and Shakespeare's work to an "irregular" (English) garden: "One can compare French tragedies to a nice, regular garden, where there are many beautiful avenues, beautiful flowerbeds, beautiful gazebos. With pleasure we walk through this garden and praise it. But we are constantly searching for something and not finding it, and our soul remains cold. . . . On the other hand, I would compare the works of Shakespeare with the works of nature itself, which delight us because of their very lack of regularity and which, with indescribable strength, act on our soul and leave an indelible impression on it" (*Moskovskii zhurnal* 3 [1791]:95).

111. Vereshchagin, p. 4. The presence of a pattern in student verses usually reflects its importance in contemporary poetry.

112. V. I. Maikov, *Torzhestvuiushchii Parnass*, pp. 3, 4, 8.

Chapter Five

1. This list is based largely on Piksanov and Bakounine. Although there have been no detailed studies of Freemasonry in eighteenth-century Russian literature as a whole, there have been a number of studies dealing with Freemasonry in individual works or providing a brief overview of the impact of the movement on this literature. See Piksanov; Pozdneev; Vlasto, "M. M. Heraskov" and "A Noble Failure"; Sakulin (whose section "Masonizm" is on the style of Masonic works); Bakunina; and Baehr, "Freemasonry in Russian Literature: Eighteenth Century." For European parallels, see Schneider. For comparison, see the following studies of Freemasonry in Russian literature of the nineteenth and twentieth centuries: Weber; Leighton, "Pushkin and Freemasonry"; Senderovich, "Khram"; and Al'tshuller, "Masonskie motivy." The following historical works have also proven very useful for this chapter: Vernadskii, *Russkoe masonstvo*; Mel'gunov and Sidorov; Pypin, *Russkoe masonstvo*; and Ryu.

2. Of major Russian writers, only Derzhavin attacked the Masons in his works. On Derzhavin and anti-Masonic literature, see Baehr, "Freemasonry in Russian Literature: Eighteenth Century."

3. The moral goals of Freemasonry were, of course, similar to those of Christianity. As one Russian Mason stated: "The similarities [of the Masonic rituals for the first three degrees] with the ceremonies and rituals of our church are so perfect and so obvious that one must inevitably conclude that both . . . flow from a single source" (quoted in Eshevskii, p. 213). Freemasonry appealed to many religious men who were dissatisfied with the low moral and intellectual level of the contemporary church. As one Mason wrote: "In the early days of Christianity the vessels were wooden but the priests were golden; nowadays, the vessels are golden but the priests are wooden" (quoted in Mazour, p. 47). Freemasonry also attracted many who sought a secular outlet for their religious feelings, reflecting the Enlightenment origins of the movement (which, as we shall see below, were later challenged by antirationalist tendencies that developed in Freemasonry in the second half of the century).

4. See, for example, *Pesni v Ierusalime: 5817*, p. 14. (Henceforth, this volume will be referred to as *Pesni*.) Although this book of songs (which gets its title from the fact that Russian Masons called Moscow "Jerusalem") was presumably published in 1801 (the year 5817 from the creation of the world according to the Orthodox Church), it contains many songs previously published in eighteenth-century Masonic journals. Indeed, most of the symbolic patterns of early-nineteenth-century Russian

Masonry were inherited from the eighteenth century.

5. Quoted in Sokolovskaia, "Masonskie pechatnye listki," p. 435. The English system was the first Masonic system of lodges, founded in England in 1717.

6. From a 1764 Masonic "catechism" by Apollon Ushakov (one of the first extant Russian Masonic manuscripts dealing with the ceremonies of an English-system lodge) in Pekarskii, p. 9.

7. Quoted in Sokolovskaia, "Lozha trekh dobrodetelei," pp. 224–25.

8. Sokolovskaia, "Masonskie risunki i vin'etki," p. 50. The square and compass with which Astraea was sometimes represented were symbolic instruments used in helping the Mason to construct an allegorical "temple of virtue" within himself. One Russian Masonic song explicitly depicted Astraea as returning to earth to live among the Masons: "Who is shining there with golden wings? It is Astraea who wants to live with us" (GBL, f. 147, No. 940.4, written addendum, p. 11).

9. The two lodges were in Petersburg (founded 1775) and Riga (founded 1785 or 1787). It is likely that the Petersburg lodge was connected with the Astraea emblem of Catherine the Great, who was on the throne at that time and who had not yet begun the anti-Masonic policies that were to incur the wrath of many Masons in the 1780's. On the Grand Lodge of Astraea, see Leighton, "Freemasonry in Russia: The Grand Lodge of Astraea."

10. Elagin, *Chtenie drevnego liubomudriia i bogomudriia, ili nauka svobodnykh kamen'shchikov,* in Pekarskii, pp. 98, 110. Part 1 of this uncompleted manuscript was to consist of a historical overview of Freemasonry from Adam, Noah, and Abraham (who, he claimed, were Masons) to the knights of the Middle Ages and, finally, the more modern systems and teachings (Vernadskii, p. 136).

11. The cult of wisdom in Freemasonry came in part from three biblical books that were important to the Masons: The Wisdom of Solomon, Proverbs, and Ecclesiastes. In higher order Masonry, as in the Wisdom of Solomon, those who follow God were portrayed as resurrecting the "higher wisdom" hidden from fallen man. See, for example, Lopukhin, *Maskonskie trudy,* p. 28.

12. GPB, O. III, No. 167, quoted in Semeka, p. 351.

13. *Moskovskoe ezhemesiachnoe izdanie* 1 (1781):x.

14. On the distinction between the English-system lodges and the various higher order systems in Russia, see Vernadskii, pp. 31–83; and Pypin, *Russkoe masonstvo,* pp. 80–135.

15. "Sostoianie cheloveka pred grekhopadeniem," *Moskovskoe ezhemesiachnoe izdanie* 2 (1781):235.

16. *Magazin Svobodno-kamen'shchicheskoi* 1 (1784):28. As a result of this

Masonic stress on a return to the perfection of Eden, the paradise myth recurs throughout Masonic songs of all orders and systems. For example, one higher order manuscript collection of songs "For All Degrees" contains different wording for each of seven degrees but repeats the same chorus: "May our desire fly up [to the heavens]: May it resound in the heavens in harmonious voices, and carry down with it a golden age for us" (GBL, f. 147, ed. khr. No. 132, pp. 2–20).

17. As one Masonic song stated: "Not malice, death, or the corruption of time can ever destroy our temple" (*Magazin Svobodno-kamen'shchicheskoi* 2 [1784]:124). On the concept of "sacred space," see Eliade, *The Sacred and the Profane*, chapter 1.

18. *Magazin Svobodno-kamen'shchicheskoi* 2 (1784):132–33. The word VIVAT ("Long live") here captures the Masonic emphasis on eternal life resulting from the rebirth of the Mason.

19. Many works emphasizing the paradisal quest of Freemasonry used imagery of doors, locks, and gates to stress the separation between the paradise of the lodge and the hell of the "profane" outside world. See, for example, *Pesni*, pp. 3–4. For a more detailed discussion of Masonic songs, see Pozdneev.

20. The theme of "death overcome" runs throughout Masonic doctrine and provides the basis for the third degree, the highest all lodges have in common; it is reflected in the duty of all members to "remember death"—the Latin term *memento mori* is frequently used—and in the symbolic skulls and skeletons displayed in important parts of the ritual. As one eighteenth-century Mason stated, "death, only death, is the beginning of life" (Z. Ia. Karneev, quoted in Vernadskii, p. 145). Masonic songs often portrayed this new life through imagery of transformation (of sorrow to bliss, death to life, matter to spirit); exclusion (of vice, death, uncontrolled passion, pride); and contrast (of the sacred Masonic space to the profane outside world, of the harmonious "here" to the chaotic "there," of paradise to hell). The main theme of such songs may be seen as the rebirth of the elect to a new paradisal life—a theme emphasized by imagery of water (a traditional birth symbol), fire (a traditional purification symbol), building, and shaping. As initiates into one higher order lodge were told (in the mystical language typical of such lodges), they would "disappear in a fire of purgation . . . and be reborn in the virginal dust of the *new heaven and new earth* in the bright transparence of *pure incorruptible paradisal being*" (Lopukhin, *Masonskie trudy*, p. 22).

21. Corcoran, p. 17.

22. *Pesni*, p. 8.

23. *Pesni*, p. 7. Masonic songs often included imagery of tasting—

perhaps allegorizing the frequent banquets that characterized the movement, representing the "communion" of the brothers through the shar-
ing of food. Members were frequently depicted as "tasting" the golden
age or Eden. For example, in one song the lodge is referred to as allowing
its members to taste "the Eden of all bliss" (*Pesni*, p. 29).

24. One song represented God ("The Wise Builder of the Entire Universe") as being "impressed into the brothers' souls" and leading them
"to joyful Eden" in order to help them "spend [their] life in bliss" (*Pesni*,
p. 51).

25. The very names of the degrees in the Scottish system and Strict
Observance system reflected the desire of the Masons to resurrect chivalry. The Scottish system had six "higher" degrees (above the three
degrees of the English system) including Knight of the East (sixth degree), Knight of the Rosy Cross (seventh degree), Knight of the Triple
Cross (eighth degree), and Knight of the Royal Arch (ninth degree). See
Longinov, p. 64; Jones, p. 130.

So strong was the relationship of the Scottish order to chivalry that
their insignia bore the letters "D.L.V." (*Dieu le veut*)—the cry of the Cru-
saders; Hugh de Payens, the founder of the Knights Templar, was even
renamed "Adam" by the order and St. Ignatius Loyola (who founded
the order of Jesuits as a group of Papal knights dedicating their services
to the Virgin Mary as knights to a lady) was called "Noah" (Longinov, p. 64). The "Strict Observance" system of Freemasonry viewed
the origin of the Masonic brotherhood in the Knights Templar, and
included the title "Knight Templar" in its sixth, seventh, and eighth
degrees (Longinov, p. 68). The Tsinendorf or Lax Observance system
based much of its opposition to the Strict Observance system on its
opposition to the Templars (Longinov, pp. 78–79).

26. *Pesni*, p. 49. The song goes on to implicitly equate this age of
chivalry with *Russian* Masonry: "The brothers, enlivened by [charity],
have raised a temple in the North [Russia]; it is evident that there has
remained in Russia the knight and true Mason" (p. 50).

27. Moorman, pp. 3–7. Moorman notes that tales of medieval knights
involved the broader pattern of "journey-initiation-quest"—the same
pattern that is involved in the ritual of Freemasonry. As I have argued
in my article "Freemasonry in Russian Literature: Eighteenth Century,"
both Masonic literature and chivalric tales embodied a larger archetype:
the emergence of the hero (p. 31).

28. As the Russian Mason Ruf Stepanov stated, "we have a hieroglyphic language in our lodge" (quoted in Sokolovskaia, "Masonskie
kovry," p. 14). The use of the term "hieroglyph" reflects the in-

direct influence of Neoplatonism on Freemasonry. On "hieroglyphs" in eighteenth-century Russia, see also the section on courtly festivals in Chapter 3 above.

29. Sokolovskaia, *Katalog*, p. 44; Sokolovskaia, "Masonskie risunki," p. 48. Hieroglyphs appeared on Masonic aprons, rugs, and other paraphernalia.

30. Sokolovskaia, *Katalog*, p. 32.

31. For a useful work on Masonic symbolism in the West, see Mackey, *The Symbolism of Freemasonry*.

32. F. L. Schroeder, quoted in Sokolovskaia, *Katalog*, p. 10.

33. Tolstoy's parody of Freemasonry is in volume 2, parts 2–3 (books 5–6 in the Maude translation). The image of Freemasonry as a "bog" occurs in part 3, chapter 7 (book 6, chapter 3 in Maude).

34. Among the many alchemical writings influencing the symbolism of Freemasonry in Russia and throughout Europe were works by Lully, Paracelsus, Fludd, Welling, and Hermes Trismegistus. See Vernadskii, pp. 126–27 and 150–53.

35. Quoted in Vernadskii, p. 156.

36. *Pesni*, p. 54. The Masons often used the morning star as a symbol of Masonic "enlightenment," e.g., in the title of Novikov's Masonic-oriented journal *Utrennii svet* (*Morning Light*, 1777–80).

37. Compare Plato's idea of knowledge as "recollection" or "reminiscence" from a previous existence, e.g., in *Phaedo*, 73A, and *Phaedros*, 247C.

38. On some of these translations, see Florovsky, pp. 152, 340–41; *Svodnyi katalog*, 1:16–18 (on Augustine). For a summary of one of these translations—John Pordage's *Fifth Tract on Paradise*—see Appendix B.

39. Augustine, *City of God*, 10.2, quoted in Martz, p. xiv.

40. Augustine, *De Trinitate*, 14.6, quoted in Martz, p. xiv.

41. As one Rosicrucian text stated, there is only a "little spark" left of man's original perfection, but such lost "sparks of light" can be regained by tearing the "shroud of corruptibility" woven by the Fall (quoted in Semeka, p. 350).

42. GPB, Q. III, No. 153; see also Semeka, p. 351. Often higher order Masonry reworded the idea of man's original state being in the image and likeness of God to state that man in paradise was *microtheos*: "Before the Fall one could call man '*microtheos*,' or 'little God,' because in truth he had been made in the image and likeness of the divine Word, i.e., the god-man or the heavenly Adam. After the Fall, however, almost nothing remained from his previous marvelous perfection" ("O grekhopadenii: Otryvok iz neizvestnogo sochineniia," IRLI, op. 44 No. 5, p.3b). See also

Ivan Shvarts (J. G. Schwarz), "O vozrozhdenii," IRLI, 4880.XXV6.47, pp. 32ff.

43. Quoted in Semeka, p. 351. According to Schwarz, after the Fall "we lost our perfection" and "made ourselves an assemblage of evil, ignorance, and imperfection"—a "rotten and stinking vessel filled with all kinds of vileness."

44. The Rosicrucians attempted to regain this "spark" in their fourth or "theoretical" degree. See Shvarts, "O vozrozhdenii," IRLI, 4880.XXV6.47, p. 32.

45. Anonymous manuscript, "Razmyshleniia o nauke masonskoi," GPB, Q. III, No. 153. See also Semeka, p. 389.

46. Lopukhin, p. 49. He goes on to state that this Golden Age will return "when that which is corruptible will clothe itself in that which is incorruptible, and that which is subject to death will clothe itself in that which is immortal, [when] death will be idle and all will be in all." Lopukhin's vision relies heavily upon the depiction in 1 Corinthians 15 of the "incorruptible" resurrection from the dead when death shall be dead and God shall be "all in all."

47. Compare with the apocryphal book of the Wisdom of Solomon, which was quite popular in Freemasonry and is explicitly mentioned in Lopukhin's text (p. 29): "For God created man for immortality, and made him the image of his own eternity, but through the devil's envy death came into the world, and those who belong to his party experience it" (Wisd. of Sol. 2:23–24).

48. The focus on a ray of light in this legend is typical of Illuminist lodges—higher order Masonic lodges influenced by European mystical thinkers like Saint-Martin. On some influences of European mysticism on Russian Masonry, see Appendix B.

49. Longinov, pp. 44, 50. As chief architect of the Temple of Solomon, Hiram Abif was responsible for paying workers. Since he had so many workers whom he had to pay at different rates, it was impossible for him to know them all; he therefore paid each according to a password reflecting a worker's skill or rank. According to Masonic legend, Hiram was murdered when he would not disclose the secret password that would give workmen higher pay. These secret words and signs supposedly became the secret signs of the various Masonic degrees, and Hiram a symbol of the Mason who holds the secrets of his organization sacred even if threatened with death. For an excellent interpretation of Pushkin's "Queen of Spades" as a parody of the Hiram Abif myth and other aspects of Freemasonry, see Weber, "Pikovaia dama."

50. The Masons sometimes claimed that their brotherhood harbored the lost Adamic language. Even in their private correspondence, mem-

bers of higher order Masonic lodges sometimes stressed the ability of Freemasonry and the works that the Masons were translating to reveal knowledge not ordinarily expressible through human words. See, for example, the February 1, 1784, letter of Prince N. N. Trubetskoi to the poet and Mason A. A. Rzhevskii in Barskov, p. 264.

51. Karamzin, 1966, pp. 58–63.

52. This inward direction reflects as well the beginnings of preromantic currents in Russia, which were to some extent hastened by Masonic concerns and translations. On the connection between Freemasonry and preromanticism, see Neuhäuser, pp. 17–25. On poetry and paradise, see also the sections The Garden in the City in Chapter 4 and The Iron Age and Early-Nineteenth-Century Russian Poetry in Chapter 7.

53. Elagin, *Uchenie*, reprinted in Pekarskii, pp. 106–7. Elagin tells his readers (serving as the lodge master talking to new initiates) that he "will go with you like Moses going from Egypt with God's people."

54. The analysis of the four Kheraskov works in this section attempts *only* to present an overview of the Masonic theme and its relationship to the paradise myth. Given the limitations of space, no attempt is made to analyze all aspects of a work.

55. Despite published data that Kheraskov joined the Masons only in 1775, Rozanov argues (in part because of the absence of official records of membership in Moscow Masonic lodges for the 1750's and 1760's) that it is possible that Kheraskov became a Mason earlier than is generally believed (p. 40). Zapadov suggests the possibility that Kheraskov was one of the leaders if not the organizer of a Moscow Masonic lodge in the early 1760's and that his group of writers, centered around the Moscow University journals of the early 1760's (*Poleznoe uveselenie*, etc.), composed a "secret Masonic circle" (introduction to Kheraskov, 1961, p. 16). Although I do not find his argument fully convincing, I do feel that his conclusion may be correct by the time of *Numa*.

56. These lodges claimed that Numa divided Rome into "corporations"—one of the most important of which was the corporation of builders, which anticipated the medieval guild of stone masons ("operative" masons) from which "speculative" Freemasonry (the brotherhood discussed in this chapter) was born. According to this legend, the corporation of builders often gathered in temples since they had close relationships with priests. See Longinov, p. 46.

57. *Tysiacha i odna noch': Skazki arabskie*, 12 vols. On the Eastern tale and on translations and imitations of the *Arabian Nights*, see Kubacheva, pp. 294–315, esp. pp. 302ff.

58. Even the non-Mason Derzhavin praised "Felitsa" (Catherine II) for "not going from the throne to the *East*" (i.e., *not* supporting the

Masons, to which many of her courtiers belonged) (Derzhavin, 1957, p. 98).

59. Like Mozart and Schikaneder's *Magic Flute*, many Masonic allegories appeal to children, perhaps because of their opposition of absolute good to absolute evil. The Masonic plot frequently resembles a fairy tale; after punishing evil, it often ends in a paradise, where good people live "happily ever after."

60. The best-known classical description of Arabia Felix was in Diodorus Siculus's *Library of History*, which was translated into Russian in 1774–75. Arabia Felix was one of three divisions made in ancient geographies for the region between Egypt, Syria, and the Euphrates: Arabia Deserta, Arabia Felix, and Arabia Petraea. Originally, Arabia Felix (the southerly parts of the Arabian peninsula) meant "the fertile part of Arabia"; the Latin word *felix* meant "fertile" or "fruitful" and received its more familiar secondary meaning of "fortunate"/"happy" from this. See Harvey, p. 35.

61. *Detskoe chtenie* 17 (1789):3.

62. A second example of Arabia Felix in a Masonic-oriented work appears in a translated Eastern tale called "Ardat and Rittsa," which tells of King Alman from "happy Arabia," who tests his two sons, Ardat and Rittsa, by sending them out to seek the secrets of life. Ardat is more philosophical and learns the secrets from a hermit; Rittsa, on the other hand, goes out to live among others. Like many Masonic works, this story shows the victory of isolation and contemplation (aided by an elderly tutor or philosopher) over the life of the outside world. In typical Masonic form, the hermit-influenced Ardat is given the throne in preference to his more gregarious brother and tries to create paradisal conditions so that in all truth his kingdom would be called "happy Arabia" (*Detskoe chtenie* 4 [1785]:42ff).

63. Some scholars have argued (following V. P. Semennikov) that Kheraskov's *Golden Wand* is a translation from a work by the French author Mme d'Aulnoy, but the editors of the *Svodnyi katalog* have maintained (3:333) that the attribution is erroneous.

64. Kheraskov, *Zolotoi prut*, pp. 1–2. The name of Kheraskov's caliph probably comes from an anonymous tale published in *Sanktpeterburgskii vestnik* for 1779 entitled "Shakh-Bagam." See Kubacheva, pp. 308–9.

65. Kheraskov is opposing here the "natural law" so popular in the Enlightenment to the "unnatural law" (i.e., grace) of Christianity and higher order Masonry.

66. Even this temporary paradise is possible only when human nature is reformed, and God bestows his grace.

67. The only significant difference between this higher order Masonic

allegory and that of the lower order is its more mystical emphasis on recovering the "secrets" of nature and uncovering the divine light that originally existed in men.

68. At first Albekir resembles Papageno in Mozart and Schikaneder's libretto for *The Magic Flute* (which was published about nine years later), reflecting the dominance of flesh over spirit. But under the influence of Magoteosopher (who represents the dominance of spirit over flesh in the true Mason), Albekir changes his ways.

69. Any satire in Kheraskov's Eastern tale seems to be directed against the court rather than Catherine herself, despite the fact that it was probably she who spearheaded the anti-Masonic policies of the 1780's. After the 1779 visit to St. Petersburg of the Sicilian charlatan Giuseppe Balsamo ("Count Cagliostro"), Catherine, whose previous attitude toward the Masons has been described as "an amused tolerance" (Madariaga, p. 524), turned strongly against the Masons. Although she at first based her opposition to the organization on its supposed support of charlatans like Cagliostro, it is likely that by the time of Kheraskov's work in 1782, this opposition reflected her fear of a possible Masonic coup to replace her with her son Paul (who may have joined the Masons in 1781 or 1782). In 1780, she published an anti-Masonic tract that ridiculed Masonic rituals and "secrets." Entitled "The Secret of the Society Opposing Absurdity" (the title of which was meant to refer to the Masons), this work was written in French but appeared in Russian and in German as well and bore a false publication date of 1759 to "prove" that Catherine had long opposed the Masons. On Catherine's opposition to and ultimate persecution of Freemasonry in the 1780's and 1790's, see Madariaga, chapter 33.

70. This detail of the defeat of an Eastern caliph by a Slav may be meant to deflect the censor's attention from the fact that some of the faults of *Russia* are represented through this Eastern country. On such projections of Russian faults onto Eastern lands (especially Turkey), see Pukhov, p. 227.

71. Kheraskov, preface to the third edition of *Vladimir vozrozhdennyi*, in *Tvoreniia*, 2:viii. Future references to *Vladimir Reborn* will be from the 1785 first edition.

72. Like the Vladimir of the Primary Chronicle and the Vladimir of Feofan Prokopovich's 1705 tragicomedy *Vladimir*, Kheraskov's Vladimir moves from damnation to salvation. Under the influence of the Primary Chronicle, where Vladimir was said to be "insatiable in vice" ("for he was a libertine like Solomon"), Kheraskov's Vladimir is at first called "a fallen Solomon" (*Russian Primary Chronicle*, p. 94, section for 6488; Kheraskov, *Vladimir*, p. 3). Green has observed some possible similari-

ties between the vices of Vladimir and those of Catherine the Great, arguing that they may reflect Kheraskov's anger at Catherine's 1785 closing of the Moscow Masonic lodges (pp. 17–18).

73. Kheraskov knew enough Greek to effectively use the *nomen omen* and play on the etymology of names. Such etymological wordplay on "Anna" and "grace" can be found in Russian literature at least as far back as Trediakovskii's 1730 "Song" to Anna Ioannovna on her coronation, where "Anna" is explicitly said to represent "grace" (*blagodat'*). See Trediakovskii, 1963, p. 55.

74. For an identification of Freemasonry with "True Christianity" (a term clearly connected with Arndt's mystical work by that name), see the lectures of J. G. Schwarz "on three types of knowledge," summarized in Shvarts, "Otryvki," or Semeka.

75. Vlasto, "A Noble Failure," convincingly suggests that Vladimir functions like Virgil's Aeneas and that Virgil is "often at the back of [Kheraskov's] mind" (p. 286). He argues that there are two intertwined themes of destiny in the work: Vladimir's personal destiny and "his destiny as the creator of a new Christian people, as Aeneas was the creator of the Roman people."

76. As Vladimir states before his conversion, "How can I rule my people? I can't even rule myself" (Kheraskov, *Vladimir vozrozhdennyi*, p. 40). This same idea is later expressed in *Cadmus and Harmonia*: "The man who has control over his own feelings, who restrains the agitations of his own passions, who governs his own spirit according to the rules of reason, is a mighty king on earth. Many wearers of crowns do not deserve this title" (quoted in Zapadov, "Tvorchestvo Kheraskova," in Kheraskov, 1961, p. 26). A similar idea was expressed in Novikov's Masonic-oriented journal *Utrennii svet*, where man was called "the ruler of the world" (*vladyka mira*, recalling the etymology of "Vladimir") since "every man can say by himself in a certain manner: 'the whole world belongs to me'" (*Utrennii svet*, 1777, 1:286, 205, quoted in Neuhäuser, p. 22).

77. On the opposition between *caritas* and *eros* in Masonic literature, see Baehr, "Freemasonry in Russian Literature: Eighteenth Century," pp. 32–33.

78. Typical of Kheraskov's works, the name *Kir* is ambiguous: the Russian name for Cyrus I (founder of the Persian empire, whose life, chronicled in Xenophon's *Cyropedia*, had become a model for the education of future kings and was quite popular in Russia in the late eighteenth century) or a possible variation on the Greek word *Kurios* (often transliterated *kirios* in Russian), meaning "God," "Lord," "Christ," "*master*," or "head of a family." Vlasto suggests that Kir is "the Lord" ("A Noble Failure," p. 284).

79. Later, the narrator states: "One road is always close to us, be it the road to Heaven or to Hell" (p. 118). It is likely that this Masonic tendency to focus on moral absolutes appealed to many Russians who, like the Masons, often believed that one had a choice only between good and evil, paradise and hell, with no middle alternative. On this Russian tendency toward "accentuated duality," see Lotman and Uspenskii, "Binary Models."

80. Compare the remark of God made earlier in the work: "There is a single ladder to reach me: that is the Word of my beloved Son; He calls all to me, *through him paradise is open to all*; His finger has already touched Vladimir" (p. 13). This "ladder" [*lestvitsa*] is simultaneously Jacob's ladder of Genesis 28:12 and the "ladder" or "staircase" of Masonic ritual, symbolizing the candidate's ascent to truth.

81. "Istolkovanie tainstv zakliuchaiushchikhsia v ieroglifakh," GPB, O. III. No. 58, p. 11.

82. Kheraskov, *Kadm i Garmoniia*, 1:iii–iv.

83. In the preface to the novel Kheraskov mentions that some people have interpreted *Garmoniia* as an allegorical representation of "the state of calmness or rejoicing of the heart" (1:iii).

84. Kheraskov was not the only Russian writer of the eighteenth century to use the name of his Masonic lodge as a literary symbol. On Maikov's use of "Urania," see Baehr, "Freemasonry in Russian Literature: Eighteenth Century," p. 32.

85. This episode recalls the frequent Masonic statement that the only escape from the labyrinth is "obedience" (*povinovenie*) to the lodge master and other Masonic officers. Among other characters functioning as lodge masters in the novel are Gifan (book 2) and Diafan (books 9–10).

86. Quoted in Vernadskii, p. 154.

87. On the role of the Cabala in Freemasonry, see Schneider, pp. 102ff. Among higher order Masons (including Rosicrucians like Kheraskov), the Cabala was seen as providing one of the key clues to the lost knowledge that would allow the regaining of paradise. As J. G. Schwarz wrote, "the light of the Cabala teaches us the sense of the holy writings and of all holy things. . . . This light is the supernatural heaven, paradise—*inluentia divina*" ("Raznye zamechaniia pokoinogo Shvartsa," in GPB, Q.III No. 112, p. 14). See also Semeka, p. 386. The importance of the Cabala in Russian Freemasonry is reflected in Ivan Elagin's decision to devote one volume of his projected five-volume work *The Study of Ancient Philosophy and Theology; or, The Science of the Freemasons* to the Cabala and the Talmud (*sic*). See Vernadskii, p. 136. Elagin, however, did not get very far, and from the sections of his manuscript that I have examined in the Lenin Library Manuscript Division, I assume that for him "Cabala" meant numerology.

The importance of cabalistic anagrams to Russian Freemasonry around the time of the composition of *Cadmus and Harmonia* is indicated by a 1785 article called "On the Science Called Cabala," which notes that there are two methods of interpretation of the Cabala: through a reworking of the syllables or letters of a word (i.e., through anagrams) or through a decoding of the meaning of each of the letters of a given word ("O nauke nazyvaemoi Kabale," *Pokoiashchiisia trudoliubets* 4 [1785]:99). The reworking of the two names Kadm and Admon into "Ad(a)m Kadmon" is an example of the first method. An example of the second method is contained in the name "Adam," which, according to the article (p. 100), the ancient Greek sibyls interpreted as an acrostic standing for the four directions of the compass: *anatole* (East), *dusis* (West), *arktikos* (North), *mesembrinos* (South). The name "Adam" thus reflects the idea that God took land from the four corners of the earth to create man. I am grateful to Professor Thomas MacAdoo for helping me with this explanation.

88. On the Adam Kadmon myth in Freemasonry, see Schneider, p. 103; Mackey, *Encyclopedia*, p. 15; and Lennhoff and Posner, p. 13. For a more detailed treatment of the legend of Adam Kadmon in the Cabala, see Scholem, pp. 104–5 and pp. 112–15.

89. Ely, *Bratskie uveshchaniia*, frontispiece. According to Sokolovskaia, Ely, the Masonic mentor of Elagin, first published this work in German in St. Petersburg ("Masonskie risunki," p. 48).

90. Sokolovskaia, "Masonskie risunki," p. 48. Sokolovskaia also interprets "A.K." to stand for Adam Kadmon. I found this article several years after publishing an interpretation of *Cadmus and Harmonia* using the Adam Kadmon myth—a coincidence that supports the probability of this explanation despite its somewhat eclectic appearance. Sokolovskaia states that the III in the center of the star represents God, replacing the more normal "G."

91. Since Masonic literature was often based on an international plot and symbolism—a transformation of Masonic ceremonies and rituals for the various degrees (especially the first three)—many of the patterns of Kheraskov's *Cadmus and Harmoniia* should appear familiar to those acquainted with the libretto written by Emmanuel Schikaneder for Mozart's Masonic opera *The Magic Flute* (1791). Both works portray an allegorical journey of discovery by a naive character who has been deceived by the forces of evil; both include initiatory trials in Egypt under the guidance of a priest of Isis, who helps the hero find the Masonic path to truth and rebirth; and both end with the hero's discovery of a Masonic paradise of brotherhood after being cleansed of sin. These common features unify many Masonic works written throughout Europe and America in the eighteenth century.

92. The interpretation of Teandra as "god-man" is also given by Vlasto, "M. M. Heraskov," p. 441, who sees this combination as representing Christ.

93. On paradise as a trap in the Renaissance epic, see Giamatti, p. 126.

94. Kheraskov, *Polidor*, 3:66.

95. Such deceptions (which often are used to emphasize the distinction between appearance and reality) are fairly frequent in Masonic literature. For example, the naive Prince Tamino in Mozart's *Magic Flute* at first assumes that the evil Queen of the Night is a paragon of virtue and that the good Sarastro is a wicked sorcerer.

96. The importance of this "internal gold" to Freemasonry is reflected in the frequent use of alchemical imagery in Masonic texts. I am grateful to Professor Savely Senderovich for showing me the relevance of the Greek word here.

Chapter Six

1. Segel, *Drama*, p. 305.

2. Shcherbatov, *Corruption*, p. 241.

3. Mannheim, pp. 192–95. For Mannheim, "ideology" refers to an ideal that in principle may contradict the existing order but in practice poses no threat to the status quo, since no effort will be made to realize it (for example, the ideal of brotherly love in a society founded on serfdom). "Utopia," on the other hand, is an ideal that is incongruous with the status quo but ultimately passes into reality, partially shattering the order of things prevailing at the time. As Mannheim notes, the idea of an other-worldly paradise that transcended history was still an integral part of medieval society; "not until certain social groups embodied these wish-images into their actual conduct and tried to realize them did these ideologies become utopian" (p. 193).

4. By the time that the first Russian translation of *Utopia* (1516) finally appeared in 1789, the panegyric "eutopia" had already been flourishing in Russia for about twenty-five years and at least one satirical utopian novel had been written. Although More was known in Russia at least by the time of Kantemir and Trediakovskii, the influence of his *Utopia* did not become great in Russia until much later. However, the *word* "utopia" was in circulation much earlier: the first use of it that I have found was by Antiokh Kantemir in a 1726 essay called "Opisanie Parizha" (Kantemir, 1867, 2:379; reference originally found in KSXVIII). As Serman has noted, Kantemir even had a copy of More's *Utopia* in his library ("Ot sotsial'no-politicheskikh utopii" p. 65). On Trediakovskii's knowledge of More, see Malein, p. 260.

It is not always possible to categorically distinguish between a satiric utopia and a panegyric eutopia. Morson (chapter 1) has even argued that the utopia is a "threshold genre" that is purposefully ambiguous. While I do not think that this is *necessarily* the case, ambiguity does occur relatively often, making classification quite difficult at times and encouraging contradictory readings. My identification of the panegyric eutopia as a genre, for example, differs significantly from the interpretations of most Soviet literary historians before the 1980's, who (largely for ideological reasons) assumed that a novel in the utopian genre *must* be satiric and *must* criticize the tsar.

5. Sipovskii, "Politicheskie nastroeniia," p. 251. Despite its promising title, Sviatlovskii's *Russkii utopicheskii roman* is (with a few exceptions like the section on Shcherbatov) inadequate in its consideration of the eighteenth century. Much better general summaries are contained in both Sipovskii works and in Serman, "Ot sotsial'no-politicheskikh utopii." Eighteenth-century literary utopianism is also treated briefly in the introduction to Varese. On utopian episodes in specific novels of the period, see Breuillard; Budgen, "Works"; Monnier; Serman, "Istoriia i prosvetitel'stvo"; and Waegemans. Several selections from eighteenth-century utopias are abridged in Guminskii.

6. This list is by no means complete, but stresses works or sections that describe ideal lands in some detail. It should be noted that the descriptions of ideal lands in a number of these works (e.g., Emin's) occupy a relatively small percentage of the whole. Sipovskii lists many additional works in "Politicheskie nastroeniia," pp. 230–67, but many of them make only fleeting reference to an ideal society.

7. As these titles suggest, major influences on eighteenth-century Russian works describing an ideal place came from several different sources: Western adventure and travel novels; Western novels of the seventeenth and eighteenth centuries; and classical Greek and Roman literature. For example the frequently translated Plutarch's *Lives* (e.g., the Lives of Numa and Themistocles) and Ovid's *Metamorphoses* (e.g., his tale of Cadmus and Harmonia) provided a skeleton that some Russian writers used to create their own works. To these sources were added strong influences from Fénelon's *Télémaque* (which had at least nine different printed editions in eighteenth-century Russia and countless manuscript editions) with its utopian tales of Salentum and Boetica; the genre of the "mirror of princes" (which itself influenced *Télémaque*); and to a lesser extent Montesquieu's *Persian Letters* (translated twice with at least two additional translations of the utopian "Legend of the Troglodytes"), Xenophon's *Cyropedia*, Swift's *Gulliver's Travels*, Terrason's *Sethos*, More's *Utopia* (which each had two editions); and Plato's *Republic*, Holberg's *Adventures of Nils Klim*, Ramsay's *New Cyropedia; or, The Voyages of Cyrus*, and Barclay's *Argenis* (which had one edition each).

On translations of foreign utopias into Russian in the eighteenth century, see Sviatlovskii, *Russkii utopicheskii roman*, p. 33; Sviatlovskii, *Katalog utopii*; Sipovskii, *Ocherki*, vol. 1, part 1, esp. pp. 121–24, 153.

8. Radishchev, *Journey*, p. 146. This is not to argue, of course, that there is no similarity between the utopia and the project. Like the project, the utopia often criticizes and satirizes existing reality. But the utopia does so by *implicit* contrast with a "good place" rather than by the explicit criticism of reality that is found in the project. Radishchev, for example, shows the need for eliminating serfdom, inequality, the privileges of the nobility, and the table of ranks but does not depict an ideal society that has eliminated them.

9. Gilarovskii, pp. 15–16. The reference, of course, is to Plato's concept of a philosopher-king guiding the ideal republic. Elsewhere in this speech Gilarovskii calls Russia "the country beloved by God" and states that the Romanov family founded Russia's "temple of happiness." He argues that Peter the Great (whom he calls the "divine lawgiver") elevated and extended this temple, that his successors "multiplied the beauty and magnificence of it," and that the current tsar, Paul I, "has been ordained to perfect . . . it," just as Solomon was chosen to "finish the temple of God in the holy city" (pp. 15–16). The implicit comparison of Russia to Solomon's temple probably reflects Masonic influence.

10. Karamzin, *Memoir*, p. 153.

11. As early as the 1740's important critics and writers, including M. V. Lomonosov, began to make exceptions to rules regarding the inadmissibility of prose for such didactic novels as Swift's *Gulliver's Travels*, Barclay's *Argenis*, and Fénelon's *Télémaque*—all of which contain utopian segments. See, for example, Lomonosov, *Kratkoe rukovodstvo k krasnorechiiu* (1748), no. 151, in Lomonosov, 1950, 7:222–23.

12. Although I have not yet found panegyric eutopias in other national literatures, the "royalist utopias" written in seventeenth-century England (one of which, *Antiquity Reviv'd* [1693], takes place, appropriately, on an island called "Astreada") have many philosophical similarities. However, since these works praise absolute monarchy *after* its disappearance, they actually are "utopias" rather than "eutopias." See Davis, chapter 10.

13. Frye compares the typical narrator of utopian fiction to the Intourist guide of pre-*glasnost'* days ("Varieties," p. 26). The rhetorical strategy of even the satiric utopia is a kind of "blame by praise"—blaming the author's society by praising the "good place," which is far removed from the society we know.

14. Manuel and Manuel, *Utopian Thought*, p. 112.

15. One probable intermediary between the Russian panegyric eutopia and the panegyric ode was the mirror of princes, which attempted

to influence the prince to model his conduct on that of God and Christ and in so doing to establish heaven on earth. In this genre, the conduct of a subject is seen to reflect the conduct of his ruler (the "mimetic ethic" of Chapter 2 above) so that the ideal state is seen as the inevitable result of the perfect prince. For an example of this genre, see the discussion in Chapter 2 above of Agapetus's "Hortatory Chapters," which combined encouragement, praise, and precepts for Emperor Justinian; it lauded him for being the philosopher-king described in Plato's *Republic* and for creating "a time of happy living" (chapter 17), while warning him of the danger of listening to flatterers (chapter 12) and encouraging him to correct and improve the human part of his nature. A similar combination is contained in a number of eighteenth-century panegyric eutopias, for example, Kheraskov's *Numa* (which may well have been influenced by the 1766 Russian translation of Agapetus). On the role of the mirror of princes in Shcherbatov's *Journey to the Land of Ophir*, see the section "Satire and Utopia" below.

16. Quoted and translated in Ransel, p. 52.

17. Translation in Madariaga, p. 39. Despite this support of law and limits, Catherine, even in her preaccession notes, did not support a constitutional monarchy and agreed with Montesquieu that the only acceptable form of government for a country as vast as Russia was autocracy (in Montesquieu's term "tyranny").

18. On this point, see, for example, Budgen, "Works," chapter 5, esp. pp. 184–92.

19. Emin, *Nepostoiannaia fortuna*, 3:348. According to Drage, this was the first original Russian novel (*Russian Literature*, p. 163).

20. "True belief" is the etymology of the Greek word "Orthodoxy"— the religion to which Miramond and Feridat convert during the course of the novel.

21. This reading generally agrees with that of David Budgen in "Fedor Emin," who adds the perceptive interpretation that the "eagles" (*orly*) are the five Orlov brothers, who helped to depose Peter III and place Catherine on the throne (p. 89n). Budgen feels that Nikita Panin and possibly Mikhail Vorontsov also play a role in Emin's allegory.

22. The image of the "hardworking bee" on Parnassus may refer to Sumarokov's 1759 journal of that name—*Trudoliubivaia pchela*.

23. Budgen, "Fedor Emin," p. 89n. Earlier in the novel Feridat attends an allegorical opera portraying Catherine ("the goddess") as the supreme monarch of Europe, to whom all other monarchs yield first place. See Emin, *Nepostoiannaia fortuna*, 2:297–300. For a more complete political analysis of this novel, see Budgen, "Fedor Emin," pp. 72–73.

24. See the preface to Emin, *Nepostoiannaia Fortuna*, and Budgen,

"Fedor Emin," p. 79. See Beshenkovskii for the many mysteries surrounding Emin's life.

25. The topos of the appeal to foreigners may be linked with the
Byzantine and old Russian rhetoric of foreign fame, which proclaimed
the monarch to be "famed in many lands" and Russia to be "a country
that is known and heard by all ends of the earth." See, for example,
Hilarion, "Slovo o zakone i blagodati," in Gudzii, *Khrestomatiia*, p. 32.

26. *Poleznoe uveselenie*, Dec. 1761, p. 184.

27. *Poleznoe uveselenie*, Mar. 1762.

28. On immigration movements to Russia, see Bartlett. See also Catherine's ukase of July 22, 1763, inviting foreign colonists to settle on the
Volga; this policy sought to settle empty lands in the South and (as was
the fashion in Europe at the time) gain greater strength through greater
population.

29. Text in V. I. Maikov, *Izbrannye proizvedeniia*, pp. 200–201.

30. *Dobroe namerenie*, June 1764, p. 249.

31. Karamzin, 1966, p. 63. It is likely that the asterisks stand for one
or more contemporary Russian poets (Derzhavin, for example) and are
used to avoid offending those poets not listed. See Chapter 5 above
regarding transformations of Masonic ideology in this poem.

32. "N.N." was also a frequent pseudonym of N. I. Novikov, who was
probably punning on his initials using this Latin emblem of anonymity.
On the basis of these initials, Pukhov has argued that the three-part
"Letter from Saturn" was probably written by Novikov (p. 117). I believe
that this is unlikely, since Novikov would be a most unlikely candidate
for writing the panegyric eutopia of section 1; also, the satire of sections
2 and 3 is much more "tame" than Novikov's usual satire.

33. *Vechera*, 1772, vol. 1, evening 6, p. 41.

34. Riasanovsky, *A History of Russia*, pp. 296–98; Alexander, pp. 122–
29.

35. Although this first part of the letter makes one wonder why the
author bothered to set his work on Saturn, the second and third parts
make an abrupt switch from political panegyrics to moral satire of the
type presented in the satirical journals of the 1760's and 1770's, focusing
on general vices rather than specific people or policies in a clear attempt to adhere to Catherine the Great's criteria for satire articulated in
Vsiakaia vsiachina. Only the empress's position could explain the general
nature of these last two letters—which satirize avarice, pride, ignorance,
and coquetry instead of making specific satiric allusions. Such satire on
general vices is most unusual in a would-be utopia.

36. Levshin, *Russkie skazki*, 10:4ff. All page numbers given in parentheses in the text are from volume 10.

37. Unlike this utopian first part, much of the second part of Levshin's tale loses sight of the ideal land, telling how Balamir helps undo a curse on Milosveta that has caused her to be unhappy.

38. Kheraskov, *Numa*, p. 147.

39. Much of this literature depicts a monarch who obeys all laws and thus provides an example for his or her citizens—a point made by Catherine in her preaccession notes, where she wrote that laws "must be sacred to the monarch." This rule was often honored in the breach.

40. Reddaway, p. 290. Spelling and punctuation have been normalized from this 1768 English translation. Future references to the *Nakaz* will be given in the text by article numbers.

41. According to Rousseau, Numa's very name derived from the Greek word for law, *nomos* (*Social Contract*, footnote to book 4, chapter 4).

Themis was sometimes confused with Astraea in eighteenth-century Russia. This confusion was to some extent caused by the fact that both were represented pictorially through the same iconography. As the 1763 Russian edition of Lacombe de Prezel's *Ikonologicheskii leksikon* stated: Astraea "holds a scale in one hand and a sword in the other, which are the signs of Themis" (p. 16). In her role as the goddess of law, Astraea functioned after Catherine's *Nakaz* more as a symbol of the paradisal condition attainable through law than as the general marker of the golden age that she had previously been.

42. Text in Vengerov, 1:317–18.

43. Like a number of other portraits by Levitskii, this picture of Catherine is more allegorical than is generally recognized. In this work, there is a metaphorical identification between foreground (Catherine) and background (Themis, represented by a statue). Indeed the statue of Themis even has facial features resembling those of Catherine.

44. Emin, *Prikliucheniia Femistokla*, p. 64. Themistocles also creates a virtual utopia in Thebes, in which he establishes an excellent system of laws, eliminates luxuries, and creates an open immigration policy.

45. For a similar point of view, see Budgen, "Works," pp. 219–20. Emin's balancing of eutopias with dystopias is mirrored in a number of other Russian eighteenth-century novels with utopian or eutopian scenes, including Kheraskov's *Numa*, which counterposes the evils of Rome before Numa with the good created by his reign.

46. Numa seems to be an idealized, composite image of Peter and Catherine, rather than standing for only one or the other. Although for much of the novel Numa seems to represent Catherine, Kheraskov portrays him as establishing a system of ranks, which are awarded by merit, much as Peter had done. As Kheraskov states in the preface, he portrays Numa "as he was and as he might have been."

47. Kheraskov's work also relies on sources ranging from Livy and Dionysus of Halicarnassus to more recent sources like David Choffin's *History of Great Rulers* and Charles Rollin's *Roman History* (all of which are referred to in Kheraskov's text). On Lycurgus and the eighteenth-century Russian utopia, see Serman, "Istoriia i prosvetitel'stvo."

48. Kheraskov, *Numa*, p. 139.

49. Piksanov, 4:79.

50. It is possible that in these last lines Kheraskov is citing a panegyric speech given by I. I. Betskii the year before, which said that "Peter the Great created men in Russia, [Catherine] gave them souls." Quoted and translated in Riasanovsky, *The Image of Peter the Great*, p. 37.

51. Elsewhere, Kheraskov notes: "And [using the example of Numa] we can be assured that glory is obtained not only through the use of weapons" (p. 171). This comment about weapons may be a warning to Catherine to avoid going to war over Poland.

52. Throughout the novel, Kheraskov criticizes scheming and deceptive courtiers (whom, he says, the monarch must observe "with an eye that never sleeps"—p. 24) and corrupt priests—groups that put self above service. But even Catherine in her *Nakaz* had criticized "flatterers who are daily instilling the pernicious maxim into all the sovereigns on earth 'that their people are created for them only.'" Like Numa, Catherine wrote that "we are created for our people" (article 520).

53. Pypin (whose comments on Kheraskov I saw only after having completed my own) shares the conviction that *Numa* is largely panegyric (*Istoriia*, 4:149). Most Soviet critics, on the other hand, stress the satirical element. See, for example, the interpretation by Kulakova in Akademiia nauk, *Istoriia russkoi literatury*, 4:328–29.

54. This combination of patriarchal and matriarchal terms during the reigns of female rulers may reflect the predominance of males on the Russian throne for a sufficiently long period that the male image of the autocratic tsar ("Father Tsar") remained inflexible in the popular mind even during the long line of female tsars in the eighteenth century. See Chapter 2 regarding the combination of imagery of Christ and Mary to refer to female tsars and Chapter 4 regarding the marriage of "Father Tsar" to "Mother Russia." In Russia, as elsewhere, such terms increased the power of the state and its ruler by encouraging family feelings toward them.

These familial terms laid the groundwork for satire in the "family quarrel" among the satirical journals of 1769. In beginning the first satirical journal in Russia, *Vsiakaia vsiachina* (*All Sorts and Sundries*), Catherine the Great adopted the persona of "Grandma" (*babushka*). In its famous 1769 polemics with *Vsiakaia vsiachina*, Novikov's *Truten'* (*The Drone*) referred to Catherine's journal (and hence, by implication, Catherine and her policies) as "our great-grandmother" (*nasha prababka*). As Gareth Jones has observed: "As the *babushka's* 'grandchildren and nephews,' the editors of the other magazines were indulgently allowed to engage in polemics under the guise of speaking within the family. Many made mordant comments on the grandmother's feebleness, smugness, and superciliousness" (*Nikolay Novikov*, p. 27). As Jones notes, there ultimately arose a "declaration of independence" of the 1769 journals from her tutelage: "We, *babushka*, although your grandchildren, have nevertheless come of age" (p. 27).

55. Thomas Hobbes, *Leviathan*, chapter 13, in Cahn, p. 365.

56. As Davis has observed, this assumption harbors an implicit paradox: "A system premised [o]n the fallibility of men must . . . assume some men infallible. . . . The perfect prince is indispensable to the perfect monarchy" (p. 278).

57. Quoted in Szamuely, p. 103. As is reflected in this statement, the patriarch externalizes the Freudian superego, ensuring compliance with authority and emphasizing an implicit use of "constraint" to get others to do what is supposed to be in their own best interests.

58. Quoted in Fliegelman, p. 4. Kant in his 1789 essay "What Is Enlightenment?" (p. 383) even defined the Enlightenment movement as a reaction against patriarchy and other forms of "self-imposed nonage."

59. The patriarchal ideal in the Russian eutopia and utopia had some diverse literary and historical precedents. In many traditional Western utopias, societies are organized into extended families ruled by a "father." Plato even abolished the private family for the Guardians of his *Republic* and required that they call the elder Guardian "father." More's *Utopia* is organized on the basis of the family and extended family, and officials there "are called fathers and share that character" (p. 114).

In Russian history, the idea of the tsar as the all-powerful father of his people was to some extent a result of the 1503 victory of the Possessors, with their doctrine that tsars ought to be "loved and obeyed as fathers were obeyed by their children" (Zernov, pp. 52, 103). As the tsar assumed the image of the father, so the state assumed the image of the family (especially the family portrayed in the *Domostroi* [*Book of Household Order*], where the father was viewed as absolute). A number of patriarchal images and titles were also used in the church after the 1589 creation of the "Patriarch," who was called "spiritual father" and even "father of the fatherland" (*otets otechestva*, a title conferred on Peter the Great only in 1721—the year he eliminated the office of Patriarch).

60. For example, the ideal Thrace in Emin's *Prikliucheniia Femistokla* is based on "the principle of an artel." Like the Slavophile ideology,

eighteenth-century utopian scenes often depicted ideal patriarchal com-
munities as highly moral and democratic, as opposed to what Masaryk
claims was the reality of the Russian commune—a "means of coercion"
established for strategic purposes (p. 15).

61. Quoted in Budgen, "Works," p. 184.

62. Earlier, in *Numa*, Kheraskov had emphasized that the good tsar
"is like a father to his citizens" (p. 25) and "rules his kingdom following
the rules of a wise father" (p. 39).

63. Sipovskii, "Politicheskie nastroeniia," p. 254.

64. Such benign patriarchs had been prefigured as early as the panegyric poetry of Simeon Polotskii, where the tsar (both the generalized
ideal tsar and Aleksei Mikhailovich) was referred to as "father" of his
state or as "a common father to all"—patriarchal images that Polotskii
directly opposed to that of the tyrant.

65. Quoted in Drage, *Russian Literature*, p. 142. Drage points out that
parental affection becomes a metaphor for the ideal Russian society in
this tale: "[J]ust as the parent cares for his children, so the 'good barin'
[landowner] cares for his peasants and the 'merciful sovereign' for all
of his citizens."

66. *Truten'*, 1770, no. 2 (Jan. 12, 1770), reprinted in Berkov, *Satiricheskie zhurnaly*, p. 185. On patriarchy in Novikov, see also Makogonenko, *Novikov*, pp. 202–10.

67. "Otryvok puteshestviia v *** I *** T ***," *Zhivopisets*, part 1, no. 5
(1772); reprinted in Berkov, *Satiricheskie zhurnaly*, pp. 295–97, 330–32.
Novikov depicts these peasants as lacking any bitterness toward their
tyrannical landlord: "May God grant him health. We rely on God.
God and the Sovereign are merciful toward us, and if only Grigorii
Terent'evich also had mercy, then we would live as in paradise" (p. 332).
There is a great deal of controversy over the authorship of this work,
with suppositions ranging from Novikov to Radishchev to Ivan Turgenev. For a short summary of this debate, see Berkov notes to *Satiricheskie zhurnaly*, pp. 560–64. On the basis of the thematic similarity with
Novikov's other works about agriculture and serfdom and the likelihood
that "I.T." stands for "*Izdatel' Trutnia*" ("The Editor of the Drone"—a
possibility suggested by L. N. Maikov in his 1889 *Ocherki*), I join many
critics (including Makogonenko, Jones, and others) in assuming that
Novikov was the author of this work.

68. "Retsepty," *Truten'*, 1769, no. 24; reprinted in Berkov, *Satiricheskie
zhurnaly*, p. 135.

69. Walicki, pp. 16–17. As Walicki has noted, "this patriarchal utopia
had little in common with the . . . ideologies of the [Western] Age of
Reason, which advocated replacing personal dependence by relations

based on impersonal, rational legislation." I am grateful to Mr. Gareth Jones for bringing this section to my attention.

70. *Moskovskii zhurnal* 8 (Oct.-Nov. 1792):13.

71. Cross, *Karamzin*, p. 108. These "patriarchal times" are paraphrastically defined as times when an "elder [*starets*] was filled with earthly blessings in the company of his large family, seeing on every face and in every glance a living expression of love and joy." This association of the patriarchal Russian family with love and joy recalls later Slavophile stress on the "bonds of love" in the Slavic (as opposed to the Western) family. On this, see Riasanovsky, *Russia and the West*, p. 132. The Slavophile ideology also stressed the familylike union of people into the Slavic commune (*obshchina* or *mir*) through "an act of love, a noble Christian act" (quote from Constantine Aksakov, in Riasanovsky, p. 135).

72. The opposition of "nature" and "nurture" is, of course, a variant on the contrast between "nature" and "art" discussed in Chapter 4.

73. Shcherbatov, *Corruption*, pp. 116–18.

74. On these qualities in Slavophile writings, see Masaryk, 1:13–16, 43; and Riasanovsky, *Russia and the West*, chapters 4–5. For a discussion of early-nineteenth-century anticipations of Slavophilism, see Al'tshuller, *Predtechi*.

75. It has been observed that in the West there has been a close relationship between the rise of interest in science and the rise of utopianism. As Gerber has commented: "The emergence of utopia coincides with periods of scientific discovery and with ages that are experimental and critical in spirit" (p. 50). While the rise of literary utopianism in Russia followed by about thirty-five years the rise of science, the relationship between science and utopian fiction in eighteenth-century Russia was more often one of estrangement than compatibility.

76. Although Chulkov's and Levshin's works were probably the first Russian *utopias* to take place on the moon, they were not the first Russian literary works to be placed there; Sumarokov's *Son* ("A Dream," 1760) also occurs on the moon. This short dream is a satire on Russian bureaucrats, who consume so much paper that the poor poet-narrator can't afford to write and thus can't describe his lunar voyage (*Prazdnoe vremia v pol'zu upotreblennoe*, part 2 [Nov. 4, 1759], p. 292). Indeed, if the narrator had not mentioned that he had "dreamed . . . that [he] was on the moon" (p. 291), the reader would not notice his location.

77. L'vov, *Rossiiskaia Pamela*, 1:i–ii. The title of L'vov's novel refers to Samuel Richardson's 1740 novel *Pamela*.

78. All three works were written by Russian nationalists who felt (as L'vov expressed it) "ardor and devotion for [their] dear homeland" (1:i). Two of the three contain the word "Russian" or "Slavic" in their

titles or subtitles, although the utopian sections never explicitly mention Russia; the third work was written by the author of a five-volume work called *Russian Tales* (Levshin's *Russkie skazki*, 1780–83). The narrator of Chulkov's *Peresmeshnik* (the collection in which his lunar utopia appears) even signs his name *Rossiianin* ("A Russian"), and says about one of the heroes of his collection: "If he had not been a Slav, he would have despaired of life on this occasion and would have died of fright on this empty shore"; but being a Slav he is "victorious over all dangers" (A. V. Zapadov, introduction to Chulkov, in Makogonenko, *Russkaia proza XVIII veka*, 1:84). An early foreshadowing of this glorification of Slavic innocence in the eutopias and utopias of the 1780's can already be found in the 1766 description by M. D. Chulkov of the mythical Slavic utopia of Vineta (see Chapter 3 above). For more on Slavic innocence, see Rogger, p. 84.

79. See L'vov's description of his peasant heroine, Maria, whom he depicts as being "like a heavenly being who had come down to earth," whose goodness "shone on her innocent forehead." Her name (that of the Virgin Mary/Mother of God in Russian) is thus probably not coincidental.

80. Both works share many common themes—presumably through the direct influence of Levshin's 1784 *Latest Journey* on his friend Chulkov's 1789 "Dream of Kidal." These two works stand in sharp contrast to most Western lunar utopias of the seventeenth and eighteenth centuries, which usually present science in a positive light. On the Western lunar tradition, see Nicolson.

81. Chulkov, *Peresmeshnik, ili Slavenskie skazki*, 5:39. "The Dream of Kidal" was one of the works added to the 1789 edition of this Slavicized *Arabian Nights*. The direct influence of the *Arabian Nights* is reflected in this tale when Kidal is brought to the moon by the roc—a mythical bird from the tales "The Third Calendar" and "Sinbad the Sailor."

82. As Levshin writes, "people who did not love work were beginning to invent . . . sciences" (*Noveishee puteshestvie*, in *Sobesednik liubitelei rossiiskogo slova*, 13:162). Levshin's utopia was serialized in volumes 13–16 for 1784 but never published separately in its entirety. It is possible that the work as published is incomplete since many details in volumes 15–16 are inadequately motivated. As Breuillard observes, volume 15 has virtually nothing in common with volumes 13–14 except its title; he even hypothesizes that parts 1–2 displeased the censor and that the editors therefore substituted another text for that of Levshin in volume 15 (p. 22). Selections from this work are published in Guminskii, pp. 69–90.

83. Quoted in Kliuchevskii, *Sochineniia*, 3:296.

84. Although Levshin's space traveler, Narsim, thinks of building a "flying machine," he is carried to the moon in a dream bearing far more relationship to classical literature than to modern science fiction. Indeed, it may not be coincidental that Lucian's *True History* and *Icaromennipus*, both of which have lunar episodes, were published in Russian in 1784—the year Levshin's work appeared. See *Razgovory Lukiana Samosatskago*, vol. 3 (St. Petersburg, 1784). I am grateful to Professor Nicoletta Marcialis of Rome University for this information.

The first work of Russian science fiction probably was F. V. Bulgarin's *Pravopodobnye nebylitsy, ili stranstvovaniia po svetu v 29-om veke* ("Probable Fables; or, Travels Around the World in the Twenty-Ninth Century," 1828), which describes the advanced state of Russian technology in the twenty-ninth century as observed by a Russian Rip Van Winkle. On Russian science fiction, see Suvin, chapter 11.

85. I employ the term "primitivism" in accordance with its usage in Lovejoy and Boas.

86. The capsule history of the earth from the golden age to the present and the flight through space both anticipate elements of Dostoevsky's "Dream of a Ridiculous Man" (1877), perhaps because of the common influence of Lucian. The argument about the earth's decline due to an increase in population and subsequent insufficiency of resources was quite common in the eighteenth century, made famous for later epochs by Thomas Malthus's 1798 "Essay on the Principle of Population."

87. In the early part of this work, Narsim says that there are no sovereigns on this moon but that fathers rule over their children in patriarchal fashion. Yet later there is a "surrogate Catherine" who is clearly a sovereign. Like Shakespeare's Gonzalo, who imagines a utopia he rules that has no sovereign (act 2 of *The Tempest*), "the latter end of the commonwealth" seems to have "forgotten the beginning."

88. A similar reversal was used by Sumarokov in his original "Chorus to a Perverted World," discussed later in this chapter, which may have provided a source for Levshin's irony.

89. Earlier it is noted that immigrant foreigners have settled in the country's newly acquired territory, and "deserts are being transformed into gardens" (16:44)—another topos from contemporary panegyric poetry.

90. See V. F. Odoevskii's statement in an 1834 article that there will ultimately be "a Russian conquest of Europe, . . . a spiritual conquest, because only Russian thought can unify the chaos of Western science" (quoted in Billington, p. 316).

91. Dobroliubov, *Sobranie sochinenii*, 5:314.

92. Quoted in Klibanov, *Social'nye utopii*, p. 6.

93. Kantemir, 1956, p. 61. Despite Kantemir's challenge to Russian panegyric culture as early as this first satire, he nevertheless reflects its omnipresence (albeit a bit halfheartedly) in his second stanza: "It is true that in our young monarch [Peter II] there is great hope for the muses; ignorance avoids him with shame." But as if to disavow such panegyrics, he continues: "But the problem is this: out of fear, many people praise in a tsar what they would strongly condemn in a subject" (lines 15–22 with omissions).

94. Text in Berkov, "Khor," pp. 198–99.

95. The anti-utopian "Fragment of a Journey to *** by I *** T ***" (noted above) focused on the abuse of serfdom on the estate as a means of criticizing serfdom in the state as a whole; but there were no *ideal* lands used for satirical purposes in Novikov's satirical journals. Given the role of the paradise myth in official ideology, its use in political satire would have been most risky.

96. See, for example, *Zhivopisets*, part 1, issue 26 (Berkov, *Satiricheskie zhurnaly*, pp. 371ff) and part 2, issues 25–26 (Berkov, pp. 465ff); and *Koshelek*, issue 9 (Berkov, pp. 506ff).

97. When occasionally used at other times in Novikov's satirical journals, the paradise myth tends to criticize *not* the Russian government or officials but other sinners. For example, in his introduction to *Koshelek*, Novikov strongly criticizes France (and hence the Russian Francophiles) through the image of hell masquerading as paradise: "And now the corruption in the morals of our teachers [i.e., the French] is so great that they have completely lost even the slightest comprehension of certain virtues and are going so far in their philosophizing that *they are hoping to find a paradise in their hell*" (Berkov, p. 478).

98. Since under Catherine the government refused to allow any obvious satire on specific persons or on political abuses, the most critical utopian satires were denied publication; to be *published*, it was desirable to be panegyric in one's orientation (at least on the surface).

99. Ransel, p. 36; Gukovskii, *Ocherki*, pp. 91ff, 127–28. The possibility of such a future-oriented panegyric is increased by the fact that Sumarokov dedicated his journal not to Elizabeth but to Catherine (then Grand Duchess), with whom Elizabeth had virtually broken after hearing rumors of her participation in discussions of a coup d'état during Elizabeth's illness in 1757–58. Gleason takes the more moderate view that the similarity between Sumarokov's "Dream" and the discussions of Catherine and Panin was probably only coincidence (p. 43).

100. Text in Malyshev and Svetlov, pp. 354–57. The middle term in this quote—*strakh* ("fear")—reflects the positive value placed on fear of a leader in Russian culture, where the word *groznyi* ("the terrible,"

but also "the majestic") was often considered a compliment to a leader, implying a tsar who "inspired fear in enemies and obedience in his citizens" (Dal', *Tolkovyi slovar'*, 1:397).

101. All quotes are from Sumarokov, 1957, pp. 279–81.

102. To increase its tax revenue, the Russian government "farmed out" to private agents contracts for the collection of taxes and other state revenues. The "tax farmer" retained receipts that were greater than the amount he had to pay for the privilege. This system was subject to a great deal of abuse and often led to extraordinary profits. Among the areas farmed out was the sale (and to some extent the production) of wine (and, after 1765, of vodka). Tax farmers were frequently the target of satire during the eighteenth century as a result of expansions of the system. For one of the better satiric treatments of this theme, see V. I. Maikov's mock epic *Elisei ili razdrazhennyi Vakh* ("Elisei; or, Bacchus Enraged," 1771), in which the main character of the title (whose name means "Elysium") is chosen by Bacchus to rebel against the tax farmers, who were raising the price of alcohol to increase their own profits. On tax farming, see Wieczynski, 26:154–56.

103. In an attempt to veil this sophisticated critique, Sumarokov's "Chorus" uses many techniques of "naive" folk literature, including parallelism in succeeding lines, fixed epithets, short forms of adjectives in oblique cases, and the device of a talking bird flying in from abroad.

104. The novel contains examples of the language of the Ophirians (supposedly Sanskrit)—a fairly frequent technique in European utopian novels from More's *Utopia* and Swift's *Gulliver's Travels* to Butler's *Erewhon*. Shcherbatov's description of the fights between the political parties of *Shapki* and *Shliapy* (Caps and Hats) in Mr. S.'s native Sweden (which recalls the battles between the Big-Endians and the Little-Endians in *Gulliver's Travels*) reflects an actual dispute in eighteenth-century Sweden.

105. Quote is from Shcherbatov, *Sochineniia*, 1:751. Unlike many other utopias of the time (including the two Russian lunar utopias discussed above), Shcherbatov's Ophir is *not* characterized by its unusual nature, animals, or birds, emphasizing the idea that this utopia is realizable.

106. Many of the geographical names in Shcherbatov's utopia are anagrams (or almost anagrams): Tervek (Tver), Evki (Kiev), the rivers Kholbo (Volkhov) and Golva (Volga). For an exhaustive reconstruction of geographical equivalents, see Chechulin, pp. 17–19. The use of such anagrams was quite frequent in utopian fiction, and Chechulin may well be correct in attributing Shcherbatov's use of this device to his reading of Denis Vairasse's 1677 utopian novel *Histoire des Sévarambes* (pp. 37–38).

The name Ophir comes from the location of King Solomon's goldmines mentioned in 1 Kings 9:28, but Chechulin attributes Shcherba-tov's use of it to his reading of an anonymous 1699 German utopia called *Königreich Ophirs* (pp. 31–37). Given the fact that the Freemasons re-ferred to Ophir in reconstructing their symbolic Temple of Solomon, it is possible that Shcherbatov's decision to use this name was reinforced by his Masonic experience. However, given the very limited Masonic sym-bolism in this work (see footnote 115 below), the Masonic connection should not be overemphasized.

107. To understand the targets of Shcherbatov's satire here and else-where in his *Voyage to the Land of Ophir*, it is useful to read the work alongside his essay *On the Corruption of Morals in Russia*. See especially the conclusion of this essay (section 10) for a parallel to this quote, where Shcherbatov states that only an "improved rule" would create "good morals in Russia"—the rule of a just, virtuous, open-minded, law-abiding, religious monarch who "rewards virtue and hates vices," hates flattery, and loves the advice of wise men. With such a mon-arch "exiled virtue" will return to Russia, and a utopia of law and good morals (where each person keeps to his own class) will result. See Len-tin's edition, p. 258.

108. Lentin notes that the hereditary monarch of Shcherbatov's utopia exists simply as a figurehead—"the personification of established law, order, and justice without true power" (p. 76). Regarding the problems caused by making monarchs feel that they are gods, see Radishchev's *Journey from Petersburg to Moscow*: "Living among such small souls and impelled towards pettiness by flattery . . . , many rulers imagined that they were gods and that everything that they touched became good and radiant" (p. 160).

109. On the mirror of princes, see Chapter 2 above. Waegemans also mentions the relevance of this genre (p. 128).

110. Compare the many preparations made by the provincial town for the visit of Gogol's Inspector General.

111. Although Shcherbatov admired, on balance, the personal sim-plicity of Peter the Great and supported Peter's goals of eliminating ignorance, complaisance, and xenophobia from Russia, Shcherbatov condemned Peter's Table of Ranks, his excessive secularization (which in the process of eliminating superstition also removed "faith in God's laws"), and especially his courtiers and officials (who introduced luxury, the pursuit of pleasure, and the practice of flattery, which Shcherba-tov felt were ultimately responsible for the "corruption of morals" in Russia). See *Corruption*, pp. 113–57, and Lentin introduction, pp. 69, 88.

112. Shcherbatov's optimism is reflected in the fact that Mr. S. arrives in the utopian Ophir on the symbolic Frigate "Hope" (*Nadezhda*).

113. Cf. the letter of May 22, 1773, written by Shcherbatov to Cath-

erine II complaining about his declining financial position as a result of his service to the state (mentioned in Lentin, p. 76).

114. To make the army a more productive class, they are required to learn farming or a trade. The army class lives in special military settlements, which, I. Z. Serman has observed, anticipate Arakcheev's military colonies under Alexander I ("Ot sotsial'no-politicheskikh utopii," p. 71).

115. The Ophirian religion combines aspects of Freemasonry (e.g., a temple built of "rough stone" [*dikii kamen'*] and references to God as "all-seeing," recalling the Masonic All-Seeing Eye) with others of an Enlightenment deistic religion. However, the Masonic aspects are contradicted by the fact that the temple is open to everyone and has "no mysteries" since all men are the children of a single God.

116. Lentin, p. 79; Raeff, "State and Nobility in the Ideology of M. M. Shcherbatov," p. 374. Cf. Shcherbatov's 1768 proposal for a law code that would give the police very broad authority in the spheres of health, morals, and individual conduct (Lentin, p. 36).

117. Shcherbatov, *Corruption*, pp. 255, 234, 240, plus Lentin introduction and notes, pp. 43, 293n. For a more complete discussion of the opposition of the Ophirian utopia to Catherine's Russia, see Chechulin (especially pp. 43ff), and Waegemans. Chechulin sees direct criticism of Catherine in Shcherbatov's depiction of Emperor Kastar ("who loved power, flattery, and luxury" and did not understand the real problems in his state) and Empress Arakiteia (whose name, as Chechulin observes, is an anagram of Ekat[e]ri[n]a [pp. 54–55]).

118. Transliterations of "Thersites" in the eighteenth century varied from "Tersit" to "Firs." See Baehr, "Who Is Firs?" The term "floating island" recalls the floating island of Morelly's utopian novel *Basiliade* and the flying island of Laputa in Swift's *Gulliver's Travels* (the home of absurd philosophical schemes such as the extraction of sunshine from cucumbers).

119. *Moskovskii zhurnal* 1 (Mar. 1791):359. Karamzin in a footnote describes *Utopia* as "The Kingdom of Happiness [*Tsarstvo schastiia*], a work by More." Although this review was of the 1790 edition (purportedly the *second* translation of More's work into Russian), there was actually only *one* translation of *Utopia* in the eighteenth century in two editions that are identical except for their titles and title pages. In his review Karamzin correctly noted that this translation had so many "gallicisms" that it could not have been translated from the English, as it claimed, but from the French. (Presumably, the publisher of this edition falsely assumed that More's work was written in English, rather than Latin, and wanted to give it an air of authenticity.)

120. Despite the dating of this episode, it was not published until considerably after the review of More's *Utopia* in *Moskovskii zhurnal*.

121. Karamzin, 1964, 1:381.

122. N. M. Karamzin, "O knigakh," *Moskovskii zhurnal* 1 (1791):80. In this review of *Cadmus and Harmonia*, Karamzin praised the novel for its "attractive mythological coating" of "moral admonitions, political exhortations, and an understanding of various things that are important for mankind."

123. *Moskovskii zhurnal* 4 (1791):65.

124. One exception to this generalization was the 1819 "Dream" by the future Decembrist Aleksandr Ulybyshev, which depicts a Russia that has finally eliminated despotism and established a good system of justice and welfare. The visions of an ideal world in three 1828 works of the conservative writer Faddei Bulgarin ("Probable Fables; or, Travels Around the World in the Twenty-Ninth Century"; "Improbable Fables; or, A Journey to the Center of the Earth"; and "A Scene from Private Life in the Year 2028") are still not "utopian" in Mannheim's sense of the word. For an overview of the Bulgarin works, see Vaslef.

Chapter Seven

1. This change of direction was accompanied by an interesting change in conceptions of literary history. For example, Trediakovskii in his 1735 article "On the Ode in General" saw the *ode* as the first literary genre; Karamzin in his 1793 article "A Word About the Sciences" wrote that "the first poetry was *elegiac*."

2. *Poleznoe uveselenie*, Mar. 1760. This journal was one of a few in the early 1760's where elegiac literature appeared as frequently as panegyric.

3. *Poleznoe uveselenie*, Oct. 1760, p. 139.

4. *Poleznoe uveselenie*, Dec. 1760, p. 201.

5. *Poleznoe uveselenie*, June 1760, p. 240.

6. Quotations are from Derzhavin, 1957, pp. 210–11. Derzhavin wrote two poems under the title "K lire," one in 1794 and the other in 1797. The 1794 poem under discussion begins "Zvukopriiatnaia lira."

7. In this work, as in many elegies of the last third of the eighteenth century, the words "gold" and "silver" connote something to be avoided, a source of unhappiness. Indeed, from the 1760's through the end of the century a poem with the word "gold" in its title was more likely to be elegiac than to be panegyric and was less likely to contain a vision of an existing golden age than a poem written earlier. For example, the poem "Zlato" ("Gold") in the January 1764 issue of *Do-*

broe Namerenie is an elegy mourning the corruption brought into man's life by the introduction of gold. Similarly, Kheraskov's 1762 elegy "On Gold" portrays the valuing of gold as "the source of all our miseries" and depicts gold as obscuring the light of the sun, blinding men with its false rays (Kheraskov, 1961, pp. 86–87). Such statements recall classical descriptions of the golden age as an age without gold.

8. Dmitriev, p. 375. The identification of Eros as "the god of Pathos" is from the commentary by G. P. Makogonenko (p. 466).

9. *Vecherniaia zaria* 1 (Feb. 1782):166.

10. Text in Derzhavin, 1864, 3:42–44.

11. *Poleznoe uveselenie*, Jan. 1762, p. 12. I am grateful to Dr. Joachim Klein for calling my attention to Jean-Baptiste Gresset's "Le siècle pastorale" as the source of Kheraskov's translation. On Gresset and the Russian pastoral, see Klein, whose work I received after completing this book.

12. Statements that the golden age never existed or was a poetic fiction purposefully destroyed what Coleridge was to call the reader's "willing suspension of disbelief" and were among the first examples in Russian literature of what the formalists would call *obnazhenie priema* ("laying bare of a device"), self-consciously drawing attention to the mechanisms of literary construction.

13. See, for example, Horace, *Odes*, I, xi, 8. Beginning with Kantemir and Lomonosov, most of the major poets of the eighteenth century translated the sixth-century B.C. poet Anacreon and his followers or wrote their own original Anacreontic works. Instead of describing the society where the good life reigns, as the paradise myth often did, Anacreontic poetry usually prescribed the means of attaining the *personal* good life and described the joys of those who had attained it. Eighteenth-century Russian Anacreontic verse thus challenged the dominance of society over the individual and hence, implicitly, the aesthetic supremacy of such genres as the panegyric ode and such conventions as the paradise myth. These oppositions are reflected quite clearly in Lomonosov's "A Conversation with Anacreon" (1758–61)—a "polemic" between the panegyric and the Anacreontic odes. On Anacreontic verse in the eighteenth century, see Drage, "*Anacreontea.*"

14. Derzhavin, 1957, pp. 90–91.

15. Cf. the last line of Derzhavin's "The Picnics" (1776): "Happiness for man is when one hour is pleasant" (Derzhavin, 1957, p. 80).

16. On *Et in Arcadia ego*, see Panofsky, who notes that the "death in Arcadia" theme, quite popular in seventeenth- and eighteenth-century European art, entered European literature (sometimes in perverted and incorrect forms and translations) by the eighteenth century.

17. *Detskoe chtenie* 18 (1789):74. The guardian uses the descriptive formula of the paradise myth discussed in Chapter 1, repeating the word "there" at the beginning of each phrase.

18. The work ends with a chorus of shepherds saying: "Do not be tormented with a desire to find Arcadia under the sun. For you can find Arcadia in a peaceful soul. Seek it there." This ending recalls the Masonic ideology that paradise is located within the individual (see Chapter 5). Some affinities of *Arkadskii pamiatnik* with Masonic doctrine are also noted by Cross, "Karamzin's Versions of the Idyll," p. 85.

19. Karamzin, 1964, 1:607–8. Liza's mother emphasizes the existence of a paradise in heaven through the use of the typical *tam* ("there") of the paradise myth: " 'Tam, skazyvaiut, budut vse vesely' " (" 'There, they say, everyone will be happy' "), where *tam* is a referent to *na tom svete* ("in the other world").

20. Karamzin stresses that the urban nobleman Erast's pastoral dreamland is literary rather than real through such phrases as "existent or nonexistent" and "if one can believe the poets." Such ironic detachment of narrator from character reflects a new sophistication beginning in Russian literature. On the clash of city and country in "Poor Liza," see Cross, "Karamzin's Versions of the Idyll," pp. 85–87; on the pastoral base of this story, see Nebel, pp. 126–27.

21. During the eighteenth century, there were two Russian translations of *Don Quixote* (1769 and 1791), both from French.

22. For the texts of these eclogues, see Sumarokov, 1787, 8:53–55 and 147–49. Nebel argues that the action, setting, and characters of "Poor Liza" (but not, of course, the conclusion) come from the pastoral tradition and that Karamzin for much of the tale even retains the plot of Sumarokov's eclogues, which depict the love of "innocent shepherdesses and not-too-innocent shepherds" (pp. 126, 57).

23. Karamzin, 1964, 2:130. As the 1790's progressed, Karamzin's attitude toward the golden age and Arcadia became more and more critical. For example, in the first edition (1791) of his *Letters of a Russian Traveler*, he portrayed the peasants of Switzerland living the idyllic existence of "the original state of man"; but in the second edition (1797) he footnoted his comments on the golden age with the words "a figment of the imagination" (cited in Cross, "Karamzin's Versions of the Idyll," pp. 77–78, 89). Cross argues that despite such attacks on the literary golden age and Arcadia, Karamzin was constructing his own *political* idyll of a Russia ruled by a wise autocrat aided by loyal and virtuous citizens who are content with their stations in life (p. 90).

24. Elsewhere in *Eugene Onegin*, Pushkin defines paradise not by its pleasures but by the presence of forbidden fruits. After Eugene sees the

transformed Tatiana at a ball and falls in love with her, Pushkin states: "O mankind! You are all like our forebear Eve. What you are given does not attract you. A snake beckons you incessantly to itself and to the mysterious tree. Give you the forbidden fruit, or paradise is not paradise for you" (chapter 8, stanza 27). Human nature, in other words, is not compatible with paradise, always leading men to seek "a place where things are better, a place where we are not," as Griboedov wrote in act 1, scene 7 of *Woe from Wit*.

25. Tynianov, "Dostoevsky and Gogol," p. 101.

26. By the 1780's and 1790's, a number of works appeared with the title or subtitle of "Parodiia" ("A Parody"). See, for example, the two works called "Parodiia" in Dmitriev, pp. 347, 351.

27. Russian text quoted in Cooper, p. 74. For another example of parody of the *raiskii krin* image, see Dmitriev, "Chuzoi tolk," *Polnoe sobranie stikhotvorenii*, p. 114.

28. Krylov, 1955, 1:442. The etymology of "Ermalafid" is suggested by W. E. Brown, p. 565.

29. Several times Krylov uses this poet's comments to parody the automatism of panegyric conventions (including those of the paradise myth) and to satirize the courtiers who take these conventional utterances for sincere feelings. As the poet states: "The ode is like a silk stocking that everyone tries to stretch to fit his leg. It has very different properties from the satire. If I wanted to write a satire on one of the viziers, then I would ordinarily have to aim at the vice to which he is most subject. . . . As for the ode, it is quite another matter: one can select as many praises as one desires to present to whomever one wishes, and there is not a vizier who would not take the description of all possible merits as the very image of his exalted self" (1:415). From this context, it is clear that the magic mirror at Kaib's court, which makes things and people a thousand times more attractive than they actually are, represents the panegyric ode.

30. Gogol, 1959, 5:15–17, 142. On Russia and Rome, see Chapter 3 above; on the appeal to foreigners, see Chapter 6.

31. On Gogol's "rather thorough acquaintance with . . . the literature of the eighteenth century in general" and especially the works of Lomonosov and Derzhavin, see Mann (quote is from p. 352). During the 1840's, Gogol even kept a notebook with excerpts from Lomonosov and Derzhavin. But in his article "On the Essence of Russian Poetry" (included in *Selected Passages from Correspondence with Friends*), Gogol condemned most of Lomonosov's followers for their cold rhetoric and pomposity. And in the article "On the Lyricism of Our Poets" (in the same collection), Gogol deplored the flattery of bad panegyric odes. Chichikov seems to have studied just such rhetorical models!

32. Gogol also parodies panegyric formulas by "quoting" a news-paper description of the illumination celebrating the opening of a town park with puny trees the size of reeds; the newspaper describes the park as "a garden consisting of shady, wide-branched trees giving coolness on a stuffy day" and the citizens as "shedding streams of tears as a sign of gratitude toward His Honor the Mayor" (5:15–16).

33. Kostanzhoglo even attacks "the fiction that life in the country is dull," beginning a tradition of anti-anti-pastoral in Russian literature.

34. On these themes, see Anchor, chapter 1.

35. Carl Becker, *The Heavenly City of the Eighteenth-Century Philosophers*, as summarized in Anchor, pp. 7–8.

36. Pushkin noted that Catherine II, despite her surface support of "Enlightenment," incarcerated or exiled most of Russia's true Enlight-enment figures; he specifically mentioned Catherine's imprisonment or exile of Novikov, Radishchev, and Kniazhnin and stated that she was afraid to touch Fonvizin because of his reputation ("Zametki po russkoi istorii XVIII veka," in Pushkin, 1962, 8:129).

37. All quotes are from Derzhavin, 1957, pp. 97–104.

38. Derzhavin, 1957, pp. 109–13.

39. John Locke, *Second Treatise on Civil Government*, chapter 2, section 13. Such statements about the humanity (as opposed to the divinity) of the monarch were typical of Enlightenment thought and echoed throughout late-eighteenth-century Russian literature.

40. Derzhavin is responding here to such poems as Lomonosov's Au-gust 23, 1741, ode to Ivan VI (called "Ivan III") where the poet explicitly referred to himself as a "most devoted slave" to the tsar (Lomonosov, 1950, 8:43).

41. Karamzin, 1966, pp. 265–70.

42. Robinson, *Bor'ba idei*, pp. 65, 91, 141, 150, 154, 156.

43. All references are from Radishchev, 1975, pp. 56ff.

44. Pushkin, 1962, 1:340. All subsequent references to Pushkin will be to this edition.

45. "Zametki po russkoi istorii XVIII veka," in Pushkin, 1962, 8:131.

46. "Poet," in Pushkin, 1962, 3:22.

47. Derzhavin, 1957, p. 233.

48. Pushkin, 1962, 3:373. On Pushkin's use of Derzhavin's "Pamiat-nik" as a prism for adapting Horace's *Ode* III, 30, see Bondi, pp. 442–76.

49. In an earlier draft of this poem Pushkin had explicitly paralleled his iconoclasm with that of Radishchev (whose ode "Vol'nost'" ["Lib-erty"] had inspired Pushkin to write his own political ode by that title in 1817): "And for a long time I will be dear to the people for the fact that . . . I praised freedom, following Radishchev, and sang of mercy" (3:477).

50. Pushkin's essay "Milton and Chateaubriand's Translation of *Paradise Lost*" lauded Milton as "the austere creator of 'The Iconoclast' and *'Defensio populi'* " (Pushkin, 1962, 7:492).

51. On "iconoclasm" in Mandel'shtam's poetry of the 1930's, see Irina Mess-Baehr, "Ezopov iazyk v poezii Mandel'shtama 30-x godov."

52. By the early nineteenth century many of the images of the paradise myth that earlier had supported autocracy became associated with poetry. See the following section for examples.

53. The concept of monarchical obligation had been embodied in Roman law under the rubric of *Lex Regia* (the law obligating a king to serve his subjects with good government and with justice) and became an early basis of social contract theory. See Michael Levin, 4:253.

54. Quoted in Lotman, "Matvei Aleksandrovich Dmitriev-Mamonov," p. 51.

55. Radishchev, 1938, 1:90. In this antimonarchical poem of almost 2,000 lines, Radishchev discusses "fathers of their people" from Noah through the fall of the Roman empire, but sees only two virtuous rulers: Titus Antoninus and Marcus Aurelius. He argues that in the sixteen centuries since Marcus Aurelius, there had not been a single comparable philosopher-king. See Zapadov, introduction to Radishchev, 1975, pp. 36–37.

56. Many images of Cato in Russian literature were strongly influenced by Joseph Addison's tragedy *Cato* (1713), which was translated into Russian several times in the late eighteenth and early nineteenth centuries. After 1789 the image of Cato also reflected the influence of the French revolutionaries, whose idealization of republican Rome led them to call each other "Cato" and "Brutus" and their opponents "Cataline" (Fleming, pp. 342–43). There were a number of "Russian Catos" in the eighteenth century—the most famous of whom was Alexander Radishchev.

57. Quoted in Lotman, "Theatre and Theatricality," p. 143. As Lotman notes, images of republican Rome frequently became part of the "theatricality" that dominated the early nineteenth century (where "players" donned "masks" including those of Cato and Brutus—conduct that later made Belinskii condemn the "Roman pomp" of the period) (pp. 147, 150). Nevertheless, such republican sentiment helped lead to the Decembrist uprising of 1825.

58. Fedorov, p. 153.

59. Quoted in Lotman, "The Poetics of Everyday Behavior," p. 93.

60. Among works dealing with Marfa Posadnitsa were title works of that name by N. M. Karamzin (1803) and F. F. Ivanov (1809). The most famous work dealing with Vadim of Novgorod was Iakov Kniazhnin's

tragedy of that name (published posthumously in 1793), portraying Vadim as a defender of Novgorodian liberty who feels that absolute monarchy and liberty are incompatible. Kniazhnin's work was written in reaction against Catherine the Great's 1786 play *A Historical Presentation from the Life of Riurik*, which portrayed Vadim as a power-hungry revolutionary who tried to topple an enlightened absolutist ruler who brought happiness to his people. The similarities in Catherine's work between Riurik and herself (both foreigners who become enlightened rulers and bring "happiness" to the Russian people) are quite clear. On these two works, see W. E. Brown, pp. 340–44.

61. Pushkin, 1962, 1:414.

62. "Rodina," translated in Leighton, "Decembrism," p. 96. This work, once attributed to Venevitinov, is no longer included in his latest *Polnoe sobranie stikhotvorenii* (Moscow, 1960). I am grateful to Professor Leighton for helping me to track down this work.

63. "Proshchai, nemytaia Rossiia," Lermontov, 1958, 1:524.

64. Blok, 1960, 3:304. I am currently conducting research on the iron age of machines and shall discuss it in a forthcoming book.

65. My comments in this section refer to Russian literature written after the patriotic fervor of the War of 1812 had died down. The poetry of 1812 repeats some of the patterns discussed in this book.

66. It is difficult to imagine a poet educated on eighteenth-century literature combining the word *vek* ("age") in the same line with one of the four basic metals (gold, silver, bronze, iron) without an implicit metaphorical reference to one of the four ages of Greek and Roman mythology.

67. Baratynskii, 1957, pp. 173–75.

68. In consonance with this winter-spring opposition, the cold of reason opposes the warmth of poetic passion and "cold Urania" (muse of astronomy, hence of the sciences) opposes "stormy-weathered [*burno-pogodnyi*, i.e., emotional] Aeolus," Aphrodite, and, implicitly, Apollo.

69. On the connection of imagery of spring and rebirth with the tsar (rather than the poet) in the eighteenth century, see Chapter 3 above.

70. Del'vig, 1959, pp. 198ff.

71. In twentieth-century Russian poetry, the land of the Hyperboreans was often connected with Russia, as in several poems by Mandel'shtam and Vaginov. This link is *not* present in Del'vig's poem.

72. Pushkin, 1962, 3:113. The riddle asked by the Sphinx of all passersby in Thebes was: "Four feet in the morning, two feet in the afternoon, three feet in the evening. Who am I?" The famous answer given by Oedipus was "man." Like Oedipus, the poet answers this riddle of the menacing sphinx (the riddle of man's life).

73. This reading of the "golden age" image is supported by an 1827 comment of Pushkin: "Del'vig's idylls are astonishing. What an imagination he must have to be able to move so well from the nineteenth century into the golden age; and what an unusual feeling for the elegant to be able to divine [*ugadat'*] Greek poetry so well on the basis of Latin imitations and German translations." Both quotes are from B. V. Tomashevskii, notes to Pushkin, 1955, 3:842.

74. On the opposition between poetry and autocracy in late Pushkin, see the discussion of Pushkin's "The Monument" above. Even Pushkin's "Bronze Horseman" implicitly identifies Eugene with a poet several times, adding another level to the opposition between Peter and Eugene.

75. Just as literature has often grouped together the golden and silver ages, so has it linked the bronze and iron ages.

76. At least two articles have noted that "The Bronze Horseman" is closely related to the eighteenth-century ode. But as far as I know, no one has argued that it is an "anti-ode"—a challenge to the autocracy that the eighteenth-century panegyric ode had supported. On "The Bronze Horseman" and the eighteenth-century ode, see Pumpianskii, " 'Mednyi vsadnik,' " and Vickery.

77. Cf. Karamzin's 1801 translation of Haydn's *Creation* under the title of *Tvorenie* in Karamzin, 1966, pp. 270–83. Pushkin's stress on the word "he," which first appears in italics in line 2 and never is given an antecedent, clearly creates the impression that this "he" is superhuman, like the godlike monarchs of the eighteenth-century ode.

78. All references are from Pushkin, 1962, 4:377ff. Since writing the initial draft of this section, I have found a somewhat similar point in Antsiferov, *Dusha Peterburga* (pp. 60–71) and *Byl' i mif Peterburga* (p. 85), who also senses the depiction of a cosmogonic act in the creation of Petersburg. The source for Pushkin's image of Peter as cosmogonic creator may be not only the general tradition of the cosmogonic monarch discussed in Chapter 3 above but, more immediately, K. N. Batiushkov's 1814 essay "Progulka v Akademiiu khudozhestv" ("A Stroll to the Academy of Arts"), which probably influenced other sections of the poem as well. Peter is portrayed in this essay as creating a great city *ex nihilo*, a city that will "conquer nature herself." The phrases *skazal on* ("said he") and *skazal i Peterburg voznik* ("said he and Petersburg arose") used in this essay may also have influenced Pushkin's syntactic choice. See Batiushkov, pp. 73–74.

79. Pypin mentions Pushkin's ambivalent attitudes toward Peter, stating that although Pushkin had at one time greatly admired Peter, he later became wary of some of his reforms (*Istoriia*, 4:397). Pypin cites a number of scholarly articles arguing that Pushkin (who was researching

a historical work on Peter at the time of *Mednyi vsadnik*) was planning a negative work. See also Riasanovsky, *The Image of Peter the Great*, pp. 87–98.

80. The passive, mystical Alexander I serves as a foil to the active, rationalist Peter in this poem. Indeed, these lines attributed to Alexander are also ambiguous. Riasanovsky plausibly sees them as representing Alexander's fatalism, which leads to the death of Parasha (*The Image of Peter the Great*, p. 98).

81. Kurganov, p. 234. Pushkin knew Kurganov's work but dismissed it as a bible for the simpleminded. See Pushkin's mockery of it in "The History of the Village of Goriukhino."

82. The war between tsar and people is represented by the scene in which Eugene makes a threatening gesture at Peter's statue (perhaps a "fig" of the type that the thief Vanni Fucci in canto 25 of Dante's *Inferno* makes at God), only to be chased by it. In this scene, the unity between monarch and subject depicted in the typical ode is destroyed, just as the odic unity between heaven and earth is destroyed in Pushkin's poem as a whole.

83. Like the statue seen in Nebuchadnezzar's dream in the Book of Daniel (and mentioned, for example, in Kurganov's section on figural interpretation), the statue of Peter consists of several symbolic metals: Peter's head is "bronze" but his bridle is "iron" (see lines 411–22). The metals representing the two best ages—those of gold and silver—are conspicuously absent from this statue, as they are from the poem as a whole.

84. On Decembrist plans for utopian colonies (e.g., those of Murav'ev and Borisov), see Mazour, p. 64.

85. Zernov, p. 105.

86. Pogiolli, pp. xxi–xxii.

87. See the comment by Fedor Burlatskii, Chairman of the Subcommittee on Humanitarian, Scientific, and Cultural Cooperation of the Supreme Soviet Committee on International Affairs, that "[b]efore the reform movement, Soviet people felt theirs was the best society in the world; today they feel it is the worst" (Kennan Institute for Advanced Russian Studies Meeting Report, Dec. 5, 1989).

Appendixes

1. This list emphasizes only essential details and those that were the most important for the eighteenth-century Russian paradise myth. Another, somewhat different listing can be found in the appendix to St. Clair.

2. This motif of men eating acorns during the golden age was popu-

larized in modern literature through Cervantes's *Don Quixote* (part I, chapter 11). Dostoevsky recognized this link when in the notebooks to his *Idiot* he wrote of "an inspired speech of the Prince (Don Quixote and the acorn)"—clearly to be a speech about the golden age. See the entry for "September 8" in his *Polnoe sobranie sochinenii*, 9:277, 468.

3. Among other seventeenth-century mystical works translated by Russian Masons that included the word "paradise" in their Russian titles were: *Raiskie tsvety* ("The flowers of paradise") by Angelus Silesius (1624–77), published in Russian in 1784; *Raiskii vertograd* (*The Garden of Paradise*) by Johann Arndt (1555–1621), appended to the translation of his *True Christianity*, published in 1784 and again in 1800–1801; *Serafimskii tsvetnik v kotorom . . . nakhodiatsia izbrannye nebesnye rasteniia i raiskie tselebnye sily* ("The flowerbed of the serafim . . . containing selected heavenly plants and the curative powers of paradise") by Jakob Boehme (1575–1624), which circulated in manuscript; and *Raiskoe zerkalo* ("The mirror of paradise") by Ambrose Miller (seventeenth century), which also circulated in manuscript.

The Russian titles, which stress the image of paradise, sometimes do not correspond to the originals. For example, Angelus Silesius's work was called *The Cherubic Traveler* in the German edition from which much of the Russian was translated. The Russian edition (which contains several of his works) is a mystical composition that occasionally uses the image of paradise as a metaphor for the rewards of faith, but it does not describe this paradise at length.

4. Hastings, 9:836ff.

5. Pordech [Pordage], *Piatyi traktat o rai*, 1787 manuscript, GPB, O. III, No. 142, pp. 20–22. Future references to this manuscript will be given in parentheses in the text.

6. Translation from L'vov, *Rossiiskaia Pamela*, 2:124–28.

Selected Bibliography

Abrams, M. H. *Natural Supernaturalism*. New York, 1973.

Adams, Hazard, ed. *Critical Theory Since Plato*. New York, 1971.

Adrianova-Perets, V. P. *Ocherki poeticheskogo stilia drevnei Rusi*. Moscow-Leningrad, 1948.

Agapit [Deacon Agapetus]. *Izlozhenie glav ili statei uveshchatel'nykh grecheskomu imperatoru Iustinianu*. Trans. S. Pisarev. St. Petersburg, 1771.

Akademiia nauk SSSR. Institut russkogo iazyka. *Slovar' russkogo iazyka XI–XVII vekov*. Ed. S. G. Barkhudarov et al. Moscow, 1975– .

——— . *Slovar' russkogo iazyka XVIII veka*. Ed. Iu. S. Sorokin et al. Leningrad, 1984– .

Akademiia nauk SSSR. Institut russkoi literatury. *Istoriia russkogo romana*. Ed. A. S. Bushmin et al. 2 vols. Moscow, 1962.

——— . *Istoriia russkoi kritiki*. Ed. B. P. Gorodetskii et al. 2 vols. Moscow-Leningrad, 1958.

——— . *Istoriia russkoi literatury*. 10 vols. in 13. Moscow-Leningrad, 1941–56.

——— . *Istoriia russkoi poezii*. Ed. B. P. Gorodetskii. 2 vols. Leningrad, 1968–69.

Alekseeva, M. A. *Feierverki i illiuminatsii v grafike XVIII veka*. Leningrad, 1978.

Alexander, John T. *Catherine the Great: Life and Legend*. New York, 1989.

Al'tshuller, Mark. "Masonskie motivy 'Vtorogo toma': Universitetskie shtudii A. A. Bloka i ikh otrazhenie v lirike 1904–1905 godov." *Revue des études slaves* 54 (1982):591–607.

——— . *Predtechi slavianofil'stva v russkoi literature: (Obshchestvo "Beseda liubitelei russkogo slova")*. Ann Arbor, Mich., 1984.

Anchor, Robert. *The Enlightenment Tradition*. Berkeley, 1979.

Anichkov, D. S. *Rassuzhdenie iz natural'noi bogoslovii*. Moscow, 1769.

Antsiferov, N. P. *Byl' i mif Peterburga*. Petrograd, 1924.

————. *Dusha Peterburga*. Petersburg, 1922.

Aristotle. *Rhetoric*. Trans. W. Rhys Roberts. New York, 1954.

Armstrong, Elizabeth. *Ronsard and the Age of Gold*. Cambridge, Eng., 1968.

Armstrong, John. *The Paradise Myth*. Oxford, 1969.

Askochenskii, V. *Kiev s drevneishim ego uchilishchem Akademieiu*. 2 vols. Kiev, 1856.

Bachelard, Gaston. *The Psychoanalysis of Fire*. Trans. A. C. M. Ross. Boston, 1964.

Baehr, Stephen L. "Freemasonry in Russian Literature." In *Handbook of Russian Literature*, ed. Victor Terras, pp. 156–57.

————. "Freemasonry in Russian Literature: Eighteenth Century." In *Modern Encyclopedia of Russian and Soviet Literature*, ed. Harry Weber, 8:28–36.

————. "Who Is Firs?: The Literary History of a Name." *Ulbandus Review* 2 (1979):14–23.

Bakhtin, M. M. *The Dialogic Imagination*. Ed. Michael Holquist. Trans. Caryl Emerson and Michael Holquist. Austin, 1981.

————. *Problems of Dostoevsky's Poetics*. Trans. R. W. Rotsel. Ann Arbor, Mich., 1973.

————. *Rabelais and His World*. Trans. Helene Iswolsky. Cambridge, Mass., 1968.

————. *Voprosy literatury i estetiki*. Moscow, 1975.

Bakounine [Bakunina], Tat'iana. *Le répertoire biographique des franc-maçons russes*. Brussels, 1940.

Bakunina, T. A. *Znamenitye russkie Masony*. Paris, 1935.

Baran, Henryk, ed. *Semiotics and Structuralism: Readings from the Soviet Union*. White Plains, N.Y., 1976.

Baratynskii, E. A. *Polnoe sobranie stikhotvorenii*. Ed. E. N. Kupreianova. Leningrad, 1957.

Barker, Ernest, ed. *Social and Political Thought in Byzantium*. Oxford, 1957.

Barskov, Ia. A., ed. *Perepiska moskovskikh masonov XVIII veka: 1780–1792*. Petrograd, 1915.

Barthes, Roland. *Sade, Lourier, Loyola*. Trans. Richard Miller. New York, 1976.

Bartlett, Roger. *Human Capital: The Settlement of Foreigners in Russia, 1762–1804*. Cambridge, Eng., 1979.

Batiushkov, K. N. *Opyty v stikhakh i proze*. Ed. I. M. Semenko. Moscow, 1977.

Baynes, Norman H. "Eusebius and the Christian Empire." In *Byzantine Studies and Other Essays*, ed. Norman H. Baynes, pp. 168–72. London, 1955.

Baynes, Norman H., and H. St. L. B. Moss, eds. *Byzantium: An Introduction to East Roman Civilization.* Oxford, 1948.
Belinskii, V. G. *Polnoe sobranie sochinenii.* Ed. N. F. Bel'chikov et al. 13 vols. Moscow, 1953–59.
Benz, Ernst. *The Eastern Orthodox Church: Its Thought and Life.* Trans. Richard Winston and Clara Winston. New York, 1963.
Bercovitch, Sacvan. *The Puritan Origins of the American Self.* New Haven, 1975.
Berdiaev, Nicholas. *The Origins of Russian Communism.* Trans. R. M. French. Ann Arbor, Mich., 1960.
Berkov, P. N. *Istoriia russkoi zhurnalistiki XVIII veka.* Moscow-Leningrad, 1952.
———. "Khor ko prevratnomu svetu i ego avtor." *XVIII vek* 1 (1935):181–202.
———, ed. *Satiricheskie zhurnaly N. I. Novikova.* Moscow-Leningrad, 1951.
Beshenkovskii, E. V. "Zhizn' Fedora Emina." *XVIII vek* 11 (1976):186–203.
Billington, James. *The Icon and the Axe.* New York, 1966.
Blagoi, D. D. *Istoriia russkoi literatury XVIII veka.* Moscow, 1945.
Blok, A. A. *Sobranie sochinenii.* Ed. V. N. Orlov, A. A. Surkov, and K. I. Chukovskii. 8 vols. Moscow-Leningrad, 1960–63.
Bogdanovich, I. F. *Stikhotvoreniia i poemy.* Ed. I. Z. Serman. Leningrad, 1957.
Bolshakoff, Serge. *Russian Nonconformity.* Philadelphia, 1950.
Bondi, S. M. *O Pushkine.* Moscow, 1978.
Bourychkine, Paul. *Bibliographie sur la Franc-maçonnerie en Russie.* Paris, 1967.
Breuillard, Jean. "Fragments d'utopies dans la littérature russe du XVIII siècle: Levshin et Xeraskov." *Revue des études slaves* 56 (1984):17–31.
Brown, William Edward. *A History of Eighteenth-Century Russian Literature.* Ann Arbor, Mich., 1980.
Budgen, David. "Fedor Emin and the Beginnings of the Russian Novel." In *Russian Literature in the Age of Catherine the Great*, ed. A. G. Cross, pp. 67–94.
———. "The Works of F. A. Emin." Ph.D. diss., Oxford University, 1976.
Bulgakov, Sergius. "Le ciel sur la terre." *Una Sancta* (1927):42–63.
———. *The Orthodox Church.* New York, 1935.
Burke, Kenneth. *A Rhetoric of Motives.* 1950. Rpt. Berkeley, 1969.
Bury, J. K. *The Idea of Progress.* New York, 1960.
Buslaev, Fedor, ed. *Russkaia khrestomatiia.* 1870. Rpt. The Hague, 1969.

Cahn, Steven M., ed. *Classics of Western Philosophy*. Indianapolis, Ind., 1979.

Carmichael, Joel. *A Cultural History of Russia*. New York, 1968.

Chechulin, N. D. *Russkii sotsial'nyi roman XVIII veka*. St. Petersburg, 1900.

Chegodaeva, N. M. "D. G. Levitskii." In *Istoriia russkogo iskusstva*, ed. I. E. Grabar', 7:40–92.

Cherniavsky, Michael. *Tsar and People: Studies in Russian Myths*. New Haven, 1961.

Chistov, K. V. *Russkie narodnye sotsial'no-utopicheskie legendy*. Moscow, 1967.

Chulkov, M. D. *Peresmeshnik, ili Slavenskie skazki*. 3rd ed. 5 vols. Moscow, 1789.

Čiževskij, Dmitrij. *History of Russian Literature from the Eleventh Century to the End of Baroque*. The Hague, 1971.

Clark, Katerina, and Michael Holquist. *Mikhail Bakhtin*. Cambridge, Mass., 1984.

Clendenning, P. H. "Dr. Thomas Dimsdale and Smallpox Inoculation in Russia." *Journal of the History of Medicine* 28 (1973):109–25.

Comito, Terry. *The Idea of the Garden in the Renaissance*. New Brunswick, N.J., 1978.

Cooper, B. F. "The History and Development of the Ode in Russia." Ph.D. diss., Cambridge University, 1972.

Corcoran, Sister Mary Irma. *Milton's Paradise with Reference to the Hexameral Background*. Washington, D.C., 1945.

Cracraft, James. "Feofan Prokopovich." In *The Eighteenth Century in Russia*, ed. J. G. Garrard, pp. 75–105.

Cross, A. G. "Karamzin's Versions of the Idyll." In *Essays on Karamzin*, ed. J. L. Black, pp. 75–90. The Hague, 1975.

———. *N. M. Karamzin*. Carbondale, Ill., 1971.

———, ed. *Russia and the West in the Eighteenth Century: Proceedings of an International Conference*. Newtonville, Mass., 1983.

———, ed. *Russian Literature in the Age of Catherine the Great*. Oxford, 1976.

Curtius, Ernst Robert. *European Literature and the Latin Middle Ages*. Trans. Willard R. Trask. New York, 1963.

Dal', Vladimir I. *Poslovitsy russkogo naroda*. 2 vols. 1862. Rpt. Moscow, 1984.

———. *Tolkovyi slovar' zhivogo velikorusskogo iazyka*. 2nd ed. 1882. Rpt. Moscow, 1956.

Danéliou, Jean. *Sacramentum futuri*. Paris, 1950.

Dante Alighieri. *The Divine Comedy*. 3 vols. Ed. Dorothy L. Sayers. Trans.

Dorothy L. Sayers and Barbara Reynolds. Harmondsworth, Eng., 1949–62.

Dashkova, E. R. *Zapiski: 1743–1810*. Leningrad, 1985.

Davis, J. C. *Utopia and the Ideal Society*. Cambridge, Eng., 1981.

Del'vig, A. A. *Polnoe sobranie stikhotvorenii*. Ed. B. V. Tomashevskii. Leningrad, 1959.

Demin, A. S., et al., eds. *P'esy shkol'nykh teatrov Moskvy*. Moscow, 1974.

Derzhavin, G. R. *Sochineniia*. Ed. Ia. K. Grot. 9 vols. St. Petersburg, 1864–83.

———. *Stikhotvoreniia*. Ed. D. D. Blagoi and A. V. Zapadov. Leningrad, 1957.

———. *Stikhotvoreniia*. Ed. A. Ia. Kucherov. Moscow-Leningrad, 1958.

Derzhavina, O. A., and V. P. Grebeniuk, eds. *Panegiricheskaia literatura petrovskogo vremeni*. Moscow, 1979.

Derzhavina, O. A., et al., eds. *Russkaia dramaturgiia poslednei chetverti XVII i nachala XVIII veka*. Moscow, 1972.

Dmitriev, I. I. *Polnoe sobranie stikhotvorenii*. Ed. G. P. Makogonenko. Leningrad, 1967.

Dmitriev, L. A., and D. S. Likhachev, eds. *"Izbornik."* Moscow, 1969.

Dobroliubov, N. A. *Sobranie sochinenii*. Ed. B. I. Bursov et al. 9 vols. Moscow, 1961–64.

Domashnev, Sergei. *Oda . . . Ekaterine Alekseevne . . . na vseradostnoe vosshestvie na prestol*. Moscow, 1762.

Dostoevskii, F. M. *Polnoe sobranie sochinenii*. 30 vols. Leningrad, 1972– .

Downey, Glanville. *Constantinople in the Age of Justinian*. Norman, Okla., 1960.

Drage, C. L. "The *Anacreontea* and Eighteenth-Century Russian Poetry." *Slavonic and East European Review* 41 (1962):110–34.

———. *Russian Literature in the Eighteenth Century*. London, 1978.

Drage, C. L., and Walter Vickery, eds. *An XVIIIth Century Russian Reader*. Oxford, 1969.

Duncan, Joseph. *Milton's Earthly Paradise*. Minneapolis, Minn., 1972.

Dvornik, Francis. *The Slavs in European History and Civilization*. New Brunswick, N.J., 1962.

Efimov, N. *Rus—Novyi Izrail': Teokraticheskaia ideologiia svoezemnogo pravo-slaviia v dopetrovskoi pis'mennosti*. Kazan', 1912.

Eleonskaia, A. S., et al., eds. *P'esy stolichnykh i provintsial'nykh teatrov pervoi poloviny XVIII veka*. Moscow, 1975.

Eliade, Mircea. *The Myth of the Eternal Return*. Trans. Willard R. Trask. New York, 1954.

———. *Patterns in Comparative Religion*. Trans. Rosemary Sheed. Cleveland, 1963.

————. *Rites and Symbols of Initiation: The Mysteries of Birth and Rebirth.* Trans. Willard R. Trask. 1958. Rpt. New York, 1965.

————. *The Sacred and the Profane.* Trans. Willard R. Trask. 1959. Rpt. New York, 1961.

Elledge, Scott, and Donald Schier, eds. *The Continental Model.* Ithaca, N.Y., 1970.

Elliott, Robert. *The Shape of Utopia.* Chicago, 1970.

Ely, Stanislaus Pinas. *Bratskie uveshchaniia k nekotorym brat'iam svbnym kmnshchkm [svobodnym kamen'shchikam], pisany Bratom Seddagom.* Moscow, 1784.

Emin, F. A. *Nepostoiannaia fortuna ili Pokhozhdenie Miramonda.* 3 vols. St. Petersburg, 1763.

————. *Prikliucheniia Femistokla.* 2nd ed. Moscow, 1781.

Empson, William. *Some Versions of Pastoral.* New York, 1950.

Eremin, I. P. "Poeticheskii stil' Simeona Polotskogo." *Trudy otdela drevne-russkoi literatury* 6 (1948):125–53.

————. "Sillabicheskaia poeziia." In Akademiia nauk SSSR, Institut russkoi literatury, *Istoriia russkoi literatury,* vol. 2, pt. 2, pp. 342–62.

Eshevskii, S. V. *Sochineniia po russkoi istorii.* Moscow, 1900.

Eusebius. *Ecclesiastical History.* Trans. Roy J. Deferrari. 2 vols. Washington, D.C., 1955.

————. "Oration in Praise of the Emperor Constantine: Pronounced on the Thirtieth Anniversary of His Rule." In *Icon and Minaret: Sources of Byzantine and Islamic Civilization,* ed. Charles M. Brand. Englewood Cliffs, N.J., 1969.

Fedorov, V. A., ed. *Sbornik dokumentov po istorii SSSR: Pervaia polovina XIX veka.* Moscow, 1974.

Fedotov, George P. *The Russian Religious Mind.* Vol. 1. 1946. Rpt. New York, 1960.

Ferguson, John. *Utopias of the Classical World.* Ithaca, N.Y., 1975.

Fleming, William. *Arts and Ideas.* 6th ed. New York, 1980.

Fletcher, Angus. *Allegory: The Theory of a Symbolic Mode.* Ithaca, N.Y., 1964.

————. *The Prophetic Moment: An Essay on Spenser.* Chicago, 1971.

Fliegelman, Jay. *Prodigals and Pilgrims: The American Revolution Against Patriarchal Authority.* Cambridge, Eng., 1982.

Florovsky, Georges. *Ways of Russian Philosophy.* Pt. 1. Trans. Robert L. Nichols. Ed. Richard S. Haugh. Belmont, Mass., 1979.

Fonvizin, D. I. *Sobranie sochinenii.* 2 vols. Ed. G. P. Makogonenko. Moscow-Leningrad, 1959.

Freeze, Gregory L. *The Russian Levites: Parish Clergy in the Eighteenth Century.* Cambridge, Mass., 1977.

Frye, Northrop. *Anatomy of Criticism*. Princeton, N.J., 1957.
———. *Fearful Symmetry*. Princeton, N.J., 1947.
———. "Varieties of Literary Utopias." In *Utopias and Utopian Thought*, ed. Frank Manuel, pp. 25–49.
Garai, Janna. *The Book of Symbols*. New York, 1973.
Garrard, J. G. *The Prose Fiction of Mikhail Chulkov*. The Hague, 1971.
———, ed. *The Eighteenth Century in Russia*. Oxford, 1973.
Geertz, Clifford. "Centers, Kings, and Charisma: Reflections on the Symbolics of Power." In *Culture and Its Creators: Essays in Honor of Edward Shils*, ed. Joseph Ben-David and Terry Nichols Clark, pp. 150–71. Chicago, 1977.
———. *Islam Observed: Religious Developments in Morocco and Indonesia*. Chicago, 1971.
Gerber, Richard. *Utopian Fantasy*. London, 1955.
Giamatti, A. Bartlett. *The Earthly Paradise and the Renaissance Epic*. Princeton, N.J., 1966.
Gilarovskii, Petr. *Istinnoe blazhenstvo Rossii*. St. Petersburg, 1799.
Gleason, Walter. "The Image of the West in the Journals of Mid-Eighteenth-Century Russia." In *Russia and the West in the Eighteenth Century*, ed. A. G. Cross, pp. 109–17.
———. *Moral Idealists, Bureaucracy, and Catherine the Great*. New Brunswick, N.J., 1981.
Gogol', N. V. *Polnoe sobranie sochinenii*. 14 vols. Moscow, 1937–52.
———. *Sobranie khudozhestvennykh proizvedenii*. 5 vols. Moscow, 1959.
Goldfrank, David. "Moscow, the Third Rome." In *Modern Encyclopedia of Russian and Soviet History*, ed. Joseph L. Wieczynski, 23:118–21.
Goodenough, Erwin R. "The Political Philosophy of Hellenistic Kingship." *Yale Classical Studies* 1 (1928):55–110.
Goodspeed, Edgar J., trans. *The Apocrypha*. New York, 1959.
Grabar', I. E., et al., eds. *Istoriia russkogo iskusstva*. 13 vols. in 16. Moscow, 1953–68.
Grebeniuk, V. P. "Evoliutsiia poeticheskikh simvolov rossiiskogo absoliutizma (ot Simeona Polotskogo do M. V. Lomonosova)." In *Razvitie barokko i zarozhdenie klassitsizma v Rossii XVII-nachala XVIII v.*, ed. A. N. Robinson, pp. 188–200.
Green, Michael A. "Kheraskov and the Christian Tragedy." *California Slavic Studies* 9 (1976):1–25.
Gudzii, N. K., ed. *Khrestomatiia po drevnei russkoi literature*. Moscow, 1973.
Guerdan, René. *Byzantium: Its Triumphs and Tragedy*. Trans. D. L. B. Hartley. New York, 1962.

Gukovskii, G. A. "Ekaterina II." In Akademiia nauk SSSR, Institut russkoi literatury, *Istoriia russkoi literatury*, 4:362–80.

——. *Ocherki po istorii russkoi literatury XVIII veka: Dvorianskaia fronda v literature 1750–1760 godov*. Moscow-Leningrad, 1936.

——. *Russkaia literatura XVIII veka*. Moscow, 1939.

——. *Russkaia poeziia XVIII veka*. Leningrad, 1927.

Guminskii, V., ed. *Vzgliad skvoz' stoletiia: Russkaia fantastika XVIII i pervoi poloviny XIX veka*. Moscow, 1977.

Hall, James. *A Dictionary of Subjects and Symbols in Art*. Rev. ed. New York, 1979.

——. *A History of Ideas and Images in Italian Art*. New York, 1982.

Harvey, Sir Paul, comp. and ed. *The Oxford Companion to English Literature*. 4th ed. Rev. Dorothy Eagle. Oxford, 1969.

Hastings, James, ed. *Encyclopedia of Religion and Ethics*. 13 vols. New York, 1917.

Hawkes, Terrence. *Metaphor*. London, 1972.

Heath-Stubbs, John. *The Ode*. Oxford, 1969.

Herrick, Robert. *Herrick*. Ed. William Jay Smith. The Laurel Poetry Series. New York, 1962.

Hippisley, Anthony. "The Emblem in the Writings of Simeon Polotskij." *Slavic and East European Journal* 15 (Summer 1971):167–83.

——. *The Poetic Style of Simeon Polotsky*. Birmingham Slavic Monographs, no. 16. Birmingham, Eng., 1985.

Homer. *The Odyssey*. Trans. E. V. Rieu. Baltimore, Md., 1945.

Horace. *The Complete Works*. Ed. Casper J. Kraemer, Jr. New York, 1936.

Hubbs, Joanna. *Mother Russia: The Feminine Myth in Russian Culture*. Bloomington, Ind., 1988.

Hughes, Robert. *Heaven and Hell in Western Art*. New York, 1968.

Hussey, J. M. *The Byzantine World*. New York, 1961.

Iunker, G. F. [Juncker, G. F. W.]. *Kratkoe opisanie onago feierverka . . . aprelia 28 dnia 1734 goda. . . .* St. Petersburg, 1734.

——. *Opisanie velikoi illiuminatsii 28 genvaria 1733 goda*. St. Petersburg, 1733.

Iz"iasnenie nakhodiashchikhsia na onom feierverke izobrazhenii . . . na den' rozhdeniia e.i.v. . . . Anny Ioannovny, 28 genvaria 1736. St. Petersburg, 1736.

Jackson, Robert L. *The Art of Dostoevsky*. Princeton, N.J., 1981.

——. *Dostoevsky's Quest for Form*. New Haven, 1966.

——. " 'Matryona's Home': The Making of a Russian Icon." In *Solzhenitsyn*, ed. Kathryn Feuer, pp. 60–70. Englewood Cliffs, N.J., 1976.

——. "The Triple Vision: Dostoevsky's 'The Peasant Marey.' " *Yale Review* 67 (Winter 1978):225–35.

Jansen, H. W. *A History of Art*. Englewood Cliffs, N.J., 1969.

Johnson, J. W., ed. *Utopian Literature*. New York, 1968.

Jones, Gareth. *Nikolay Novikov: Enlightener of Russia*. Cambridge, Eng., 1984.

Jonson, Ben. *Ben Jonson's Plays and Masques*. Ed. Robert M. Adams. New York, 1979.

Juncker, G. F. W. *See* Iunker, G. F.

Jung, Carl. *The Basic Writings of C. G. Jung*. Ed. Violet Staub de Laszlo. New York, 1959.

Kaisarov, P. *Oda. Blagodenstvie Rossii*. . . . Moscow, 1795.

Kant, I. "What Is Enlightenment?" In *The Enlightenment: A Comprehensive Anthology*, ed. Peter Gay, pp. 383–91. New York, 1973.

Kantemir, A. D. *Sobranie stikhotvorenii*. Ed. F. Ia. Priima and Z. I. Gershkovich. Leningrad, 1956.

——— . *Sochineniia, pis'ma i izbrannye perevody*. Ed. P. A. Efremov and V. Ia. Stoiunina. 2 vols. St. Petersburg, 1867–68.

Kantorowicz, Ernst. *The King's Two Bodies*. Princeton, N.J., 1957.

Kanty na vysochaishee eia imp. velichestva v Sviato-Troitskuiu lavru prishestvie. Moscow, 1762.

Kapnist, V. V. *Izbrannye proizvedeniia*. Ed. G. V. Ermakova-Bitner and D. S. Babkin. Leningrad, 1973.

Karamzin, N. M. *Izbrannye sochineniia*. Ed. P. N. Berkov and G. P. Makogonenko. 2 vols. Moscow-Leningrad, 1964.

——— . *Karamzin's Memoir on Ancient and Modern Russia*. Ed. and trans. Richard Pipes. Cambridge, Mass., 1972.

——— . *Polnoe sobranie stikhotvorenii*. Ed. Iu. M. Lotman. Moscow-Leningrad, 1966.

Karlinsky, Simon. *Russian Drama from Its Beginnings to the Age of Pushkin*. Berkeley, 1985.

Kheraskov, M. M. *Epistola k . . . imp. Ekaterine Alekseevne v den' tezoimenitstva eia*. Moscow, 1762.

——— . *Izbrannye proizvedeniia*. Ed. A. V. Zapadov. Leningrad, 1961.

——— . *Kadm i Garmoniia*. 2 vols. Moscow, 1789.

——— . *Khram rossiiskogo blagodenstviia*. Moscow, 1775.

——— . *Numa, ili Protsvetaiushchii Rim*. Moscow, 1768.

——— . *Oda . . . Ekaterine Aleekseevne na ustanovliaemye vnov' premudrye zakony*. . . . Moscow, 1767.

——— . *Oda . . . Elizavete Petrovne . . . na den' vozshestviia na prestol*. . . . Moscow, 1753.

——— . *Oda na den' vozshestviia na prestol e.i.v. Ekateriny Vtoroi*. . . . Moscow, 1764.

——— . *Plody nauk*. Moscow, 1761.

———. *Polidor, syn Kadma i Garmonii.* 3 vols. Moscow, 1794.

———. *Tvoreniia Mikhaila Kheraskova, vnov' ispravlennye i dopolnennye.* 12 vols. Moscow, 1796–1803.

———. *Veseliashchaiasia Rossiia.* Moscow, 1776.

———. *Vladimir vozrozhdennyi.* Moscow, 1785.

———. *Zolotoi prut.* Moscow, 1782.

Klein, Joachim. *Die Schäferdichtung des russischen Klassizismus.* Wiesbaden, 1988.

Klibanov, A. I. *Narodnaia sotsial'naia utopiia v Rossii: Period feodalizma.* Moscow, 1977.

———. *Social'nye utopii v russkikh krest'ianskikh dvizheniiakh.* Moscow, 1966.

Kliuchevskii, Vasilii O. *Peter the Great.* Trans. Lilian Archibald. New York, 1961.

———. *Sochineniia.* 8 vols. Moscow, 1956–59.

Kokorev, A. V., ed. *Khrestomatiia po russkoi literature XVIII veka.* Moscow, 1965.

Krasovskaia, V. M. *Russkii baletnyi teatr ot vozniknoveniia do serediny XIX veka.* Moscow-Leningrad, 1958.

Kratkaia literaturnaia entsiklopediia. Ed. A. A. Surkov. 9 vols. Leningrad, 1962–78.

Krylov, I. A. *Sochineniia.* Ed. N. L. Stepanov. 2 vols. Moscow, 1955.

Kubacheva, V. N. "Vostochnaia povest' v russkoi literature XVIII-nachala XIX veka." *XVIII vek* 5 (1962):294–315.

Kurganov, N. *Rossiiskaia universal'naia grammatika, ili vseobshchee pis'moslovie.* St. Petersburg, 1769.

Kurilov, A. S., ed. *Lomonosov i russkaia literatura.* Moscow, 1987.

Lacombe de Prezel, Honoré. *Ikonologicheskii leksikon.* Trans. Ivan Akimov. St. Petersburg, 1763.

Ladner, Gerhart B. "The Concept of the Image in the Greek Fathers and the Byzantine Iconoclastic Controversy." *Dumbarton Oaks Papers* 7 (1953):1–34.

———. *The Idea of Reform.* Cambridge, Mass., 1959.

Leighton, Lauren G. "Decembrism." In *Handbook of Russian Literature,* ed. Victor Terras, pp. 94–96.

———. "Freemasonry in Russia: The Grand Lodge of Astraea (1815–1822)." *Slavonic and East European Review* 60 (1982):221–43.

———. "Pushkin and Freemasonry: The Queen of Spades." In *Studies in Nineteenth-Century Russian Prose,* ed. George J. Gutsche and Lauren G. Leighton, pp. 15–23. Columbus, Ohio, 1982.

Lennhoff, Eugen, and Oskar Posner, eds. *Internationales Freimaurerlexikon.* Zurich-Leipzig-Vienna, 1932.

Lentin, A. Introduction to M. M. Shcherbatov, *On the Corruption of*

Morals in Russia. Cambridge, Eng., 1969.

Leont'ev, Nikolai. *Oda . . . Ekaterine Alekseevne . . . na vseradostneishee vozshestvie na prestol*. St. Petersburg, 1762.

Lermontov, M. Iu. *Sobranie sochinenii*. 4 vols. Moscow-Leningrad, 1958–59.

Levin, Harry. *The Myth of the Golden Age in the Renaissance*. New York, 1972.

Levin, Michael. "Social Contract." In *Dictionary of the History of Ideas*, ed. Philip P. Wiener, 4:251–63.

Levshin, V. A. *Noveishee puteshestvie*. In *Sobesednik liubitelei rossiiskogo slova*, 1784, 13:138–66; 14:5–33; 15:5–33; 16:38–45, 49–53.

———. *Russkie skazki*. 10 vols. Moscow, 1783.

Likhachev, D. S. *Poetika sadov*. Leningrad, 1982.

Lomonosov, M. V. *Izbrannye proizvedeniia*. Ed. A. A. Morozov. Moscow-Leningrad, 1965.

———. *Polnoe sobranie sochinenii*. Ed. S. I. Vavilov et al. 10 vols. Moscow-Leningrad, 1950–59.

Longinov, M. N. *Novikov i moskovskie martinisty*. Moscow, 1867.

Lopukhin, Ivan. *Maskonskie trudy I. V. Lopukhina*. Ed. V. F. Savodnik. Moscow, 1913.

Lotman, Iu. M. "Matvei Aleksandrovich Dmitriev-Mamonov." *Uchenye zapiski Tartuskogo universiteta* 78 (1959):19–92.

———. "The Poetics of Everyday Behavior in Eighteenth-Century Russian Culture." Trans. Andrea Beesing. In Iu. M. Lotman, L. Ia. Ginzburg, and B. A. Uspenskii, *The Semiotics of Russian Cultural History*, pp. 67–94.

———. "The Theatre and Theatricality as Components of Early Nineteenth-Century Culture." Trans. G. S. Smith. In Lotman and Uspenskii, *The Semiotics of Russian Culture*, pp. 141–64.

Lotman, Iu. M., L. Ia. Ginzburg, and B. A. Uspenskii. *The Semiotics of Russian Cultural History*. Ed. Alexander D. Nakhimovsky and Alice Stone Nakhimovsky. Ithaca, N.Y., 1985.

Lotman, Iu. M., and B. A. Uspenskii. "Binary Models in the Dynamics of Russian Culture (to the End of the Eighteenth Century)." Trans. Robert Sorenson. In Lotman, Ginzburg, and Uspenskii, *The Semiotics of Russian Cultural History*, pp. 30–66.

———. "Echoes of the Notion 'Moscow the Third Rome' in Peter the Great's Ideology." Trans. N. F. C. Owen. In Lotman and Uspenskii, *The Semiotics of Russian Culture*, pp. 53–67.

———. "Myth-Name-Culture." In *Semiotics and Structuralism: Readings from the Soviet Union*, ed. Henryk Baran, pp. 17–32.

———. *The Semiotics of Russian Culture*. Ed. Ann Shukman. Ann Arbor, 1984.

Lovejoy, Arthur, and George Boas. *Primitivism and Related Ideas in Antiquity.* 1935. Rpt. New York, 1965.

L'vov, P. Iu. *Khram istiny.* St. Petersburg, 1790.

―――. *Rossiiskaia Pamela, ili Istoriia Marii.* 2nd ed. 2 vols. Moscow, 1794.

Lyons, John. *Introduction to Theoretical Linguistics.* Cambridge, Eng., 1969.

Mackey, Albert. *An Encyclopedia of Freemasonry and its Kindred Sciences.* New York, 1913.

―――. *The Symbolism of Freemasonry.* New York, 1869.

Madariaga, Isabel de. *Russia in the Age of Catherine the Great.* New Haven, 1981.

Maddison, Carol. *Apollo and the Nine.* Baltimore, Md., 1960.

Magazin svobodno-kamen'shchicheskoi. 1 vol. in 2 parts. Moscow, 1784.

Maggs, Barbara Widenor. "Firework Art and Literature: Eighteenth-Century Pyrotechnic Tradition in Russia and Western Europe." *Slavonic and East European Review* 54 (1976):24–40.

Maiakovskii, V. V. *Polnoe sobranie sochinenii.* 13 vols. Moscow, 1955–61.

Maikov, L. N. *Ocherki iz istorii russkoi literatury XVII i XVIII stoletii.* St. Petersburg, 1889.

Maikov, V. I. *Izbrannye proizvedeniia.* Ed. A. V. Zapadov. Moscow-Leningrad, 1966.

―――. *Torzhestvuiushchii Parnass.* Moscow, 1775.

Makogonenko, G. P. *N. I. Novikov i russkoe prosveshchenie.* Moscow-Leningrad, 1952.

―――, ed. *Russkaia literatura XVIII veka.* Leningrad, 1970.

―――, ed. *Russkaia proza XVIII veka.* Moscow-Leningrad, 1950.

Makogonenko, G. P., and I. Z. Serman, eds. *Poety XVIII veka.* Biblioteka poeta, Malaia seriia, 3-e izdanie. 2 vols. Leningrad, 1958.

Makogonenko, G. P., I. Z. Serman, et al., eds. *Poety XVIII veka.* Biblioteka poeta, Bol'shaia seriia, 2-oe izdanie. 2 vols. Leningrad, 1972.

Malein, A. I. "Izdaniia i perevody *Utopii.*" In Mor, pp. 257–63.

Malinin, V. *Starets Eleazarova monastyria Filofei i ego poslaniia.* Kiev, 1901.

Malyshev, I. V., and L. B. Svetlov, eds. *N. I. Novikov i ego sovremenniki: Izbrannye sochineniia.* Moscow, 1961.

Mann, Iu. V. "M. V. Lomonosov v tvorcheskom soznanii N. V. Gogolia." In *Lomonosov i russkaia literatura,* ed. A. S. Kurilov, pp. 351–71.

Mannheim, Karl. *Ideology and Utopia: An Introduction to the Sociology of Knowledge.* Trans. Louis Wirth and Edward Shils. London, 1952.

Manning, Clarence, ed. *Anthology of Eighteenth-Century Russian Literature.* 2 vols. New York, 1951.

Manuel, Frank, ed. *Utopias and Utopian Thought.* 1967. Rpt. Boston, 1972.

Manuel, Frank, and Fritzie P. Manuel. "Sketch for a Natural History of Paradise." *Daedalus* 101 (Winter 1972):83–123.

————. *Utopian Thought in the Western World*. Cambridge, Mass., 1979.

Marinelli, Peter V. *Pastoral*. London, 1971.

Martz, Louis L. *The Paradise Within: Studies in Vaughan, Traherne and Milton*. New Haven, Conn., 1964.

Marvell, Andrew. *Selected Poems*. Ed. Joseph H. Summers. New York, 1961.

Masaryk, T. G. *The Spirit of Russia*. Trans. Eden Paul and Cedar Paul. 2 vols. New York, 1968.

Maschkowzew, N. G., ed. *Geschichte der russischen Kunst*. Dresden, 1975.

Massie, Suzanne. *Land of the Firebird*. New York, 1980.

Mathew, Gervase. *Byzantine Aesthetics*. New York, 1971.

Mazour, Anatole. *The First Russian Revolution, 1825: The Decembrist Movement*. Stanford, Calif., 1961.

Medlin, William K. *Moscow and East Rome*. Geneva, 1952.

Medlin, William K., and Christos G. Patrinelis. *Renaissance Influences and Religious Reforms in Russia: Western and Post-Byzantine Impacts on Culture and Education (16th–17th Centuries)*. Geneva, 1971.

Mel'gunov, S. P., and N. P. Sidorov, eds. *Masonstvo v ego proshlom i nastoiashchem*. 2 vols. St. Petersburg, 1914–15.

Mess-Baehr, Irina. "Ezopov iazyk v poezii Mandel'shtama 30-x godov." *Russian Literature* 29, no. 3 (1991).

————. "'Soldattskaia' satira i allegoriia v neizdannykh antinapoleonovskikh stikhakh Derzhavina." *Study Group on Eighteenth-Century Russia Newsletter* 8 (1980):70–85.

Meyendorff, Baron, and Norman H. Baynes. "The Byzantine Inheritance in Russia." In *Byzantium: An Introduction to East Roman Civilization*, ed. N. H. Baynes and H. St. L. B. Moss, pp. 369–91.

Meyendorff, John. *Byzantine Theology*. New York, 1974.

————. "The Church." In *An Introduction to Russian History*, ed. Robert Auty and Dmitri Obolensky, pp. 315–30. Cambridge, Eng., 1976.

Miller, Madeline G., and J. Lane Miller, eds. *Harper's Bible Dictionary*. 7th ed. New York, 1961.

Milton, John. *Paradise Lost and Other Poems*. Ed. Edward Le Comte. New York, 1961.

Miner, Earl. *Studies in Seventeenth-Century Imagery*. Los Angeles, 1971.

Monnier, André. "Une utopie russe au siècle de Catherine." *Cahiers du monde russe et soviétique* 23 (1982):187–95.

Moorman, Charles. *A Knyght There Was: The Evolution of the Knight in Literature*. Lexington, Ky., 1967.

Mor, Tomas [More, Thomas]. *Utopiia*. Ed. A. I. Malein. 2nd ed. Moscow, 1953.

More, Thomas. *Utopia*. Trans. and ed. Edward Surtz. New Haven, 1964.

Morozov, A. A. "Emblematika barokko v literature i iskusstve petrov-
    skogo vremeni." *XVIII vek* 9 (1974):184–226.
———. "Lomonosov i barokko." *Russkaia literatura*, 1965, no. 2, pp.
    70–96.
Morson, Gary Saul. *The Boundaries of Genre: Dostoevsky's "Diary of a
    Writer" and the Traditions of Literary Utopia*. Austin, 1981.
Murray, Henry A., ed. *Myth and Mythmaking*. Boston, 1968.
Nebel, Henry M., Jr. *N. M. Karamzin: A Russian Sentimentalist*. The
    Hague, 1967.
Neuenschwander, Dennis B. "Themes in Russian Utopian Fiction."
    Ph.D. diss., Syracuse University, 1974.
Neuhäuser, Rudolf. *Towards the Romantic Age: Essays on Sentimental and
    Preromantic Literature in Russia*. The Hague, 1974.
Nicolson, Marjorie Hope. *Voyages to the Moon*. New York, 1960.
Novikov, N. I. *Satiricheskie zhurnaly N. I. Novikova*. Ed. P. N. Berkov.
    Moscow-Leningrad, 1951.
Novyi entsiklopedicheskii slovar'. 29 vols. St. Petersburg/Petrograd, 1911–
    16.
Oda, pripisannaia v pokhvalu Raify. Moscow, 1771.
Okenfus, Max. "The Jesuit Origins of Petrine Education." In *The Eigh-
    teenth Century in Russia*, ed. John G. Garrard, pp. 106–30. Oxford,
    1973.
Opisanie koronatsii . . . Anny Ioannovny. Moscow, 1730.
*Opisanie oboikh triumfal'nykh vorot postavlennykh v chest' . . . Elizavety Per-
    voi. . . .* St. Petersburg, 1742.
Orgel, Stephen. *The Illusion of Power*. Berkeley, 1975.
———. "The Poetics of Spectacle." *New Literary History* 2 (1971):367–89.
Orthodox Eastern Church. *The Festal Menaion*. Trans. Mother Mary and
    Archimandrite Kallistos Ware. London, 1969.
———. *Service Book of the Holy Orthodox-Catholic Apostolic Church*. Comp.
    and trans. Isabel Hapgood. 4th ed. New York, 1965.
Ouspensky, Leonid. *Theology of the Icon*. Anonymous translation from
    the French. Crestwood, N.Y., 1978.
Panchenko, A. M. *Russkaia stikhotvornaia kul'tura XVII veka*. Leningrad,
    1973.
Panofsky, Erwin. "Et in Arcadia ego." In *Pastoral and Romance*, ed.
    Eleanor Terry Lincoln, pp. 25–46. Englewood Cliffs, N.J., 1969.
Patch, Howard Rollin. *The Other World According to Descriptions in Medi-
    eval Literature*. Cambridge, Mass., 1950.
Pekarskii, P. P. *Dopolneniia k istorii masonstva v Rossii*. St. Petersburg,
    1869.
Perepechin, A. I. *Oda na . . . den' vozshestviia na prestol . . . imp. Ekateriny
    Alekseevny . . . .* Moscow, 1765.

Pesni v Ierusalime: 5817. Moscow, n.d.

Peter I (the Great), Emperor of Russia. *Pis'ma i bumagi Petra pervogo.* St. Petersburg/Petrograd/Leningrad, 1887–1964.

Piksanov, N. K. "Masonskaia literatura." In Akademiia nauk SSSR, Institut russkoi literatury, *Istoriia russkoi literatury,* 4:51–84.

Pipes, Richard. *Russia Under the Old Regime.* New York, 1974.

———. Introduction to Karamzin, *Karamzin's Memoir on Ancient and Modern Russia.*

Plato. *Great Dialogues of Plato.* Trans. W. H. D. Rouse. New York, 1956.

———. *The Republic of Plato.* Trans. and ed. Francis Macdonald Cornford. New York, 1945.

Pogiolli, Renato. "On Goncharov and His Oblomov." In Ivan Goncharov, *Oblomov,* pp. v–xxiii. New York, 1960.

Pokotilova, O. "Predshestvenniki Lomonosova." In *Lomonosov: Sbornik statei,* ed. V. V. Sipovskii, pp. 66–92. St. Petersburg, 1911.

Polotskii, Simeon. *Izbrannye sochineniia.* Ed. I. P. Eremin. Moscow-Leningrad, 1953.

Popov, Andrei. *Istoriko-literaturnyi obzor drevne-russkikh polemicheskikh sochinenii protiv latinian (XI–XV vv.).* 1875. Rpt. London, 1972.

Popov, Mikhail Ivanovich. *Dosugi, ili Sobranie sochinenii i perevodov.* 2 vols. St. Petersburg, 1772.

Pordech, Dzhon [Pordage, John]. *Piatyi traktat o rai.* GPB, O. III, No. 142.

Pozdneev, A. V. "Rannie masonskie pesni." *Scando-Slavica* 8 (1962):26–64.

Preobrazhenskii, A. *Etymological Dictionary of the Russian Language.* New York, 1951.

Prokopovich, Feofan. *Sochineniia.* Ed. I. P. Eremin et al. Moscow-Leningrad, 1961.

Prolog v den' rozhdeniia e.i.v. predstavlennyi v gimnaziiakh blagorodnymi uchenikami. Moscow, 1765.

Prutskov, N. I., ed. *Idei sotsializma v russkoi klassicheskoi literature.* Leningrad, 1969.

Pukhov, V. V. "Zhanry russkoi satiricheskoi prozy vtoroi poloviny XVIII veka." Kandidatskaia dissertatsiia, Leningrad Pedagogical Institute, 1968.

Pumpianskii, L. V. "Kantemir." In Akademiia nauk SSSR, Institut russkoi literatury, *Istoriia russkoi literatury,* 3:176–213.

———. "'Mednyi vsadnik' i poeticheskaia traditsiia XVIII veka." *Vremennik pushkinskoi komissii* 4–5 (1939):91–124.

Pushkin, A. S. *Polnoe sobranie sochinenii.* 3rd ed. 10 vols. Moscow, 1962–65.

———. *Stikhotvoreniia.* Ed. B. V. Tomashevskii. 3 vols. Leningrad, 1955.

Pyliaev, M. I. *Staroe zhit'e.* St. Petersburg, 1892.

Pypin, A. N. *Istoriia russkoi literatury*. 4 vols. 1903. Rpt. The Hague, 1968.
———. "Lomonosov i ego sovremenniki." *Vestnik Evropy*, 1895, No. 3, 295–342; No. 4, 689–732.
———. *Russkoe masonstvo (XVIII i pervaia chetvert' XIX v.)*. 1916. Rpt. Düsseldorf, 1970.
Radishchev, A. N. *A Journey from Petersburg to Moscow*. Trans. Leo Wiener. Ed. Roderick Page Thaler. Cambridge, Mass., 1958.
———. *Polnoe sobranie sochinenii*. 3 vols. Moscow-Leningrad, 1938–52.
———. *Stikhotvoreniia*. Ed. V. A. Zapadov. Leningrad, 1975.
Raeff, Marc. "In the Imperial Manner." In *Catherine the Great: A Profile*, ed. Marc Raeff, pp. 197–246.
———. *Origins of the Russian Intelligentsia*. New York, 1966.
———. "State and Nobility in the Ideology of M. M. Shcherbatov." *American Slavic and East European Review* 19 (1960):363–79.
———, ed. *Catherine the Great: A Profile*. New York, 1972.
Ransel, David L. *The Politics of Catherinean Russia*. New Haven, 1975.
Raznye sochineniia Tverskiia seminarii . . . 26 maia 1777. Moscow, 1777.
Reddaway, W. F., ed. *Documents of Catherine the Great*. New York, 1931.
Riasanovsky, Nicholas V. *A History of Russia*. 2nd ed. New York, 1972.
———. *The Image of Peter the Great in Russian History and Thought*. New York, 1985.
———. *Russia and the West in the Teaching of the Slavophiles*. 1952. Rpt. Gloucester, Mass., 1965.
Robinson, A. N. *Bor'ba idei v russkoi literature XVII veka*. Moscow, 1974.
———, ed. *Razvitie barokko i zarozhdenie klassitsizma v Rossii XVII-nachala XVIII v*. Moscow, 1989.
Robinson, A. N., et al., eds. *Pervye p'esy russkogo teatra*. Moscow, 1972.
Rogger, Hans. *National Consciousness in Eighteenth-Century Russia*. Cambridge, Mass., 1960.
Röhling, Horst. "Illustrated Publications on Fireworks and Illuminations in Eighteenth-Century Russia." In *Russia and the West in the Eighteenth Century*, ed. A. G. Cross, pp. 94–101.
Rosenberg, Karen. "The Quarrel Between the Ancients and Moderns in Russia." In *Russia and the West in the Eighteenth Century*, ed. A. G. Cross, pp. 196–205.
Rosenmeyer, Thomas G. *The Green Cabinet: Theocritus and the European Pastoral Lyric*. Berkeley, 1969.
Røstvig, Maren-Sofie. *The Happy Man: Studies in the Metamorphoses of a Classical Ideal*. Oslo, 1962.
Rousseau, Jean-Jacques. *Discours*. Ed. Gaston Meyer. Paris, 1968.
———. *The Social Contract*. Trans. Maurice Cranston. Harmondsworth, Eng., 1968.

Rovinskii, D. A. *Opisanie feierverkov i illiuminatsii (1674–1891)*. In *Obozre-nie ikonopisaniia v Rossii do kontsa XVII veka*. St. Petersburg, 1903.

Rozanov, I. N. "M. M. Kheraskov." In *Masonstvo v ego proshlom i nastoia-shchem*, ed. S. P. Mel'gunov and N. P. Sidorov, 2:38–51.

Runciman, Steven. *The Byzantine Theocracy*. Cambridge, Eng., 1977.

———. "Byzantium and the Slavs." In *Byzantium: An Introduction to East Roman Civilization*, ed. Norman H. Baynes and H. St. L. B. Moss, pp. 338–68.

The Russian Primary Chronicle: Laurentian Text. Translated and edited by Samuel H. Cross and Olgerd P. Sherbowitz-Wetzor. Cambridge, Mass., 1953.

Ryu, In-Ho Lee. "Freemasonry Under Catherine the Great: A Reinter-pretation." Ph.D. diss., Harvard University, 1967.

Rzhevskii, A. A. *Oda e. i. v. . . . Ekaterine Alekseevne na den' rozhdeniia eia*. Moscow, 1763.

Said, Edward W. *Beginnings: Intention and Method*. New York, 1975.

Sakulin, P. N. *Teoriia literaturnykh stilei*. Moscow, 1928.

Salaville, Sévérien. *An Introduction to the Study of Eastern Liturgies*. Trans. John M. T. Barton. London, 1938.

Sankovskii, V. *Oda e.i.v. tsesarevichu Pavlu Petrovichu*. Moscow, 1762.

———. *Stikhi na den' tezoimenitstva . . . Ekateriny II*. Moscow, 1763.

Sazonova, L. I. "Ideino-esteticheskoe znachenie 'myslennogo sada' v russkom barokko." In *Razvitie barokko i zarozhdenie klassitsizma v Rossii XVII-nachala XVIII v.*, ed. A. N. Robinson, pp. 71–103.

———. "Ot russkogo panegirika XVII veka k ode M. V. Lomonosova." In *Lomonosov i russkaia literatura*, ed. A. S. Kurilov, pp. 103–26.

Schneider, Heinrich. *Quest for Mysteries: The Masonic Background for Lit-erature in Eighteenth-Century Germany*. Ithaca, N.Y., 1947.

Scholem, Gershom G. *On the Kabbalah and Its Symbolism*. Trans. Ralph Manheim. New York, 1965.

Schroeder, F. L. *Katalog masonskoi kollektsii D. G. Burylina*. St. Petersburg, 1912.

Segel, Harold B. "Classicism and Classical Antiquity in Eighteenth- and Early-Nineteenth-Century Russian Literature." In *The Eighteenth Cen-tury in Russia*, ed. J. G. Garrard, pp. 48–71.

———. *Twentieth-Century Russian Drama*. New York, 1979.

———, ed. *The Literature of Eighteenth-Century Russia*. 2 vols. New York, 1967.

Semeka, A. V. "Russkie rozenkreitsery i sochineniia Ekateriny II protiv masonov." *Zhurnal ministerstva narodnogo prosveshcheniia*, 1902, no. 2, section II, pp. 343–400.

Senderovich, Savely. "Chudo Georgiia o zmie: Istoriia oderzhimosti

Chekhova odnim obrazom." *Russian Language Journal* 39 (1985):135–225.

———. "Potaennyi khram Vasiliia Zhukovskogo." *Wiener Slawistischer Almanach* 14 (1984):179–205.

Serman, I. Z. "Istoriia i prosvetitel'stvo v russkoi obshchestvennoi mysli i literature XVIII veka." *Slavica Hierosolymitana* 5–6 (1981):81–98.

———. "Ot sotsial'no-politicheskikh utopii XVIII v. k ideiam sotsializma v nachale XIX v." In *Idei sotsializma v russkoi klassicheskoi literature,* ed. N. I. Prutskov, pp. 62–77.

———. *Poeticheskii stil' Lomonosova.* Moscow-Leningrad, 1966.

———. *Russkii klassitsizm.* Leningrad, 1973.

Ševčenko, Ihor. "Agapetus East and West." *Revue du sud-est Européen* (Bucharest) 16 (1978):3–44.

———. "A Neglected Byzantine Source of Muscovite Political Ideology." In *The Structure of Russian History,* ed. Michael Cherniavsky, pp. 80–107. New York, 1970.

———. "On Some Sources of Prince Svjatoslav's *Izbornik* of the Year 1076." In *Orbis Scriptus: Festschrift für Dmitrij Tschižewskij zum 70 Geburtstag,* pp. 723–38. Munich, 1966.

Seznec, Jean. "Myth in the Middle Ages and Renaissance." In *Dictionary of the History of Ideas,* ed. Philip P. Wiener, 3:286–94.

———. *The Survival of the Pagan Gods.* Trans. Barbara F. Sessions. New York, 1953.

Shafer, Robert. *The English Ode to 1660.* 1918. Rpt. New York, 1966.

Shcherbatov, M. M. *On the Corruption of Morals in Russia.* Ed. and trans. A. Lentin. Cambridge, Eng., 1969.

———. *Sochineniia.* Ed. I. P. Khrushchev and A. G. Voronov. 2 vols. St. Petersburg, 1896.

Shklovskii, Viktor. *Chulkov i Levshin.* Leningrad, 1933.

Shubinskii, S. N. *Istoricheskie ocherki i rasskazy.* St. Petersburg, 1903.

Shvarts, I. G. [Schwarz, Johann Georg]. "Otryvki iz lektsii pokoinogo professora I. G. Shvartsa." *Drug iunoshestva,* 1813, no. 1.

———. "O vozrozhdenii." IRLI, 4880.XXV6.47.

———. "Raznye zamechaniia pokoinogo Shvartsa." GPB, Q. III, No. 112.

Silbajoris, Rimvydas. *Russian Versification: The Theories of Trediakovskij, Lomonosov, and Kantemir.* New York, 1968.

Simon, Ulrich. *Heaven in the Christian Tradition.* London, 1958.

Sipovskii, V. V. *Ocherki iz istorii russkogo romana.* 1 vol. in 2 parts. St. Petersburg, 1909–10.

———. "Politicheskie nastroeniia v russkom romane XVIII veka." *Izvestiia otdeleniia russkogo iazyka i slovesnosti imperatorskoi Akademii nauk* 9 (1904):230–67.

Skripil', M. O. "Legendarno-nravouchtel'nye povesti i dukhovnye sti-khi." In Akademiia nauk SSSR, Institut russkoi literatury, *Istoriia russkoi literatury*, vol. 2, part 2, pp. 287–301.
Smirnov, I. V. "Zabolotskii i Derzhavin." *XVIII vek* 8 (1969):144–61.
Smith, Barbara Herrnstein. *Poetic Closure*. Chicago, 1968.
Smith, Mary Grace. *The Art of the Dance in the USSR*. Notre Dame, Ind., 1968.
Sobolevskii, A. "Kogda nachalsia u nas lozhno-klassitsizm?" *Bibiliograf*, 1890, 1:1–6.
Sofronova, L. A. "Mif i drama barokko v Pol'she i Rossii." In *Mif, fol'klor, literatura*, ed. V. G. Bazanov et al., pp. 67–80. Leningrad, 1978.
Sokolovskaia, T. O. "*Kapitul Feniksa*" (*Vysshee tainoe masonskoe pravlenie v Rossii: 1778–1822*). Petrograd, 1916.
———. *Katalog masonskoi kollektsii D. G. Burylina*. St. Petersburg, 1912.
———. "Lozha trekh dobrodetelei i eia chleny dekabristy." *Russkii arkhiv*, 1908, no. 3, pp. 224–29.
———. "Masonskie kovry." *More*. 1907, no. 13–14, pp. 417–34.
———. "Masonskie pechatnye listki v pervuiu chetvert' XIX veka." *Russkii arkhiv*, 1916, no. 4, pp. 425–51.
———. "Masonskie risunki i vin'etki." *Starye gody*, 1909, no. 1, pp. 46–51.
Soloviev, Alexander V. *Holy Russia: The History of a Religious-Social Idea*. The Hague, 1959.
St. Clair, Foster York. "The Myth of the Golden Age from Spenser to Milton." Ph.D. diss., Harvard University, 1931.
Staehlin, Jakob von. *Original Anecdotes of Peter the Great*. 1788. Rpt. New York, 1970.
Stepanov, V. P., and Iu. V. Stennik, comps. *Istoriia russkoi literatury XVIII veka: Bibliograficheskii ukazatel'*. Ed. P. N. Berkov. Leningrad, 1968.
Stremooukhoff, Dmitri. "Moscow the Third Rome: Sources of the Doctrine." *Speculum* 28 (1953):84–101.
Strong, Roy. *Splendor at Court*. Boston, 1973.
Stuart, John. "The Flowering of Moscow." In *Art Treasures in Russia*, ed. Bernard Myers and Trewin Copplestone, pp. 73–97. New York, 1970.
———. *Ikons*. London, 1975.
Stupperich, R. "Kiev—das zweite Jerusalem." *Zeitschrift für slawische Philologie* 12 (1935):332–54.
Sumarokov, A. P. *Difiramv . . . Ekaterine Alekseevne na den' tezoimenitstva*. St. Petersburg, 1763.
———. *Izbrannye proizvedeniia*. Ed. P. N. Berkov. Leningrad, 1957.
———. *Novye lavry: Prolog*. St. Petersburg, 1764.
———. *Polnoe sobranie vsekh sochinenii v stikhakh i proze*. 10 vols. Moscow, 1781–82; 2nd ed., 1787.

———. *Pribezhishche dobrodeteli. Ballet.* 1759. Rpt. St. Petersburg, 1764.
———. *Stikhotvoreniia.* Ed. A. S. Orlov. Leningrad, 1935.
Suvin, Darko. *The Metamorphosis of Science Fiction.* New Haven, 1979.
Sviatlovskii, V. V. *Katalog utopii.* Moscow-Petrograd, 1925.
———. *Russkii utopicheskii roman.* Petrograd, 1922.
Svirin, A. "O roli prirody v russkom inter'ere XVIII veka." In *Khudozhestvennaia kul'tura XVIII veka.* Moscow, 1974.
Svodnyi katalog russkoi knigi grazhdanskoi pechati XVIII veka: 1725–1800. Ed. I. P. Kondakov et al. 5 vols. plus supplement. Moscow, 1963–75.
Sydorenko, Alexander. *The Kievan Academy in the Seventeenth Century.* Ottawa, 1977.
Szamuely, Tibor. *The Russian Tradition.* Ed. Robert Conquest. New York, 1974.
Tayler, Edward William. *Nature and Art in Renaissance Literature.* New York, 1964.
Teatral'noe predstavlenie, prazdnestvo Roze, Izobrazhaiushchei istinnuiu dobrodetel'. St. Petersburg, 1783.
Terras, Victor, ed. *Handbook of Russian Literature.* New Haven, Conn., 1985.
Tertz, Abram [Andrei Siniavskii]. *"The Trial Begins" and "On Socialist Realism."* New York, 1965.
Thompson, David, ed. *The Idea of Rome: From Antiquity to the Renaissance.* Albuquerque, N.M., 1971.
Tillyard, E. M. W. *The Elizabethan World Picture.* New York, n.d.
Titunik, I. R. "Classicism." In *Modern Encyclopedia of Russian and Soviet Literature* ed. Harry B. Weber, 4:217–33.
Toliver, Harold B. *Pastoral Forms and Attitudes.* Berkeley, 1971.
Torzhestvennye pesni . . . Aleksandru pervomu. Moscow, 1801.
Torzhestvo Belogradskikh muz. Moscow, 1801.
Torzhestvuiushchaia Minerva, obshchenarodnoe zrelishche . . . v Moskve 1763 goda. Reprinted in *Moskvitianin,* 1850, no. 19, pp. 111ff.
Torzhestvuiushchaia Rossiia: Balet pantomimo-allegorichnyi. St. Petersburg, 1770.
Treadgold, Donald W. *The West in Russia and China: Religious and Secular Thought in Modern Times.* Vol. 1. *Russia: 1472–1917.* Cambridge, Eng., 1973.
Trediakovskii, V. K. *Izbrannye proizvedeniia.* Ed. L. I. Timofeev and Iu. M. Strochkov. Moscow-Leningrad, 1963.
———. *Sochineniia.* 3 vols. St. Petersburg, 1849.
———. *Stikhotvoreniia.* Ed. A. S. Orlov et al. Leningrad, 1935.
Tuveson, Ernest Lee. *Redeemer Nation: The Idea of America's Millennial Role.* Chicago, 1968.

Tuzov, Vasilii. *Oda . . . Ekaterine Alekseevene . . . na vseradostnyi den'* *rozhdeniia*. St. Petersburg, 1769.

Tynianov, Iurii. "Dostoevsky and Gogol: Towards a Theory of Parody." In *Dostoevsky and Gogol: Texts and Criticism*, ed. Priscilla Meyer and Stephen Rudy, pp. 101–17. Ann Arbor, Mich., 1979.

―――. "The Meaning of the Word in Verse." In *Readings in Russian Poetics*, ed. L. Matejka and K. Pomorska, pp. 136–45. Cambridge, Mass., 1971.

Uspenskii, B. A. "Historia sub Specie Semioticae." In *Semiotics and Structuralism: Readings from the Soviet Union*, ed. Henryk Baran, pp. 64–75.

―――. *See also* Lotman, Iu. M.; and Zhivov, V. M.

Varese, Marina Rossi, trans. and ed. *Utopisti Russi del primo Ottocento*. Napoli, 1982.

Vasil'ev, V. N. *Starinnye feierverki v Rossii (XVII-pervaia chetvert' XVIII veka)*. Leningrad, 1960.

Vaslef, Nicholas P. "Bulgarin and the Development of the Russian Utopian Genre." *Slavic and East European Journal* 12 (1968):35–43.

Vengerov, S. A., ed. *Russkaia poeziia*. Vol. 1. St. Petersburg, 1897.

Vereshchagin, I. A. *Oda kotoroiu imperatorskii Moskovskii universitet iz"iavliaet svoiu radost' o vozvrashchenii . . . Shuvalova, chrez glas . . . studenta Ivana Vereshchagina*. Moscow, 1777.

Vernadskii, G. V. *Russkoe masonstvo v tsarstvovanie Ekateriny II*. 1917. Rpt. Düsseldorf, 1970.

Vernadsky, George. *Kievan Russia*. New Haven, 1973.

Vickery, Walter. " 'Mednyi vsadnik' and the Eighteenth-Century Heroic Ode." *Indiana Slavic Studies* 3 (1963):140–62.

Virgil. *Eclogues, Georgics, Aeneid*. Trans. H. Rushton Fairclough. 2 vols. Cambridge, Mass., 1935.

Vivanti, Corrado. "Henri IV: The Gallic Hercules." *Journal of the Warburg and Courtauld Institutes* 30 (1967):176–97.

Vlasto, A. P. "M. M. Heraskov: A Study in the Intellectual Life of the Age of Catherine the Great." Ph.D. diss., Cambridge University (King's College), 1952.

―――. "A Noble Failure—Kheraskov's *Vladimir Vozrozhdyonny*." In *Gorski Vijenac: A Garland of Essays for Professor Elizabeth Mary Hill*, ed. R. Auty et al., pp. 276–89. Cambridge, Eng., 1970.

Voltaire [François Marie Arouet]. *Candide, Zadig, and Selected Stories*. Trans. Donald M. Frame. New York, 1961.

Voyce, Arthur. *Moscow and the Roots of Russian Culture*. Norman, Okla., 1969.

Vozvrashchenie zlatago veka pri . . . gosudarstvovanii Ekateriny Vtoryia. Moscow, 1763.

Waegemans, Emmanuel. "Ščerbatov's Ideal of the Future: The First Rus-
    sian Utopia." In *Just the Other Day: Essays on the Suture of the Future*,
    ed. Luk De Vos, pp. 125–38. Antwerp, 1985.
Walicki, Andrzej. *A History of Russian Thought: From the Enlightenment to
    Marxism.* Trans. Hilda Andrews-Rusiecka. Stanford, Calif., 1979.
Walker, Roy. *The Golden Feast.* New York, 1952.
Ware, Timothy. *The Orthodox Church.* Baltimore, Md., 1967.
Watts, Alan W. *Myth and Ritual in Christianity.* Boston, 1968.
Weber, Harry B. "*Pikovaia dama*: A Case for Freemasonry in Russian
    Literature." *Slavic and East European Journal* 12 (1968):435–47.
———, ed. *Modern Encyclopedia of Russian and Soviet Literature.* 9 vols. to
    date. Gulf Breeze, Fla., 1977–.
Weidlé, Vladimir. *Russia: Absent and Present.* Trans. A. Gordon Smith.
    New York, 1952.
Wieczynski, Joseph, ed. *Modern Encyclopedia of Russian and Soviet History.*
    53 vols. to date. Gulf Breeze, Fla., 1976–.
Wiener, Philip P., ed. *Dictionary of the History of Ideas.* 4 vols. New
    York, 1974.
Williams, George H. *Wilderness and Paradise in Christian Thought.* New
    York, 1962.
Wilson, Elkin Calhoun. *England's Eliza.* 1939. Rpt. New York, 1966.
Wolff, Robert Lee. "The Three Romes: The Migration of an Ideology and
    the Making of an Autocrat." In *Myth and Mythmaking*, ed. Henry A.
    Murray, pp. 174–98. Boston, 1968.
Yates, Francis. *Astraea: The Imperial Theme in the Sixteenth Century.* Lon-
    don, 1975.
———. "Bacon and the Menace of English Literature." *New York Review
    of Books* 12 (1969):38–40.
———. "Queen Elizabeth as Astraea." *Journal of the Warburg and Cour-
    tauld Institutes* 10 (1947):27–82.
Zapadov, A. V. *Russkaia zhurnalistika XVIII veka.* Moscow, 1964.
Zenkovskii, V. V. *A History of Russian Philosophy.* Trans. George L. Kline.
    2 vols. New York, 1953.
Zernov, Nicolas. *The Russians and Their Church.* 3rd ed. New Rochelle,
    N.Y., 1978.
Zhivov, V. M., and B. A. Uspenskii. "Tsar' i bog: Semioticheskie as-
    pekty sakralizatsii monarkha v Rossii." In *Iazyki kul'tury i problemy
    perevodimosti*, ed. B. A. Uspenskii, pp. 47–154. Moscow, 1987.
Zuev, V. F. *Pedagogicheskie trudy.* Moscow, 1956.

Index

In this index an "f" after a number indicates a separate reference on the next page, and an "ff" indicates separate references on the next two pages. A continuous discussion over two or more pages is indicated by a span of page numbers, e.g., "57–59." *Passim* is used for a cluster of references in close but not consecutive sequence.

261; "A Scene from Private Life in 2028," 261
Butler, Samuel: *Erewhon*, 258
Buzhinskii, Gavriil, 28
Byzantium, 16–19, 24, 47f, 191ff, 196

Cabala, Jewish, 92, 108, 243f
Cadmus (founder of Thebes), 106. *See also under* Kheraskov, Mikhail M.
Caesar, Julius, 55, 161f, 187
Cagliostro, Count (Giuseppe Balsamo), 241
Calendar rituals, 43
Campanella, Tommaso, 187
Campion, Thomas, 4
Caritas, 93, 105, 168, 236. *See also* Agape versus eros
Carnival, 57, 59, 217f; and "Minerva Triumphant" masquerade, 61–63
Carousel, allegorical, 58
Carpe diem, 150
Catherine II ("the Great"): identified with Mother of God, 28, 38, 39–40, 227; as transfigured Christ, 30–31; as Moses, 33; as Astraea, 38–40, 147, 206, 208, 234; as Minerva, 39–40, 61–62, 82, 116, 119, 207; and *Nakaz*, 39, 115, 120–24 *passim*; as "risen Elizabeth," 39; and "Greek Project," 48–49, 212; and imperial expansion, 49, 54–57; and science, 60, 78, 82; and satirical journals, 63; wedding of, 71–73; as lily of paradise, 75, 153; literary works by, 75–76, 212, 241, 267; as "Felitsa," 76, 158–59; and Freemasonry, 103, 234, 241; criticism of, 112, 120, 124, 140, 160, 265; reforms of, 115, 120; and immigration policy, 115; as Numa, 123, 250; as Themis, 206
Catholicism, 119
Cato the Younger, 161, 266
Catullus, 225
Caussin, Nicolas, 218

Censorship, 63, 141, 143
Cervantes, Miguel de: *Don Quixote*, 151, 270
Chaadaev, Petr Ia., 162
Chaos, 43f, 61f, 125–26, 141, 166, 210
Charles I, king of England, 12–13, 189
Cherub, 15, 22
Chesme, battle of, 223
Childhood, 10, 209
Children's literature, 75, 240
Chiron, 107
Chivalry, 93, 97–98, 104, 207, 234, 236. *See also* Freemasonry
Christ: comparison of ruler to, 16–18, 27–31, 36–37, 42, 166, 191, 197f, 226; representation in dome church, 26, 191; as phoenix, 47; as alchemist, 96; in Freemasonry, 96, 245; as gardener, 222. *See also* Transfiguration
Christianity, 14–40 *passim*
Chulkov, Mikhail, 52; *The Mocker*, 52, 255; "The Dream of Kidal," 129–33 *passim*, 255
Church Fathers. *See* Patristic writings
Church Slavonic, 210
"Church Militant, The" (icon), 20–21
Cincinnatus, 161
City: versus country, 69–70, 151–52, 223f, 231, 263; as paradisal garden, 84–85
"Classicalization," 33
Clement of Alexandria, 190
Clio (muse of history), 159. *See also* History
Coats of arms: as symbols, 73, 118–19, 216
Columbus, Christopher, 47
Commedia dell'arte, 62, 221
Communalism, 125, 128f, 131, 176
Community: ideal, 9; individual and, 10
Consent in Russian culture, x, 183, 263
Conservatism in Russia, x, 127, 131, 144

32, 195, 197; "Ode for the Royal Favor . . . ," 86, 231; "Ode . . . on the Taking of Khotin," 227; "Ode on the Wedding Day . . . of Peter and Catherine," 71–73; *A Short Introduction to Rhetoric*, 72, 226, 247; "Speech in Memory of Peter the Great," 28, 57; "To Tsarskoe Selo," 86–87

Lopatinskii, Feofilakt, 28
Lopukhin, Ivan, 97–98
Louis XIV, king of France, 31, 186
Love, garden of, 69, 70–74, 224f
Loyola, Saint Ignatius, 236
Lucian: *Icaromennipus*, 256; *True History*, 256
Lukin, Vladimir I., 90
Lunar utopias, *see under* Utopia
Lycurgus, 54, 121f, 132

Machine, image of, 83, 163
Magic, 78–79, 208, 211
Maikov, Vasilii: as Mason, 90; as satirist, 136. Works: 1775 Accession Day Ode, 54; "Parnassus Triumphant," 88; "Ode on the Selection of New Delegates," 117–18; "Elisei," 258
Malthusianism, 132, 256
Mandel'shtam, Osip E., 161, 267
"Manifest Destiny," 212–13. *See also* World empire
Manna, 176
Maps, medieval, 187–88
Marcus Aurelius, 50, 266
Mardi Gras, *see* Maslenitsa
Marriage ceremony: Orthodox, 73; of tsars, 74, 226
Marriage odes, *see* Epithalamiums
Maslenitsa, 59, 62, 221
Masquerade, allegorical, 58–62 *passim*. *See also* "Minerva Triumphant" masquerade
Mayakovsky, Vladimir, 112, 217
Memento mori, 235
Menshikov, Aleksandr, 31
Messianic pattern, 6–7, 12–13, 231; irony and, 8
Messianism, 19, 29, 31–33, 119, 133,

156, 210. *See also* Appeal to foreigners; Nationalism
Metaphorical pattern, 4
Milk and honey, land of, 2, 33, 63, 168, 172, 174, 176, 201f. *See also* Promised land; Paradise
Milton, John, 75, 161, 266
Mimetic ethic, 29, 158, 199, 248. *See also* Image and likeness
Minerva, 37, 38–40, 207. *See also* Wisdom; Science; *under* Elizabeth, empress; Catherine II
"Minerva Triumphant" masquerade, 61–64, 89, 117, 122, 136, 220f
Mirror of princes (literary genre), 17, 138, 192, 246ff
Mohyla, Petr, 34, 207, 229
Momus the Mocker, 61f, 64
Monarchy, government by, 97, 123–24, 142–43, 161, 266. *See also* Aristocracy, government by; Absolutism; Autocracy, Russian; Tsar, literary depiction of
Montaigne, Michel de: "On Cannibals," 8, 129
Montesquieu, 157, 248; *Spirit of the Laws*, 125; *The Persian Letters*, 246
Moon, 10, 118, 129, 130–33, 200, 254f
More, Thomas: *Utopia*, 5, 35, 112f, 141, 187, 245f, 252, 258, 260f
Morelly, abbot: *Basiliade*, 260
Moses, 32f, 121, 200ff, 239
Mother, image of, 61, 73–77 *passim*, 225, 251; "Mother Russia," 71, 73–74, 225f; Great Mother, 76–77, 227f. *See also* Mother of God
Mother of God, 42, 188, 255; as "spiritual garden," 23, 226; linked with female rulers, 23, 28, 38–40, 207, 227; as intercessor between heaven and earth, 26; linked with classical deities, 39, 206; as lily, 74, 226; as rose without thorns, 226
Mount Tabor: tsar's throne as, 30. *See also* Transfiguration
Mozart, Wolfgang A.: *The Magic Flute*, 240f, 244
Mysticism, 92, 175–76, 238

Library of Congress Cataloging-in-Publication Data
Baehr, Stephen Lessing.
    The paradise myth in eighteenth-century Russia : utopian patterns
in early secular Russian literature and culture / Stephen
Lessing Baehr.
        p.   cm.
    Includes bibliographical references.
    ISBN 0-8047-1533-5
    1. Russian literature—18th century—History and criticism.
2. Utopias in literature.   3. Freemasonry in literature.   4. Soviet Union—
Intellectual life—18th century.   5. Paradise in literature.   I. Title.
PG3010.5.U85B3   1991
891.709'372—dc20
90-27015
CIP
(rev.)

⊗ This book is printed on acid-free paper